A HISTORY OF ANCIENT COINAGE

A HISTORY OF ANCIENT COINAGE

700—300 B.C.

BY

PERCY GARDNER, Litt. D., F.B.A.

WITH ELEVEN PLATES

GYAN

Published by

GYAN

Gyan Publishing House
5, Ansari Road
Daryaganj, New Delhi-110002
Phone: 011-47034999, 9811692060
E-mail: books@gyanbooks.com

Distribution Network
gyanbooks.com
India, USA, Canada, UK, Australia, France

ISBN : 978-81-212-9974-9 (PB)
First Published, 1918

2nd Impression 2021

Printed at: Gyan Press, Delhi.

A History of Ancient Coinage
700—300 B.C.
Author: Percy Gardner

A HISTORY OF ANCIENT COINAGE

700–300 B.C.

BY

PERCY GARDNER, Litt.D., F.B.A.

LINCOLN AND MERTON PROFESSOR OF CLASSICAL ARCHAEOLOGY IN THE UNIVERSITY OF OXFORD

WITH ELEVEN PLATES

OXFORD
AT THE CLARENDON PRESS
1918

INSCRIBED TO

BARCLAY VINCENT HEAD

AS A MEMORIAL

OF

SIXTEEN YEARS

OF COMMON TOIL

AND

UNINTERRUPTED FRIENDSHIP

PREFACE

In the course of the last fifty years the science of Greek coins, ancient numismatics, has undergone great developments. Up to about 1860 the study had been gradually taking shape, and many able scholars and numismatists, such as Sestini, Eckhel, and later Millingen and others, had opened up great fields of study, and showed much penetration and erudition in the discussion of the various classes of coins and their relations to the cities which issued them. Yet these writers had scarcely founded a science of ancient numismatics. Methods had still to be sought out and established. The pioneers of numismatic method were Mommsen, in the opening chapters of his *Geschichte des römischen Münzwesens* (1865), and Brandis, in his *Münz-, Mass- und Gewichtswesen in Vorderasien* (1866). These writers clearly saw that for the formation of numismatics as a branch of historical science two points were fundamental. First, it was necessary to determine not only the cities which struck each group of coins, but also the date and occasion of each issue. And secondly, as coins were measures of value and a medium of exchange, the one most important fact in regard to them was the quantity of precious metal which each contained; in fact their weight. Eckhel in his great *Doctrina Numorum Veterum* (1792–8), which is still valuable as a storehouse of learning and a model of good sense, had but a very vague notion of the dates of coins; and their weights had not been seriously considered. The works of Brandis and Mommsen were epoch-making; but they could not carry very far, because the essential point of the dates of issues had not been satisfactorily gone into.

In the period 1870–90 a fresh turn was given to the study by a series of more thorough attempts to connect the successive issues of money with the history of the mint-cities to which they belonged. In this field B. V. Head's *Coinage of Syracuse* (1874) may be said to have opened the door. It is only a monograph of eighty pages, but its value was at once recognized in the Universities of Europe; and it proved the first of a number of similar treatises, which tended gradually to introduce into numismatics the true historic method. The work was in a remarkable degree international. In Holland J. P. Six, in Switzerland F. Imhoof-Blumer, in France W. H. Waddington and Théodore Reinach, in Germany A. von Sallet and R. Weil, in England A. J. Evans, may be specially mentioned as having made very useful contributions. And when in 1887 Mr. Head published his *Historia Numorum* he was able, as a result of combined labours, to present the coins of the Greeks as orderly series under each mint-city or kingdom. The new edition of the *Historia* (1911) shows a great number of alterations and additions in consequence of the discoveries and researches of twenty-four years; but it is astonishing how well the main lines of the book have endured. On similar principles to Mr. Head's, but on a much larger scale, M. Babelon is now publishing, volume by volume, a complete digest of the published coins of the Greek world, down to 300 B.C., ranged under mints and rulers (*Traité des Monnaies grecques et romaines*).

A still more elaborate work, a *Corpus* of Greek Coins, is in progress under the auspices of the Prussian Academy of Sciences. In proposing this work, as far back as 1887, Mommsen wrote: 'It is beyond doubt that students who plan some study in the field of Antiquity, whether concerned with History, Language, Religion or Art, or any other subject, find no more serious hindrance and constant impediment than the want of a rationally ordered collocation of ancient coins.' The *Corpus* has the able assistance of Dr. Imhoof-Blumer, of Winterthur, with whom work very competent scholars. But the penalty resulting from their attempt to include every known coin, and to go carefully into every detail, is that the *Corpus* moves very slowly. A few parts only, dealing with the coins of a few cities and districts of Northern Greece, have appeared. If carried on thus, the work will not be completed, literally, for several centuries.

A talented numismatist, M. Théodore Reinach, has written:[1] 'Nous avons des catalogues dont quelques-uns sont des œuvres scientifiques de premier ordre, des monographies, des manuels disposés suivant l'ordre géographique ou systématique.' '*L'histoire* de la monnaie chez les Grecs n'a jamais été écrite.' I am ambitious enough to try to put together at least the outlines of such a history.

The plan followed by Mr. Head and M. Babelon, though perhaps the best for their purpose, has certain disadvantages. It gives the succession of monetary issues under each state and city, but it does not include the comparison together of the coins of different cities, even when the cities lie near together and the coins are contemporary. Each city is treated as if it were quite independent of its neighbours. For example, in the *Historia Numorum*, Rhegium appears on p. 107, and the closely kindred Chalcidic colony of Messana on p. 151: Byzantium is considered on p. 266, and Calchedon, only divided from it by the Bosporus, on p. 511. It is not easy, without much investigation, to trace political or commercial influence of one city on another. Especially it is hard to determine, on the evidence to be found in the book, why one city uses the Aeginetan standard for its coin, another the Corinthian, another the Attic, and so on. M. Babelon is clearly aware of this defect; and in the recent volumes of his great work he has commonly

[1] *L'Histoire par les Monnaies*, 1894, p. 4.

prefixed to the account of the coinage of the cities of each district a general sketch of its character. This is excellent; but even so, the means for following lines of numismatic connexion is incomplete.

It seems that there is need for another history of coinage constructed on a different plan, taking cities in groups rather than separately, tracing lines of trade influence from district to district, trying to discern the reasons why particular coin standards found acceptance in one locality or another. Head's book is really a history of the coinages of cities and states; it is desirable as a supplement to trace at least the outlines of the history of Greek and Asiatic and Italian coinages as a continuous activity. This is the plan of the present work. It could not have been attempted if such works as the *Historia Numorum*, M. Babelon's *Traité des Monnaies grecques*, and the *Catalogue of Greek Coins in the British Museum* (27 volumes) had not lain ready to hand. Such works furnish abundant material; but the material can only be used by those thoroughly familiar with the coins themselves.

I have been unable at present to continue this history into the Hellenistic age. The truth is that, in the case of coins, as in the case of politics, religion, and all else, the problems of the Hellenistic age are not the same as those of the autonomous age. We have kingdoms in the place of city-states. The question of coin standards becomes far simpler in consequence of the wide adoption of the Attic weight. But the question of mints becomes infinitely more complex, and in fact is full of difficulties at present insoluble, because the mint-cities seldom place their names on their money, more often a monogram difficult of interpretation.

It is unfortunate that while continental scholars have all written the weights of coins in grammes, English numismatists have used the Troy measure of grains. As the British Museum Catalogues go by grains, I have felt bound, whenever I give a weight, to express it according both to the English and the continental methods. I have not, in giving these weights, attempted minute accuracy, as I think such accuracy misleading, since coins of the same group differ considerably in weight, and it is quite clear that ancient mints did not attain to great accuracy, even in the case of gold coins. Silver coins from the same dies often differ markedly in weight; and bronze coins are usually only token-money, of which the weight is unimportant. It appears that in antiquity, as in the Middle Ages, the number of coins struck out of a talent or mina of metal was more regarded than the weight of individual specimens. To weigh coins, as some numismatists have done, to the thousandth of a gramme seems to me absurd; and the result is to give to their calculations an exactness which is quite illusory.

The plates are arranged to give a general view of the coins of districts and periods. It was quite impossible to figure every coin mentioned in the text. In order to supplement the plates, I have added references to the plates of the British Museum *Guide to Greek and Roman Coins* (B. M.) and to those of M. Babelon's *Traité des Monnaies grecques et romaines* (B. T.) in the case of coins figured in those works.

Parts of some of the following chapters have already appeared in print in less developed form: two papers on the origins of coinage in the *Proceedings of the British Academy*; papers on the coinages of the Ionian Revolt and the Athenian Empire in the *Journal of Hellenic Studies*. These have been largely rewritten.

I should add that the dates I have accepted in the text for events in Greek history are only approximate, taken from ordinary books of reference, unless when any of my arguments depended on an exact date. It is clear that if I had tried to determine the exact date of events in

Greek history, it would have involved endless research, and the result when reached would have been only conjectural. Nor would the investigation have been in the line of my work.

It is with great satisfaction that I have inscribed this work to the memory of Barclay Head, as he inscribed the *Historia Numorum* to the memory of Joseph Eckhel. For sixteen years (1871–87) my desk at the British Museum was within a few feet of Head's, and almost daily in those years we discussed together problems of Greek numismatics. That he valued my collaboration is proved by the acknowledgement of it, expressed with characteristic generosity, in the Introduction to his *Catalogue of the Coins of Attica.*[1] But my obligations to him are greater, because, while I had a variety of interests, his whole mind was concentrated on the subject of our study. My dedication must stand as a memorial of a friendship never clouded. I must add that to watch the science of ancient numismatics taking form year by year, and constantly improving in methods and results, was an experience of a rare and very instructive kind.

I have to thank Dr. George Macdonald for kindly reading my proofs, and making many useful suggestions. The very full and useful General Index I owe to Miss Edith Legge.

P. G.

[1] p. lxix.

CONTENTS

INTRODUCTION

I. Greek Trade-routes.

The history of Greek commerce has yet to be written. There are, indeed, in existence a few books which professedly treat of it;[1] but they are necessarily built on inadequate foundations, since the preliminary studies, which should furnish them with a basis, have scarcely been made. The data for a construction of a history of Greek commerce would include not merely an examination of the works of ancient writers, and a detailed survey of geography, but also a fuller investigation of published inscriptions, and, in addition, of all the results of excavation on classical soil. The results of such excavation, down to the middle of the last century, were not adequately recorded. Even since then they have only in some cases been recorded in sufficient detail: objects in themselves uninteresting, and of no money value, such as unpainted vases and common bronze utensils and tools, have been often thrown away. Yet such objects might be of great value for indicating the lines of ancient commerce. Coins, however, which are also of inestimable importance for commercial inquiries, have been carefully examined and published; and the value of such works as Head's *Historia Numorum* has been generally recognized. It is the object of this book to make the facts of coinage useful for the knowledge of commercial intercourse.

[1] E. Speck (1905) devotes a volume of his *Handelsgeschichte des Altertums* to Greece; and his work is of value. Of course, there are many smaller works and monographs which throw light on particular fields of ancient commerce. An excellent book, though now somewhat out of date, is Büchsenschütz, *Besitz und Erwerb im griech. Altertum*, 1869. It is to be regretted that Mr. A. E. Zimmern, in his recent work on the *Greek Commonwealths*, has, in the chapters devoted to commerce, frequently followed untrustworthy modern authorities who put theories in the place of facts.

I will begin by sketching the main features of Greek commerce.

Attempts have been made by some recent writers to trace the trade-routes, and to track the commerce of the Minoan and Mycenaean ages.[1] The results reached by them are somewhat speculative. In the absence of literature, attempts to utilize pottery and schemes of ornament for proof of trade influences and ethnographic connexions are meritorious, but they are risky. Peoples, even if unrelated, at the same stage of civilization often produce implements and earthenware of closely similar character; nor does the imitation by one people of the rude art products of another prove identity of race. In any case, the subject of the present book being the coins of the Greeks, I cannot investigate the civilization which prevailed in Hellas before the Greeks came in.

In the Homeric age commerce can scarcely be said to have existed among the Greeks.[2] The state of society was such as scarcely to require it. The Homeric nobles produce on their own lands nearly all that they require for their rude mode of living. The chief necessary which they had to go to the town and fetch seems to have been iron.[3] Luxuries they imported, or rather bought of the foreign merchants who visited their shores. The chief riches of the Homeric chiefs consisted in their flocks and herds and their slaves. These alone they could offer to merchants in exchange for wares. Hence prices are always in Homer reckoned in oxen; and we are told that when a cargo of Lemnian wine reached the Greek camp before Troy, the chiefs purchased amphoras of it for cattle and hides.[4] The real resources of Greek lands, the purple-fisheries of Cythera, the copper-mines of Cyprus, the gold-mines of Thasos, seem to have been in the hands of Phoenicians; and from the

[1] See especially W. Leaf, *Troy, a study in Homeric geography*; V. Berard, *Les Phéniciens et l'Odyssée.*

[2] A great part of this and the following two sections is repeated from Gardner and Jevons, *Manual of Greek Antiquities*, pp. 386 and foll., with the permission of the publishers.

[3] *Il.* xxiii. 835.

[4] *Il.* vii. 474.

Phoenicians came most of the articles of manufacture and luxury used by the Greeks of that age. Vases for unguents and vessels of bronze, and clothes dyed with purple, the skilful Sidonians manufactured themselves; ivory they brought from Egypt, and tin from Britain or the East. Slaves, in those days the most important article of commerce, they bought and sold everywhere. Their factories were to be found on many shores where any gain was to be made by trading, and their voyages reached as far as Britain.

They did not, however, possess a monopoly of trade. Ruder peoples organized expeditions, partly for piratical purposes, and partly for trade. The Taphians and Teleboans,[1] who are supposed to have lived in the neighbourhood of Corcyra, traded in metal and slaves with the opposite inhabitants of Italy and Sicily; and the Phaeacians, supposing them to have been a real and not an imaginary people, seem to have possessed an extensive and lucrative trade. The Lemnians exported their wine in their own ships, and the Cretans were celebrated as bold sailors and organizers of piratical expeditions as far as the coasts of Africa.[2] In the traditions of the Argonautic expedition we may see proof that even the Achaeans did not shrink from long and venturesome expeditions, though they had as yet small idea of trading; rather they endeavoured to surprise and sack the cities of richer peoples and to bring home wealth and honour. The gold, which we know to have been used in some parts of Greece in Homeric times, may have either been thus acquired or brought over the sea by wealthy Phoenicians or Lydians.

It was doubtless the pressure of population which caused the Greeks about the eighth century before our era to turn their attention to the spreading of colonies over the shores of the Mediterranean, and, as a consequence, to commerce. We may call this a consequence, because in most cases communication was kept up between the mother-city and the colony; the latter, finding itself in the midst of a new set of surroundings and productions, acquired new wants

[1] *Od.* xv. 427.

[2] *Od.* xiv. 245.

and new tastes, and then communicated these wants and tastes to its parent, together with the materials for their satisfaction. Thus a lively trade between old and new Greek cities arose throughout the Levant; and the Greek traders, by a process which we can but rarely trace in history, gradually ousted the Phoenicians from many of their factories and trading stations, inheriting their traditions and their relations to the barbarous tribes of the interior. For the western trade Corinth became the most important city. The incomparable position of this city, the Acropolis of which is placed on a lofty rock commanding both the eastern and western seas of Greece, gave it marvellous advantages. No trireme could be dragged across the isthmus which divided the two seas without permission of the Corinthians; and as the Greeks dreaded the open sea of Cape Malea, they eagerly sought such permission. By the colonies of Corcyra and Dyrrhachium, Corinth commanded the Adriatic Sea, and pushing on, founded mighty cities in Italy and Sicily, including Syracuse itself. Scarcely less active in the same region were the people of Chalcis in Euboea, who founded Naxus and Catana in Sicily. On the coast of Macedonia a whole district was settled by these same Chalcidians, and received its name from them. Miletus took as a special province the Euxine Sea and studded its shores with flourishing towns. Greek settlers occupied the coasts of Cyprus, and even the distant Libya received a colony in Cyrene. In the time of the Persian wars, the people of Phocaea sailed as far as Massilia and settled there. Before the Persians conquered Egypt the Greeks had settled in large numbers at Naucratis on the Nile, and had in their hands much of the trade of that rich country.

The history of Greek commerce may be most aptly divided into three periods. The first comprises the time when no Greek city was specially pre-eminent above the rest, although Corinth in the west and Miletus in the east took usually the lead. The second period begins with the fall of Miletus and with the sudden expansion of Athenian commerce, the Athenians inheriting Milesian supremacy in the Euxine and forming a strict commercial confederacy in the Levant. This period begins with the Persian wars and ends with the taking of Athens by Lysander. The third period includes the rise and activity of the city of Rhodes, which was founded about 408 B.C., and almost immediately became a centre of Greek commerce, continuing to be wealthy and flourishing until the Romans were supreme in all parts of the Mediterranean Sea.

It is into these three periods that the history of coinage also divides itself; the Persian wars of 490–480 B.C., and the fall of Athens in 405 B.C., with the contemporary destruction of the cities of Sicily, forming strong dividing lines. In the body of the present work these three periods are kept separate, except in some districts, such as Lower Italy, Cyrene, and Peloponnesus, where the line is harder to draw. In these districts the later two periods are treated together.

Two cardinal points must be always borne in mind in any consideration of Greek commerce. Firstly, the interior of the country being rough and mountainous, and scantily provided with roads, while the sea on the other hand is gentle and alluring, the greater part of Greek trade was always sea-borne. The inland trade was largely carried on, not with wagons, but with sumpter beasts, ponies and mules, which climbed up the narrow paths leading from town to town. Secondly, Greek ships at sea always hugged the land. The storms in the Mediterranean are sudden and violent, but they soon pass. When they came on, the ships ran for the shelter of an island, as steamers often do to this day. Creeping along the coast from headland to headland, or passing from island to island in the Aegean, ships made their journeys slow but sure. Such stretches as that between Corfu and Italy, or that between Crete and Egypt, seemed to the Greek sailors long and perilous.

Taking Athens, Aegina, and Corinth as the centre, we find radiating from it four principal courses of trade. The first led in a north-easterly direction past the coasts of

Macedon and Thrace, through the Bosporus into the Euxine Sea. This line of trade was perhaps to the Greeks the most important of all. The shores of Macedon, Thrace, Pontus, and Bithynia were to the Greeks what the wide plains of North and South America are to ourselves. Thence came their supply of food and the raw materials of manufacture, and, above all, slaves, the largest and most profitable object of ancient commerce. In ancient as in modern days, the plains of Southern Russia produced a plenteous harvest of corn, and fed innumerable herds of oxen, which supplied the Greek tanners with hides. At the mouth of the Borysthenes and in the Propontis were some of the most productive fisheries known to the Greeks, supplying them with immense quantities of salt fish, which, with bread, was the staple of their food. The vast forests of Bithynia and the Danube valley furnished an inexhaustible supply of timber for house and ship building, while even at that period Greece was poor in forest; as well as tar and charcoal. Flax and hemp also came largely from the Euxine. The great bulk of these products the Greek colonists did not produce on their own lands, but procured by barter from the barbarous tribes of the interior. The tribes of Scythians, who dwelt on the northern shores of the sea, learned to cultivate corn for export, and to breed cattle; and bringing these to the Greeks, obtained in return oil and bronzes, and more especially wine, which was very necessary to their enjoyment, and yet could not be grown so far north. Their kings were generally on good terms with the Hellenic colonists; and in our own day the tombs of these chiefs in the Crimea have been in many cases opened, and found to contain elegant pottery, jewelry, and ornaments, which exhibit Greek art almost at its best. The influence of Athens in particular is very clear in these elegant luxuries; a fact which reminds us that at Athens the public police force consisted of slaves imported from Scythia, the τοξόται.

In all periods the city which controlled the gates of the Euxine, of which the most important was guarded by Byzantium, was commercially the most important in Hellas.

We can trace a succession of dominant cities: Miletus down to 500; then Aegina; Athens at the time of the Athenian Empire; Sparta, Athens, and Persia alternately in the early fourth century; then Rhodes. It is worth while, in passing, to correct an absurd mistake, into which some recent writers have fallen, of supposing that whereas Athens exported oil and pottery, she exported the oil in the fragile and delicate painted vases abounding in our museums, which are hopelessly unfit for such a purpose.

The second great line of trade was that of which at successive periods Rhodes and Delos were the emporia, and which led from Hellas past Rhodes and Cyprus along the coast of Phoenicia to Egypt. This route was the more important because along it came the products of the Far East, of India and Arabia, and Babylon. Before the foundation of Alexandria, the great cities of Phoenicia retained the commerce of Farther Asia in a great degree in their own hands, but at a later period it was more widely spread, and shared by Antioch on the north and Alexandria on the south. Babylon furnished the Greeks with carpets and other stuffs, India with precious stones, silk, and ivory, Arabia with frankincense and various spices. The valley of the Nile exported both in later Greek and in Roman times immense quantities of corn, as well as writing-paper and linen made of the papyrus plant, ivory, and porcelain. Phoenicia supplied the Greeks with fewer and fewer articles as their own resources developed; but cloth of purple, alabaster flasks of ointment, and fragrant woods seem to have been exported through Tyre and Sidon until Roman times. Cyprus furnished not only an abundant supply of copper, but in addition manufactured cloth of both finer and coarser texture. Cyrene, which could be reached either through Egypt or direct by way of Crete, supplied wool and silphium, an article very much used in ancient medicine, and found nowhere but in the Cyrenaic district. The people of Peloponnesus sailed to both Cyrene and Egypt by way of Crete.

The third line of trade, which was always largely in the

hands of Corinth and her colonies, passed through that great commercial metropolis, and led through the Corinthian gulf, past the coasts of Acarnania and Epirus to the various ports on both sides of the Adriatic Sea. Although the Adriatic was reckoned a very dangerous sea, both on account of its frequent storms and because of the hardihood of the Illyrian pirates, yet it produced great gain to the merchants who ventured on it. They exchanged Greek wine and manufactured goods for the produce of agriculture and grazing offered them by the farmers of the Epirote and Italian coasts. On the Italian side the harbours of Adria and Ancona lay open, and offered access to the peoples of Eastern Italy.

More celebrated and frequented was the fourth line of trade, which led either from the Corinthian Gulf or round the promontory of Malea across to Sicily, and through the Straits of Messina to the western coasts of Italy, to Gaul and Spain. As far to the north as Cumae this route passed a continuous succession of Greek colonies, and even in Gaul and Spain Massilia and Emporiae stood ready to harbour the Greek merchants, and to give them facilities for obtaining the produce of the interior. Corn and cheese were obtained from Sicily, wood from the forests of Southern Italy. The merchants who were so venturesome as to penetrate to Spain reaped a rich reward in the shape of gold, with which Spain at that time abounded. But the jealousy of Carthaginians and Etruscans prevented the commerce of the Greeks from ever spreading in force to the west and north of Cumae. To Italy and Sicily the Greeks of Hellas brought in return for the products of the soil wine, pottery, and articles of manufacture.

These four routes were the chief lines by which the riches of the barbarians flowed into Greece. Of course, among the great Greek cities themselves, scattered over the coasts of Asia Minor, Sicily, and Italy, and the mainland of Hellas, there was constant intercourse and a continual exchange of goods, for particular classes of which special cities and districts were famous. Thus Chios exported the finest wine, as did Cnidus and Thasos; the wool of the Milesians, probably derived from Phrygia, was universally appreciated; Corinth and Chalcis supplied the Greek world with articles of bronze; Athens with painted pottery and with silver from the Laurian mines, with oil, honey, and figs; Thessaly with horses; Arcadia with asses; Sparta and Epirus with dogs; Boeotia with eels from the Copaic lake; the district about Mons Pangaeus with silver. The internal trade of the Peloponnese was mainly in the hands of astute natives of Aegina, who travelled as pedlars over the country, carrying wares adapted to the needs of the hardy peasantry.

Besides the sea-routes there were a few long land-routes leading to far countries, the beginnings, if not the ends of which were known to the Greeks. From the Greek colonies of the Crimea ways led north to the Baltic, whence amber was derived. Greek coins have been found at Bromberg in Prussia, and a notable hoard of gold ornaments of Ionian work at Vettersfelde. Again, starting from the Sea of Azov, a line of trade ran up to the Ural mountains, whence gold was to be had. Most eastern caravan routes, until the time of Alexander, reached the Mediterranean at Tyre and Sidon, and this trade was in Phoenician hands; but the Royal Road from Ephesus to Sardes and thence to the cities of Persia was trodden by Greeks, both politicians and traders, at all periods.

Such in its general features was the frame on which was woven the fabric of Greek commerce.

II. Classes of Traders.

Plato in the *Politicus* [1] distinguishes two classes of dealers. The first consists of those who sell only the goods they themselves produce (αὐτοπῶλαι). The second consists of those who buy in order to sell again at a profit. In the latter class are included both shopkeepers or hucksters (κάπηλοι), whose business is retail, and merchants [2] (ἔμποροι)

[1] *Polit.* 260 c. [2] *Repub.* 371.

who deal wholesale between market and market, or city and city.

We are told that among the Locrians[1] the second and third of these classes were wanting; that the husbandmen sold their products one by one to the consumer and not in the mass to dealers. Such a state of things could exist only in a very simple society; and among the Greeks generally the two classes of hucksters and merchants were numerous and clearly distinguished one from the other.

In poor and mountainous or barren districts, such as Arcadia, the hucksters usually moved from place to place carrying with them a pack of goods for sale. But wherever the Greek population gravitated, as it normally did, into cities, these petty dealers did not acquire wandering habits, but remained attached to a certain spot in the market-place. Here their booths stood side by side with the factories of those who made articles for sale, sandal-makers, for instance, or wreath-makers. Among the most numerous classes of them were dealers in wine, oil, and fish. Sometimes covered halls were erected in order to contain a certain class of them, halls which thenceforth became the markets for a particular class of goods, the wine-market, for instance, or the fish-market. In large cities there might be found in the market-place several detached halls of this character, near together but disconnected. Even where everything was sold in the open Agora, dealers in the same commodities would naturally gravitate to the same quarter of it, forming what were termed *κύκλοι* for the sale of such and such goods. The Agoras were not always in the cities; sometimes they were situated on a convenient spot on the boundaries of two or more states, to be used in common by them; sometimes they were in the neighbourhood of celebrated temples, which attracted crowds of votaries.

Not all times were equally devoted to marketing. Special days were set apart in many cities for fairs, the first of the month being a favourite time. On the occasion of all great festivals, and more especially of the Olympic,

[1] Heracleides, *Polit.* 30.

Nemean, and Pythian games, the assembly offered an irresistible opportunity to petty dealers of all sorts, who turned the place of meeting into a great fair, and provided the visitors with goods to carry away in memory of the feast. The meeting of the Amphictionic council, the annual assemblies of the Achaeans and Aetolians, and all other such gatherings were used in the same way. It is generally regarded by numismatists as established that it was on the occasion of these festivals that many issues of coins appeared. The coins which bear the name of the Eleians, for example, were almost certainly struck on the occasions of the Olympian festivals, and their types bear a close relation to the worship of the Olympian Zeus, and his messenger Victory. Finally, armies on the march were accompanied by crowds of hucksters ready to provide the soldiers with the necessaries of a campaign in return for the booty they might acquire, and especially to buy up the numerous enemies who should be captured and reduced to a condition of slavery. In passing through a friendly country, the army would halt in the neighbourhood of a city, and the inhabitants would come out and form a temporary Agora without the walls, where the soldiers could buy what they required. Hence generals in the field were obliged to constantly issue a supply of money, and in a large number of the coins which have come down to us we find traces of a military origin.

With regard to the transactions of merchants we get much information from the Attic orators, which is well summed up by Büchsenschütz, from whose work[1] the following is an extract:

'The merchant embarks certain goods for a place where he is sure of disposing of them, or at least has reasonable expectations of doing so; and either makes the journey on board the ship, or commits the goods to a trustworthy person whom he sends with them. As he thus runs the risk of finding under certain circumstances at the destination no market for his goods, he is in that case compelled to repair to another port which offers better prospects, unless on the

[1] *Besitz und Erwerb*, p. 459.

journey he has already received news of the altered circumstances and changed his plan in accordance with them. It is obvious that the merchants must have sought means of gaining news as to favourable or unfavourable conditions in the markets to which they intended to send their wares, as well as to the prices of the goods they intended to purchase in exchange. In the speech against Dionysodorus, Demosthenes gives a clear outline of the way in which a company of corn merchants keep themselves informed by correspondence of the current prices of corn, in order thence to determine whither to send their cargoes from Egypt. For the forwarding of such news, as well as for the buying and selling of goods, merchants kept agents at important places. For instance, we find it stated that a merchant resident at Athens sends word to a partner at Rhodes, giving him directions as to a corn-ship on her way from Egypt which is to call at Rhodes; a merchant of Heraclea has an associate at Scyros, who makes thence business trips; in another case the son and the partner of a merchant resident at Athens pass the winter at the Bosporus, probably with a stock of goods or to make purchases; at least it is stated that they were commissioned to receive payments.'

The Greek merchant would not be able, as a rule, to dispose of his whole cargo to one purchaser, but would sell it by portions to the various retail dealers. Sometimes indeed a speculator would try to buy up all of a particular commodity, such as corn or olives, which was in the market, in order to gain the control of the supply of that commodity and raise the price against the consumers. No behaviour was so unpopular in antiquity as this, and those who attempted it were very often victims of the general indignation. But there does not seem to have been, as among us, a class of general dealers or speculators intervening between merchant and shopkeeper.

On receiving payment for his goods in money, the merchant might sometimes sail home with it. This, however, took place seldom, partly because the money current at one seaport was usually not taken at another, except at a considerable reduction, every city having its own types and monetary standard. There were certain kinds of coin which had a more general circulation, as the silver coin of Athens and afterwards that of Alexander the Great in the Levant, the money of Corinth in Sicily and on the Adriatic, and the gold coins of Philip in Central Europe. But usually the money received by merchants had to be either expended by them in the same or a neighbouring port, or else taken away and melted down in order to pass as bullion. Therefore, after disposing of his cargo, the merchant would search about for a new stock of goods such as he might judge to be in demand at his native city or elsewhere; and thus the process already described would be repeated. It will be evident from this description that merchants among the Greeks could not usually confine themselves to dealing in one or two classes of goods, but must be ready to purchase whatever was cheap. There were, perhaps, exceptions in case of dealers who attended specially to classes of goods in demand everywhere, such as corn and slaves. Transactions among Greeks took place for money, but, in dealing with the barbarians, the Greeks retained barter at all periods of their trade.

That which produces the greatest differences between ancient and modern trade is the fact that in ancient times buying and selling took place not on credit but for cash. This makes the mechanism of ancient trade extremely simple. But it does not follow that a merchant must have then possessed a large trading capital. A large part of his working capital could be borrowed on the security of his goods.

III. Bankers.

As a large proportion of the wealth of many Greeks consisted in gold and silver money, they sought from the earliest times to turn it to account by lending it to those persons who could profitably employ it, and receiving interest in return. This lending was accompanied in various cities by various ceremonies, the chief object of which was to secure witnesses of the transaction and to prevent the borrower from denying the loan. Sometimes the contract was made in the presence of a sort of notary appointed by the State; more frequently it was arranged before witnesses summoned by the parties. At Athens the terms of the loan, the amount, rate of interest, and period were carefully stated in a document which was sealed by both parties and deposited in the custody of some trustworthy person. It is said that in the city of Cnossus[1] the borrower made a pretence of stealing the money lent him, in order that, if he did not repay it in time, the lender would have him in his power. A more usual precaution would be to require a person of respectability as surety for the repayment. As regards the goods which are the material security of a loan, Büchsenschütz,[2] whose chapters on these subjects are admirable, remarks that they may be either handed bodily over to the lender of money, in which case they would by us be called pledged, or retained by the borrower, whose creditor acquired certain rights over them, a condition to which we give the name of mortgage. Furniture, slaves, or horses might be given in pledge; lands, houses, or ships would usually be mortgaged. The nature of pledges is simple, and they need not occupy us further, if we only observe that he who lent money on a living pledge, such as a horse or slave, ran great risk of its dying, and of his security becoming thus worthless. Mortgages were more usual and of more importance.

Money-lenders in Greece were of two classes, either private individuals who had to live on the interest of their property, and possessed that property in the form of money, or else *τραπεζῖται* or *ἀργυραμοιβοί*, money-changers. Indeed, private persons usually intrusted these latter with spare capital, their professional habits and business abilities rendering them able to make better use of it than the owners could, while the money-changers gave good security to their creditors and allowed them a fair rate of interest.[3] As in Greece every considerable city had its own coinage,

[1] Plutarch, *Quaest. Gr.* 53. [2] *Besitz und Erwerb*, p. 485.

[3] Compare Matt. xxv. 27, 'Thou oughtest therefore to have put my money to the exchangers, and then at my coming I should have received mine own with usury'.

money-changers must have had a very large stock of gold and silver; and they would naturally constitute *par excellence* the class with money to lend. Further, their profession compelled them to live in the market-place at a spot known to all. Hence all in need of funds resorted to them, and they become bankers almost in our sense of the word. Some of them attained great wealth and world-wide credit. Thus Pasion[1] employed a capital of fifty talents, of which eleven belonged to his depositors. Merchants would without witnesses, such was his reputation for probity, deposit sums of money with him, which he at once entered in his books. On the credit of his name money could be procured in any Greek town, and deeds of all classes were deposited with him for safe custody. It was customary for merchants to make payments one to another, when they could not meet, by leaving the sum with a *trapezites*, with orders to him to deliver it to the proper person, who was also obliged, before receiving it, to prove his identity.

It was the *trapezitae*, then, who usually lent on mortgage (ὑποθήκη). The security was sometimes a manufactory with slaves in it. A still better class of security was the lands and farming capital of the citizens. It was usual to set up on mortgaged lands an inscription on stone stating the name of the creditor and the amount due to him. In some states there seems to have been a less primitive arrangement in the shape of a register of mortgages kept by authority. In case of default of payment on the part of the owner of the land, the holder of the mortgage apparently had the right to occupy it, even although the value of the land exceeded the amount of the debt. It would hence appear that foreigners and *metoeci*, being incapable of holding land, could not lend on this sort of security, or, if they did so, must do without the customary remedy.

To commerce the trapezitae were of the utmost importance, since without such aid as they afforded merchants could only have traded to the amount of their actual

[1] Demosth. *pro Phorm.* 5.

capital in coin. The ordinary course of proceeding was as follows: A merchant, say at Athens, wishes to carry a cargo to the Euxine. He finds a trapezites willing to lend 8,000 drachmas on the outward cargo on condition that he undertakes by written contract to make that cargo of the value of 12,000 drachmas. The rate of interest is fixed for the whole voyage at so much per cent. Either an agent of the trapezites sails with the ship, or else he appoints some person at a port on the Euxine to receive the money. When the cargo is sold on arriving at its destination, principal and interest are paid. If, on the other hand, the cargo is lost at sea, the trapezites loses his venture. Thus the system of borrowing on cargoes served, so far as the merchant was concerned, the purpose of insurance, besides increasing his available capital and so extending trade. The rate of interest was, of course, high and proportioned to the risks of the voyage, the course of which was carefully specified beforehand; in the contract it was sometimes also stated that if the voyage were prolonged into the winter season the rate of interest should be higher. In the case we have supposed, our merchant, after disposing of his cargo on the Euxine, and paying his debt with the proceeds, would find himself deprived of means for the return voyage unless he could again find a lender. It was therefore far more usual for those who sailed from Greek ports to borrow for the double journey, out and home, and repay the loan to the original lender on their return. Unfortunately, Greek commercial honour never being very high, this course of proceeding gave opportunity for a great deal of dishonesty and fraud. Various means of self-defence were adopted by the lenders, such as sending an agent on board or requiring a surety who remained at home, but their chief reliance was on the strictness of the laws, which were very severe against those who attempted fraud, more especially at Athens.

Sometimes capitalists, instead of lending on a cargo, would lend money on the ship herself. This was in most respects less risky, the value of a ship being easier to discover. Accordingly, while lenders would advance not more than two-thirds of the stated value of a cargo, which might easily suffer depreciation, we find that they would lend on a ship up to its full worth. But there was, of course, much risk of its being lost, a danger no doubt taken into view in fixing the rate of interest.

The functions of temples in regard to finance must not be overlooked. As the interests of the state and of the deities who protected it were identical, it was not unnatural that the temples should be the place where the revenues of the state were stored. The tribute from the allies at Athens was laid up in the precinct of Athena. Athena received her share of it, but the rest was used for revenue or for war.

It is commonly stated that besides being capitalists and lending money, temples received sums on deposit for safe keeping and restored them to the lenders on demand. The temple of Artemis at Ephesus seems to have been especially used for this purpose, and some writers go so far as to compare its position in the commercial world to that now held by the Bank of England. This, however, is gross exaggeration. As a rule, money placed in a temple became sacred and could not be withdrawn, or at least could only be taken for purposes of state. Most of the passages quoted in defence of the view just mentioned refer to peculiar cases. Xenophon, for example, deposited a sum of money in the Ephesian temple and afterwards withdrew it, but it was in order to found a new temple of Artemis in Peloponnese. In other instances we hear of money left by states and individuals in the hands of the people of Ephesus and by them honourably returned. They may have kept the treasures in the temple or its vicinity; but lending to the Ephesian state was another thing than lending to the estate of the goddess. It is obvious that if it had been lawful to place money in temples for security and withdraw it at pleasure, such a privilege would have been very frequently used, and the priests would have become regular bankers, which they never were. It was, however, maintained by

E. Curtius that the earliest coins were issued by temples which felt the need of a ready currency, and this theory, though not proved, is not impossible.

In a somewhat different category must be placed the wealth belonging to the temples of many of the great deities of Greece, notably in that of Athena at Athens. In the opinion of the Greeks the deities of a state were quite as much concerned in its preservation as were the citizens themselves; the state therefore did not hesitate in times of straits to borrow money from the sacred treasuries, to be repaid at some more convenient season. We have an Athenian inscription [1] which records such a transaction. It appears that in the time of the Peloponnesian war, during the eleven years 433–422 B.C., considerable sums of money were advanced to the Athenian state by the treasurers of Athena and of the other gods; and that, after the conclusion of the peace of Nicias in 421 B.C., this money was repaid with interest. This was probably no isolated case; but the same thing, at least as far as the borrowing was concerned, would have taken place in other cities. But, on the whole, the Greeks respected these deposits; and when temple treasures were violated, as by the Pisatae when they obtained possession of Olympia, and by the Phocians when they seized Delphi, all that was best in the race was scandalized, and a speedy vengeance of the offended gods fell on the violators.

Interest (*τόκος*) was reckoned among the Greeks in one of two ways, either by stating the number of drachms to be paid per month for the use of each mina,[2] or by stating the proportion of the whole sum lent to be paid yearly or for the period of the loan. The rate of interest was, of course, higher than among us, 12 per cent. per annum being considered a very low rate, and instances occurring in which 24 per cent. was charged. At Athens interest was generally paid monthly, at the new moon.

[1] *C. I.* No. 273.

[2] As the mina contained 100 drachms, a drachm in the mina per month would be twelve per centum per annum.

We find 10 or 12 per cent. paid for a loan on a single voyage from Athens to the Bosphorus; but we must remember that a part only of this amount represents interest on money; the remainder was paid for risk. For, as already shown, if the ship were wrecked at sea, or captured by pirates, or otherwise lost, the capitalist who had lent money on her cargo was the chief sufferer, recovering no part of his venture. The rate of interest being thus high, we can understand how private persons in the great cities, possessing no lands but only capital in the shape of money, managed to live in comfort on the interest of it.

Throughout the period of Greek autonomy the value of money, that is, of gold and silver, fell steadily. A scale is given by the rate of payment of those who at Athens attended the ecclesia. Towards the end of the fifth century it was only an obolus; it rose to three obols by 390 B.C., and stood at a drachm in the time of Alexander. Boeckh calculated that in the period from Solon to Demosthenes prices increased fivefold.

In the time of the Athenian Empire skilled workers or mercenary soldiers would be paid from half a drachm to a drachm a day. Assuming a drachm a day to be sufficient to keep a family in ordinary comfort, this indicates an expenditure of 360 drachms a year. At 12 per cent. interest such an annual revenue would be provided by a capital of 3,000 drachms or half a talent, corresponding in weight of silver to about £120 to £130 of our money.

The denominations of coins in Greece were simple. At Athens eight oboli went to the drachm, a hundred drachms to the mina, sixty minas to the talent. The term stater was vaguely applied to any standard coin in general use; such as the daric in Persia, the tetradrachm at Athens, the didrachm at Aegina. A simple and rough, but sufficiently accurate scale of values to keep in mind would equate the daric, or the Attic gold stater, with the English sovereign; the twentieth part of the daric, the silver shekel, with the English shilling; the Attic drachm with the French franc. The purchasing power of money was, of course, much greater in Greece than in modern times; but to determine the exact purchasing value of Greek coins as compared with our own is, of course, an insoluble problem. Many luxuries which the modern artisan buys for a few pence would have been beyond the reach of Croesus; while, on the other hand, a Greek could have bought for a drachm a terra-cotta figurine for which a modern collector would give hundreds of pounds. The equation above given that a family could live comfortably on a drachm (a franc) a day gives the best practical test of purchasing power.

IV. Early Measures of Value.

Aristotle, in language on which the best instructed political economist could scarcely improve, has explained the true origin of a metallic currency.[1]

'As the benefits of commerce were more widely extended, by importing commodities of which there was a deficiency, and exporting those of which there was an excess, the use of a currency was an indispensable device. As the necessaries of nature were not all easily portable, people agreed, for purposes of barter, mutually to give and receive some article which, while it was itself a commodity, was practically easy to handle in the business of life, some such article as gold or silver, which was at first defined merely by size and weight, although finally they went further, and set a stamp upon every coin to relieve them from the trouble of weighing it, as the stamp impressed upon the coin was an indication of quantity.'

Aristotle is, of course, right in the main; but he is wrong when he supposes the need for a coinage to press most on merchants and shippers. Those who dispose of great quantities of goods (*ἔμποροι*) need a coinage less than the stall-keepers and pedlars, *κάπηλοι*, to whom small change is almost a necessity. Thus it was the Aeginetans, the pedlars of Greece, who first struck money in Europe. The great mercantile cities of Tyre, Sidon, and Carthage adopted the invention much later.

[1] *Politics*, i. 6, 14. Welldon's translation.

We can trace, though not in detail, three stages through which trade passed in early Greece, in the development of a coinage:

(1) The pre-metallic stage. Among the more backward races of the world even now, or until very recently, the medium of exchange or measure of value has been some article which was portable, and the value of which was recognized by all. Every reader of travels in Africa knows that, in the interior of that continent, the yard of cloth is or was the unit of value: the traveller bargains with a chief as regards the number of yards he must pay for permission to pass through the chief's territory. In China, shells passed as currency, as in parts of Africa and South Asia: we are even told that compressed cubes of tea passed as currency in Turkestan. Much curious lore of this kind is to be found in Ridgeway's *Origin of Currency*. The only pre-metallic unit of value which we can clearly trace in Greece is cattle, the ox in particular, which served as the measure of wealth to the Homeric Achaeans. The well-known Homeric line, 'Arms worth a hundred kine for arms worth nine,' proves this. In the early laws of Rome, as well as in the laws of Draco, fines were assessed in oxen. And the very word *pecunia*, which is closely related to *pecus*, a flock, bears record of a time when in Latium wealth was calculated in flocks and herds, as was wealth in Palestine in the days of Job.

(2) The next stage in currency is the use of the precious metals by weight. When once gold, silver, and bronze circulated freely, their superior fitness as currency enabled them to drive out all competitors. An ox is well enough to reckon by, but when it comes to halves and quarters of the unit a difficulty arises; the half of an ox would be a most inconvenient thing to take in payment. But metals can easily be divided and lose nothing in the process. In fact, in the ancient world most nations which had passed beyond the stage of barter used the precious metals by weight in their trade. This fact is made familiar to us by several passages in Genesis. 'Abraham weighed to Ephron the

silver, which he had named in the audience of the children of Heth, four hundred shekels,'[1] on a recognized standard. This custom of weighing the precious metals recurred both in ancient and mediaeval times, when the currency of coin had been debased beyond a certain point, and had become unworthy of trust. It is even carried on at the present day at the counter of banks, where gold is weighed before it is accepted.

(3) The third stage concerns us more closely. It consists in the circulation of the precious metals, no longer in bars or ingots to be cut up as occasion demanded, but in units of fixed amount. In Egyptian wall-paintings there is frequently represented the weighing of rings of gold or silver. These rings the records show to have been of fixed weight. The form is very suitable, because if a ring be everywhere rounded, it is almost impossible to 'sweat' it without detection. Rings of fixed weight could be used alike for ornament and for currency. The servant of Abraham at the well gave Rebekah a gold ring half a shekel in weight, and two bracelets of ten shekels weight.[2] In Syria to this day women carry much of their wealth thus on their persons, and it can be readily spent.

The Greek fashion, however, in early times, seems to have been to use, not rings, but bars or pellets of fixed weight. In gold, they would be pellets; in bronze or iron, bars of recognized size. From the gold pellet, when once the notion had been started of stamping it to guarantee weight and fineness, there sprang the electrum coinage of Ionia. From the bars or spits (ὀβελοί) of bronze or iron sprang, as we shall see in a future chapter, the silver coinage of Greece Proper.

In the *Iliad* we read of talents of gold. Achilles proposes as the first prize for a race a vessel of silver, for the second an ox, for the third a half talent of gold.[3] And as the third prize might well be of half the value of the second, this at once suggests that the talent of gold and the ox would be of equal value. Certainly, since at the time both oxen and

[1] Genesis xxiii. 16. [2] Genesis xxiv. 22. [3] *Iliad*, xxiii. 750.

fixed weights of gold were in use as measures of value, some kind of relation between the two would have to be recognized, and equality is the simplest of all relations. A writer on Talents at Alexandria of about A. D. 100[1] roundly says that the Homeric talent was of the same weight as the later daric, that is to say, contained 130 grains (grm. 8·42) of gold. But it is hard to see whence a writer of the Roman Age can have learned such a fact: it must almost certainly be a theory of some earlier writer on metrology. In itself it is very probable[2]; but the majority of modern scholars decline to allow that the Homeric talent had any fixed weight or value. It ought to mean the equivalent in gold of the amount of bronze which a man could conveniently carry: whether it had become conventionalized as a fixed weight it is not easy to determine. But however the word *talent* may be used in Homer, it may be regarded as very probable that pellets of gold of the weight of the later darics were in use as early as the eighth century, and probably much earlier.

Julius Pollux tells us[3] that at the Delian festival the prizes to be given were announced as to be in oxen, according to ancient precedent; but that, in fact, for each ox was substituted a didrachm of Attic weight. But there can be little doubt that by this phrase is meant an Attic didrachm of silver (135 grains, grm. 8·74); so that if the passage proves anything, it indicates that an ox was only of the value of two silver drachms, which is certainly too low. An Attic didrachm of gold was of nearly the same value as a daric; but such coins were not issued until the fourth century, and so they can scarcely have directly succeeded oxen.

It has been suggested that bars of bronze, if of well-known diameter, might be estimated by length only, a foot or an inch having a recognized value. Butter is thus sold at Cambridge in the market. But it seems a fatal objection to this view that the bronze oboli were spits, coming to

[1] Hultsch, *Metrologici Scriptores*, i, p. 301.

[2] See Ridgeway in *Journ. Hell. Stud.*, 1887, p. 133.

[3] *Onomasticon*, ix. 61.

a point, and thus cannot have been of an uniform diameter throughout.

V. The Origin of Coin-standards.

The question of the ultimate origin of the weight standards used for coins in Hellas is a very complicated and difficult one. Several recent German writers, such as Brandis, Hultsch, Lehmann-Haupt, and Haeberlin, have worked out most elaborate theories, deriving these standards from those in use in the great Empires of the East. A brief account of these theories will be found in the Introduction to the *Historia Numorum*, and in Mr. Hill's *Handbook of Greek and Roman Coins.*

Not only do such writers believe in an accurate transmission of measure and weight from Babylon to the West, but they also think that the Greeks made in their turn, in the times before the Persian Wars, elaborate and complicated systems of weights and measures, the talent being of the weight of a cubic foot of water, and the measures of length, surface, and weight fitting together in a coherent scheme.

Attempts have been made, for example, to show that the weight of the Attic talent, used for silver coin, corresponds to that of water filling a cube of the Attic foot. Whether this view be sound or not I cannot here inquire; but if it be a fact, it may very probably result from an adjustment of the foot in the fifth century, long after the introduction of the Attic coin-weight.

It has even been maintained that a study of the French system of mètres and litres, introduced in the time of the Revolution, and based on scientific investigation, is a necessary preliminary to understanding ancient weights and measures. The contrary is the truth. The modern scientific methods of determining weights and measures are completely foreign to peoples in the mental condition in which the Greeks were when coinage began.

We English, who retain in a modified form the mediaeval

weights and measures, the mile of 1,760 yards, the perch, the fathom, the quarter of corn, troy, avoirdupois, and apothecaries' weights and the like, are far more nearly in touch with ancient ways of measuring. The attempt to squeeze Greek coin-weights into metric systems is misleading. We must take them as they stand, in all their irregularity and inaccuracy, and try to discover how they worked, not according to preconceived theory, but in commercial practice. Only so can we approach the historic facts of Greek money-changing and commerce.

As I have above given to Mommsen and Brandis the credit of first introducing method into the metrology of coins, I must express regret that their followers in Germany have often made in this matter schemes which are merely fantastic. Mr. Hill's sober judgement is that 'the least satisfactory department of ancient numismatics is that which is occupied with questions of metrology'.[1] Beloch is still more severe. 'Ancient metrology', he writes,[2] 'seems on the point of losing all solid ground under its feet, and becoming a meeting-place of wild fancies.' Brandis began by inventing for Babylon, besides the mina of 60 shekels, a mina of 50 shekels, which never really existed. Subsequent writers have improved upon this, and tried by raising or diminishing a standard of weight by some proportion, a fifth or a sixth, or it may be a twenty-fourth, to derive other standards. As Beloch observes, by such a process it is easy to derive any weight from any other, and he proceeds by way of *reductio ad absurdum* to derive the French kilogram from the Egyptian kite. But unfortunately Beloch, while rightly rejecting these extravagances, falls into a pit of his own digging. He produces the fact, on which we shall comment later, that at Delphi the Attic mina was officially equated with 35 Aeginetan didrachms (just about its true value), and draws from it the unjustified inference that the Aeginetan mina, instead of consisting of 100 drachms, contained only 70. Now we have several extant weights which follow a mina (9,700 grains, grm. 628·5)

[1] *Handbook*, p. 26. [2] *Griech. Geschichte*, i. 2, 333.

which can scarcely be any but the Aeginetan; but for an Aeginetan mina of the same weight as the Attic there is no authority whatever. He goes on to make a mina at Thasos of 45 Thasian staters of 150 grains, grm. 9·70, also equal to the Attic mina; a Milesian mina of 30 staters, and so on. He writes [1]: 'All the Greek systems which were widely accepted before Alexander the Great stand in the closest relations one to another; they all are based on a mina of 436·6 grammes, 6,700 grains, or on one half as heavy again, and differ only as this mina is variously divided.' This is mere fancy.

A useful corrective to the *a priori* metrologists is furnished by Professor Ridgeway's *Origin of Currency and Weight Standards*, which is a broad and comparative survey, and contains a great amount of interesting information. But unfortunately Ridgeway has adopted the theory that the weights of silver coins in Greece were fixed by a continuous series of attempts so to adjust them as to make them stand in a convenient relation to the gold shekel of 130 grains (grm. 8·42). This theory I hold to be, save in a few instances, quite baseless [2]; and thus, while the earlier part of Ridgeway's book is useful, the latter part is of a much lower order of value. He is much more at home in dealing with the practices of primitive peoples than in explaining Greek customs.

I feel that in skirting a shore thus strewn with wrecks I cannot be too careful in adhering closely to that for which we have definite evidence. And if sometimes I have to propound hypotheses, I will at all events let it be clearly seen on what facts I base them.

In regard to the coinage of Greece, as in regard to sculpture, vase-painting, and other developments of Hellenic civilization, there are, and probably will always be, two views: the view of those who derive the origin of Greek civilization from the East, from the old and established cultures of Babylon and Egypt in the eighth and seventh

[1] *Griech. Geschichte*, ii. 1, 345.

[2] See chs. v and xvi, below.

centuries B.C., and the view of those who think it more or less continuous from the pre-Hellenic civilizations, which we now call Minoan and Mycenaean. In my view there was little actual survival from prehistoric to historic times. The invasions of the Hellenes from the North seem to have made an almost complete end of the Mycenaean culture; a few centuries of comparative barbarism intervened; after which fresh seeds of culture were imported by the Greeks from their Asiatic neighbours.[1]

What positive evidence have we as to the weights in use in Minoan and Mycenaean Greece? It is put together by Sir Arthur Evans in a paper in the *Corolla Numismatica*.[2] But weights, unless they bear an inscription, are very hard to identify as belonging to this or that system; and we have not yet attained to certainty. In Evans's opinion the Kedet system of Egypt, the gold shekel system of Babylon, and the Phoenician silver shekel system were all in use in the Minoan world. But apparently the Minoans had no native system of their own. From this point of view the question is only whether the Greeks received these oriental weights through the Minoans, or whether they derived them direct from the east. But there are a few other data. Professor E. A. Gardner weighed the gold rings found in the Acropolis graves at Mycenae[3]; but the weights he records are so varied and erratic that it does not seem safe to base any conclusion on them. More important are certain dumps or pellets of silver, one of which was found in the magazines of the palace at Cnossus. These are of forms very similar to that of the earliest electrum coins, of which Evans is disposed to consider them the forerunners. The weight of the Cnossian example is 56·4 grains (grm. 3·65). Three other examples were found in the Mycenaean cemetery at Salamis in Cyprus. The weights are: 132·9 grains (grm. 8·60); 72·9 grains (grm. 4·72); and 72·2 grains (grm. 4·67). If these pellets of metal had all conformed to one standard, their evidence would have been important. As it is, though

[1] See especially Poulsen, *Frühgriechische Kunst*. [2] p. 336 and foll.
[3] *Journ. Hell. Stud.*, x. 90.

severally they can be fitted into various scales of weight, the first to the Phoenician, the second to the Egyptian, the third and fourth to the Babylonic, yet they do not prove the use of pellets of silver of fixed weight as currency; certainly they do not prove that it was from the primitive inhabitants of Hellas that the Ionians and the Dorians derived their monetary standards.

The view maintained in this book is that there were three chief original monetary systems in the Greek world, whence all, or almost all others were derived:

(1) The gold system, exemplified in the gold staters issued by Croesus and the Persians

(2) The silver system, exemplified in the silver staters issued by the people of Aegina.

(3) The bronze system, in partial use in the Greek cities of Italy and Sicily, and probably derived from the original inhabitants of those countries.

Of these the first is the most important: the third is important for Rome, but not for Hellas.

(1) The coinage of Lydia and Ionia starts, so far as we can judge, with a gold stater of 130 grains (grm. 8·42); though the actual gold of Lydia is about four grains lighter, and the coinage of Phoenicia seems to take its origin from a gold stater of double the weight, 260 grains (grm. 16·84). These two staters correspond with the sixtieth part of two minae, weights representing which were actually found by Layard at Nineveh. The heavier standard, with a mina of about 1,010 grammes (15,600 grains), was represented by bronze lions, bearing inscriptions both cuneiform and Aramaic. The lighter standard, with a mina of about 505 grammes (7,800 grains), was represented by stone ducks, bearing cuneiform inscriptions. Whether these minae (manahs) were formed by multiplication of the above-mentioned staters, or whether the staters were arrived at by dividing the minae, is not certain, but the latter view seems clearly preferable. Two lion weights are inscribed respectively: (1) 'Five manahs of the King', in cuneiform; 'Five manahs weight of the country', in Aramaic; (2) 'Two

manahs of the King', in cuneiform; 'Two manahs weight of the country', in Aramaic. The Aramaic legends are important, as they seem to show that the standard which they represent was in use in Mesopotamia and Syria, and this is confirmed by other evidence. But the lighter mina was historically more important, as the whole coinage of Lydia and Ionia is dominated by it. In discussing the early electrum coinage of Asia, I shall show how the weights of the early coins of Asia Minor, gold, electrum, and silver, are related to the Lydian gold shekels.

That the Homeric Greeks equated this shekel with their older measure of value, the ox, is probable; but it is likely that this equation was only a rough adjustment for practical purposes. It must have been quite conventional, since obviously oxen differ very much one from another in value; and it is quite natural that when once the Ionians had accepted the current gold pellet as the standard of value, it soon, in virtue of its greater stability and definiteness, would drive out the old method of reckoning in cattle or other units of value, or cause it to fall into line.

(2) It might not be unreasonable to suppose that the tradition of Mycenae had some influence on the origin of the one really Greek system of weights and coinage—that of Aegina—a system which, with small exceptions, was not applied to gold but only to silver. On the other hand, the Pheidonian weights, which were the regulating condition of that coinage, may have been of pure Hellenic origin, and come in with the Hellenes from the north. To this question I will return when I treat of the Aeginetan coinage. However this be, it is certain that between the Ionian coinage, which started with the gold stater, and divided it, or its equivalent in electrum, into thirds, sixths, twelfths, and twenty-fourths, and the Aeginetan coinage, which started with the bronze or iron spit, and went on to the silver drachm and didrachm, there was a broad line of distinction. The one represented the Ionian, the other the Dorian stream of influence. In coinage, as in architecture and in sculpture, and, in fact, in every department of civilization, the

Ionian and the Dorian contributions were the two elements which made up the Hellenic whole.

We may perhaps find a silver standard independent of that of Aegina in use at Samos and at Cyrene in the sixth century. This question is discussed below, where I have conjectured its derivation from the Egyptian Kat.

(3) The unit of value in Italy and Sicily, before the establishment of the Greeks in those countries, was the litra or pound of bronze. This had indeed been the case in Greece Proper before the coming in of the Aeginetan and Euboic silver; but in Greece after that time the bronze unit of value seems to vanish; while the iron unit held its place only in Sparta. In Italy and Sicily, owing to the tenacity of the native population, reckoning in pounds of bronze went on at the same time as reckoning in silver. But in Sicily, when the bronze litra had been equated with 13·5 grains of silver (grm. 0·87), and the drachm of silver made equal to five litrae, a simple and easy way of double reckoning was set up, and it was not until the issue of gold coins at Syracuse, at the end of the fifth century, that the equivalence of a round number of litrae with coins of fresh denominations was seriously aimed at.

In Italy, as we know from the history of the Roman coinage, bronze as a measure of value better held its own, as indeed would be expected from the stronger character of the native population. At Tarentum, for example, Evans has proved the use of the bronze litra and its equivalent in silver. In Etruria, silver and bronze lived on equal terms, and every silver coin had a value in bronze, commonly indicated by numerals on the coin itself. We may suspect that the continuous fall in the standards of the silver coins of the Greek cities of South Italy, a fall not easy to understand, and presenting a marked contrast to the strict maintenance of full weight in the cities of Sicily, may have been due to the influence of bronze.

It is often by no means easy to determine to which standard a given coin belongs. We cannot, in assigning it to one or another, go merely by the weight, since with time coins may either gain weight by oxidation or lose it by friction or decay. One has to use the reason as well as the scales; and in so doing there is, of course, a danger of importing erroneous theory into the question.

It is also difficult to assign names to the various standards in use. The names at present in use are often unsatisfactory. I have as far as possible taken a safe line by naming each standard after the city from which it seems to proceed, or indeed the most important city which used it. It is much more satisfactory to speak of the standard of Miletus or Corinth or Abdera, than of the Graeco-Asiatic or the Babylonic standard. In fact cities, in adopting some standard for their coins, usually modified it; and then commonly preserved their own version for centuries. This is a procedure we could hardly have expected. But such is the fact. It is astonishing how little cities such as Athens, Ephesus, Syracuse, vary the weights of their coins over long periods of time. Some other cities, such as Abdera, have not unfrequent changes in standard; and the reasons for such changes have to be carefully sought.

VI. Mutual Relations of Precious Metals.

It is obvious that the functions of coins in the commerce of the Greek states cannot be traced, unless we are able with some confidence to determine the mutual relations in value of the metals used for money: for coins in Greece were merely bullion, with an official stamp to guarantee weight and fineness. In a great empire the money of the state may circulate for a time at a fictitious value. In the Middle Ages kings were able to compel their subjects, by threats of punishment, to take their depreciated coin at its nominal value, though in the long run such artificial inflation failed. But the case was different in Greece. Each city had its coinage, but it had no means whatever of forcing it into circulation beyond the limits of the city's territory, except by taking care that the coin was of full weight and pure metal. Tyrants like Dionysius of Sicily attempted to tamper with the state coinage, but their success must have been both slight and transient.

Fortunately we are able, within certain limits, to fix the relative values of gold, silver, electrum, and bronze in different regions at successive periods of history. I propose in this place to give a summary of our knowledge of the matter which in future chapters I can expand.[1]

As regards the proportional values of the three metals, gold, silver, and electrum, in the ancient world we owe an excellent summary of our knowledge to an investigation by M. Théodore Reinach.[2] On nearly all points the conclusions of M. Reinach, based as they are upon a careful examination of ancient texts and inscriptions and of extant coins, seem to me to be solidly established.

In Asia, from the beginning of coinage down to the middle of the fourth century, the ratio of value between gold and silver was $13\frac{1}{3}$ to 1. This is a view maintained by Mommsen and Brandis, and it seems trustworthy. It is indeed established by induction from a consideration of the Persian coinage. The gold daric or stater in that empire weighed up to 130 grains (grm. 8·42) and the silver shekel up to 86 grains (grm. 5·57). Now we know on the definite authority of Xenophon[3] that twenty of the silver coins passed as equivalent to one of the gold; so we have the formula 1,720 grains of silver are equivalent to 130 of gold, and the relation between these numbers is nearly $13\frac{1}{3}$ to 1. The same equation holds in the Lydian coinage which preceded the daric; and we cannot doubt that it was an old-established equivalence. Herodotus, it is true, in his account of the revenues of Persia,[4] says that gold was thirteen times as valuable as silver; but this is clearly only an approximate statement. The relation $13\frac{1}{3}$ to 1, although at first glance

[1] Especially useful are papers by M. E. Babelon, *Origines de la monnaie*, 1897, chs. 6–8, and by M. Théodore Reinach, *L'Histoire par les monnaies*, 1902, chs. 4 and 5.

[2] *L'Histoire par les monnaies*, 1902, ch. 4.

[3] *Anab.* i. 7, 18. Cyrus pays 3,000 darics in discharge of a debt of ten talents of silver, or 60,000 shekels.

[4] Hdt. iii. 95, 1.

more complex, is in reality simpler, for by working on it the silver shekel is almost exactly two-thirds of the weight of the daric; and this fact would greatly simplify the process of weighing (86 + 43 = 129).

It appears from Egyptian inscriptions that gold was in Egypt regarded as twelve or thirteen times as valuable as silver.[1] Of course, however, the ratio varied from time to time. And we know that in very early times gold was plentiful in Egypt in comparison with silver. But Ridgeway is not justified in thinking that in Hellas a higher proportion than 14 to 1 prevailed between the two metals.

But there was in use in Asia as a measure of value a third metal, electrum, a mixture of gold and silver; of which, in fact, the earliest coins are composed. The same authorities who have established the proportionate values of gold and silver have shown that electrum was not regarded as a compound, but as a separate kind of metal, and reckoned in Asia as of ten times the value of silver and three-fourths of the value of pure gold. Hence electrum coins were usually struck not on the standard used for gold, but on that used for silver. We are told by Herodotus that the bricks of electrum or white gold dedicated by Croesus at Delphi were of the same size as the bricks of pure gold, but weighed only four-fifths as much. An easy calculation based on the specific gravities of gold and silver respectively shows that these electrum bricks contained 70 per cent. of gold and 30 per cent. of silver, approximately. Isidore of Seville[2] says that electrum contained three-fourths gold and one-fourth silver. But we do not know whence he gained this information. Pliny states that the term electrum is applied to all gold mixed to the extent of at least one-fifth with silver.

The question of the relation in value between gold and electrum nevertheless offers problems which, in the present state of our knowledge, we are scarcely able to solve. What has caused the utmost perplexity to numismatists is

[1] E. Babelon, *Origines de la monnaie*, p. 311. [2] *Orig.* xvi. 24.

the very remarkable fact that the proportion between gold and silver in the composition of the coins varies greatly, and with it their intrinsic value. It is possible by weighing, first in air and then in water, to determine the specific gravity of electrum coins; and from the specific gravity it is possible to deduce, within certain limits, their composition, the proportion of gold and silver which they contain. In 1887 I applied this method to a number of electrum coins of Cyzicus; and in the same year B. V. Head made a series of similar investigations as regards other electrum coins.[1] The results are extraordinary, and very disconcerting. Instead of the proportions of gold and silver being fixed, they vary in an extreme degree. In the case of a set of electrum coins of Cyzicus of various ages, I found the percentage of gold to vary from 58 to 33 per cent. Mr. Head, ranging over a wider field, found that the percentage of gold in early electrum coins varied from 72 to 10 or even 5 per cent. Thus of coins of the same weight, one might be sixfold the value of another.

J. Hammer has analysed a far larger number of coins with similar results.[2] The view which he accepts is that electrum was coined as it was found in the rivers. He shows that modern investigations prove that gold thus found contains up to 40 per cent. of silver. Yet it is hard to believe that Lydians and Greeks, even in the sixth century, were unaware of a process for separating the two metals. It is still harder to suppose that the same disability existed in the case of the people of Cyzicus down into the fourth century. The Greeks, even at an early period, were perfectly well aware of the methods for mixing gold and silver; and they used touchstones, found in the very district of Lydia where coinage originated, which enabled them to determine with considerable accuracy the degree of alloy in coins professedly of gold. How then is it possible that they can have accepted debased coins of electrum as of equal value with coins of good quality?

The view of Brandis and Mommsen, that electrum was

[1] In the *Numism. Chronicle.*

[2] *Zeitschr. f. Numism.*, xxvi, p. 47.

originally regarded as a metal apart, and conventionally accepted as of ten times the value of silver, or three-fourths of the value of gold, strange as it may seem, is after all probably the true one. For, remarkable as it may be that Greek merchants should be willing to accept coins not guaranteed by any king or city at a fixed and conventional rate, it is still more improbable that they should have to value every piece of money offered them by means of the touchstone, and make the simplest bargain into a very elaborate arithmetical problem. In the latter case, one cannot see what advantage the electrum coinage would possess over bars or rings of gold or silver, which as a matter of fact it superseded in commerce.

It is, however, improbable that this conventional value of electrum lasted after the sixth century. In the case of the electrum coins issued by the cities which took part in the Ionian Revolt, and still more in the case of the later Cyzicene and Lampsacene electrum staters, it is probable that the value in exchange better conformed to intrinsic value. At a relation of 10 to 1 a Cyzicene stater of 254 grains would be nearly the equivalent of 38 Attic silver drachms, and we know, as is shown below, that 25 drachms was much nearer to its actual valuation.

M. Reinach maintains that as the value of gold in relation to silver fell in Greece, the value of electrum fell also, retaining its proportion to gold of three-fourths. Thus in the early part of the fourth century electrum was in Greece no longer ten times as valuable as silver, but nine times, or three-fourths of twelve times. And in the days of Alexander, on the same principle, electrum fell to seven and a half times the value of silver. This view seems plausible, but it does not agree with the facts in regard to Cyzicene staters.

While, however, electrum coinage thus offers unsolved difficulties, this is not really the case with gold and silver issues. Habit was of infinitely greater power in the ancient than in the modern world, and conventions were more readily accepted. Thus there is no difficulty in supposing that the proportionate value of gold and silver as maintained by the Lydians and the Persians might persist for an indefinite period. In France, in the nineteenth century, the proportion of 15½ to 1 was long maintained in coinage, and was only overturned by the vast output of silver in America.

As the Treasurers at Athens sometimes required gold for dedications, we find in the Athenian treasure-lists a fairly complete account of the value of gold at Athens at various periods. It is true that these treasure-lists which have come down to us are usually mutilated or fragmentary, but it has been possible to collect their testimony. They prove that when the gold and ivory statue of Athena was being constructed, 438 B.C., gold was bought at the rate of 14 to 1. But when, towards the end of the fifth century, gold coins began to be struck at Athens, it is almost certain that the rate had fallen to 12 to 1. For not only the drachm was struck in gold, but also the third and the sixth of the drachm. If gold were at 12 to 1 these would be equivalent respectively to a tetradrachm and a didrachm in silver; but at any other proportion they would not work in. In the pseudo-Platonic dialogue *Hipparchus*[1] the value of gold in relation to silver is distinctly stated to be twelvefold. And this relation seems to have persisted until the great issues of gold coins by Philip of Macedon, and the dissipation of the gold treasures of the Persian kings by Alexander, brought down the value of gold in Greece to 10 to 1, a value confirmed by the Athenian accounts of 306 B.C.

These values held in Greece Proper as a rule.

In Sicily, gold seems to have retained its value better than in Greece. In the time of Timoleon it was still twelve times as valuable as silver.[2]

VII. Rights of Coinage.

At what period the right to issue coin came to be regarded as belonging only to autonomous cities, tribes

[1] p. 231 d.

[2] Head, *Coinage of Syracuse*, p. 28.

and kings is not an easy question. M. Babelon has maintained that the earliest coins were minted not by cities but by capitalists and merchants, and he cites many mediaeval and modern parallels.[1] This question I have discussed in my chapter on the earliest electrum coinage. However that be, it is certain that in the course of the sixth century, if not earlier, private issues ceased and civic coinages took their place.

Besides autonomous cities, it would seem that in early times the great religious centres of Greece sometimes issued coins. This was natural enough. Many of the shrines of Greece, notably those at Delphi, Delos, Olympia, and Miletus, were possessed of great wealth, drawing revenues from lands and houses as well as by the exercise of religious functions. As the great temples exercised some of the functions of modern banks in lending money on lands or goods, it is not unnatural that they should have struck coin bearing as device an attribute or the effigy of the deity to whom they were consecrated. Ernst Curtius sought here the origin of the religious character of the types commonly borne by coins; and though this view is an exaggeration, and the civic devices were usually religious as well as those of the temples, yet we are in a position, in a few cases, to prove the striking of coins by the religious corporations of temples. A coin of Miletus, struck in the fourth century, bears the legend *'Εγ Διδύμων ἱερή*, where *δραχμή* is probably understood. This must clearly have been struck on some special religious occasion, very probably at the time of the rebuilding of the temple of Apollo in 334 B.C. And as the weight, 27 grains (grm. 1·75), is just half of that of the Rhodian drachm then current, it seems to prove that a special issue was made on a reduced standard. The Jews, in Roman times, struck sacred coins for offerings in the Temple, whence money-changers set up their tables in the precincts to provide such coin in exchange for foreign money. Olympia was not a town, but only a sacred site, hence when we find coins inscribed

[1] *Origines de la monnaie*, pp. 93–134.

'Ολυμπικὸν (i.e. νόμισμα) we may be sure that such coins were issued in the sacred precincts, probably to provide memorials for the visitors who thronged the sacred place at the time of the festival.[1] In fact, the whole coinage which bears the name of the people of Elis probably belonged to the temple and the festival, with which the types which it bears are closely connected, Zeus, Hera, the eagle, the thunderbolt, and the like. In the same way, the abundant coins issued at Heraea in the fifth century, and inscribed Ἀρκαδικόν, were probably issued on the occasion of the festival of Zeus Lycaeus. At the time the people of Arcadia had no federal union, and cities such as Mantinea and Psophis struck their own coins, so that it seems certain that the issue at Heraea was a religious rather than a civic one. The coins, again, issued at Delphi after the sacred war, and bearing the legend Ἀμφικτιόνων,[2] are certainly no federal issue, but temple coins, perhaps struck on the occasion of the Pythian festival of 346 B.C.

The great mass of Greek coins, however, at all events after the Persian conquest of Asia Minor, was struck by the civic authorities of the Hellenic cities.

Students of Greek coins are apt to receive the impression that each Greek city-state, and each independent tribe, issued coins, choosing their types and their weights in a perfectly arbitrary way. M. François Lenormant puts this view as follows[3]: 'Every city had its coins, which it struck and regulated at will, acting in the matter with complete independence, in the isolation of its own sovereignty, and without caring what course was taken by its nearest neighbours.' The number of mints was certainly great, between 1,500 and 2,000. More than fifty Greek cities in Sicily struck coins. The little island of Ceos, not ten miles across, had three active mints. Some towns are only known to have existed by their extant coins. Nevertheless the statement of Lenormant is an extreme exaggeration. The Greeks have always had a keen commercial instinct, and

[1] Head, *H. N.*, p. 420. [2] Ibid., p. 342.

[3] *Histoire de la monnaie dans l'antiquité*, ii, p. 54.

when one reflects on the chaos which must naturally have resulted in trade, if cities really used their autonomy in this unbridled fashion, one sees that there must have been restrictions of some kind, else the work of money-changers in commercial centres would have been impossibly complicated; and the Greek world, like the Roman world at certain periods, would have fallen back on only accepting the precious metals by weight, and not as currency. There must have been in all important markets predominant coinages, and other coinages of any importance would have to stand in some defined relationship with these. If we look at the coins of the less wealthy Greek cities, we often find that they seem to have been issued only on two or three occasions in the history of those cities. Of course, it is not easy to prove a negative, or definitely to assert that since no coins of other periods have survived, therefore they were not struck. But where negative evidence is cumulative, it may demand acceptance. It is contrary to common sense, and to our evidence, to suppose that cities took no account of their neighbours' coin-standards in fixing their own. If that had been the case, the present book would have been without basis. But in our days no historic student believes that events happen by accident: we look for lines of influence and connexion everywhere, and attach special value to indications of commercial influence.

It will be well to begin with instances in which we have actual evidence of the restriction of the right of coinage.

It is the view of nearly all numismatists[1] that the great King of Persia allowed in his dominions no issues of gold coins save the royal darics. There is no definite statement of an ancient historian to be quoted to this effect; but the survey of ancient coinage seems clearly to establish the fact. Darius prided himself, as Herodotus tells us, on the purity of his gold coin[2]; and no other coins in pure gold were

[1] M. Babelon is an exception. *Traité*, ii. 2, 5.
[2] Hdt. iv. 166.

issued in Asia until about 400 B.C., though the Greek cities of the coast struck money in silver freely; and a few of them issued coins of electrum. Persian satraps also struck silver money in Cilicia on the occasion of military expeditions, but no gold. At a later time this monopoly of gold coinage was taken on by the Romans as part of their policy, and rigidly guarded through all their history.

A second example may be found in the monetary policy of Athens in the time of her empire, 476–405 B.C. Here we have the authority, not only of numismatic facts but of inscriptions, for the statement that it was a part of Athenian state policy to prohibit the issue of coins in all places which were under the Athenian dominion, and to force the subject cities to use the silver *owl* coins of Athens. (See Chap. XIV.)

A third example may be found in the coinage of Boeotia. Mr. Head has shown[1] that for sixty years from the battle of Coroneia (447 B.C.) to the peace of Antalcidas (387 B.C.) Thebes used her position as head of the Boeotian League to monopolize the coinage. During these sixty years all coins struck in Boeotia bear the name and the types of the dominant city. Whether Corinth moved on the same lines will be discussed below.

We cannot doubt that when the history of Greek coinage is better known to us we shall find abundant instances of this restriction by dominant cities of the privilege of coinage in states controlled by them. How far the motive was commercial, and how far merely pride and a love of dominance, is a difficult question. At Athens certainly the finance of the state was largely based on the resources obtained from the silver mines of Laurium and Thrace, and the utilization of these resources in the form of coin; but it does not follow that this motive held in all other cases.

As regards rulers and tyrants it appears that, generally speaking, the issue of coins with the ruler's name is a proof of a claim to complete autonomy. But there are exceptions to this rule. One of the most noteworthy is found in the case of Themistocles. When he went over to the King

[1] *Numismatic Chronicle*, 1881, p. 206.

of Persia, the latter assigned to him some of the Greek cities of Asia Minor as a possession. In the city of Magnesia he struck coins with his own name (Θεμιστοκλέος) and no sign of Persian overlordship. Other Persian satraps, such as Pharnabazus and Orontes, followed the example; and in the fourth century the Persian admirals and generals at the head of military expeditions struck in the cities of Cilicia silver coins which bore their names. When the Phoenician kings of Citium in Cyprus issued in the fourth century gold money bearing their names, it may fairly be considered as a proof that they threw up their allegiance to the Great King; but the same does not hold of issues of silver money.

Often, it appears, while a predominant ruler or city imposed coin of large denomination in a district, to the lesser cities was left the privilege of striking small silver or bronze coins for local circulation. The small divisions of the early Attic money are seldom found in the hoards of Sicily or Asia, in which Athenian tetradrachms are of frequent occurrence, but seem to have been meant only for Attica; and in the later time of the first Athenian Empire, when Attic tetradrachms passed everywhere in the lands around the Aegean, a number of towns in the Propontis, Mysia, Troas, and elsewhere issued small silver coins, sometimes following the Attic standard and sometimes departing from it. As to bronze coin, it may be said to have been in all Greek lands a mere money of account, struck to meet the needs of local markets, and having no circulation beyond them. There is in this respect a strong contrast between Greece and Rome, as the Roman coinage began with the *as* or pound of bronze, and bronze coins were for centuries state issues of wide circulation.

In the Hellenistic age the matter became more complicated. Philip, Alexander, and the kings who followed Alexander, Seleucus, Ptolemy, and the rest had regular state coinages uniform through their dominions; and the mint-cities where the coins were struck are indicated on the coins at most by a few letters, a monogram, or a small subsidiary device. At that time the appearance of a civic coinage bearing the name of a city at length is important, indicating some survival of autonomy, or grant of autonomy by a king. This, however, is a matter which lies outside the scope of the present work, though it would well repay investigation.

VIII. Monetary Alliances.

Confederacies of cities in earlier Greece, and the federal unions of later Greece, such as the Achaean and Aetolian Leagues, naturally affected or even brought to an end the autonomous issues of coins. The early confederacies were of various degrees of closeness, varying from a mere monetary convention to a close political alliance; and this variety is reflected in the issues of coins.

Sometimes groups of cities merely had an understanding in regard to the weights of their coins and the fabric. Such uniformities do not necessarily prove any close political relations, though, of course, they do not disprove it. Two good examples in the time before the invasion of Xerxes are to be found among the cities of Magna Graecia and the Ionian cities of Asia.

A number of the Hellenic foundations in South Italy adopted at the time when they first issued coins, about the middle of the sixth century, an identical standard and fabric. These issues I consider in more detail in Chapter XI. The standard is that of Corinth, with a stater of 130 grains (grm. 8·42) and a drachm of 43 grains (grm. 2·80). The fabric is notable as presenting on the obverse the ordinary civic device of the issuing city, on the reverse the same type incuse. How far these cities had a political union is a question of much controversy; but that it was in any case not at all close is shown by the further fact that we have coins belonging to the class which testify to a closer alliance within the group of several pairs of cities, Siris and Pyxus, Croton and Sybaris, Sybaris and Poseidonia, and the like. These alliances would seem to have been of short duration, and were probably entered into for special reasons, as when Croton and Sybaris united for the conquest of Siris.

The alliance of the Ionian cities against Persia in the movement called the Ionian Revolt was certainly closer, since these cities had a common fleet, and Herodotus expressly applies the term *συμμαχία* to their confederation. They also struck coins of uniform weight and identical fabric (see Chapter III), while retaining the civic types.

When we find at Himera in Sicily, in the early fifth century, the crab, the civic type of Agrigentum, on the reverse of the coins which bear on the obverse the ordinary Himeraean type,[1] the cock, we cannot hesitate to regard this innovation as a memorial of the domination at Himera, in 480–472 B.C., of Theron, the ruler of Agrigentum. Such cases are not rare, and indeed they furnish us with one of our most trustworthy indications for the dating of coins.

A close alliance of cities is definitely indicated when the coins, in addition to identity of coin-standard, bear a common type or the legend *Συμμαχικόν*.

The term *Συμμαχικόν* is found in the case of two important series of coins. After Conon's victory over the Lacedaemonians at Cnidus in 394 B.C., a league was established, no doubt for mutual defence, by some cities of Ionia which threw off the Spartan yoke. (See Chap. XVI.) These cities placed on the reverse of their coins the letters ΣΥΝ and the type of young Heracles strangling the serpents, which seems to have been adopted from the coinage of Thebes, at that time the most prominent enemy of Sparta. They also adopted a new monetary standard. When Timoleon, about 340 B.C., was occupied in the liberation of the cities of Sicily from Carthaginian domination, several of those cities adopted on their coins the legend *Συμμαχικόν*; and these coins, largely of bronze, are of uniform size and fabric.

A still closer union is indicated by the coinages of the cities which composed the Leagues of later Greece. These belong mostly to Macedonian times, but some are earlier.

[1] Head, *H. N.*, p. 144.

As early as the sixth century the cities of Phocis and of Boeotia, respectively, struck money of federal type—that of Phocis bears the name only of the district, ΦΟ or ΦΟΚΙ. That of the Boeotian towns has an identical type, the Boeotian shield; but the initial of the striking city is usually introduced on obverse or reverse, Α for Acraephia, 𐌇 for Haliartus, ⊕ for Thebes, Τ for Tanagra, and so on. The Chalcidian League in Macedon, of which Olynthus was the chief city, issued early in the fourth century very beautiful coins bearing the legend *Χαλκιδέων*. And the Achaeans seem, even before the formation of the later league about 280 B.C., to have struck money with the legend *Ἀχαιῶν*.[1]

From these alliances and confederations which had a political bearing we must distinguish others which appear to have been merely commercial. These may have been common, but it is scarcely possible to establish their existence only on the evidence of the coins. Fortunately one inscription has survived which gives us the particulars of a purely commercial monetary agreement. In the latter part of the fifth century Phocaea and Mytilene agreed to issue in alternate years hectae of electrum of identical weight and alloy.[2] It is stipulated that the coins shall circulate indiscriminately at the two cities. Any degradation of weight or fineness is to be punished by the death of the moneyer who is responsible. We possess a great series of these coins, proving their wide circulation.

That similar conventions existed in regard to the issue of the electrum staters of Cyzicus, Lampsacus, and other cities is clear; but the documents have unfortunately disappeared.

IX. Mother-city and Colony.

A special case of the dominance of one city over another in the matter of coinage is that of mother-city and colony. And here it seems that a few observed rules can be laid down with some confidence.

[1] Head, *H. N.*, p. 416.

[2] Hicks and Hill, *Greek hist. inscr.*, p. 181.

Already in my *Types of Greek Coins* (1883) I had reached views on this subject which still seem to me valid[1]:

'Coin-types and coin-weights are the two matters in which we may look for signs of connexion between mother-city and colony. But the connexion which is indicated by identity of type considerably differs from that indicated by identity of monetary standard. When a colony keeps the types of its mother-city it thereby attaches itself to the deities of its home and their temples. On the other hand, by retaining the monetary system of the mother-city, the colony merely shows that it remains in close commercial intercourse with her, and is one of the depots of her trade.'

In the case of colonies founded before the invention of coinage, very few examples can be found in which a colony has the same types as the mother-city. Naxos, the earliest of the Greek colonies in Sicily, seems to be an exception, since it was founded before coins came into use in Greece; and yet the type which it presents, the head of Dionysus, must be derived from that island of Naxos from which the city took its name, and which was specially devoted to the God of wine. The coins of the island of Naxos also have Dionysiac types; but it is not from them but from some religious connexion that the Sicilian city takes its types. Croton also was founded before the Achaean mother-cities had any coins. Its type, the tripod, connects it with Delphi and Apollo, and we observe that the city was founded at the immediate prompting of Delphi.

But such cases are quite exceptional. The Chalcidian and Achaean colonies in Italy and Sicily, and the Aeolic and Ionic cities of the Asiatic coast, usually took types referring rather to deities whom they found in possession of the sites which they occupied than to the gods of the mother-city. The types of the coins founded by Chalcis in Macedonian Chalcidice seem to have no relation to Euboea. If in many cases in the fifth and later centuries the deities of the founding city appear on the coins of the colony, as the head of Apollo at the Delphic colony of Rhegium, it

[1] *Types*, p. 36.

need not imply any political influence on the part of the metropolis, but rather a religious veneration.

The case is somewhat different when at the time of the founding of the colony the mother-city already possessed a coinage. The classical example is Abdera, which was founded by the people of Teos in Ionia about 544 B.C., when they were flying from the conquering Persians. Teos already possessed a silver coinage bearing the type of the griffin, which was probably Apolline. This type the colonists took with them, and kept on their money. In fact, if they had not, as we shall presently see, changed the standard on which the money was minted, it would be no easy matter to distinguish the coins of Abdera from those of Teos. A notable instance of the carrying of a type from Ionia to the West is to be found at Velia or Hyele in Italy, a city founded by the people of Phocaea in Ionia, when they fled from the Persian conquerors of Asia Minor. An usual type at Hyele is a lion tearing the prey, which is certainly a Phocaean coin-type. Somewhat later, after the failure of the Ionian revolt, a body of Samians fled to the straits between Italy and Sicily, being invited by Anaxilaus, Tyrant of Rhegium. How they fared there and what they founded is hard to make out, as the accounts of the ancient historians are contradictory.[1] But it cannot be a mere coincidence that at just this period there appear upon the coins of Rhegium and the neighbouring Zancle quite new types, a lion's scalp and a calf's head, which seem certainly derived from the coinage of Samos.

Another example may be found in the case of Thurium, a colony established on the site of Sybaris by Athens in the time of Pericles. The new city combined on its money the head of Athena of Athens with the bull (probably Poseidonian) which had been the old type of Sybaris.

Some of the colonies of Corinth, notably Leucas and Anactorium in Acarnania, struck from their first foundation (not before the sixth century) coins bearing the types of the mother-city; in fact differing from the coins of Corinth

[1] See a paper by Mr. Dodd in *Journ. Hell. Stud.*, 1908, p. 56.

only in inscription. In the same way the Corcyrean colonies, Apollonia and Dyrrhachium, struck coins only different from those of Corcyra in inscription. Corcyra herself, it must be observed, had been founded by Corinth before that city had any coins, and, according to the rule we have already mentioned, the types are purely local, not Corinthian. Nor does Syracuse, the other great colony of Corinth, use during the fifth century the types of Corinth, but such as were connected with the worship of Persephone and Arethusa.

When we come to the relationship of the weight or standard in coinage between mother-city and colony, we cannot in the same way draw a line at the existence or non-existence of coin in the founding-city at the time of the foundation. For, of course, before actual coin was struck every city had a recognized monetary standard according to which the precious metals were weighed. Presumably the colony would under ordinary circumstances take it to the new home. But it seems that it was not long retained if the colony found itself in new trade surroundings which made a change of standard expedient.

Here again Abdera and Teos offer us a striking example. The standard used at Teos in the sixth century was the Aeginetan, at that time universally used in the Cyclades, as well as in Caria, but by scarcely any of the Ionian cities. Abdera from the first did not continue to use this standard, but adopted instead a variety of the standard of Phoenicia, midway between the standard used by Chios in Northern Ionia and that used by Miletus, Samos, and Ephesus in Southern Ionia. The facts are in this case clear and decided, but the reasons which caused the people of Abdera to take the particular line which they did take are anything but clear. At the time only the cities of Chalcidice and the island of Thasos, in the whole stretch of the coast of Thrace, struck coins, and in neither of these places was the standard which the Abderites adopted in use. This matter will be further considered in Chapter X.

At the same time that the people of Teos migrated to

Thrace, those of Phocaea sailed for the far West, and after many adventures came to stay at Massilia in Gaul and Velia (Hyele) in Italy. They took with them the Phocaean weight standard, stater, 256 grains (grm. 16·6), which hitherto had been little used except for electrum. A few silver coins seem to have been struck at Phocaea in the early part of the sixth century on the Aeginetan standard, and apparently also a few on the Phocaean standard. The money used by the Phocaean colonists has been found in a great hoard at Auriol in France, as well as in Italy.

The colonists from Euboea who settled in Chalcidice in Macedonia naturally took with them the Euboic standard, according to which their silver was struck: it bears in its types no traces of the influence of Chalcis. But it is shown in the present work[1] that the inhabitants of Chalcidice, possibly as a result of the influence of Potidaea, a colony of Corinth which was in their midst, divided their staters by three, on the Corinthian, not by two, on the Euboic plan. The small coins which they struck belong to a system in which the unit or drachm weighs 45 grains (grm. 2·91) as at Corinth, and not 67 grains (grm. 4·34) as at Athens and Euboea.

The same combination of the Attic or Euboic and the Corinthian standards took place more evidently and on a larger scale in South Italy and Sicily, as shown below.[2]

When the Athenians founded Thurii in Italy, in the time of Pericles, the coinage of Athens was not only well established but dominant in the Aegean. It is natural that the colonists should have adhered to the Attic standard, which differed slightly from that of the neighbouring cities of Magna Graecia, and should have used as their standard coin the tetradrachm, instead of the (debased) Attic didrachm (or Corinthian tridrachm), which was the usual currency in South Italy. The influence of Thurii caused the neighbouring city of Metapontum exceptionally to issue tetradrachms.

[1] Chapter X. [2] Chapter XI.

X. Standard Currencies.

The question of the existence and the exercise in cities of the right of coinage is evidently a very complicated one, which underlies every page of the history of ancient coins. But equally difficult and even more complicated questions arise from the fact that often classes of coins attained what may be called an international circulation, not from any political reason of overlordship, but as a mere matter of convenience in trade. The trapezitae, or money-changers, who had their seats in the Greek market-places, must have usually kept in stock certain kinds of specie generally recognized and universally appreciated, to form a basis for their trade. What these were it is hard to ascertain. The historians seldom help us: we have usually to resort to such evidence as the composition of hoards, or the inscriptions which are the financial records of temples.

Among the most notable of these cosmopolitan issues were the electrum staters of Cyzicus. We know, alike from the financial inscriptions of Athens and from the statements of such writers as Xenophon and Demosthenes, that these staters had a wide circulation alike in Greece and in Asia, and especially were used in the Pontic trade and for the payment of Greek mercenaries. Why Cyzicus, a city of moderate importance, should have possessed, and retained, for at least a century and a half, a practical monopoly in the issue of these staters (for the staters of Lampsacus and Mytilene are comparatively scarce) we do not know. Nor do we know how far Athens officially recognized them. The hectae, or sixths of an electrum stater, struck in alternate years at Mytilene and Phocaea, seem also, from their great abundance, to have circulated far beyond the limits of the cities which issued them.

As regards silver coin we have a few instances in which we can trace the dominance of widely circulated issues. The cities of Italy and Sicily, in the later sixth and fifth centuries, used the coins of Athens and of Corinth in great quantities as currency. This is abundantly proved by the finds which have been discovered in those countries. The cities of South Italy, notably Metapontum, sometimes used Corinthian staters as blanks in their mints, to be stamped with the local dies. In the fourth century we have less abundant evidence of the use in Italy and Sicily of the Athenian coins. But the Pegasus staters of Corinth constitute a considerable part of Sicilian hoards at that period. They were imitated in all the Corinthian colonies of Epirus and Acarnania, and even in cities such as Leontini and Rhegium, which do not seem to have had political relations with Corinth, and which must have adopted the types of Corinth merely because Corinthian money was the most ordinary currency in their districts.

At a later time the coins of Rhodes seem to have attained wide recognition. And later still the cistophori, so called because they bear as type a Dionysiac cista or chest, issued by Greek cities in the domains of the kings of Pergamon and in the Roman Province of Asia, were the main currency of Asia Minor, as we may see from the enormous quantities of them carried in the triumphal procession of the conquerors of Antiochus III of Syria. They seem to have been first struck at Ephesus.

In a valuable paper contributed to the *Mémoires* of the French Académie des Inscriptions[1] M. Théodore Reinach has put together such extant texts and inscriptions as give some light on the difficult question of the exchange of coins in the market. The comic poet Diphilus, describing the ways of the Athenian fish-market,[2] says that the dealers in fish, if the price were fixed in oboli, were apt to demand Aeginetan oboli; but if they had to give change, gave it in Attic oboli, the Attic obolus being little more than two-thirds of the value of the Aeginetan. We have evidence that at Delphi at one time in the fourth century Attic money passed at a premium of 5 per cent.: at Tenos in the second century Rhodian silver commanded the same pre-

[1] *Mémoires*, 1911, p. 351. *L'Anarchie monétaire.*
[2] Keil, *Fragm. com.*, ii. 563; fragment 66.

mium. And we have a decree of the Amphictyons, of about 95 B.C., ordering that the Athenian tetradrachms are to be accepted throughout Greece as legal tender.

The Treasurers of Delphi in the fourth century, having frequent dealings with coins of both Attic and Aeginetan standard, established a convention that the Attic mina, which contained, of course, 100 Attic drachms, should be regarded also as equivalent to 70 Aeginetan drachms.[1] This valuation closely conforms to the actual weights of the respective issues, and therefore we are not surprised to find that it was recognized not only at Delphi but in other places. Reinach has shown that it was accepted also at Orchomenus in Arcadia, at Gortyna in Crete, and at Epidaurus in Argolis. At an earlier time a similar valuation lies at the basis of the Solonian reform of the Attic coinage; in fact it seems to have been generally accepted, much as the equation of an English sovereign with twenty-five francs is accepted in Latin countries now.

Thucydides[2] tells us that when troops were raised by the Confederacy formed against Sparta by Corinth and Argos in 421 B.C. it was stipulated by treaty that the foot-soldiers should receive half an Aeginetan drachm a day, and the horse-soldiers a drachm: in Attic money this would have been equivalent to four and eight obols respectively; in Corinthian money to a drachm and two drachms respectively, or a little more.

Proof of the international acceptance of a class of coins is to be found if there exist in its case barbarous imitations. Of the coins of Athens such imitations are common, especially in three periods—first, at the time of the Persian invasion (probably struck by the Persians); secondly, in the time of Alexander the Great; thirdly, in the later age when the coinage came to a final end at Athens, and the trading tribes of Arabia, used to that currency, issued curious imitations of it to fill the gap.[3] The gold coins of Philip of

[1] T. Reinach, *L'Histoire par les monnaies*, p. 100. [2] v. 47.

[3] See *Numismatic Chronicle*, 1878, p. 273; also a paper by Mr. Hill in the *Proceedings of the British Academy* for 1915.

Macedon were imitated from tribe to tribe across Europe, even to remote Britain. And the silver coins of Alexander were copied, not only by remoter peoples of Asia, but also by the Greek cities of the Ionian coast when, after the victory of the Romans at Magnesia, they were free from the dominion of Antiochus III. Such imitation was sincere flattery, proving the reputation of the coins copied.

XI. Monometallism and Bimetallism.

Two plans are possible for a government which strikes both gold and silver coins. The one plan is monometallic; one of the two metals is made the official standard, the legal tender; and the other metal is used only in a subsidiary way in relation to it. England is monometallic; gold is the legal tender, and silver is only used in subordination to it for payments of small amount. The English shilling is not really worth a twentieth of the sovereign; it is a money of account. India is monometallic; the silver rupee is the standard coin, and gold is only a matter of commerce.

The other plan is bimetallic. Two metals, usually gold and silver, are both made legal tender; and a fixed relation between their values is fixed by law. A man who has to pay a debt may pay it in coins of either metal. France before 1872 was bimetallic, the proportionate value between gold and silver being fixed at 15½ to 1.

Both the monometallic and the bimetallic systems are found in modern days to have great disadvantages in consequence of the fluctuating value of gold and silver. But no remedy for this has yet been found.

In ancient times commerce was less active than with us, and custom and convention were far more powerful, so that the troubles arising from the monometallic and the bimetallic systems were less serious. Both systems were in use at various times and places.

When coinage began in Asia, bimetallism was in possession; and it held its ground in Asia as long as the Persian empire existed. The daric and the shekel were both of a weight which did not vary, and one daric passed as of the value of twenty shekels. Whether the shekel was accepted in large payments we do not know. On the coast of Asia Minor the relations between silver and electrum, the electrum being ten times the value of silver, appear to have persisted, at all events until the time of Croesus.

In Greece Proper, on the other hand, from the time when silver coins superseded the ancient bars of bronze, that is from the seventh century B.C., those coins were the standard of value, and gold and electrum coins passed only as metal of fixed weight. Whereas Asia was bimetallist, Greece was monometallist. No gold coins of any importance were struck in the West until the fall of Athens, which city had strongly adhered to the use of silver, and promoted its dominance.

Some writers have been disposed to find traces of bimetallism in Greece. For example, Ridgeway has suggested that the early coins of Aegina in silver were originally intended to pass at the rate of ten staters (1,950 grains) for one gold shekel of 130 grains, giving a ratio of 15 to 1 for the proportionate value of gold to silver. This view I have decidedly rejected (see Chapter V) on the ground that the gold shekel (daric) was purely Asiatic and had no dominance in Greece Proper. A more plausible suggestion is that we may trace in the changes of monetary standard at Abdera in Thrace in the fifth century an attempt at bimetallism, a purpose so to regulate the weight of the silver staters of the city, that a round number of them should be equivalent to a daric, or two darics. This view has at first sight some plausibility, as numismatically Thrace belonged, at all events before the Persian wars, rather to Asia than to Europe. Even Mr. Head was half converted to the view. I have below (in Chapter XIV) carefully considered it, but it does not bear examination. The Thracian coast was a source of gold, as Herodotus was aware;[1] but what became of the gold is quite unknown. It was certainly not minted into coin at Athens or at Thasos. It may have passed in the

[1] Hdt. vi. 46, 47.

form of bars of bullion, or possibly it may have been used for the issues of electrum coins at Cyzicus and Lampsacus. In any case it is clear that the daric exercised no influence on the coinage of Hellas, and that it had no fixed value at places like Athens and Corinth. When the authorities at Athens wanted gold for the adornment of their Goddess, or for any other purpose, they bought it with silver like any other merchandize.

What is still more remarkable is that the silver coinage of cities of Asia sometimes followed the Aeginetan or the Attic standard, and had no relation, so far as we can judge, to the value of the daric. We can, in a measure, trace the respective supremacies of Persia and Athens in Asia Minor in the fifth and fourth centuries by the predominance in the coinages of cities and districts of the Persian daric or the Athenian silver stater. How devoted the Athenians were to their silver, and how completely it excluded other metals may be judged from Xenophon's work on the *Revenues of Athens.*[1] He regards it as the first duty of the city to exploit the mines of Laurium, considering silver as the only commodity of which one can never have enough. Even gold and copper, he thinks, may be superabundant, but silver never.

The silver coin issued by the cities of Greece was extremely pure, even the small amount of alloy was probably accidental. In the paper of J. Hammer already referred to there are tables of the proportion of alloy in the silver coins of various cities. Only two or three cities, Mytilene, Phocaea, and Cyzicus, for example, which had been in the habit of issuing electrum coins, struck in the sixth century billon coins, containing about 40 per cent. of silver, and so bearing to pure silver coins the same relation which electrum coins bore to pure gold.

The reasons for the purity of the coin are obvious. Generally speaking, the Greek cities had no way for procuring acceptance of their coins beyond the limits of the city, save by making it good, though perhaps beauty might

[1] Chapter IV.

help. In later days, under the rule of Greek and Parthian kings, and in the days of the Romans, those in authority tried, like the rulers in the Middle Ages, to force base coin into circulation. It is to the credit of the Athenians that, even in the days of their somewhat tyrannical empire, they made no such attempt, but preserved intact the high reputation of their money.

When coins of gold and silver were struck at one time in a city, the normal rates of the two metals would naturally govern their weights. We can scarcely suppose that the gold coins would belong to one commercial system and the silver coins to another, and that there would be no easy relation between them. To this question we shall return on occasion in future chapters.

But in the business of the money-changers, no doubt, there would usually be an *agio.* Coins in demand, because of their purity and wide acceptance, would command a premium. Some examples of the practical preference for certain kinds of coin are given above. The *agio* might greatly vary in different districts owing to the difficulty and risk of conveying gold and silver from one place to another. This held also in more modern days in a measure; but when the Mediterranean Sea was bordered by nests of pirates, and sea-voyage was attended by many risks, the difficulty of conveying coin might cause a great temporary appreciation or depreciation of particular kinds of money.

A fact which has caused great perplexity to modern writers is that there is great inexactness in the weight of the gold and silver coins of the Greek cities. It is true that the divergency may be partly accounted for by changes wrought by time, by the oxidation which silver undergoes when buried in the earth. But when a number of silver coins are found together in exactly the same state of preservation, these variations in weight still exist. And they even exist, though in a lesser degree, in the case of gold coins which are not liable to oxidation.

It is probable that the ancient moneyers were more successful in striking so many coins to the pound weight than in keeping their blanks all of one size. The process of forming these blanks was a rough one, and did not lend itself to exactness, so that silver coins struck at the same place and time may vary in weight as much as a quarter of a gramme (four grains), or even more. Gold coins or silver issues of the standard types, such as the staters of Athens or of Alexander, vary less; but even these show an extraordinary variety, from the modern point of view. We find it hard to understand how a gold coin of 130 grains and a gold coin of 135 grains can have passed, when struck at the same time and mint, as of identical value; and we are disposed to suspect that the scales were commonly in use, and light coins taken only at a discount. But we must not project our strict commercial notions into antiquity. It is more likely that coins of recognized classes passed as if of standard weight, even when they were short of it. As we have seen, there is a far greater difficulty of the same kind attaching to the general use of electrum coins, which differed in intrinsic value in a remarkable degree.

In Sicily, and in some cities of Italy, there was in the fifth century some attempt at a double standard of silver and bronze. At Syracuse, for example, the silver litra, weighing 13·5 grains (grm. 0·87), was struck as the equivalent of a pound of bronze. And this silver coin remained for centuries the basis of the Syracusan coinage, being the tenth part of the Corinthian silver stater, and the twentieth part of the Syracusan tetradrachm. Whether a parallel currency in actual litrae of bronze was in use we do not know: the bronze coins of Sicily bearing marks of value diminish rapidly in weight, and evidently passed only as money of account. (See Chapter XX.)

XII. The Dating of Greek Coins.

I have already in my *Types of Greek Coins* (1883) described the way in which numismatists proceed in order to arrange the coins of any Greek city in chronological order. A consideration of the style of the coins is, of course, fundamental; and their weights and the composition of hoards in which they are found are of importance. But our chief reliance must always be on the fixing on historic grounds of the dates of certain issues, and thus gaining fixed points whence we may work upwards and downwards in the series. For example, the archaic decadrachm of Syracuse struck by Gelon in 479 B.C., and named after his wife Damarete, furnishes us with a fixed point in the coinage of Syracuse: we may fairly suppose that the pieces of earlier style at Syracuse may be dated before 480, and the pieces of later style after 478. In the same way, when we find the name Simos on a coin of Larissa in Thessaly,[1] and with reason identify the name as that of one of the four tetrarchs set up by Philip of Macedon in Thessaly, 352–344 B.C., we may regard this coin as marking a fixed point in the coinage of Larissa. Or at a later time, it is reasonable to follow Evans[2] and attribute the coins of Tarentum, which bear the figure of an elephant, to the time of Pyrrhus in Italy, 281–272 B.C.; as Pyrrhus first brought the elephant into the country. The dates of the destruction of the cities of Sicily at the time of the Carthaginian invasion of 409–405 give us fixed dates for the latest issues of such cities as Gela and Camarina. Other examples abound.

But in the present work we are endeavouring to pass beyond the arrangement of coins under separate cities to their classification in commercial groups or geographical districts. From this point of view it is most important to point out how the arrangement of the coins of any city in chronological order, with definite points of division, helps us to arrange in the same way the series of all cities which had any connexion with it, either political, commercial, or even artistic. Thus the science of numismatics becomes rapidly progressive, and coinage after coinage falls into its proper place and time.

To return to an instance already given, the Damareteion not only makes a dividing point in the series of coins of

[1] *Brit. Mus. Cat., Thessaly*, Pl. VI. 9: cf. ch. xviii.

[2] *Horsemen of Tarentum*, p. 136.

Syracuse, but it also enables us to divide the coins of Leontini. For at Leontini was issued a tetradrachm, so closely similar in style to the Damareteion (having also the same figure of a lion in the exergue), that we confidently give it to exactly the same period, and so gain a fresh fixed date in another coinage. Similarly, the occurrence of coins bearing the type of young Heracles strangling the snakes, in several of the cities of Asia, just after the Athenian victory at Cnidus in 394 B.C., can be used with great effect as a means of dating coins. Not only does this issue of money make a clear dividing line in the coinages of Samos, Byzantium, Ephesus, and Cnidus, but the occurrence of a closely similar type on the coins of Lampsacus, and even of the distant Croton, furnishes us with a means for dating some of the issues of those cities also. If one sets side by side Mr. Head's scheme for the arrangement of the coins of Ephesus and my own for the arrangement of the money of Samos,[1] it will be seen how each of these arrangements helps the other. Ephesus appears not to have issued coin at all during the period of the first Athenian empire: Samos, on the other hand, continued its coinage all that time, though the conquest of Samos by Pericles in 439 has left unmistakable traces on the coin. Both cities belonged to the Cnidian League (394), and accepted the Chian or Rhodian standard about that time. But again Samos passes through the crisis of a second Athenian conquest, and the issue of money in the island is intermitted, 365–322 B.C., while Ephesus has a continuous coinage during the fourth century. On the other hand, while at Samos after 322 there is an undisturbed period of coinage, at Ephesus there is a decided break in the time of Lysimachus (288–280 B.C.), who renamed the city after his wife Arsinoe and changed both the types and the standard of the coin. Each city has crises, but they are not usually the same crises; so that to arrange the successive issues of the two cities side by side gives one

[1] *Ephesus*, by B. V. Head, 1880; *Samos*, by P. Gardner, 1882. Both originally printed in the *Numismatic Chronicle.*

much more information than either city can furnish separately.

There is no district of the Greek world where changes in the coin standards were more frequent than in Thrace. And there the influence of city upon city in their adoption and abandonment is sometimes clearly to be traced, but more often can only be surmised as a probability. If the cities of the southern coast of Thrace be taken one by one, the history of their coinage is a complicated one, and a clue to the labyrinth is scarcely to be found. If they are considered in groups in connexion with the commercial history of the time, this history can, at least in its main outlines, be traced, and will usually be found to be not inexplicable. (See Chapters X, XIV, and XVI.)

XIII. Hoards.

No more valuable evidence in regard to the dates and the circulation of coins can be had than that which is furnished by finds or hoards. There can be no doubt that hoards of coins have been at all times constantly discovered in lands which were once Hellenic. But in the great majority of cases, and in fact in almost every case until lately, the coins so found were either at once melted down or divided among the finders and sold piecemeal. In such cases the evidence is of course destroyed. We have now a fairly accurate account of a certain number of hoards, but the misfortune is that the evidence which they furnish must be used with great caution. Such evidence is in the nature of things cumulative; a series of finds in a particular district may give us much information; but each taken by itself is obviously too much the result of chance, or rather of unknown causes, to be much relied on.

It is very natural that, when an enemy advanced into a country, or other danger impended, the inhabitants should bury their valuables, and especially their money. Frequently, when these inhabitants were slain, or carried into slavery, the hiding-place was never revealed, and the hoards remained underground to our day. In a few cases, military chests or the capital of bankers have thus survived. But, generally speaking, finds consist of comparatively few coins. A few examples may be cited.

Archaic period. First in importance and interest come the finds in Egypt. No native Egyptian coins were issued until the time of the Ptolemaic kings. Gold and silver seem usually to have gone by weight, even after the time of the Persian conquest, though the Persian darics and sigli may have circulated to some extent. At various sites in Lower Egypt a quantity of archaic Greek coins has been found, some of them broken and some defaced, which were almost certainly intended for the melting-pot.

These coins are mostly scattered and isolated examples from the mints of many cities on the Aegean Sea and the southern coast of Asia Minor. At Myt Rahineh [1] was found a treasure including coins of Lete, Maroneia, Corinth, Naxos, Chios, Cos, Cyprus, and Cyrene. At Sakha was discovered a deposit,[2] including coins of Dieaea, Lete, Aegina, Corinth, Naxos, Paros, Chios, Clazomenae, Ialysus and Lindus in Rhodes, and Cyrene. As with these coins were found fragments and bars of silver, the destination of this hoard for the melting-pot has been conjectured. The coins included in it belong to the most usual currencies of the eastern Mediterranean. A small find of coins of Cyrene from near Ramleh emphasizes the close connexion affirmed in historic records between Egypt and Cyrene.

Another hoard, found in the Delta,[3] is very similar in composition to those above mentioned. It included a few coins of Athens, and examples of the coinages of Corinth, Thasos, Lete, Mende, Miletus, Chios, Samos, Cos, Cyprus, Cyrene, and other places; the date being seldom later than 500 B.C.

Some of these coins are rough, and appear to be barbarous imitations. M. Babelon [4] thinks that they were made at

[1] *Rev. Numism.*, 1861, p. 414.
[2] *Num. Chron.*, 1899, p. 269; *Zeitschr. f. Num.*, 1900, p. 231.
[3] *Num. Chron.*, 1890, p. 1.
[4] *Traité*, ii. 1, p. 1572.

Naucratis itself; and certainly not dissimilar copies of Egyptian scarabs were made by the Greeks of Naucratis. But it does not appear why the people should have taken the trouble to make copies of coins only in order that they should be melted down. Barbarous work is not unusual in many series of archaic coins, and they may often be most simply explained by the supposition that the moneyers at the city mints were often careless or worked under pressure. At Athens, however, we seem to have clear proof of imitation by the Persians, as will be shown in its place.

The site of Naucratis has yielded a small hoard,[1] supposed to have belonged to a silversmith, buried about 439 B.C., including coins of Lycia, Chios, Samos, Aegina, Athens, Cyrene, and—a notable fact—one of Syracuse of archaic style. Of the other early coins found scattered on the site the overwhelming majority (86 out of 97) were tetradrachms of Athens, struck mostly at the time of the Athenian empire, when Athens almost monopolized the coinage of the Aegean. Probably at that time the Athenian money passed by tale and not by weight in Egypt.

Near the harbour of Tarentum was found a few years ago[2] a large jar containing about 600 early Greek silver coins, together with bars of silver, indicating that the whole was intended for melting down. M. Babelon fixes the date of burying at about 510 B.C. The coins came from almost every part of the Greek world. Some cities of Italy and Sicily were represented, Selinus, Himera, Metapontum, Sybaris, Croton, Poseidonia, Velia; but more abundant were the coins of Aegina, Athens, Eretria, Potidaea, Acanthus, Lete, Thasos, Peparethus, Carthaea in Ceos, Naxos, Chios, and other places. This hoard gives us most valuable information as to the dates of the coins comprised in it; but it does not give us data as to the course of commerce at Tarentum.

A celebrated hoard is that discovered at Thera (Santorin)

[1] *Naukratis*, i (W. M. F. Petrie and others), p. 63.

[2] *Rev. Numism.*, 1912, 1. Babelon.

in 1821,[1] consisting of 760 coins of the Aegean Islands and the coasts of Thrace and Asia Minor. Of these, 541 were of Aegina, showing how in the seventh and sixth centuries that city dominated the coinage of the Aegean. Among the mints, Naxos, Paros, Siphnos, and a few others can be identified; but the attribution of many of the coins, in the absence of inscriptions, is doubtful.

Another similar hoard, found about 1889 at an undetermined place,[2] included 114 coins of Aegina, and a few examples of Carthaea in Ceos, Paros, Siphnos, Chios, Cos, and some Ionian mints.

The want of inscriptional evidence mars the value of another noted find made at Auriol, near Marseilles in France.[3] M. Babelon, in describing the class of hoards, of which this is one, writes as follows: 'Besides finds of isolated pieces, several hoards all of one character have come to light; at Velia in Lucania, at Volterra, near Rosas and Ampurias in Spain,' and other Spanish sites. 'The examination in detail of all these hoards allows us to discover in them two categories of coins; one class, generally broken and worn in circulation, may be assigned to the Greek cities where they originated; the most numerous coins in this category are of Phocaea and Mytilene in Lesbos, from which cities originally came the Phocaean settlers of the western Mediterranean. The other category, by far the most considerable, is composed of silver pieces which are imitations of those already mentioned,' and which seem to have been struck on the spot.

The types of the little coins composing these hoards are very various; and it seems doubtful whether, even when they repeat the recognized types of cities in Greece and Asia Minor, they really come from those cities. We may compare a hoard of small electrum coins found by Mr. Hogarth

[1] *Num. Chron.*, 1884, p. 269, Wroth. Compare *Brit. Mus. Cat.*, *Crete*, *&c.*, p. xlii.

[2] *Num. Chron.*, 1890, p. 13.

[3] A full account in Babelon, *Traité*, ii. 1, p. 1571.

at Ephesus,[1] which also bear a great variety of types, yet which may belong to one district, or even one city.

Later period. Of somewhat later date is a very interesting hoard, supposed to have been discovered in Cilicia, and published by Mr. E. T. Newell.[2] Unfortunately the place of its discovery is not recorded, nor can we be sure that the coins were all found together. The date of burial is fixed at about 380 B. C.: most of the coins are defaced with gashes on one or both sides, apparently to unfit them for further circulation, which looks as if they had been destined for melting. Many of them also bear small stamps or counter-marks which Mr. Newell regards as private marks of certain bankers or traders: we know that such marks are very common on the Persian silver sigli and the coins of several cities of southern Asia Minor.[3] The three classes of coins most common in this hoard are: first, Persian sigli; second, coins of Athens of the fifth century;[4] third, coins issued in the cities of Cilicia by Persian Satraps, especially Tiribazus. Besides these there are coins of the later fifth and earlier fourth centuries, struck at Byzantium, Calchedon, Sinope, Miletus, Samos, Aspendus, Side, Teos, Celenderis, Soli, Mallus, Issus, Aradus, Tyre, and the kings of Salamis and Citium in Cyprus. The collocation of these coins gives us useful information as to the dates of issues in all the cities represented; and by carefully recording which examples were fresh-struck and which had been worn in circulation, Mr. Newell makes our information more precise.

It is mainly by the evidence furnished by hoards found in Sicily that Sir Arthur Evans[5] has succeeded in more accurately dating the series issued at Syracuse, and the money issued by Phoenicians in Sicily. These data, so far as they concern the purposes of the present work, are considered in the chapters below dealing with Sicilian coins.

[1] *Excavations at Ephesus*, 1908, p. 74.

[2] *Num. Chron.*, 1914, p. 1.

[3] Compare a find of Persian silver sigli published by Mr. Milne in *Num. Chron.*, 1915, p. 1.

[4] One is of the early fourth century, with the later type of the head of Athena.

[5] *Num. Chron.*, 1890, 1891.

In the following pages, it is needless to say, the evidence of hoards is used whenever it is available.

XIV. Fabric.

As regards the process of coining, I may begin with a quotation from a recent traveller in the native states of India, where ancient ways of manufacture still survive[1]:

'Under a little, open, whitewashed roof, there are two or three tiny furnaces, two or three small anvils, and two or three nearly naked workmen. Three iron pegs, six inches high, with flattened heads, looking rather like exaggerated golf-tees, spring from the stone floor. The workman takes a lump of bullion in his hands, heats it in the furnace, cuts off a round or moderately round disk, and carries it with his pincers to the die, and hammers on it until he has got a sufficient impression; then he casts it aside upon a little heap to get cool, and to be conveyed into the royal treasury.'

If this, or anything like this, was the method by which coins were commonly struck in Greece, we need not be surprised at their variations in fineness and in weight.

There is, however, a notable distinction between the method of providing blanks at Jodhpur, by cutting slices from a bar, and the method generally in use in earlier Greece, which consisted in casting, as bullets are cast, in a mould. By this means certainly more exactness would be attained than by the Indian method, but not nearly so much exactness as is attained in modern days by the use of a collar. But until modern writers rid themselves of our natural presuppositions, and realize more completely how rough and ready were, as a rule, the methods of the ancient mints, they will always be making theories far too exact to fit the facts. For example, numismatists often try to give the standard weights of particular classes of coins to the third decimal place in grammes. There is no indication that the controllers of ancient mints worked with anything like this accuracy. I therefore have nowhere made any

[1] Sidney Lee, *Vision of India*, p. 106. The mint described is that of Jodhpur.

attempt to give more than an approximate statement of the weights of any classes of coins. Further refinement gives the appearance of great accuracy without its reality, and tends only to mislead.

It has been shown by Dr. Macdonald[1] that in the Middle Ages 'Decrees generally prescribe, not that coins shall be struck of such and such a weight, but that so many coins shall be struck out of such and such a quantity of metal'. We can scarcely doubt that this was the case also in ancient Greece. This would explain considerable variation in the weights of individual coins. If the mint-master found that the coins he was producing were above the standard, he would at once take measures to diminish the size of the blanks: if he found that the coins were light, he would move in the opposite direction. Except in the case of gold coins a small excess or deficiency would not be serious.

At the beginning of coinage it would seem that the type was engraved on the head of the anvil, which may have been, as at Jodhpur, an iron peg let into the floor, and the rude incuse which marks the other side of the coins may have been produced by the head of a punch which by a hammer was driven into the round or oval blank which was to be the coin. At a later time there were two neatly engraved types, let the one into the anvil, the other into the punch. But it is impossible by a mere description to make clear the history and the peculiarities of the technique of coin-striking. Knowledge on the subject can only come from practical familiarity with coins. In assigning a mint and a date to coins the numismatist is necessarily largely guided by peculiarities of technique, often so minute that he is scarcely able to describe them in words. But to do justice to this subject would require a technical treatise fully illustrated.

One innovation recently introduced by Mr. Hill in the British Museum catalogues[2] is to state in what positions relatively to one another the obverse and reverse dies of a

[1] *The Evolution of Coinage*, p. 70.

[2] See the Preface to the *Brit. Mus. Catalogue of Coins of Phoenicia.*

coin stand. No doubt such statistics give us valuable information. But no mere statistical information can ever be used mechanically, and without common sense. Mechanical principles of arrangement may well serve to give us suggestions, or to decide doubtful points, but one must be prepared to disregard them when they conflict with well-established inductions. The respective placing of obverse and reverse dies may in some cases be the result of a system, but in others may be only the result of habit in a particular workman.

CHAPTER I

EARLY ELECTRUM

§ 1. Origin of Coinage.

It is generally thought, alike by numismatists and historians, that the coinage of the western world took its origin on the coast of Asia Minor in the eighth or at latest in the seventh century B.C., in those primitive and rude coins of electrum, which are now abundant in our museums. Of this coinage I do not propose to treat in detail, as it has been the subject of able papers by Head, Babelon, and other writers,[1] nor is it possible fully to discuss it without taking into account a multitude of small numismatic considerations, the introduction of which would thwart the purpose of the present treatise, which is to give a broad historic sketch. I will, however, give a brief summary of the principal discussions which have arisen in regard to it.

In the first place, it has been disputed to whom belongs the honour of the first invention of coins. We know from Julius Pollux that this question was much discussed by his learned authorities. He writes[2] that it was disputed 'whether coins were first issued by Pheidon of Argos, or by the Cymaean Demodice, wife of the Phrygian Midas, who was daughter of Agamemnon, King of Cyme, or by the Athenians, Erichthonius and Lycus, or by the Lydians, as Xenophanes asserts, or by the Naxians, according to the view of Aglaosthenes'. Some of these views are now out of court, especially those which give the origination of coins to

[1] Head in *Numismatic Chronicle*, 1875; *Catalogue of Greek Coins in the British Museum: Ionia*, Introduction. Babelon, *Traité des Monnaies grecques et romaines*, Part II, vol. i, where further references; also *Revue Numismatique*, 1894 and 1895.

[2] *Onom.* ix. 83.

Pheidon of Argos or to Athens. It is universally allowed that money first appears on the western coast of Asia Minor. But it may still be doubted whether it originated with the wealthy Mermnad kings of Lydia or with Miletus and other Ionian cities of the coast.

In favour of the Lydians it may be argued that Herodotus supports their claim. He writes of the Lydians,[1] *πρῶτοι ἀνθρώπων, τῶν ἡμεῖς ἴδμεν, νόμισμα χρυσοῦ καὶ ἀργύρου κοψάμενοι ἐχρήσαντο· πρῶτοι δὲ καὶ κάπηλοι ἐγένοντο.* There seems to be some connexion between the clauses of the sentence: that is, the fact that the Lydians were pedlars or hucksters was the reason for their invention of coin. And here it may be allowed that we can cite a parallel: the great extension of the Aeginetan currency is explained by the fact that the Aeginetans were the pedlars of Greece Proper. At the same time the words of Herodotus are too ambiguous to be pressed. To say that the Lydians first struck coins in gold and silver is not the same thing as to say that they first issued money of mixed gold and silver or electrum. There is thus some justification for those who, with J. P. Six, take the words of Herodotus to mean that the Lydians were the first to issue coins, not of electrum, but of gold and silver separately. This separation was, as we shall see, a feature of the coinage of Croesus; and it is possible that Herodotus was thinking of the money issued by Croesus. On the other hand, we may take the words *χρυσοῦ καὶ ἀργύρου* closely together, as implying a coinage of mixed gold and silver or electrum; and if we take this view, the authority of Herodotus will be on the side of the origin of coinage in Lydia. Xenophanes, according to Pollux, takes the same view, and Xenophanes was probably a contemporary of Darius, and near to the time of the origin of coinage.

Another ancient authority for the Lydian origin of coins has been found in the phrase of Julius Pollux,[2] who speaks of *Γυγάδας χρυσός* in the same breath with darics and staters

[1] i. 94.

[2] *Onomasticon*, iii. 87.

of Croesus; for this passage has been taken as a proof that the early electrum staters were issued by Gyges. To this argument, however, there lies an insuperable objection in the fact that in another passage[1] Pollux speaks of the gold of Gyges as notable for purity; it could not, then, have been electrum. Gyges, as we are told by Herodotus,[2] dedicated at Delphi many objects in gold, and it was from this that his gold had its reputation. Certainly no coins of pure gold of the time of Gyges are known.

The mere fact that Lydia possessed in great abundance the raw material of the electrum coinage can scarcely weigh very heavily, since that material was also easily accessible to the Ionians. The only alleged proof of an early issue of coins in Lydia is furnished by the legend FAΛFEI in archaic letters read (first by M. Six) on some electrum coins, as the name of King Alyattes of Lydia. To these coins I will presently return. Meantime it is clear that, even if we accept M. Six's reading, all that it would prove would be that Lydian coins were issued in the reign of Alyattes, 610–561 B.C., not that coins originated with the Lydians. Quite as early as these coins is the remarkable stater of electrum[3] which bears the name of Phanes, and which was almost certainly struck in one of the cities of Ionia. (**Pl. I. 2, B. M. I. 7.**)

Most numismatists—Lenormant, Six, Head, and others—are disposed to assign the earliest electrum coins to early Lydian kings, Gyges and his successors. But the most recent writer on the subject, M. Babelon, prefers, alike from the probabilities of the case, and the evidence of extant coins, to think that coinage originated with the Greeks of Asia. I am disposed to support this view. It would be strange if the Lydian horsemen anticipated the quick-witted and versatile Ionians in so remarkable a discovery as that of striking coins. Moreover, in addition to the intrinsic probability of Babelon's view, the balance of evidence to be drawn from existing coins is in its favour.

[1] *Ibid.*, vii. 98. [2] i. 14.

[3] *B. M. Cat. Ionia*, Pl. III. 8.

It may well seem strange that the Greek world contrived to do without coins until the eighth century B.C. We now know what a highly developed civilization flourished in Crete and in Peloponnesus at a much earlier time. But there are abundant examples of an elaborate civilization without money. The great empires of Egypt and Assyria had no coins. The Phoenicians did not issue money for centuries after its invention, though they may have used the coins of Persia and of Greece. It is conjectured from a survey of the places where Persian gold coins are found, that they were but little used in the eastern provinces of the Persian Empire, but almost exclusively in Asia Minor. And we have modern parallels for indifference to the use of coin. In China, down to our own days, only copper and iron coins have been issued by authority, gold and silver still passing by weight, whether in the form of bars or of foreign coin.

§ 2. Ionia.

The early electrum coins of the Ionic coast are bean-shaped, bearing usually on one side a type, on the other punch-marks enclosing smaller devices. (**B. M. I. 1–12.**) The metal is hard; the art and fabric primitive. They present us with a series of problems, which cannot at present be said to be solved.

The stater of electrum is the ordinary large unit. It is divided according to Asiatic, and not according to Greek customs. In Greece the unit is the drachm, larger pieces are didrachms and tetradrachms, smaller pieces the half-drachm, and so on. But electrum coins are quite independent of the drachm. Half-staters were not unknown, but the ordinary method of division was by three. There was the tritê or third, the hectê or sixth, the twelfth, the twenty-fourth, and so on, down to the ninety-sixth. But the third and sixth were by far the most common divisions; the smaller units were at the time of the Ionian revolt and later superseded by silver coins.

The question has been much discussed whether these

coins were issued by cities or by temples or by private persons. It was perfectly natural that numismatists, accustomed to the fact that in later historic times every Greek city had one or two easily recognized devices which stamped its coin as belonging to it only, should have begun by trying to assign the early electrum also to city mints, by help of the types which the coins bear. The lion was held to be the mark of Miletus, the lion's scalp of Samos, the stag of Ephesus, and so forth. But there are grave reasons for thinking that this procedure was mistaken, or at least was carried much too far. Thus the lion, the lion's head and his scalp, appear on a large number of electrum coins, which differ so widely in style and in monetary standard that they can scarcely come from any one mint. To suppose that the lion is always the regal sign of the Lydian kings is a view which cannot be maintained. Again, there are on electrum coins many devices—the cock, the chimaera, the fox, the human head, and others—which cannot be satisfactorily assigned to any known mint. It therefore seems probable that the custom of issuing money by state authority, and impressing upon all coins so issued the civic badge as a type, had not yet arisen, or at all events had not become usual. An overwhelming impression that the types of early electrum coins are not civic arises from a consideration of the specimens found in the temple of Artemis at Ephesus in 1905.[1] The types borne by these coins were the lion, the goat, the cock, the stag; heads of the bull, the horse, the gryphon, a human head; the seal, the beetle. Of these types only two could be assigned to a mint-city with any probability (the stag to Ephesus, and the seal to Phocaea). It seems by far most probable that all were struck at Ephesus or in the neighbourhood.

A confirmation of this view may be found in the fact that even in the case of the later issues of electrum coins, such as those of Cyzicus and Mytilene, there is no uniform type, as on the coins of most Greek cities, but an almost unlimited

[1] *British Museum Excavations at Ephesus.* The Coins, pp. 74–93 (Head).

number of devices, which do not indicate place of mintage, but far more probably belong to the monetary magistrates.

Thus the types of early electrum coins are no safe indication of their place of mintage. And since, with one or two exceptions, they are uninscribed, there is a dearth of clues to direct us to their place of origin.

It is maintained by M. Babelon that these primitive coins were not state-issues at all, but struck by the bankers of Ionia and Lydia for the purposes of trade, and stamped with their private signets.[1] He has several historic parallels to cite. He shows that among the Franks of the Merovingian age money was issued by private coiners, and varies remarkably in alloy, and even in weight. And he brings forward examples in which trading companies in America in the eighteenth and nineteenth centuries issued great quantities of coin in their own name, and on their own responsibility.

It must also be noted that large classes of coins in Persian times, especially the Persian silver shekels or sigli, and the money of Aspendus in Pamphylia, bear a multitude of small stamps or countermarks which seem to be the marks of bankers, or possibly of local financial officers, guaranteeing the quality of the coin.[2] This custom might well be the successor of a system of private coinage. Terrien de la Couperie observes[3] that on early coins of China we find many private marks. 'The exchange being generally limited to the region of the issuers, they used on their currency to put as their marks names of regions, places, families, individuals, or things.' In early India also small ingots circulated bearing many countermarks, which may have been stamped on them either by financial authorities or else by private capitalists.[4]

I cannot examine in detail the theories of M. Babelon as

[1] *Origines de la Monnaie*, pp. 93–134.

[2] This custom may be well studied in the case of the Cilician find published by Mr. Newell (*Num. Chron.*, 1914).

[3] *B. M. Cat. Chinese Coins*, Introd., p. 4.

[4] E. Thomas, *Ancient Indian Weights*, p. 52.

to the way in which the Ionian bankers stamped the coin; and in that matter I do not think his particular views can be maintained. But as regards the probability that many of the types of early coins are only private marks, I agree with him. Certainty is not to be attained; it is, however, at the least quite possible that private issues made their appearance before the rise of the regular civic coinages. Long ago Professor Ernst Curtius called attention to the probability that in some cases, at all events, very early issues of coins may have taken place in connexion with the wealthy temples of Ionia, where specie tended to accumulate. And this view has been generally accepted, even by Professor Ridgeway,[1] who is generally disposed to deny the religious origin of coin-types.

But however much truth there may be in the view that the earliest coins belong to bankers or temples, we have good reason for thinking that not later than about 600 B.C. the Greek cities of Asia were beginning to take the issue of electrum into their own hands, and to stamp it with an official seal.

Some account must here be given of the monetary systems according to which the early electrum coins were minted.

The basis of the Asiatic systems was bimetallic: they started from the gold unit, or shekel, and assumed a fixed proportion in value between gold and silver. As to electrum, it has been clearly made out that it was always, or almost always, minted on a silver and not on a gold standard. We must therefore start from the gold unit, thence to reach the standards used both for silver and for electrum.

We may fairly consider the fixed conventional weight of the shekel of gold as 130 grains (grm. 8·42), being the sixtieth of a Babylonic mina of 505 grammes,[2] or the double of this shekel, which also was in use. The prevailing view, started by Mommsen and Brandis, and satisfactorily established, is that the weights of silver and electrum coins were

[1] *Origin of Currency*, p. 215.
[2] Head, *Hist. Num.*, ed. 2, p. xxxvi.

derived from this stater, the proportionate values of th metals being—

AV.	EL.	AR.
1	$\frac{4}{3}$	$13\frac{1}{3}$
$\frac{3}{4}$	1	10
$\frac{3}{40}$	$\frac{1}{10}$	1

Hence we derive—

I. From the double or heavy gold shekel of 260 grain (grm. 16·84):

$260 \times 13\frac{1}{3} = 3{,}466$ grains of silver,
= 15 silver shekels of 230 grains (grm. 14·90
or $1\frac{1}{2}$ of electrum.

Thus is derived the Phoenician or Graeco-Asiati standard for silver and electrum.

II. From the single or light gold shekel of 130 grain (grm. 8·42):

$130 \times 13\frac{1}{3} = 1{,}733$ grains of silver,
= 10 silver shekels of 173 grains (grm 11·20), or 20 shekels of 86 grain (grm. 5·60), or 1 or 2 of electrum.

Thus is derived the Babylonic or Persian standard fo silver and electrum.

In the Introduction I have briefly considered the questio of these relations of value, which certainly suggest som questions at present unsolved. The weight-standards whic we have above reached, the Phoenician and the Persian a we may perhaps best call them, are the commonest in us in early times for electrum coins.

The classification of these coins is at present difficul and very tentative. It was first clearly set forth b Mr. Head[1] that certain classes of electrum coins may b distinguished as belonging to different districts of Ioni and following different monetary standards. M. Babelo has further developed this view, and shown that the fabri

[1] *Numismatic Chronicle*, 1875.

of the various classes, with the form of incuse, is different and characteristic.[1] We may distinguish four classes:

(1) There is a very primitive class of coins following the Phoenician standard of weight (stater, grm. 14·90–14·40, grains 230–222). Some of these have scarcely any type; and the fabric of the earliest of them is rude. Their pale colour indicates, what is confirmed by analysis, that they contain but a small proportion of gold. They belong to cities in the neighbourhood of Miletus and Ephesus in the south of Ionia. (**Pl. I. 1, 2; B. T. I. 15–19; B. M. I. 2, 3, 6, 7.**) To this class also belong the numerous electrum coins found by Mr. Hogarth on the site of the Artemisium at Ephesus.[2] These bear a great variety of types, as we have above seen, but the types seem to be no indication of mint.

It is highly probable, considering the political and commercial importance of Miletus in the seventh and sixth centuries, that a large proportion of the pale electrum coins were minted in that city. On this subject I must refer to the detailed arguments of M. Babelon.[3] On the other hand, I can by no means accept the view of this writer that the coins belong to the times of Croesus. On the contrary, it was against their circulation, as we shall presently see, that the royal coinage of Croesus was directed. In another place[4] M. Babelon rightly observes that if the people of Phocaea took with them to Massilia, even in the sixth century, their coins of silver, as seems to be the case, the electrum of Phocaea, being earlier than the silver, must be given to the seventh century. But it is certainly not earlier than the electrum of Miletus. We shall speak of it presently.

The earliest electrum coins of Chios are of this class:

Obv. Sphinx of archaic style. *Rev.* Small incuse square. (**B T. VIII, 6, 8.**)

[1] *Revue Numismatique*, 1894–5, four papers.

[2] *British Museum Excavations at Ephesus*, pp. 74–93.

[3] *Traité*, ii. 1, pp. 11–54. [4] *Ibid.*, p. 96.

These staters are of Milesian weight: they have a ver archaic look, and one would be disposed to attribute ther to the earlier part of the sixth century. A later exampl was in the Vourla find, which belongs mainly to the tim of the Ionic revolt.[1]

A similar uncertainty prevails in regard to another earl electrum coin of Milesian standard, that which bears th inscription of which the best reading seems to be φάνο ἐμὶ σῆμα (Pl. I. 2). We may regard it as having been issuec with his own stamp, by some Phanes. If so, there is n reason to think that the stag indicates the mint of Ephesu: On the other hand, the coin is too early to have been issue by the Phanes known to history who was a contemporar of King Cambyses in Egypt, and who was tyrant of Hali carnassus.[2] More probably Ephesian is a third of a state bearing the type of a bee, with two rectangular incuses o the other side: weight 72–68 grains[3] (grm. 4·64–4·37).

That the Lydian kings at their capital of Sardes issue electrum coin is in the highest degree probable, for th Lydians as a people seem to have possessed the commercia instinct.[4] Yet it is not possible with certainty to assig to any of the Mermnad kings any electrum coin. Th classification of electrum money to each of them by Françoi Lenormant is little more than a work of imagination.

M. J. P. Six has indeed read on some pale electrum coin bearing as type a lion's head,[5] the name of King Alyatte of Lydia. The letters, so far as they can be made out, seem t be FAΛFEI. Whether these letters can stand for the nam

[1] See an elaborate paper on the early coins of Chios by J. Mavrogordato i the *Numismatic Chronicle*, 1915, p. 29.

[2] The coin, however, is stated by Mr. Borrell, its first possessor, to hav been found at Halicarnassus.

[3] Babelon, *Traité*, ii. 1, p. 66.

[4] Babelon, *Rev. Num.*, 1895, p. 20. The whole of M. Babelon's two articl on early electrum coins in this volume is important.

[5] *Numismatic Chronicle*, 1890, p. 204; *B. M. Cat. Lydia*, p. xviii; Babelo *Traité*, p. 227. In his most recent publication, in the volume published b the British Museum on excavations at Ephesus (p. 91), Mr. Head allows th probability of M. Six's reading. Babelon, however, adduces strong reason mainly philological, against it.

of the king is a problem for philologists. At the same time, the fabric of the coins and the nature of their incuse connects them closely with the coins of Croesus, shortly to be mentioned. And, as M. Six observes, the use of the digamma seems to exclude the notion of an Ionian mint. We may therefore regard the attribution to Alyattes as not impossible. The issue, however, was not important, as were those of Croesus.

'The reverse of primitive electrum coins is often in a measure an indication of the mint. At Miletus it is a rectangle between two small squares, at Teos a small square, at Smyrna a large square, at Phocaea a larger and smaller square, side by side.'[1] These observations of M. Babelon are valuable as suggestions, but they must not be taken as final.

(2) There is another class of early coins, also of pale electrum, which is generally referred to the Euboic standard.[2] The principal examples are as follows:

1. *Obv.* Two lions' heads, back to back.[3] *Rev.* Two oblong incuses. Weight, 269 grains (grm. 17·43). Paris.[3] (**B. T. IX. 14.**)
2. *Obv.* Same type. *Rev.* Incuse square and oblong. Weight, 133·5 grains (grm. 8·65). Six. (**B. T. IX. 16.**)
3. *Obv.* Lion's head facing. *Rev.* Incuse square and triangle. Same weight. Brit. Museum. Found at Priene. (**B. M. I. 5.**)
4. *Obv.* Lion's head facing. *Rev.* Incuse square. Weight, 66·2 grains (grm. 4·29). Brit. Museum. Found at Mytilene. (**B. T. IX. 19.**)
5. *Obv.* Head of lioness l. *Rev.* Incuse square. Weight, 67·6 grains (grm. 4·37). Brit. Museum. Found in Lydia.
6. *Obv.* Bull's head r. *Rev.* Incuse square. Weight, 133·4 grains (grm. 8·62). Berlin. (**B. T. IX. 26.**)

[1] Babelon, *Traité*, ii. 1, p. 132.

[2] See Head, *Notes on Electrum Coins, Num. Chron.*, N. S. xv, p. 270; Babelon, *Rev. Num.*, 1894, p. 253, Pl. X.

[3] This type is obscure, and has been variously interpreted: by Müller as silphium (and given to Cyrene); by Head as the device of Corcyra.

7. *Obv.* Bull's head r. *Rev.* Fylfot in incuse. Weight, 129·5 grains (grm. 8·39). Berlin. (**B. T. IX. 27.**)
8. *Obv.* Fylfot among globules. *Rev.* Incuse square. Weight, 45 grains (grm. 2·92). Brit. Museum. (**B. T. IX. 18.**)

The provenience of these coins, so far as I know, is always the neighbourhood of Samos. M. Babelon proposes to attribute them all to Samos. And as a hoard containing several of them[1] was actually found on the island, there is much to be said for this attribution. When, however, M. Babelon gives them to the time of the Tyrant Polycrates, he certainly brings them too low. They are of very early fabric, the incuses being decidedly of the kind in use before the time of Croesus. Wealthy tyrants like Polycrates are usually more advanced than their period in the style of their coins: compare, for example, the coinages of Gelon of Syracuse and Peisistratus of Athens. The attribution to Samos is further confirmed by the fact that some of the very early silver coins usually given to Samos are struck on exactly the same standard:

1. *Obv.* Forepart of bull. *Rev.* Incuse square. Weight, 135 grains (grm. 8·74). Brit. Museum.[2]
2. *Obv.* Lion's head facing. *Rev.* Incuse square. Weight, 63 grains (grm. 4·08). Brit. Museum. (**B. T. XI. 9.**)
3. *Obv.* Lion's scalp facing. *Rev.* Incuse square. Weight, 39·1 grains (grm. 2·53). Brit. Museum. (**B. T. XI. 19.**)
4. *Obv.* Head and neck of bull. *Rev.* Incuse square. Weight, 32·7 grains (grm. 2·11). Brit. Museum. (**B. T. XI. 22.**)

This standard is commonly assumed to be the Euboic. But here there is a difficulty, which has been passed over by numismatists.

The Euboic standard, as used in the seventh and early sixth centuries at Chalcis and Eretria in Euboea, Athens and Corinth, does not reach for the stater more than

[1] See Head, *l. c.*

[2] *Cat. Ionia*, p. 350. Mr. Head observes that the weight and the style of the incuse is rather Lycian than Samian. For such reasons the coin was omitted in my paper on Samian Coins, *Num. Chron.*, 1882.

130 grains at most (grm. 8·42). The Babylonic gold standard, with which Herodotus equates it, also reaches 130 grains as a maximum, and is almost always somewhat below that. But the standard for the electrum coins which we are considering is quite clearly higher than this. Its normal full weights seem to be—

	Grains.	*Grammes.*
Double stater	269	17·43
Stater	133	8·61
Half	67	4·37
Third	45	2·92
Sixth	22	1·46

These are the weights, not of the Euboic standard, but of the Attic standard introduced by Pisistratus, as I try to show in Chapter VIII, about the middle of the sixth century, and adopted from Athens by Euboea and Corinth, and in Sicily. As these electrum coins are certainly much earlier than any coins of the same weights in Greece, we must needs suppose that they were issued on the standard of the city which struck them, whether Samos or another, and that this standard was imported into Greece by Pisistratus.

Some numismatists may be disposed to regard this standard as one handed down to later Greece from the Mycenaean Age. Thus Professor Ridgeway,[1] in drawing up a list of the weights of some gold rings found at Mycenae, regards a group of them as following an unit of 135 grains, 8·75 grammes. Sir A. Evans[2] regards a ball or 'dump' of gold from Salamis in Cyprus and some carnelian duck weights from Palaikastro as evidencing the use of this standard in prehistoric times. It will, however, be found, on examining the rings of Mycenae, that their weights are too irregular to allow of any satisfactory deduction. And Evans regards all the weights used at Cnossus as derived from Egypt, so that in any case the derivation of the standard we are considering may be from that most ancient empire, whether through Crete and Argos or not.

[1] *J. H. S.* x. 90. [2] *Corolla Numismatica*, p. 365.

When we reach the coins of Cyrene we shall see that the same monetary standard was in vogue there from 600 B.C. onwards. It is almost certainly derived from Egypt, where a *Kedet* of the weight of 139 grains (grm. 9·0) was in use in the Delta[1] at Heliopolis. The Samians, who were among the most important of the peoples who founded Naucratis, seem to have there adopted the local weight for silver, and transferred that weight to electrum, electrum coinage being, as we know, usually issued on a silver standard.

(3) Next to these coins of Samian weight we must place a few very early staters of pale electrum which follow the standard afterwards called Persian.

Obv. Irregular transverse furrows. *Rev.* Three incuses; in the middle one, which is the largest, one can trace the figure of a fox. Weight, 10·81 grm., 167 grains. *B. M. Cat. Ionia*, p. 183, Pl. III.[2] (B. M. I. 1.)

Mr. Head doubts whether the fox in the incuse can really be made out. He attributes the coin, doubtfully, to Miletus. But this attribution, in view of its weight, is most improbable. It is of the same weight as the silver coins, and a few of the gold coins of Croesus; and for that reason M. Babelon[3] would give it to the time of Croesus. But the fabric is as fatal to this attribution as is the weight to Mr. Head's. The coin contains but a small proportion of gold (according to its specific gravity only 2 per cent.), and it may have passed as silver, in which case it would be an early and exceptional prototype of the silver coinage of Croesus. Considering the coin thus, the objection to the attribution to Miletus would be lessened; but it is much more probable that it was struck at Sardis.

(4) There is a somewhat later class of coins which follow the lead of Phocaea. These coins are of somewhat darker colour, and contain a larger proportion of gold. (B. M. I. 10, 11.) Indeed, Mr. Head has suggested that they were intended to pass as gold, not as electrum. Their standard,

[1] Petrie, *Proc. Soc. Bibl. Archaeol.*, xxxiii, p. 378 and foll.

[2] *Corolla Numismatica*, p. 365.

[3] *Traité*, ii. I, p. 19.

which in common with other numismatists I call Phocaean, is the double of the gold stater or shekel (260 grains; grm. 16·84). It is partly for this reason that Mr. Head has maintained these coins to be really intended for gold; since in nearly all other cases electrum coins are minted on a silver standard. They can be assigned in some cases to mints with considerable confidence. I mention a few staters; at Phocaea and Cyzicus there are also smaller denominations.

Phocaea.

Obv. ⊙ (Φ) Seal (phoca). *Rev.* Two square punch-marks. Brit. Museum, Munich. Weight, 255 grains (grm. 16·50). (Pl. I. 3.)

Cyzicus.

Obv. Tunny bound with fillet. *Rev.* Two punch-marks; in one a scorpion. Brit. Museum. Weight, 252 grains (grm. 16·32). (Pl. I. 4.)

Dr. von Fritze, in an elaborate monograph on the coins of Cyzicus,[1] denies, on account of the character of the incuse on the reverse, that this coin belongs to the city. The coins which he attributes to Cyzicus in the sixth century have on the reverse a single, rather rough, incuse square. They will be found on Pl. I of his paper: they have a variety of types, part of which is always a tunny or the head of a tunny. Among the more remarkable devices are a winged fish and a male or female winged figure. These coins, dating from about 600 B.C., are regarded by von Fritze as the earliest examples of the great series of electrum coins so prominent in the fifth century. He thinks that the issue was uninterrupted; but I prefer the view that in the latter part of the sixth century electrum issues came to a stop until the Ionian revolt.

There is also a stater of this weight with the type of the griffin's head and the inscription ΙΣΟΜ (*Ζιος?*) which has been given with some probability to Teos.[2] Other attribu-

[1] *Nomisma*, Part VII.

[2] Babelon, *Traité*, ii. 1, p. 119; Pl. V. 2.

tions, of a less convincing kind, to Methana and Mytilene in Lesbos, Smyrna, Cyme, and other cities are proposed by M. Babelon. All these coins belong, so far as we can judge, to cities to the north of Smyrna; and they may be mostly assigned to the period mentioned by Eusebius in his list of thalassocracies as the time of the greatest sea-power of Phocaea, 578–534 B.C. It is also the time of the foundation of the Phocaean colonies Velia and Massilia.

To the same class of electrum staters, though of lower weight, belong the early staters of Lampsacus. These bear on the obverse the forepart of a winged horse, usually with traces of a vine-wreath, and have on the reverse an incuse square, sometimes quartered, sometimes having only two of the four divisions sunk.[1] The weight is 15·15 grammes (234 grains) or less, which weight is also in use for the Lampsacene staters issued in the fifth century. It is very remarkable how cities in Asia preserved their monetary standard unchanged through successive periods.

Such are the principal issues of electrum coins in the seventh and sixth centuries. The question of the date of their cessation will be considered in the next chapter.

[1] See Babelon, *Traité*, ii. 1, p. 183, Pl. VIII. 1–2; Nos. 3–5 of the plate belong to later issues.

CHAPTER II

LYDIAN AND PERSIAN COINAGE

§ 1. Gold of Lydia.

There is no proof that the earlier Mermnad kings of Lydia, whose power was rapidly increasing in the seventh and sixth centuries, showed any desire to interfere with Ionian issues of electrum. If, as is probable, they issued electrum coin of their own at Sardes, they seem to have allowed it to take its chance with the rest, and did not stamp it distinctively as a royal issue. But when Croesus came to the throne he seems to have determined to take another line. It may be that the inherent faults in the electrum coinage of Ionia were unfitting it for its purpose. It may be that with great sagacity he grasped the notion that by concentrating the issue of coin in his own hands he could strengthen his political power. It may be that he merely wished, with commercial instinct, to make the most of his great stores of gold. Whatever the motive, he certainly initiated one of the greatest of all the political movements which the world has known—the issue of a state coinage.

It is true that the proofs that this action was due to Croesus are not absolutely conclusive. Holm is even disposed to call them in question. They are circumstantial rather than direct. But in my opinion they are ample. This is the only view which brings consistency and order into the arrangement of facts. And since Julius Pollux talks of the staters of Croesus in the same line with the noted gold staters of Philip and the darics, he bears testimony to the existence of well-known gold coins named after Croesus. These can only be the coins long attributed by numismatists to the king, which are the following:

Obv. Foreparts of lion and bull facing each other. *Rev.* Two incuses side by side. **(Pl. I. 5, 6; B. M. I. 13–16; B. T. X. 1–12.)**

These coins were issued in gold on two standards, a stater of 10·89 grm. (168 grains), with its fractions of a half, a third, a sixth, and a twelfth; and a stater of 8·17 grm. (126 grains), with corresponding divisions, and on one standard in silver with an unit of 10·89 grm. (168 grains), again with corresponding fractions.[1]

The gold and silver employed are extremely pure: the specific gravity of the gold being that of unmixed gold.

If we accept the current view as to the proportionate value of gold electrum and silver as $13\frac{1}{3} : 10 : 1$, we can easily calculate the values of the Croesean coins in currency in relation to the existing electrum. The gold piece of 168 grains (grm. 10·89) would be equivalent to ten silver pieces or one electrum piece of the weight of 224 grains. The gold piece of 126 grains (grm. 8·17) would be equivalent to ten silver pieces or one electrum piece of 168 grains (grm. 10·89). The Phocaean gold or electrum coins of 260 grains (grm. 16·84) can scarcely have been regarded as equivalent to two Croesean staters of 126 grains (grm. 8·17) since the gold of the latter is far purer.

The gold of Croesus, and of the Persian kings who succeeded him, seems to have superseded the electrum coinage. It is not easy to prove this, because it involves the negative proof, that of the electrum coins which have come down to us none belongs to the second half of the sixth century. This would scarcely be generally conceded, and it is of course quite possible that the Persian kings may have in the sixth century, as they certainly did in the fifth, allowed to a few Greek cities of the coast the privilege of issuing money of electrum. All that we can do is to examine the electrum coins of such well-known mints as Chios, Cyzicus, Phocaea, and Lampsacus, to see if we can there discern a break or gap in the series which might

[1] See Babelon, *Traité*, ii. 1, p. 227.

correspond to the period 540–500 B.C. This may easily be done by the help of the earliest plates of M. Babelon's great work. The identification of the coins of the Ionian Revolt shows us the state of monetary art in Asia Minor in 500 B.C.

Chios. Mr. Mavrogordato, in his careful paper on the coins of Chios,[1] observes that the coinage of electrum must have ceased under the Persian rule. The coins are quite consistent with that view.

Lampsacus. There certainly seems to be a considerable interval of time between the very early electrum staters (Babelon, Pl. VIII. 1, 2) and Babelon, Pl. VIII. 5, which is of the time of the revolt. Nos. 3 and 4 of this plate, where the half-horse is surrounded by a vine-wreath, are certainly of the fifth century.

Cyzicus. Here, if anywhere, we should expect to find a continuous and uninterrupted coinage of electrum. And the most recent writer on the coins of Cyzicus, Dr. von Fritze,[2] arranges them in consecutive series from 600 B.C. onwards. If, however, we turn to von Fritze's plates, we may discern a distinct gap between Pl. I. 38 and I. 39. Coins 1–38 on that plate are marine in character, with very few exceptions. The tunny, body or head, appears on them all; and fish swimming or flying appear usually. A few winged human monsters make up the tale. The incuse of the reverse is rough and primitive. Coins I. 39 onwards are of quite a different type; the tunny comes in as mint-mark, but the types are very varied, animals or the heads of animals being usual. The incuse has become a mill-sail pattern. It is true, as von Fritze points out, that some of the human heads in this series are decidedly archaic in character, such heads as II. 13 and 19. But some types, of which the reverse bears the same mill-sail incuse as these, must be dated well into the fifth century. I am disposed to think that the facts of the coinage of Cyzicus do not compel us to suppose that the coinage was continuous through the sixth century; it is more probable that it intermitted.

[1] *Num. Chron.*, 1915, p. 35.

[2] *Nomisma*, Part VII.

Phocaea. The early electrum of Phocaea must almost certainly have come to an end when the bulk of the inhabitants left their city to sail westwards. The coinage was resumed under the Athenian Empire.

It seems then that the electrum coinage of Asia Minor came to an end generally, if not universally, soon after the middle of the sixth century. As we shall see later, it was revived for a while at the time of the Ionian Revolt, and continued at a very few mints, such as Cyzicus, Phocaea, and Lampsacus, in the fifth century; and even, at Cyzicus, Phocaea, and Mytilene, down to the time of Alexander the Great.

§ 2. Gold of Persia.

When the kingdom of Croesus fell, about 546 B.C.,[1] the royal coinage at Sardes probably ceased. Before long, its place was taken by the royal darics and sigli, or staters of gold and drachms of silver, issued by the Persian kings. The daric stater was a few grains heavier than that of Croesus, following the Babylonic standard, also a little less pure in metal. It was current until the fall of the Persian empire, and governed the trade of Asia Minor for ages. The issue of gold coin was the exclusive privilege of the Great King, a privilege jealously guarded and enforced. Satraps of the Persian Empire were allowed to strike silver coins freely for the needs of military expeditions, and the Greek cities of the coast struck silver for ordinary purposes of trade. But no issue of gold coin was allowed, save under exceptional circumstances.

Although this view is generally accepted,[2] yet it is not easy to establish it by quotations from ancient writers. Herodotus seems under the influence of such a view when

[1] All the dates in early Greek and Oriental history are only approximate. Winckler prefers for the date of Croesus' fall 548 B.C. As the exact year in which events took place is a matter of small importance to the purpose of the present work, I have not judged it necessary to enter into chronological discussions, but usually accept the ordinary view, except in a few cases where there are numismatic data to come in.

[2] M. Babelon, however, does not allow it. *Traité*, ii. 2, p. 5.

he writes,[1] 'Darius wished to leave such a memorial of himself as no king had ever left before: therefore, refining his gold to the last degree of purity, he issued coins of it'. But this is, of course, no assertion of a principle of state, that no one else should issue coin. Nor in fact is it likely that the issue of gold coin was from the first looked upon as something quite exceptional. The first issue of pure gold was due to Croesus, not to Darius. It seems likely that the principle that the issue of gold coin was the first privilege of authority was one which made its way slowly and perhaps almost unconsciously. From age to age it became more solidly fixed, and the Roman Empire maintained it even more rigidly than did that of Persia.

The type of the darics is well known. It is a figure of the king, kneeling, or perhaps rather running, holding spear and bow, and wearing the royal crown, the kidaris. The reverse is an oblong incuse, in which occasionally a device may be made out; but more often the search for such a device is quite fruitless. (**Pl. I. 7; B. M. I. 17; B. T. X. 13–23.**)

Some metrologists, such as Lehmann-Haupt, have regarded the Croesean and daric staters as of different origin, the former being derived from the common gold mina of the Babylonians, the latter from the royal gold mina, which was heavier by one thirty-sixth. But it seems that in fact the two were nearly equivalent, since the Croesean coin was of purer metal than the daric. The most recent investigation of the specific gravity of these coins (by Mr. Hunkin) shows that the fineness of the Croesean staters is about 0·99, and that of the darics about 0·98. On this basis the daric would be slightly more valuable.[2]

The date of the first introduction of the daric is a matter of some uncertainty. The word daric is a Greek adjective, formed from Darius, and it is expressly associated by Julius Pollux with the name of that king,[3] but that fact does not

[1] iv. 166.

[2] *Num. Chron.*, 1887, p. 303; 1916, p. 258.

[3] *Onom.* iii. 87 *οἱ Δαρεικοὶ ἀπὸ Δαρείου.*

necessarily prove that darics were not issued before the accession of Darius in 521 B C. For it is quite maintainable that the Greeks named the coin after the Persian king best known to them, even if they were issued before his reign.[1]

It is certainly in itself improbable that Asia Minor had to wait until the reign of Darius for a satisfactory gold currency. The coinage of Persia is confessedly modelled on that of Lydia; and it is difficult to believe that the 25 or 30 years which elapsed between the overthrow of Croesus and the reforms of Darius passed without the issue by Cyrus and Cambyses of coins to take the place of the Lydian money. Indeed, so improbable does this seem, that some writers, such as François Lenormant and B. V. Head, have supposed that the Persian governors of Sardes continued to issue money of the types and the standard of Croesus.[2] This is of course not impossible, and parallels may be found; but it is improbable, and the view is rightly rejected by M. Babelon.[3] Herodotus[4] asserts the purity of the coin issued by Darius, but does not at all imply that he was the first to issue a Persian gold coinage. Thus it seems most probable that the Persian darics were issued immediately after the conquest of Lydia, and were the institution of Cyrus rather than of Darius.

It has been supposed that half-darics also were struck, because Xenophon records, in his account of the expedition of the younger Cyrus,[5] that the latter promised to raise the pay of his soldiers from a daric a month to a daric and a half, *τρία ἡμιδαρεικά*. Since, however, no half-darics are known to exist, it is probable that the half-daric was a

[1] Attempts have been made to show that similar words to daric were used for money in Assyria in pre-Persian times. In any case, though the adjective *δαρεικός* is regularly formed in Greek from Δαρεῖος, it may be what is called a Volksetymologie, and really have nothing to do with that king. Cf. Harpocration (Hultsch, *Metrol. Script. reliquiae*, p. 310), ἐκλήθησαν δὲ Δαρεικοὶ οὐχ, ὡς οἱ πλεῖστοι νομίζουσιν, ἀπὸ Δαρείου τοῦ Ξέρξου πατρός, ἀλλ' ἀφ' ἑτέρου τινὸς παλαιοτέρου βασιλέως.

[2] Lenormant, *Monn. royales de la Lydie*, p. 198; Head, *Coinage of Lydia and Persia*, p. 23.

[3] Babelon, *Traité*, p. 242.

[4] Hdt. iv. 166.

[5] *Anabasis*, i. 3. 21.

money of account. Double darics have in recent years been discovered in considerable numbers, especially in the Far East. They certainly belong to the very latest time of Persian rule. M. Babelon thinks that they were issued shortly before the time of Alexander, and that he continued to strike them; but numismatists have generally been more disposed to think that they were struck only by Alexander and his generals.

The main subsidiary coins to the daric were silver coins of the same type and form, the sigli or shekels weighing about 86 grains (grm. 5·57), which, as we know from the testimony of Xenophon,[1] passed at the rate of 20 to the daric. It is strange indeed to find thus, at the beginning of consecutive history, the primary coinage of Asia consisting of gold coins of nearly the weight of an English sovereign, divided into twenty sigli, each nearly of the metal weight of a shilling, or a German mark.

Very rarely, fractions of the daric and the siglos seem to have been struck, of the same types as the larger coins. Twelfths of the daric are mentioned by M. Babelon,[2] weighing 10·5 to 11·5 grains (grm. 0·65 to 0·75). Also a small fraction weighing grm. 0·155 (2·4 grains), and bearing only the head of the king.

Several ancient historians bear witness to the enormous extent of the daric currency of the Persian Empire. In the reign of Xerxes, as Herodotus[3] informs us, a wealthy Lydian named Pythius had amassed four millions of darics, lacking seven thousand. The Persian archers, as the darics were called because they bore the type of the king holding the bow, were but too well known and too potent in the domestic affairs of Greece. The vast stores of them found by Alexander at Ecbatana and Susa[4] inundated the whole Greek world with gold, and doubtless formed the material out of which many of Alexander's own coins were struck.

[1] *Anabasis*, i. 7. 18, where the talent of silver (6,000 sigli) is equated with 300 darics.

[2] *Traité*, ii. 2, p. 46.

[3] Hdt. vii. 28.

[4] At Susa Alexander captured 9,000 talents of darics, besides unminted gold and silver. Diodorus, xvii. 66.

A century ago the daric was a comparatively rare coin in our museums, the obvious reason being that those found were concealed by the finders, and at once melted down. A great abundance of them has appeared in recent years. To determine their find-spots is almost impossible; but they certainly range over a great part of western Asia.

Can they be classified as regards period? Lenormant tried to find on them the portraits of the successive reigning monarchs of Persia. Mr. Head, with his usual sanity and moderation, writes [1]: 'A close examination of the gold darics enables us to perceive that, in spite of their general similarity, there are differences of style. Some are archaic, and date from the time of Darius and Xerxes, while others are characterized by more careful work, and these belong to the later monarchs of the Achaemenian dynasty.' More recently, M. Babelon [2] thinks that he has found a clue in a hoard of 300 darics discovered in the canal of Xerxes by Mount Athos, which he ventures to divide, on the ground of minute differences in the portrait and beard, between Darius and Xerxes. For my part I prefer to stop at the point marked by Mr. Head.[3] An exceptional coin has as type the king not bearded but beardless. M. Babelon proposes to attribute it to the younger Cyrus; but there appears no sufficient reason for such assignment. In fact, several of the Persian kings came to the throne young. And the extreme rarity of the coin in question is a strong reason against supposing that it was issued by Cyrus, who must have used gold coins in great quantities to pay his Greek mercenaries, who received a daric or more a month. Moreover, the weight of the example in Paris (grm. 8·46: 130·5 grains) seems to point to the period of Alexander the Great.

[1] *Lydia and Persia*, p. 28.

[2] Babelon, *Traité*, ii. 2, p. 51 : Pl. LXXXVI, 16–18.

[3] The arrangement of M. Babelon is inconsistent with the data of the find in Cilicia published by Mr. Newell in *Num. Chron.*, 1914.

CHAPTER III

THE COINAGE OF THE IONIAN REVOLT[1]

In a paper published in the *Proceedings of the British Academy*[2] I tried to show that the cities of Ionia which took part in the revolt against Persia in the years 500–494 B.C. issued an uniform coinage in electrum. So far as I am aware, this discovery has met with general acceptance. I propose here to state my view somewhat more in detail, and to trace certain corollaries.

I need not go through the story of the Ionian Revolt, as narrated by Herodotus: it is fair to assume that every scholar is familiar with it. It may, however, be well here to mention the cities, the names of which occur in this section of the story of Herodotus, with the definite facts recorded of them, as the issues of coins would probably be civic issues. It was Miletus, under the guidance of Aristagoras, which began the revolt (Hdt. v. 35). It spread rapidly to Mylasa and Termera in Caria, as well as to Mytilene and Cyme. The Ionian cities expelled their tyrants, and set up *στρατηγοί* in their place (v. 37). The Athenians and Eretrians, at the invitation of Aristagoras, land at Ephesus, and burn Sardes (v. 101). The Ionians compel the people of Byzantium and the Hellespont, and the Carians, including the Caunians, to join them (v. 103). The Cyprians join them willingly (v. 104), but are reconquered (v. 115). Daurises the Persian reduces Dardanus, Abydus, Percote,

[1] This chapter is reprinted, with certain omissions and modifications, from the *Journal of Hellenic Studies* for 1911. It is somewhat disproportionately long: my excuse must be the importance of the class of coins, which I was the first to identify.

[2] Vol. iii, 1908.

Lampsacus, and Paesus in the Troad and Mysia (v. 117). He attacks the Carians unsuccessfully (v. 121). Hymeas the Persian reduces Cius and Gergithus and other places in the Troad (v. 122). The Persians take Clazomenae and Cyme (v. 123). Aristagoras departs in despair to Thrace, where he dies, leaving the government of Miletus to Pythagoras (v. 126). The Chians capture Histiaeus, but afterwards release him, and he goes to Lesbos, thence to Byzantium (vi. 5). The battle of Lade, in which Miletus has 80 ships, Chios 100, Samos 60, Priene 12, Myus 3, Teos 17, Erythrae 8, Phocaea 3, Lesbos 70. [Notably absent are Ephesus and Lebedus] (vi. 8). Flight of the Samians and Lesbians. Desperate resistance of the Chians: Persian victory (vi. 15). A band of Chian fugitives cut off by Ephesians (vi. 16). Taking of Miletus (vi. 19). Samians sail to Sicily (vi. 22): their temples spared (vi. 25). Histiaeus gains possession of Chios (vi. 26). The Persians reduce Chios, Lesbos, and Tenedos, also the cities of the Hellespont, Chersonesus, Perinthus, Selymbria, and Byzantium. The people of Byzantium and Chalcedon escape to Mesembria. The people of Cyzicus had already submitted unattacked to the Persian satrap of Dascylium (vi. 33). Mardonius the Persian comes to Ionia: he puts down the tyrants, and establishes democracies (vi. 43). Artaphernes having already established a federal system among the cities, so that their disputes should be amicably settled, measured out their territories, and arranged tribute on the basis of that which they had paid before the revolt: an arrangement which endured (vi. 42).

Such being the facts recorded by Herodotus, let us next see what is the extant numismatic evidence. There is a well-marked and homogeneous set of coins in electrum, evidently contemporary one with another, and struck on the coast of Asia Minor about 500 B.C. Some of them are of certain, or almost certain, attribution: others are of quite uncertain mint. The reverse of all is uniform: an incuse square divided into four squares. The weight is also uniform: they are staters of the Milesian standard, weighing from 216 to 218 grains, grm. 13·98 to 14·09. The obverse types are as follows:[1]

1. Sphinx seated to r.
2. Forepart of bull r., looking back.
3. Eagle to l. looking back, standing on hare.
4. Eagle to l. looking back; in front a dolphin.
5. Forepart of winged boar to r.
6. Forepart of winged horse to l.; above, leaf-pattern.
7. Horse galloping to l.; beneath, leaf.
8. Sow walking to r.
9. Cock to r.; above, palmette.
10. Head of Athena in close-fitting helmet.[2]

The similarity of these coins one to another in fabric and art, in weight, and even in colour had long ago struck numismatists. In 1890 M. J. P. Six maintained that they were all issued from the mint of Chios.[3] M. Babelon[4] did not accept this view; but he held that the coins, in view of their identical fabric, must have been issued either from a single mint, or by a group of closely allied cities.

As to their date the authorities differ rather widely. M. Six thinks of the end of the fifth century: M. Babelon gives them to 'une époque assez avancée dans le cinquième siècle'. These views seem to me impossible. The art, though fine, is distinctly archaic, and after 490 B.C. there were no issues of electrum staters in Asia, except at the privileged mints of Cyzicus, Phocaea, Lampsacus, and Mytilene.

Mr. Head's view of date is much nearer the mark. As early as 1887[5] he accepted for the coins of this class the date of the beginning of the fifth century B.C. In 1892 he observed[6] that they probably began to be struck before

[1] Pl. I, 8–13. It does not seem necessary to give a detailed list of examples: such a list will be found in Babelon, *Traité*, ii. 1, pp. 191–8; Head, *Cat. Ionia*, pp. 7–8; Six, *Num. Chron.*, 1890, pp. 215–18.

[2] *Revue Numism.*, 1911, p. 60.

[3] *Num. Chron.*, 1890, p. 215.

[4] *Traité*, ii. 1, p. 198.

[5] *Num. Chron.*, 1887, p. 281.

[6] *B. M. Cat. Ionia*; Introduction, p. xxv.

500 B.C. But if we accept, as I think we must, the view that this group of coins was issued on the Ionian coast about 500 B.C. by a group of allied cities, that is tantamount to saying that they are the money of the Ionian Revolt. It is strange that numismatists should have missed so obvious a corollary.

The question of the exchange value of these staters, and their relation to the contemporary silver drachms, is one of considerable difficulty. They are of more uniform weight and composition than the early electrum of Asia Minor. They contain from 40 to 20 per cent. of gold, and from 60 to 80 per cent. of silver.[1] If we reckon their average contents as 30 and 70 per cent. respectively, and compute gold as $13\frac{1}{3}$ times more valuable than silver, we shall find that the staters were intrinsically worth about 76 grains of gold or 1,012 grains of silver, which is nearly twenty silver drachms of the Milesian standard.

If these equations were established, we should have a proof of the view maintained in the Introduction that the convention fixing the value of electrum at ten times that of silver did not outlast the sixth century.

It is very probable that the choice of electrum as the material for the coinage of the League was dictated by a determination to be free from the tyranny of Persian gold. Electrum was the ancient currency of the Ionian cities, and in time of crisis they seem to have reverted to it. At an earlier time the stater of 224 grains had probably passed as the equivalent of the gold coins of Croesus;[2] and it is not impossible that the revolting cities may have had a hope that their new coins would attain the value of the daric: but it is very improbable that this hope ever came to fruition.

At a somewhat later time, as we learn from the *Anabasis* of Xenophon, a daric or a Cyzicene stater per month was the ordinary pay of a mercenary soldier. Xenophon tells us that, when the Greek mercenaries of Cyrus learned that

[1] Six, in *Num. Chron.*, 1890, p. 218.

[2] See above, p. 84.

they were to march against the Great King, they demanded higher pay; and Cyrus promised them a daric and a half a month, in the place of a daric, which they had so far received.[1] Later these Greek soldiers were offered, by Timasion, a Cyzicene stater a month;[2] and Seuthes the Thracian made a similar offer.[3] This being the case, it seems not unreasonable to think that the coins which we are considering, of somewhat lower value than the daric and the Cyzicene, represent each a month's pay of a mercenary. No doubt the sailors and soldiers of the Ionian fleet were in the main not mercenaries, but citizens. Yet the poorer would require pay.

The issue of an uniform coinage by a set of allied cities is in later Greece an ordinary phenomenon. There is the set of coins struck by Rhodes, Samos, Ephesus, and other cities of the Ionian coast after the victory of Conon at Cnidus, and the expulsion of Spartan governors in 394. In that case the type of reverse is the same, young Heracles strangling the snakes; and the inscription ΣΥΝ (*συνμαχία*) records the alliance. Later we have the coinage of the Achaean League, of the Lycian League, and other confederacies. The earliest issue of the kind took place among the Greek cities of Southern Italy about the middle of the sixth century: each of the cities retaining its own types, while the fabric of the incuse reverse (obverse type reversed) is identical in all, as is usually the monetary standard. Numismatists suppose that the appearance of this uniform coinage proves some kind of understanding to have existed among the Greek cities; but the nature of it is doubtful.[4] I think that those who suppose it to prove the existence of some sort of Pythagorean brotherhood throughout Magna Graecia go beyond the evidence; for we do not know that the influence of Pythagoras had much effect on politics. It is clear, however, that this Italian coinage might serve as a precedent to the Ionian cities. In the case of these latter we have more definite proof not merely of a confederation

[1] *Anab.* i. 3. 21. [2] v. 6. 23. [3] vii. 3. 10.

[4] See G. Macdonald, *Coin-types*, p. 12.

of cities, but even of a federal unity. For Herodotus represents the envoys sent by the Ionians to stir up a revolt in Cyprus as saying Ἡμέας ἀπέπεμψε τὸ κοινὸν τῶν Ἰώνων (v. 109): and this word κοινόν implies a close union.

The assignment of the coins above mentioned to particular cities involves some difficulty. No. 1 bears the ordinary type of Chios, the sphinx, and was almost certainly struck in that city. The early electrum coinage of Chios is by no means easy to arrange; but the excellent paper of J. Mavrogordato [1] facilitates matters. A Chian stater was actually found at Vourla in company with other coins of the Revolt.[2] It seems, however, almost impossible in view of its style and fabric to assign it to a period much later than the middle of the sixth century. It seems that the coins of the class of the Vourla stater may well be the prototypes of all the staters of the League. A somewhat later and much finer stater of Chios may well be of the time of the League (*Num. Chron.*, 1915, Pl. II. 10). I must mention that the stater which in my previous paper (*J.H.S.* xxxi, Pl. VII. 1) I selected as being of the time of the Revolt is now regarded as a forgery, and I wish to withdraw it in favour of the stater last mentioned. It is to be observed that these pieces of Chian electrum are continuations of a series of staters of Milesian weight which began at Chios in the seventh century; it is at once suggested to us that it is Chios which is the true originator of the whole coinage, other cities merely falling into line and adopting the Chian standard. This completely accords with the position taken by the Chians among the allies: they furnished the largest contingent of the fleet, and were the last to fly at Lade. In the sixth century Chios was very flourishing; and the works of the Chian sculptors Archermus and his sons had influence far and wide.

Indeed, some numismatists might even be disposed, in view of the great uniformity of the coins, to give them, as did M. Six, all to the mint of Chios; to hold that Chios

[1] *Num. Chron.*, 1915. [2] *Ibid.*, Pl. I. 7.

became the banker of the League, and struck money for the various cities with their own types. This is possible, but improbable: it is far more likely that each city issued its own coins. To take the nearest parallel, we do not suppose that the early incuse coins of South Italy were issued at a single mint; but their fabric is even more notably uniform than is the case in Ionia.

No. 2 is almost certainly Samian. The half-bull is the ordinary type of Samos in later times: the reversion of the head is according to the fashion of art at the time.

No. 3 is probably of Abydos, the type of which city is an eagle. No. 4 may also be of Abydos; but the eagle standing on a dolphin is the ordinary type of the Pontic city of Sinope, a colony of Miletus, which may have followed the fortunes of the parent city. Abydos joined the Ionian League, but was soon reduced by Daurises.

No. 5 bears the type of Clazomenae, which city was also reconquered by the Persians before the battle of Lade.

No. 6 is certainly of Lampsacus. It is of different standard from the other electrum coins of Lampsacus,[1] which are of Phocaean weight, and was evidently struck on a special occasion. M. Babelon observes that it 'permet d'affirmer que Lampsaque conclut, à un moment donné, avec Chios et, sans doute, d'autres villes, un traité d'alliance monétaire'. It is strange that, having gone so far, M. Babelon should not have thought of the Ionian Revolt; doubtless he would have done so but for his opinion of the late date of the coins.

No. 7 may be of Cyme in Aeolis, the usual type of which city is in later times the forepart of a horse. Cyme and Lampsacus both joined the Ionian Revolt at first.

No. 8 is sometimes attributed to Methymna in Lesbos. This attribution is, however, very doubtful, as the early type of the city is a boar not a sow; and in relation to mythology the distinction of gender is important.

[1] Babelon, *Traité*, ii. 1, p. 187.

No. 9 is given, with more reason, to Dardanus. Dardanus was one of the cities reduced by Daurises. Pollux (ix. 84) states that the monetary type of Dardanus was the cock; and this statement is borne out by the coins of the city. Not impossibly, however, the cock, the connexion of which with the sun-god is natural, may be the type of the city of Miletus.[1]

No. 10 was discovered, after my paper was published, at Vourla (Clazomenae), with other electrum coins of the League, and was published by M. R. Jameson in the *Revue Numismatique* for 1911. It was almost certainly struck at Priene, which city contributed twelve ships at Lade. In the same find were silver coins of Clazomenae of the class mentioned below: their attribution to the time of the League is thus confirmed. Hectae of electrum, with the type of a bull's head and neck, were also found. Samos is their probable mint.

It thus appears that all the coins of the series which we are considering are attributed either with certainty, or at least with some degree of probability, to cities which joined the Revolt. But it is noteworthy that several of these cities were reconquered by the Persians some time before the battle of Lade: the monetary convention then must have been formed quite early. And the notable phrase in which Herodotus speaks of the Ionians at the beginning of the revolt as *τὸ κοινὸν τῶν Ἰώνων*, suggests that there was formed from the first a regular federation; the alliance was not a mere collection of detached cities, but a deliberate attempt to create an Ionian nationality. It was in some senses an anticipation of the League of Delos. That no electrum coins have yet made their appearance which we can attribute with confidence to Miletus, Teos, or Mytilene may of course be merely an accident: we must be on the look-out for them.

The Ionian coinage was in a manner continued after the suppression of the revolt. The well-known and beautiful

[1] See above, p. 75.

series of the electrum staters of Cyzicus begins just at the time when the Ionian coinage ceases, and goes on to the middle of the fourth century. The Cyzicene staters do not follow the Milesian standard, nor do they stand quite alone; Lampsacus, Mytilene, Phocaea all issue electrum staters or hectae on certain occasions. But the position of Cyzicus in coinage is unique. This may be to some extent explained by the fact that Cyzicus alone among the revolted cities came back to Persian rule without resistance and without punishment. Generally speaking, the Ionian cities were treated with clemency, an exception being made in the case of Miletus. Indeed, the Persians treated them with far more leniency than they would have shown to one another in case of capture, and the coinage of Cyzicus may be regarded as at first a general Ionian currency, and later as a coinage specially favoured and protected by Athens, especially for the commerce of the Euxine.[1] The King of Persia jealously guarded for himself the issue of gold coin; and the Athenians put down so far as they could the issue of silver money by the cities belonging to their Empire. But the electrum money of Cyzicus seems to have been tolerated both by Persia and Athens.

I have as yet spoken only of the electrum staters of the Ionian cities. These constituted the main issues, a fact which would fit in well with my conjecture that each stater represents a month's pay of a sailor or a marine. Fractions in electrum are published by M. Babelon[2] as belonging to this series: at Chios twelfths; at Cyme (?) twelfths and twenty-fourths with a horse's head for type; at Abydos forty-eighths. In my opinion these coins are of earlier date, and do not belong to the group. But I think we are able to identify certain silver coins as having been struck as fractions of the staters.

The most distinctive of these are certain silver coins of *Lampsacus*—

[1] Demosthenes, *Against Phormio*, p. 914.

[2] *Traité*, ii. 1, pp. 190–8.

Obv. Forepart of winged horse. *Rev.* Incuse square.
Weight, 103–105 grains (grm. 6·67–6·80) (*J. H. S.*, 1911, Pl. VII. 8).
Weight, 19–20 grains (grm. 1·23–1·29) (ibid. 11).
B. M. Cat. Mysia, p. 78, Pl. XVIII. 4–6.

These coins are given in the catalogue to 500 B.C., and their fine careful archaic style well suits that period. But a noteworthy fact is that they follow the Milesian standard, of which they are didrachms, and probably diobols, respectively. The Milesian standard of weight is usually confined to Southern Ionia, to Samos, Ephesus, Rhodes, &c. This standard is not used for other coins of Lampsacus, nor by other cities of the Propontis. There is only one period at which such coins are likely to have been issued, and that is the time of the Ionian Revolt, when the Milesian standard was for a time accepted as national. Closely similar to these are coins of *Erythrae*:—didrachms and tetrobols.

Obv. Horseman on horse cantering to r. *Rev.* Incuse square.
Weight, 108–9 grains (grm. 7–7·06) (*J. H. S.*, 1911, Pl. VII. 9).
Weight, 36 grains (grm. 2·33) (ibid. 12).
B. M. Cat. Ionia, p. 118, Pl. XV. 1.

Clazomenae:—didrachms, drachms, and diobols. **Pl. I. 14.**

Obv. Forepart of winged boar flying to r. *Rev.* Incuse square.
Weight, 104–108 grains (grm. 6·75–7) (*J. H. S.*, 1911, Pl. VII. 14).
Weight, 41–51 grains (grm. 2·65–3·30) (ibid. 13).
Weight, 15–18 grains (grm. ·97–1·16) (ibid. 15).
B. M. Cat. Ionia, p. 17, Pl. VI. 1–3.

These coins are in style and fabric identical with the above-cited coins of Lampsacus. The incuse of the reverse at first sight looks somewhat early. But the types are careful and highly finished. The editors of the British Museum catalogues give them to the time 500–480 B.C., and it can scarcely be doubted that this is right. The art is just like that of the Ionian staters. Erythrae after 490 B.C. goes over to the Persian monetary standard. Clazomenae either ceases to coin, or strikes small divisions of Attic weight.[1] Probably 20 silver drachms went to the stater of electrum.

A little searching brings to light other silver coins which seem to belong to the same time:

Miletus.[2] Tetrobols and diobols.

Obv. Lion to r. *Rev.* Star in incuse.

Weight, 31–32 grains (grm. 2·0–2·07) (*J. H. S.*, 1911, Pl. VII. 16).

Obv. Forepart of lion with head turned back. *Rev.* Star in incuse.

Weight, 16–19 grains (grm. 1·03–1·23) (ibid. 18).

Mr. Head gives these coins to the period after 478 B.C. But the larger denomination corresponds in weight (roughly) with the coin of Erythrae: the smaller denomination with the coins of Clazomenae. And as Miletus was utterly destroyed in 494, and the surviving inhabitants carried away to the mouth of the Tigris, it is probable that the coinage then ceased, and indeed was not renewed until the break-up of Athenian domination at the end of the fifth century.[3] The coins of other cities, such as Ephesus, which ordinarily used the Milesian standard, are not easily dated with exactness.

Chios. Tetrobols.

It may have been on this occasion that Chios issued the series of silver coins having on the obverse a sphinx and an amphora, and on the reverse an incuse square quartered, which have the weight of 36–40 grains (grm. 2·33–2·60). *B. M. Cat. Ionia*, p. 329, Pl. XXXII. 5. For the other coins of these types, belonging to the middle of the fifth century, are of a much heavier standard, 50–56 grains (grm. 3·24–3·62).

Such are the coins of electrum and of silver which I have

[1] *B. M. Cat. Ionia*, pp. 18, 119.

[2] *B. M. Cat. Ionia*, pp. 185-6. Pl. XXI. 3, 4.

[3] Several of these coins of Miletus occur in a find of coins in Egypt, of which few are later than about 500 B.C. *Num. Chron.*, 1890, p. 4.

up to the present been able to connect with the Ionian Revolt. The search may perhaps be carried further. In any case the establishment of fixed dates for coins at so many cities must needs help us considerably in the arrangement of the monetary issues of those cities in chronological order. Fixed dates are the first necessity of the historically minded numismatist.

A certain amount of objective light is thrown back on the character of the Revolt. Herodotus, carried on by his dramatic genius, is naturally disposed to exaggerate the part taken in the history of the Revolt by interesting personalities. Nothing could be more impersonal than the coins. They bear no names of leaders, nor even of cities: they belong primarily to the *κοινὸν τῶν Ἰώνων*; and they suggest that had the Revolt succeeded, other things than coins would have been held in common by the cities, perhaps even a powerful State might have arisen. Indeed, we have in Herodotus a hint that, though the attempt failed, it yet had some result in counteracting the excessive autonomy of the cities of Ionia. He records to our surprise the leniency of the Persian victors, who, in place of selling the people as slaves, delivered them from their tyrants, established something like a federal arrangement among them,[1] and put upon them no heavier tribute than they had borne before the Revolt. It may be that this leniency was a piece of Persian policy, in view of the contemplated invasion of Hellas. If so, it was very successful; for a great part of the fleet of Xerxes at Salamis consisted of Ionian ships; and some of them were zealous in the Persian service. Xerxes is said to have treated the accusation of treason brought by the Phoenicians against the Ionians as a vile calumny. It is quite in accord with this that an international or inter-civic coinage in electrum by Cyzicus was allowed by the Satrap of Dascylium. If at most cities of the Ionian coast silver coinage is rare in the fifth century, the fault lies not in Persian oppression but in the jealousy

[1] Hdt. vi. 42 *συνθήκας σφίσι αὐτοῖσι τοὺς Ἴωνας ἠνάγκασε ποιέεσθαι, ἵνα δωσίδικοι εἶεν, καὶ μὴ ἀλλήλους φέροιέν τε καὶ ἄγοιεν.*

of the Athenians, who wherever they were able stopped native issues of coins to the profit of their own silver *owls*, abundant materials for which were furnished by Thrace and Laurium.

Thucydides[1] tells us that it was at the special and earnest request of the Ionians that the Athenians, setting aside the hegemony of Pausanias, founded the Delian League, which may thus in a sense be considered the political outcome of the Ionian Revolt, just as the coinage of the Cyzicene staters may be regarded as the monetary outcome of the Revolt. That the Ionian cities so readily transferred their loyalty, first to Persia, and then to Athens, may be explained by the fact that in each of the cities there was a Medizing party and an Atticizing party, which gained power in turn accordingly as the star of Persia or of Athens was in the ascendant. But after the crushing defeat of Lade, the hope of founding an Ionian commonwealth was extinct. Perhaps we may regard the alliance proved by coins to have existed between Rhodes, Ephesus, Samos, Cnidus, Iasus, and other cities, after the victory of Conon at Cnidus in 394 B.C., as a short-lived attempt to galvanize the corpse.

[1] i. 95.

CHAPTER IV

SUPPOSED ELECTRUM COINS OF EUROPEAN GREECE

SINCE the earliest coins of Asia Minor are all of electrum, we are obliged to consider the question whether the same may not have been the case in Greece also. There are various electrum coins of early style which have been attributed to cities of Hellas on a variety of evidence, which, however, is seldom conclusive.

If there be any district west of the Bosphorus in which we should be disposed to look for electrum coins, it is certainly the southern coast of Thrace and Macedon, in the neighbourhood of the island of Thasos. On the mainland opposite Thasos, in the district of Mount Pangaeus, were gold mines, the wealth of which was notorious in antiquity. And in the seventh and sixth centuries B.C. Thrace had closer relations with the Asiatic than with the European shores of the Aegean. Along that coast passed the armies of Darius and Xerxes on their way to European conquests. The earliest Greek colonies on the coast were founded from Ionia. Maronea was settled by men from Chios, Abdera by men from Teos; and still earlier a colony from Paros had settled at Thasos and succeeded to the wealth of the Phoenician factory there. Histiaeus of Miletus, late in the sixth century, occupied and enlarged Myrcinus in the Pangaean district; and Aristagoras tried to found a city on the site where later stood Amphipolis. Thus it would seem to be equally probable that the electrum of Miletus circulated in the district, and that electrum coins were struck in the towns of Thrace.

In an able and important paper,[1] Mr. Svoronos has tried

[1] *Journal Internat. de l'Archéologie Numism.*, XV.

to establish the second of these alternatives. His arguments are, first, that electrum coins are often found on the Thraco-Macedonian coast, or, as he would prefer to say, in the district of Paeonia, and second, that their types seem to show that they were local issues.

As regards the first point, F. Lenormant mentioned as found on the coast and preserved in the collection of L. Caftanzoglu at Salonica several small electrum coins of the type of an ingot of metal, a fish's head, and a cock's head.[1] (B. T. I. 1; VI, 4–12.) L. Friedländer mentioned that electrum coins reached him from Thrace and Macedon, having as type a rose or floral type (*Sternblume*); and one with a swan and a lizard, which he attributed to Eion on the Strymon.

As regards the second point, Mr. Svoronos picks out several types which he regards as distinctively Paeonian, the rose (Babelon iii. 5, 7), the shield (Babelon iii. 4, 6), the Gorgon head (Babelon v. 20), the cow and calf (Babelon iii. 1), the Centaur carrying a nymph (Babelon v. 17). But he confesses that at present our knowledge of the places where these coins are found is so imperfect that we cannot make any confident statement.

Certainly the matter is at present undecided. But there are weak points in Svoronos's arguments. He does not keep apart the pale electrum of Milesian standard and the dark electrum of Phocaic standard, but supposes that both standards might be used in Paeonia. This, however, is improbable. If coins on both standards are found locally, it is more likely that they were imported than that they were locally struck. And some of the coins mentioned were almost certainly imported. For example, the coins bearing the head of a fish were probably minted at Cyzicus (Phocaic standard). Coins with the type of a cock were found at Ephesus, and belong to Southern Ionia. The coin bearing the cow and calf is far more likely to have been minted in Ionia than in Paeonia.

[1] See Svoronos, *l.c.*, pp. 274–5.

The coins which seem to have the best claim to a Paeonian origin are those of Milesian standard bearing the type of a flower or a shield (which are sometimes hardly to be distinguished), and the gold stater of Phocaic standard which bears on the obverse the type of a Centaur carrying off a woman, and on the reverse a square incuse roughly divided into four.[1] It contains 64 per cent. of gold. Its assignment to Thrace, however, rests on no solid basis. The reason for such assignment is that, on early silver coins of the people of the Pangaean range, the Orrescii, Zaeelii, and Letaei, we have a not dissimilar type of a Centaur carrying a woman in his arms. But a comparison of the electrum with the silver coins shows at once differences far more striking than the general likeness. On all the Thracian silver coins the Centaur runs or kneels and bears the woman lying at length in both arms so that her head is in front of him. On the electrum coin he is walking, and turns round to greet the woman, who is seated on his back. The motive is thus quite different. The incuse of the reverse also is quite different from the flat mill-sail-like incuse of the Thracian silver coins, which are in fact quite a century later than the electrum coin. M. Babelon regards this coin as of Ionic origin.[2] Whether it was actually struck in Ionia or Thrace, it belongs beyond doubt to the Phocaean, or North Asia Minor, circle of influence; and has no relation to the coins of Greece Proper. Thrace, indeed, at that time was more exposed to the influence of Asia than that of Europe. This is clearly indicated by the fact that when the cities of Thasos and Lete began striking silver coins, they struck them on a different standard from those of Euboea, Aegina, and Corinth, a standard peculiar to Asia.

Hectae and fractions of hectae of Phocaean weight have been attributed to Eion on the Strymon[3]:

[1] Weight, 252·5 grains (grm. 16·35), *B. M. Cat. Ionia*, p. 9, Pl. II. 3; B. M. IV. 1, B. T. V. 17.

[2] *Traité*, ii. 1, p. 134.

[3] Babelon, *Traité*, ii. 1, p. 139; and Friedländer in *Zeitschr. f. Num.*, vi. p. 8.

1. *Obv.* Goose looking back; behind, lizard. *Rev.* Incuse square. Weight, 39 grains (grm. 2·55). (**B. T. V. 25.**)
2. *Obv.* Goose looking back. *Rev.* Incuse square. Weight, 20 grains (grm. 1·29).
3. *Obv.* Head of goose. *Rev.* Incuse square. Weight, 5 grains (grm. 0·33).

The reason of the attribution is the type, which is that of a class of silver coins given to Eion, not on the ground of inscriptions, but only because they are found on the site of Eion. Some of the electrum coins also have come from the same district; others from Smyrna. The chief objection to giving them to Eion lies on the historic side. The city does not appear to have been founded before the time of Darius, which is after the time of the early electrum issues.

We turn next to the electrum coin attributed to Aegina. It is an unique electrum stater weighing 207 grains (grm. 13·45) at Paris. (**B. T. III. 2.**) The type of the obverse is a tortoise: on the reverse are two deep oblong incuses side by side. This particular form of incuse is rare: I know it only for Calymna, Cos, Rhodes, and other Carian mints, in the sixth century. This electrum coin has been regarded as the earliest coin of Aegina, and indeed as remains of the bridge by which coinage passed from Asia to Greece. But the type is not the sea-turtle, as on the earliest Aeginetan money, but a land tortoise, and neither the incuse nor the weight is Aeginetan. Its attribution is therefore very doubtful. It may be of Asia Minor; indeed, it is more probable that it is Asiatic than that it is European.

Other electrum coins of the Euboic standard have been given to cities of Greece:

1. *Obv.* Owl to l. *Rev.* Incuse. Weight, 21 grains (grm. 1·36). (**B. T. V. 23.**)
2. *Obv.* Eagle devouring hare. *Rev.* Incuse. Weight, 44·4 grains (grm. 2·87).
3. *Obv.* Eagle flying. *Rev.* Incuse. Weight, 22·1 grains (grm. 1·43). (**B. T. IX. 17.**)
4. *Obv.* Wheel of four spokes. *Rev.* Incuse. Weight, 21·8 grains (grm. 1·41).

The reverse device of No. 1 is in some examples remarkable, consisting of two rectangles and three triangles. These coins have sometimes been set aside as modern forgeries. U. Koehler, however, has maintained their genuineness.[1] He mentions several examples, one of which was found in the bed of the Ilissus, one at Piraeus, others at Athens.

If we grant the genuineness of these coins, we must regard them as an attempt to introduce into Athens the electrum coinage of the Ionian coast. The coins are sixths of the Euboic stater of 130 grains; they thus follow the Asiatic system of division by thirds and sixths, and not the European system of division by halves and quarters. They have not the appearance of being very early; certainly they are not as archaic as the earliest silver of Aegina. They stand apart from the silver coinage of Athens, and seem to have exercised no influence upon it. The other coins were formerly by Mr. Head given to Chalcis in Euboea,[2] mainly on account of silver coins of Chalcis: Eagle flying, with serpent in beak: ΨAL (XAΛ), wheel. Tetradrachms, tetrobols. But more recently he has retracted that attribution,[3] observing that they are found in Asia Minor, No. 2 at Priene. The recent discovery of a hoard of electrum coins at Ephesus with a great variety of types has decidedly increased our disinclination to regard type in early electrum coins as a satisfactory indication of mint.[4] It is therefore far more probable that these eagle and wheel coins belong to Asia than to Europe. Thus it seems that any electrum issue in Europe is more than doubtful, or if any such took place (at Athens, for example) it was rather in the way of a tentative issue for special purposes than as a regular state currency.

[1] *Athen. Mittheil.*, 1884, 359.

[2] *B. M. Cat. Central Greece*, p. lii; *Num. Chron.*, N. S. xv, Pl. VIII, 16–18. Cf. Babelon, *Traité*, ii. 1, p. 670.

[3] *B. M. Cat. Ionia*, p. xxxi; *Hist. Num.*, ed. 2, p. 357.

[4] Compare Macdonald, *Coin-types*, p. 49.

CHAPTER V

PHEIDON AND PELOPONNESUS

§ 1. Coinage at Aegina.

The problem as to which king or which city of Hellas first issued coin was much discussed in antiquity. Before considering the evidence offered by extant coins, which is of course by far our most valuable source of knowledge, we must consider the testimony bequeathed to us on the subject by ancient historians, and such historic documents as the Parian Chronicle.

The grammarian Julius Pollux, though he wrote in the reign of Commodus, and can have had no direct knowledge of early Greek coins and weights, is yet of value to us, because he had access to a considerable range of literature, much of which has disappeared. Only such of Pollux's statements as refer to coins of Greece Proper concern us here. He mentions an opinion that coins were first struck at Athens by Erichthonius and Lycus. It is, however, the universal opinion of modern numismatists that coins did not make their appearance at Athens until the sixth century, and that the money of various other cities is earlier in fabric. And, indeed, the very fact that two mythical heroes like Erichthonius and Lycus were credited with the first issue of coins appears to be in itself a proof that there was no tradition connecting the earliest issue of coins in Greece with historic persons at Athens. We are told by Plutarch that Theseus issued money with the type of a bull; but here again we are in mythic surroundings. The laws of Draco mention oxen as the measure of value in case of fines, which clearly shows that in his time

(620 B.C.) the Athenians did not ordinarily use coins, though at that time they were certainly in use at Aegina and Corinth. Pollux also tells us that Aglaosthenes ascribed the earliest issue of coins to Naxos, of which island the writer was probably an inhabitant. Early coins of Naxos are known to us; but they appear to be imitations of those of Aegina, and less archaic. Both of these attributions are probably due to patriotic feeling, which often induced Greek writers to attribute to their own city the origin of great inventions.

A more serious claim to the origination of a coinage in Europe is put forward on behalf of Pheidon of Argos. The whole question of the position of Pheidon in early Greek history and of the nature of his policy is a difficult one. Here we need only consider his date, and his connexion with early weights, measures, and coins.

In reviewing the statements of ancient writers in regard to this matter, I propose first to mention them in historic order, and afterwards to examine them briefly, to judge of their respective value and their truth.[1] Herodotus, our earliest authority in point of time, makes two statements. He says that Pheidon established the measures (*τὰ μέτρα ποιήσας*) of Peloponnesus;[2] and that his son Leocedes was one of the suitors of Agariste, daughter of Cleisthenes of Sicyon (about 595 B.C.). The next authority in order of date is Ephorus, who is quoted in this connexion by Strabo.[3] He says that Pheidon of Argos, who was tenth in descent from Temenus, invented the measures and the weights called Pheidonian, and struck coins, both silver and other, that is, presumably, gold or electrum.

In another place[4] Strabo cites Ephorus as authority for the statement that silver was first issued by Pheidon at Aegina. The *Etymologicum Magnum*[5] makes the same

[1] This has already been done by M. Théodore Reinach (*L'Histoire par les Monnaies*, p. 35; *Revue Numismatique*, 1894) and others. I have preferred to make an independent investigation; but my results are much like those of M. Reinach.

[2] Hdt. vi. 127.

[3] p. 358.

[4] p. 376.

[5] *s. v.* ὀβελίσκος; cf. Orion, *s. v.* ὀβελός.

assertion, and adds that Pheidon dedicated in the Argive Heraeum the spits (of iron or bronze) which had hitherto served as a currency, but were now demonetized. Pausanias gives us a valuable statement as to the date of Pheidon when he says that that tyrant in conjunction with the people of Pisa celebrated at Olympia the eighth occasion of the festival: 748 B.C. The Parian Chronicle says that Pheidon was the eleventh in descent from Herakles, whereas Ephorus makes him the tenth from Temenus, and so the fourteenth from Herakles. The Parian Chronicle would thus date him to about the middle of the ninth century, according to the ordinary Greek way of reckoning by generations, Ephorus to the middle of the eighth century. Thus various authorities place Pheidon in the middle of the ninth, the middle of the eighth, and the end of the seventh centuries.

Confused by these conflicting authorities, modern historians have given very various dates to Pheidon. Some, following Weissenborn and Curtius, have assigned him to the twenty-eighth Olympiad (668 B.C.) rather than the eighth. Others have accepted the date of Herodotus,[1] as determined by the appearance of Pheidon's son among the wooers of Agariste. But the date of Weissenborn is an unsatisfactory compromise, a mere correction of the text of Pausanias, and the whole story told by Herodotus of the wooing of Agariste has the air of fable rather than of fact.[2] It is not at all difficult to suppose that Herodotus may have missed out a few generations, or confused an earlier with a later Pheidon. On the other hand, the date given by Pausanias, 748 B.C., is consistent with that given by Ephorus, which works out as 757 B.C. And it is almost certain that Pausanias had seen at Olympia some documentary authority for his date; though no doubt the records of the early Olympiads were of no great historic value.[3] On these grounds we may regard it as at least very probable that

[1] So formerly did I. See *Types of Greek Coins*, p. 7.
[2] Compare the note of E. Abbott on Hdt. vi. 127.
[3] See especially Mahaffy in *Journ. Hell. Stud.*, ii. 164.

Pheidon belongs to the middle of the eighth century B.C. And it is even more probable that he had to do with a reform or regulation of the measures of Peloponnesus. Not only Ephorus, but Aristotle [1] and the Parian Chronicle speak of certain measures as fixed by and named after Pheidon. So much then we may regard as historic fact. That he regulated weights as well as measures is extremely probable, since there is a close connexion between the two. We are justified in ascribing to him the weights used in commerce for a long time not only in Peloponnesus, but in Athens also, which are known to us by many extant examples,[2] following the so-called Aeginetan standard. The phrase of the Parian Chronicle is *ἐδήμευσε τὰ μέτρα . . . καὶ ἀνεσκεύασε.* This regulation would naturally take the form of making weights and liquid measures consistent one with the other; that is to say, equating his standard of weight with a certain cubic measure of water. This sounds a somewhat complicated proceeding for so early a time, but it is the readiest way of producing a system of weights and measures; and it was probably by doing this that Pheidon attained his fame in Greece. It is probable that he merely regularized existing measures and weights, not inventing them, but making them systematic and consistent.

These Pheidonian weights are in all probability the same that were used in Greek commerce, until the time of Alexander the Great and later, in Northern Greece and Peloponnesus. Several specimens have reached us from Athens. And they were no doubt used by Pheidon for bronze and iron, as for other commodities. According to them were regulated the old *ὀβελοί* in those metals which circulated in Greece before the invention of silver coin. And when silver coin came into existence it went by the same standard, though probably with new denominations. This standard is that which we are accustomed to call Aeginetan, because it is made familiar to us through its adoption by the people of Aegina.

[1] In Pollux, x. 170.

[2] Smith, *Dict. of Antiq.*, art. *Pondera*, p. 452.

But the assertion that Pheidon issued coins at Aegina is a statement which we cannot accept. In the first place, no coins of Greece proper seem to be so early as the eighth century; and in the second place, Pheidon never had any authority in Aegina. Probably the Aeginetans were the first people in Greece to strike money; and their money was on the Pheidonian standard: hence a natural confusion. It was the weights, not the coinage of Greece, which were due to Pheidon.

We turn next from the literary to the archaeological evidence. It is at once clear that the compiler of the *Etymologicum Magnum* would scarcely have asserted that dedicated obeli were preserved in the Heraeum of Argos, unless one of his authorities had seen them there. The Heraeum, as we know, was burned in 423 B.C., when there is a probability that dedications of bronze would be melted and disappear, in which case the obeli preserved in the later temple could scarcely be genuine, but rather restorations. However that may be, it is certain that the excavations conducted by the American School of Athens on the site of the Heraeum have brought to light a great quantity of votive bronzes of early date. Many of these were spits, and many pins for the hair or garments.[1] Sir C. Waldstein suggests that these were the original bronze currency; but as there is no record of their weights the theory is hard to verify. On the other hand, a mass of iron was discovered, which was found to consist of numerous rounded bars of metal coming to a point, and which was held together at either end by an iron coil tightly twisted round. It is hard to regard these iron spits as anything but obeli dedicated after being demonetized. This discovery would seem to refute the suggestion of T. Reinach,[2] that the obols exhibited in the temple were really standard-weights kept in the temple for reference. Mr. Svoronos has made diligent search for these iron spits in the Museum at Athens, and

[1] *The Argive Heraeum*, i. 61; ii. 330.

[2] *L'Histoire par les Monnaies*, p. 38.

discovered them.[1] They are much broken and decayed, so that their present weight gives us little information. It is, however, desirable to record that in Mr. Svoronos' opinion the length of the spits was about 1·29 mètres (four feet); and the weight 495–302 grammes (7,650–4,675 grains), a Pheidonian mina being about 622 grammes (9,600 grains). Supposing that these iron bars were a remnant of early currency, that currency, being dedicated in the Heraeum of Argos, would naturally be not Aeginetan but Argive. If I have rightly assigned the date of Pheidon, their dedication would be later than his time. For it appears that until the seventh century, and even later, the currency of Peloponnesus consisted of literal obeli or bars of metal. These were of bronze or of iron: the iron, of course, being heavier and less valuable. This currency was everywhere except at Sparta replaced later by the Aeginetan coins, at all events for large payments. The dedication, therefore, must belong to the seventh or sixth century.

The Aeginetan standard as known to us from extant weights and coins is as follows:

Talent	37,320 grammes	576,000 grains.
Mina	622 ,,	9,600 ,,
Drachm	6·22 ,,	96 ,,
Obol	1·03 ,,	16 ,,

But while this is certainly the standard which passed in later times as Pheidonian, and must have been connected with Pheidon, it is a system based upon the weight of the silver drachm. In discussing its origin, we had best take our start, not from the perplexing traditions as to Pheidon, but from the known facts as to the earliest coins.

At a far earlier date even than that of Pheidon, regular systems of weights and measures had been in use in the great empires of the East, Babylon, Assyria, and Egypt. That they were in use also in prehistoric times in Crete and Mycenae is in itself very probable, and is maintained by Sir A. Evans in a paper contributed to *Corolla Numis-*

[1] *Journ. Intern. de Numism.*, ix, p. 196.

natica.[1] He examines the weights in use at Cnossos, and hows that in every case the standard used was taken from Egypt, though in some cases it may be traced beyond Egypt to Babylon. That a system approximating to the ight Babylonic gold standard was in use in Egypt, in Crete, and in Argolis in the second millennium B.C. seems o be clearly made out. The use of a standard corresponding to that of Aegina is, however, not proved for prehistoric imes. What Evans has called the heavy Egyptian gold standard is certainly followed in Crete in the case of several weights which bear marks of value, showing an unit of 12·30 to 13·98 grammes (188 to 215 grains). At first sight this may seem a probable source for the weight known as Aeginetan, with a drachm of 96 grains (6·22 grammes), and a didrachm of 192 grains (12·44 grammes). But it is very doubtful whether there is here any line of connexion. In the first place, the weights generally are much nearer to the higher than to the lower limit, and so are not at all close to the Aeginetan standard. And in the second place the break between Mycenaean and historic Greece is so complete, it is so clear that a period of barbarism and poverty separates one from the other, that we may well doubt whether so civilized an institution as a weight-standard would survive.

Mr. Head[2] is disposed to regard a group of weights found at Naucratis, which seems to follow the Aeginetan standard, as indicating that that standard may have come from Egypt. But Naucratis was not of very early foundation; and there is no reason for thinking that the weights in question are earlier than the date of Pheidon, or even than the first issue of coins at Aegina.

Talents and minas of gold and silver and electrum, together with the stater of electrum, which was a fraction of the mina, and its divisions $\frac{1}{3}$, $\frac{1}{6}$, $\frac{1}{12}$, $\frac{1}{24}$, had long been known in Asia, and used by the Ionians of the coast of

[1] *Minoan Weights and Currency*, pp. 336–7.

[2] *Hist. Num.*, 2nd edition, xliv: cf. Petrie, *Naukratis*, i, p. 78.

Asia Minor. But the comparatively rude inhabitants of Peloponnesus had been content with a currency of bronze pieces, sometimes round, in the shape of a πέλανορ, but more often long, in the form of a bar or spit (ὀβελός).[1] Originally, it may be, these bars were real spits, used for roasting meat; but by degrees their weight became fixed, and their value conventional. A handful (six) of these bars made up a drachm (δραχμή). In larger payments bronze was probably weighed out, as was the *aes rude* of Italy.

It was this rude currency which Pheidon regulated, without, so far as we can judge, superseding it. But later, in the seventh century, this primitive system was out of date. Probably the bars of bronze were very irregular in shape, and perhaps in weight. They were not suited to the growing commerce of the Greek islands. The people of Aegina, at that time in the front ranks of commerce, must have known all about the electrum coins of Ionia. Electrum, however, was not native to Greece. Silver, on the other hand, was procurable from Spain, Thrace, and elsewhere. The Aeginetans decided to strike in silver coins which should represent the bronze obeli which were current. The silver obol would stand for one such bar; the silver drachm for a handful of such bars, that is for six; the silver didrachm would stand for twelve.

Setting aside the notion that Pheidon was connected with the earliest coinage of Aegina, we may claim for Aegina the precedence in European coinage, on the ground of the extremely rude and primitive character of the oldest examples of Aeginetan coinage, and because they seem to have served as models for all the coins of the islands of the Aegean. In the noteworthy find at Santorin, in 1821, 760 early coins of the Greek coast and islands were found, and of these 541 were of Aegina, while many other coins showed in fabric and type signs of an attempt to conform to the Aeginetan pattern.[2] To this find we will presently return.

[1] So *Etym. Magn.*, *s. v.* δραχμή and ὀβελίσκος.

[2] *Num. Chron.*, 1884, pp. 269–80 (Wroth).

Though the question of the origin of the standard used ,t Aegina for silver coin has been a subject of much dis-ussion, the discussion has not been fruitful, mainly because t has not proceeded on scientific lines. It has been carried n by numismatists solely in relation to coins: the inquiry ias been why the Aeginetans struck coins weighing 192 or .94 grains, when no people used that standard for money efore. The question, however, is really a much wider one, ncluding the whole question of the origin of currency and veights in Peloponnesus.

We may begin by dismissing the current views as to the rigin of the silver weight of Aegina. One view[1] is that it s the weight of the South Ionian stater (224 grains), some-vhat reduced. And in support of this theory the fact has een brought forward that one of the very early Aeginetan ilver coins weighs as much as 211 grains. That coin, owever, stands quite by itself and, as Mr. Head suggests, nay be a mere accident. No explanation of the degradation f weight-standard by twenty grains has been given, nor ny reason why the South Ionian standard should have been dopted at Aegina when it was not adopted at any other European mint. It is a mere guess, without any evidence o justify it. The same may be said of Prof. Ridgeway's iew that the object of issuing coins of the Aeginetan veight was that ten of them should be of the value of Homeric talent or Euboic gold coin of 130 grains. He uggests that 130 grains of gold, at the rate of 15 to 1, vould be equivalent to ten silver coins weighing 195 grains. This view is based upon two assumptions, both of which re arbitrary. It is assumed that the standard of value in Aegina was a gold coin or talent. This was not the case; he standard of value was, according to our authorities, bar of bronze or of iron. And it is assumed that gold nd silver passed in the proportion of 15 to 1. This is nlikely to have been the case. When the Athenians eeded gold for the Parthenos statue of Pheidias, they

[1] So Head, *Hist. Num.*, p. xxxviii. In the second edition of his great work, owever, Mr. Head takes another view.

bought it with silver at the rate of 14 to 1; but this is the highest rate of exchange of which we hear in Greece Proper: the rate usual in the Persian Empire was 13 or $13\frac{1}{3}$ to 1.[1] A more probable view is that adopted by Flinders-Petrie, that the Aeginetan standard is derived from a somewhat heavier standard in use in Egypt. He mentions a weight found in Egypt, bearing the name of Amenhotep I (seventeenth century B.C.), marked as 'gold 5', which gives a standard of 207·6 grains (grm. 13·45). Other Egyptian weights with marks of value give a somewhat lower standard than this. The chief difficulty in the way of this derivation is the fact that this seems to be a gold standard: and what we are in search of is a silver standard; and gold and silver standards were in antiquity usually distinct.[2]

One more suggestion is that the Aeginetan stater is derived from the Euboic mina[3] of 6,700 grains (grm. 434), of which it is in fact one thirty-fifth. This equation can be but fortuitous. Passing these conjectures, let us consider the real circumstances of the case.

In adjusting the new silver currency to the existing currency of bronze, two courses were possible. The Aeginetans either could strike coins of such a weight that a round number of the bronze obeli, say ten or twenty, would go for one of them. In that case they might have originated a new standard of weight for coinage, other than the Pheidonian. Or they could strike silver coin on the Pheidonian standard, leaving the question of the number of bronze bars which would exchange for each to settle itself.

We know that other states when they issued coins in a fresh metal, say in silver or in gold, sometimes, like the kings of Lydia and Persia, used different standards for the two metals, in order that a round number, ten or twenty, of the silver coins should pass for one of the gold. And sometimes, like the Athenians and like Alexander the Great, they used one standard for the two metals.

[1] See T. Reinach's paper in *L'Hist. par les Monnaies*, pp. 41–73.
[2] *Encycl. Brit.*, ed. 11, xxviii. 487.
[3] Beloch, *Griech. Geschichte*, i, p. 294.

It was the latter of these systems which was adopted by the people of Aegina. They issued their silver money on the already familiar Pheidonian standard. The weight of these early silver staters is well known to us. The didrachm weighed about 192 grains (grm. 12·44), the drachm 96 grains (grm. 6·22), the obol, which was the sixth of the drachm, 16 grains (grm. 1·03). These weights correspond with the standard of numerous weights of Pheidonian type which have come down to us.

At the same time the Aeginetans fitted the new coins into the old currency by equating the new obol of silver with the old obelus or spit of bronze. In primitive societies it is easy and usual to find some simple proportion between various objects used as measures of value; for example, a slave may be equated with three oxen, an ox with ten sheep, and so on. We have reason to think that the relation established between the values of silver and bronze at Aegina was 120 to 1. We have an indication of this in the facts of the regular currency of Sparta. At Sparta the current obeli were not of bronze; the currency consisted of iron bars, the so-called πέλανορ, which were of the weight of an Aeginetan mina, 9,600 grains.[1] According to Plutarch and Hesychius, these minae of iron were worth only half an obol of silver. In that case iron would be in relation to silver only as 1 to 1,200. Hultsch, however, gives reasons for thinking that the original value of these bars was an obol, giving a relation of 1 to 600. Now bronze was in Greece about five times as valuable as iron. Haeberlin[2] has given reasons for thinking that in Italy in the third century the relations of value between silver and bronze were 120 to 1. If the same proportion held in Greece in earlier times, the silver obol of 16 grains would be equivalent to an obol of bronze weighing 1,920 grains (grm. 124), or twenty Aeginetan drachms. This corresponds to the reason and probability of the matter. The bronze bars would in that case have weighed about a quarter

[1] Hultsch, *Metrologie*, p. 535.
[2] *Systematik des ält. röm. Münzwesens* (1905).

of a pound; a drachm or handful of six of them would weigh about $1\frac{2}{3}$ pounds, somewhat less than a kilogram.

The early currency of Peloponnesus seems to have consisted of bars both of bronze and iron, bronze for larger, and iron for smaller payments. At Sparta iron only was allowed. But it would appear that this regulation was not a primitive one, but introduced in the course of Spartan history: for in the Homeric age, as we know, iron was very valuable; and its value could not have become despicable until well on in the Iron Age. At Byzantium, and in Peloponnesus, iron bars or coins were retained for small payments until the fourth century B.C. In other places, as at Clazomenae, we hear of iron coins as a merely fiduciary issue.

The Aeginetan talent, consisting of 60 minae, or 6,000 drachms, or 36,000 obols, must have reference to minae, drachms, and obols of silver, not of bronze. For 36,000 × 16 grains weighs about 82 pounds, or 37 kilograms, which would be about what a man might easily lift. If a talent had been formed from the bronze obelus of 1,920 grains, it would be a weight 120 times as great, which would be quite out of proportion to a man's capacity for lifting. So the drachm which was in weight the hundredth of a mina, and the obol which was in weight the sixth of a drachm, only came into existence when silver began to be coined. The drachm and the obol as coins appear to have been invented by the Aeginetans. They were borrowed by all the systems of silver coinage which came into use in Hellas. This is abundantly proved by the marks of value which the coins of Peloponnese bear in the fifth century.[1] And even in Asia it became usual to strike drachms or obols of Persian or Phoenician standard. But originally, as the Aeginetans from the first went by the drachm and the obol, so the Ionians of Asia used the stater and its parts.

A difficulty remains. Why in that case should the Aeginetans have struck at first, not the drachm of 96 grains, but the didrachm of 192 grains? The answer, I think, is

[1] *B. M. Cat. Peloponnesus*, p. xvii.

ultimately this, that man has two hands and not one only. A didrachm is the equivalent of the bars of bronze which a man carries when he has both his hands full of bars, six in each. It stands for a man, while a drachm represents only half a man.

We may observe a parallel phenomenon in regard to the talent. Students of metrology are puzzled at finding that the various talents in use in Asia, and even in Europe, have two forms, light and heavy; and the heavy is of exactly double the weight of the light. Now a talent, usually weighing some 60 or 80 of our pounds, is what a man can lift: the root of the word is τλα: τλάω meaning I bear. But a man can lift in two hands double as much as he can lift in one. What a man can carry in one hand is a light talent: what he can carry in two hands is a heavy talent.

At Aegina the mina is an arbitrary division, $\frac{1}{60}$ of the talent, or 100 silver drachms. The name shows it to be of Asiatic origin: it is a stepping-stone in European systems of weight between talent and drachm. But the talent is a natural weight, almost as natural as a weight as the foot and the fathom are as measures of length. And like them it varies in various countries between certain limits, following the local notion as to what a man can be expected to lift. As the yard represents the length of the King's arm, measured from the breast-bone, so the royal talents of Assyria represented what the King could comfortably lift in one hand or in two. In a sense the drachm also is a natural measure, for given the usual size of a bar of metal, it would not be convenient to carry more than a certain number of them in the hand. The bars of Peloponnese were of such a size that six could be conveniently carried.

The early coins of Aegina are well known. (**Pl. II. 1.**) Their type is the sea-tortoise, which probably refers to the worship of Aphrodite as sea-goddess. Pheidias made for the people of Elis a statue of Aphrodite Urania, resting her foot on a tortoise.[1]

[1] Pausanias, vi. 25. 1.

§ 2. Influence of Aegina.

The Aeginetan standard for coin spread in several directions before 480 B.C. It spread to the south of Asia Minor, to Cnidus, Rhodes, and some of the Greek cities of the south coast, as well as to the cities of the Euxine Sea. It was adopted by most of the Aegean islands between Europe and Asia. It spread through Greece Proper as far north as North Thessaly. And it spread southward to Crete. The reason for this wide and rapid diffusion was doubtless the fact that the Aeginetans were the hucksters (*καπηλοί*) of Greece, and took with them their native currency for the purpose of bargaining. We may observe that Aegina was the only city of Greece Proper which took part in the foundation of Naucratis.

An especially noteworthy fact is the issue, in the sixth century or even earlier, by most of the larger islands of the Aegean, of an abundant coinage, which not only follows the Aeginetan weight, but also in its types shows an intention of imitating the tortoise of Aegina. This fact was proved by the discovery at Santorin in 1821 of a large hoard of coins.[1] It comprised in all 760 pieces, of which 541 were of Aegina. Others were almost certainly minted at Naxos, Paros, and Siphnos.[2] As the coins have no inscriptions, it is not possible to identify all the mints with certainty; but it is probable that Andros, Ceos, Tenos, and other islands issued money on the Aeginetan standard. In another island find, described in the *Numismatic Chronicle* for 1890, the mass of the coins was of the mint of Aegina, but there were also a few pieces of Andros, Paros, and Siphnos; as well as of some of the islands of the Ionian coast, Chios, Cos, Lindus in Rhodes, and Poseidion. These latter coins are further considered under the head of Silver of Asia.

Since it was the weights and measures of Peloponnesus, not of Argos only, that Pheidon regulated, we cannot be surprised that all the cities of Peloponnesus, with a few

[1] See *Num. Chron.*, 1884, pp. 269–80.

[2] *B. M. Cat. Crete*, &c., Pls. XXV, 7–8; XXVI, 1; XXVII, 9.

exceptions, used the Aeginetan or Pheidonian standard for their coins, when they issued any, down to a late period. The most notable exception is of course Corinth, which city, with its colonies, formed a distinct commercial confederacy.

These facts seem to lead to a very interesting conclusion. The coinage of Aegina seems to have been the earliest silver coinage ever issued. It was from Aegina that the invention spread, first to other islands of the Aegean, later to some of the cities of Asia Minor. At first, as was natural, the weight went with the coinage. And as the Aeginetan weight-standard was entirely independent of all Asiatic systems, it seems to follow that some of the Asiatic cities at first issued coins which bore no proportional value to the electrum which was current in Asia Minor.

It is noteworthy that some cities used in their early coinage not the didrachm of Aeginetan scale, but the drachm or half-drachm. The cities of Thessaly used the drachm, Argos the drachm and hemidrachm, Heraea the hemidrachm. This question was no doubt determined by the circumstances of the local commerce.

As the talent and the mina passed from Asia to Europe, so in return the drachm and the obol passed from Europe to Asia, superseding, at least in Greek cities, the older shekel or siglos. This we shall see when we treat of the silver coinage of Asia in the sixth century in Chapter IX.

CHAPTER VI

EARLY COINS OF EUBOEA

The cities of Chalcis, Eretria, and Cyme in Euboea were among the great colonizing cities of Greece at the beginning of the Olympiads. Cumae in Italy was a foundation of the people of Chalcis and Cyme,[1] and the earliest of all Greek settlements in Italy; and Italy, Sicily, and Chalcidice in Macedon were dotted with Euboean colonies. The Euboeans would not be likely to be far behind the Aeginetans in the issue of coin. And being more detached from the Greek mainland, and in closer relations with the people of Ionia, where Cyme in Aeolis was a colony of Euboea, it is probable that their earliest issues would have a closer resemblance to those of Asia Minor.

The standard which was derived from Babylon and was largely used for gold coins in Asia, was known to the Greeks, including Herodotus, as the Euboic standard. This does not, of course, imply that the Babylonic standard was adopted from Euboea. The opposite line of derivation is the only one probable or indeed possible. It does, however, prove that it was through Euboea that the Greeks gained knowledge of the standard of Babylon.

The issue of silver coins on a gold standard is a remarkable phenomenon. In Asia, gold and silver were in the sixth century, and earlier, minted on different standards, in order that a round number of the silver coins should exchange against one or two of the gold coins. The issues of Croesus and of the Persian kings, for example, were so arranged that twenty of the silver pieces passed for one of the gold pieces. And this custom has generally prevailed,

[1] Modern historians are generally agreed that it was Euboean Cyme, and not Cyme in Aeolis, which took part in this settlement.

down to our days. The Euboeans took another line, which was later adopted by the Athenians and by Alexander the Great. They issued silver money of the same weight as the gold which was current. Not much gold would pass in Greece, but such as there was would no doubt pass by the Babylonic weight, which indeed had struck such deep roots that no gold coins (with insignificant exceptions) were struck on any other standard than the Euboic and its Attic variant down to Roman times. The price of the gold stater in silver coins of the same weight was left to be determined, not by any authority, but by the demand, and the circumstances of the time. It is a characteristic difference between Asia, where the will of kings regulated all things, and Europe, with its free cities.

But though the Euboeans accepted the Babylonic weight for their stater, they did not divide it, on the Asiatic plan, into thirds and sixths and twelfths, but into halves and twelfths, drachms and obols. This was the Pheidonian system of division. Herein, as we shall see, they differed from the Corinthians.[1] And they succeeded in making their coinage thoroughly European and national.

This is the simplest, and I think the true, view of the origin of the Euboic weight. It is not, however, wholly free from difficulty. That it was bronze, not gold, which was the early standard of value in Greece I have insisted in speaking of the early coins of Aegina. And the Aeginetans adapted their issues of silver to a bronze and not to a gold currency. Why should the Euboeans have taken another course? Dr. Lehmann-Haupt[2] has maintained that the Euboeans also adapted their silver to bronze; but in my opinion he does not prove this satisfactorily. He supposes that Chalcis, being as its name implies a city abounding in copper, and commanding copper mines, was able to force copper to a higher comparative value than it had elsewhere.

[1] In the trinal divisions of the silver coins of Chalcidice, I should see not Euboean influence, as Dr. Imhoof-Blumer, but Corinthian. See below, Ch. X.

[2] *Hermes*, 1892, p. 549; *Zeitschr. f. Numism.*, 27, 125. This writer does not clearly distinguish copper and bronze.

The ordinary relation between copper and silver in the Levant being 120 to 1, a mina of silver would ordinarily pass, he says, where the Babylonic silver weight was used, for two talents (120 minae) of copper. But if the Chalcidians were able to force copper up to a value of 1 to 96 in comparison with silver, then these two talents of copper would be equivalent only to $\frac{96}{120}$ or $\frac{4}{5}$ of a Babylonic mina of silver. Now $\frac{4}{5}$ of a Babylonic mina of silver is nearly an Euboic mina of 436·6 grm. (6,750 grains).[1] Thus the writer supposes that the greater value given to copper resulted in the invention of a new and lighter standard for silver. It will however be observed that Dr. Lehmann-Haupt's theory is entirely conjectural; and is built upon the astonishing assumption that, when you have a greater quantity of goods to dispose of, you can raise the price of the goods, which is entirely contrary to economic experience. Of course, if Chalcis had a monopoly of copper, it would be somewhat different; but even then, why should the people who bought copper at a high price in Euboea sell it at a lower price in Asia Minor? Moreover, Chalcis had no monopoly, but only valuable mines. The theory in question therefore is utterly baseless and inacceptable. Only one plausible argument can be urged in its favour, that at Athens the χαλκοῦς was one ninety-sixth of the didrachm, since eight chalci went to the obol and six obols to the drachm. But this argument has no weight. The chalcus was probably a late-invented fraction of the obolus: in some places six went to the obol, in other places eight: there is no indication that at Chalcis the obol in bronze was originally of the weight of a didrachm, as the theory requires.

Mr. Head[2] is disposed to think that the Euboic standard came to Euboea from Samos, where it had already been used in early times for electrum; and the use for electrum would be a natural stage on the way to its use for silver. The chief objection to this view is that the early electrum

[1] This is a false value for the Euboic mina, which really weighed 421 grm. (6,500 grains).

[2] *Hist. Num.*, ed. 2, p. xlvi.

coins in question, attributed by Mr. Head to Samos, are not really struck on the Babylonic gold standard, but on a somewhat heavier standard, stater 135 or 270 grains (grm. 8·75 or 17·50), which was in use later at Cyrene and was introduced at Athens by Peisistratus. This standard I regard as of Egyptian origin: I consider it below, under *Athens*. Thus a Babylonic origin of the Euboic standard is by far the most probable.

I have already discussed, and dismissed, the view that the earliest coins of Euboea were struck in electrum.

The earliest silver coins which can be attributed with certainty to Chalcis are the tetradrachms, didrachms, and smaller divisions bearing as type on one side a flying eagle, on the other a wheel in a triangular incuse.[1] The weight of the tetradrachm is 258·7 grains (grm. 16·76); that of the didrachm just half this. The attribution of these coins to Chalcis is guaranteed by the appearance on them of the letters ᐯΑΨ (ΧΑΛ in some later specimens). These certain examples, however, can scarcely be given to an earlier date than the middle of the sixth century; and the uninscribed coins, some of which probably belong to Chalcis, must begin at least half a century earlier.

The earliest coins which can with certainty be attributed to Eretria are tetradrachms and lesser coins bearing on one side a cow scratching her head with a hind foot and the letter E; on the other side a cuttlefish in an incuse. The weight of the tetradrachms varies from 260 to 267 grains (grm. 16·84–17·27): their date would begin probably when Eretria was rebuilt after the Persian destruction of 490 B.C., say about 485 B.C.[2] These coins show the raising of the standard which is so general in Greek cities about the middle of the sixth century. Carystus issued coins at the same period.

It is, however, almost certain that the coins which I have

[1] Babelon, *Traité*, p. 667.

[2] As Mr. Head points out, *Cat. Central Greece*, Introd. p. lviii, Eretria must have been speedily rebuilt, as Eretrian ships were present at the battle of Artemisium, 480 B.C.

mentioned were not the earliest issues of Chalcis and Eretria. A large and varied series of uninscribed silver coins was first attributed to the cities of Euboea by F. Imhoof-Blumer and E. Curtius.[1] It consists of what have been called in Germany *Wappenmünzen* (heraldic coins), didrachms of Euboic weight (130 grains, grm. 8·42), bearing on one side a very simple type, often enclosed in a linear circle, on the other side an incuse square divided into four triangles by crossing lines.

The types are as follows:[2]

1. Gorgon-head—Didrachm, obol, tetartemorion.
2. Ox-head, facing—Didrachm, hemiobol.
3. Owl to l.—Didrachm, obol. (**Pl. II. 6.**)
4. Horse, standing, unbridled—Didrachm.
5. Forepart of bridled horse r. or l.—Didrachm.
6. Hinder part of horse to r.—Didrachm, drachm.
7. Amphora—Didrachm, obol.
8. Astragalus—Didrachm.
9. Wheel. Sometimes of archaic type, one transverse crossed by two supports; sometimes with four spokes, with or without supports—Didrachm, drachm, obol. (**Pl. II. 4.**)
10. Triskeles of human legs—Didrachm, drachm, triobol.
11. Scarabaeus—Didrachm, obol.
12. Frog—Obol.

These types are by Mr. Head conjecturally assigned as follows to the cities of Euboea:[3]

Chalcis—Wheel, triskeles.
Eretria—Gorgon-head, ox-head.
Cyme—Horse; fore- or hind-part of horse.
Athenae Diades—Owl, astragalus.
Histiaea—Amphora.

These attributions, however, are anything but certain; and the whole question must be seriously considered.

We begin by identifying the coins of Eretria, which

[1] *Hermes*, x. 215; *Monatsber. der Pr. Akad.*, 1881.
[2] Babelon, *Traité*, ii. 1, pp. 674–723, Pls. XXXI–III.
[3] *B. M. Cat Central Greece*, p. xlix.

form the most important class of early Euboean money. They form a series thus:

Didrachms.

Obv. Gorgon-head. *Rev.* Incuse (in one case, lion's head in incuse). (Pl. II. 3.)

Obv. Bull's head. *Rev.* Incuse.

Tetradrachms.

Obv. Gorgon-head. *Rev.* Bull's head. (Pl. II. 5.)

Obv. Gorgon-head. *Rev.* Face and forepaws of panther.

Later Coinage, after Persian wars.

Obv. Cow scratching herself. *Rev.* Cuttle-fish in incuse square.

As regards this later coinage, it can be given with confidence to Eretria, as we have seen. But the earlier series, between which and the later there is no point of direct contact, presents more difficulty. It stretches over a considerable period of time, the style showing gradual development, and the incuse giving way to a second type. Only two attributions are suggested for the series, Athens and Eretria. And the conclusive reason for assigning it to Eretria rather than to Athens is that many of the coins are certainly later than the earliest coins bearing the head of Athena and certainly of Athenian origin, and that it is not to be supposed that two sets of coins of quite different types and fabric would be issued contemporaneously from the Athenian mint.

This argument may be enforced and made more definite by a careful consideration of the weights of the coins. The earliest didrachms above mentioned seldom exceed 130 grains in weight. The specimens in the British Museum average 129·5 grains (grm. 8·39). The tetradrachms bearing the Gorgon-head and another type, the head of a panther, are heavier, the average of six examples being 2 × 130·6, or if we omit one abnormal example, 2 × 131·4; these latter, then, constitute the coinage of Eretria contemporary with the early Athena type at Athens.

In treating of the coins of Athens I shall try to show

that these two-type pieces were first struck in the time of Peisistratus, who raised the monetary standard from the Euboic level (130 grains for the didrachm) to the Attic level (135 × 2 grains for the tetradrachm). If that view be correct, it will follow that the tetradrachms of Eretria are later than the middle of the sixth century, and the didrachms which preceded them presumably earlier than that date. We shall find in dealing with the coins of Corinth that in the middle of the sixth century Attic influence in that city also appreciably raised the weight of the coins. Thus the Peisistratid issue of tetradrachms turns out to be of great value as evidence for the arranging and dating of the coins of Greece proper.

On some of the tetradrachms given to Eretria there are two globules in the field.[1] These can scarcely be taken for anything but marks of value. M. Six and M. Babelon regard their presence as proving that the coins in question were issued as didrachms—double, that is to say, of the drachm of 130 grains which they regard as used at Athens between the time of Solon and that of Hippias. M. Six draws the further conclusion that they were struck at Athens, there being no evidence for the existence of so heavy a drachm elsewhere. In my opinion, however, there is no satisfactory evidence for the currency, even at Athens, of a drachm of the weight mentioned. I regard the globules on the Eretrian coins as merely showing that they were of double the value of the coins which had up to that time circulated at Eretria, and which were without doubt Euboic didrachms. The people of Eretria in the archaic period, just like the people of Aegina, thought not in drachms, but in staters or didrachms. At Delphi, at a much later date, and at other places, expenses were ordinarily reckoned in staters.

Another series, that of the owl, has been attributed, not without reason, to Athens. As M. Babelon has well observed, if a numismatist were asked what coinage would

[1] *B. M. Cat. Central Greece*, p. 121; Babelon, *Traité*, Pl. XXXI. 14, 16.

naturally at Athens precede the Athena-type, the only reply he could make, remembering the analogy of other series would be, a coinage with owl for type.[1] Examples have been found both in Attica and Euboea. The amphora type would also be very appropriate to Athens. On the later issues of the city the owl stands on an amphora; and the amphora naturally would represent the oil which was the great gift which Athena had bestowed upon men. The olive-spray marks the Athenian coinage almost throughout, and the amphora would have the same significance. The astragalus might also be Athenian, as the device occurs frequently on the well-known weights and tesserae of Athens.

M. Babelon tries to show the appropriateness to Athens of some of the other types. He would connect the horse-type and the wheel, as shorthand for a chariot, with the legend which narrated that Erechtheus was the inventor of chariots. It might have been better to seek in these types some allusion to the great festival of Athena, with its processions of chariots. But, in any case, little weight can be assigned to what may be called literary or mythological arguments. If a type is actually used on Athenian monuments, as are the owl and the amphora, there is some reason to expect it on the early coins. But the mere fact that a type has a legendary connexion with the city goes for very little. I would therefore regard the horse coins as rather Euboean than Attic.

The wheel series has been given by M. Svoronos to Megara.[2] For this also there is some show of reason. The type of Mesembria, a Megarian colony in Thrace, is a radiate wheel, apparently a symbol of the sun-god. The types at Megara would certainly be Apolline; on the coins of the fourth century they are the head of Apollo and the lyre; but it is possible that the wheel may have been an earlier type at Megara. It is scarcely to be supposed that Megara, the outpost of the Dorians against Athens, and a great

[1] Babelon, *Traité*, ii. 1, p. 705.

[2] *Journ. int. d'Archéol. numism.*, 1898, p. 273.

colonizing city in the seventh century B.C., should have been without coins when Aegina, Corinth, and Athens, her three neighbours, were all issuing them.

In view of the occurrence of the wheel on coins given with certainty to Chalcis one might be disposed to give these wheel coins to that city. But they are scarcely earlier than the coins of Chalcis of which I have spoken; and it is improbable that the city would issue at the same time two dissimilar sets of coins. The claim of Megara would therefore seem to be stronger than that of Chalcis, but not without difficulty, as Megara was not on good terms with her Ionic neighbours, and would not be very likely to form a monetary convention with them.

It is doubtful whether in the case of these series, just as in the case of the early electrum of Asia, we are justified in regarding the types as regular civic stamps. Indeed, the variety of types is so considerable, and the similarity of fabric so great, that Beulé declared they must all of them, or none, come from the mint of Athens. They seem from the evidence of finds to have circulated together with the regular early tetradrachms of Athens and Euboea. For example, a hoard found at Eleusis[1] consisted of an early triobol of Athens, a didrachm and triobol of the recognized coinage of Eretria, three obols bearing the wheel, one the Gorgon-head, and a half-obol bearing the bull's head. A hoard found near Cyme in Euboea consisted of tetradrachms and lesser coins of Eretria, many archaic tetradrachms of Athens, and the following *Wappenmünzen*: wheel (1), owl (1), hind-part of horse (1), fore-part of horse (1), standing horse (1), Gorgon-head (2). Another hoard found at Eretria contained tetradrachms and didrachms of Eretria, early Athenian tetradrachms, a tetradrachm with Gorgon-head, and several examples of *Wappenmünzen* (types not stated).[2]

[1] Köhler, *Athen. Mitth.*, 1884, p. 357.

[2] Köhler, *l. c.* It is noteworthy that in these hoards there were found no coins of Chalcis. Eretria and Athens stood together: Chalcis stood apart from them, with Corinth.

It is thus clear that these coins had a wide and general circulation; and it seems almost certain that they point to a monetary convention of some kind. In the sixth century Athens and Eretria were closely associated. But on the other hand there was hostility between Athens and Megara.

To Euboea and Athens therefore I would attribute the series, though certainty is impossible. We can separate one class as Euboean, and another as probably Attic; but such types as the horse, the wheel, the frog must remain of doubtful attribution.

The coins of Euboea, of the time of the Persian wars, are dealt with in Chapter XIV.

An extremely interesting numismatic discovery of recent years is that of the early coins of Peparethus, an island situated near the coast of Thessaly, a little to the north of Euboea. These coins were put together by Mr. Wroth in the *Corolla Numismatica*.[1] They are tetradrachms of Attic weight, having on one side a bunch of grapes, on the other various types, Dionysus seated, the head of Herakles, &c. The class of coins which stands nearest to them is the tetradrachms of Eretria and Carystus, which have types on obverse and reverse. Their date is between the latter part of the sixth century and the rise of the Athenian Empire, when the coinage of Peparethus ceases. That the island should have adhered to the Attic standard, when Thessaly on one side, and the Aegean islands on the other, adopted the Aeginetan standard, is an interesting historical indication. Peparethus is small and produces little save wine, which must have been exported to Athens or Euboea.

[1] p. 90.

CHAPTER VII

EARLY COINS OF CORINTH AND CORCYRA

§ 1. Corinth.

That the coinage of Corinth began very early is sufficiently proved by its extremely early art and fabric. It is easy to prove that it began at an earlier time than that of Athens. For the earliest tetradrachms of Athens are almost on the same level of art as the coins of Corinth on which the head of Athena appears on the reverse; and these are preceded at Corinth by at least two regular series of coins, stretching over a considerable space of time, as is shown by their variety and abundance.

But these coins of Athens can be dated with reasonable certainty to the middle of the sixth century. The coins of Corinth then must reach back to the seventh century, probably to the reign of Cypselus. They can scarcely, however, be so early as the time of the foundation of Corcyra, or the Corcyrean coin would have probably started under their influence.

Mr. Head's assignment of the early coins of Corinth is as follows:

Time of Cypselus, 657–625 B.C.

1. Ϙ Pegasus with curled wing = incuse square, of similar pattern to that on coins of Aegina. Stater (130 grains; grm. 8·42.) (Pl. II. 7.)

It is curious that some of the very earliest coins of Corinth, found in Egypt,[1] are of very light weight (102–104 grains, grm. 6·60–6·70). There must have been some loss of weight by chemical process

[1] *Num. Chron.*, 1899, p. 274.

Time of Periander and later, 625–500 B.C.

2. ♀ As last = incuse developing into the mill-sail pattern. Stater and drachm (43 grains; grm. 2·78). (Pl. II. 8.)

On the hemidrachm of this class a half Pegasus occurs, on the obols a Pegasus, on the hemiobol the head of Pegasus.

After 500 B. C.

3. An archaic head of Athena appears on the reverse of the staters; an archaic head of Aphrodite on the drachm. The diobol bears the mark of value Δ, the trihemiobol the letters TPIH, the hemiobol H.

It appears to me that as Mr. Head has placed the archaic coins of Athens bearing the head of Athena too early, so he has placed the earliest staters of Corinth bearing the same head too late. Von Fritze [1] has well pointed out that there cannot be much difference in date between the two series, as the style of art is closely similar. We cannot place the Athenian series much earlier than, nor the Corinthian series much later than, the middle of the sixth century.

Some of the earliest flat coins of Metapontum (*Br. Mus. Cat. Italy*, p. 239) are restruck on coins of Corinth of the second type. These Metapontine coins belong to the second half of the sixth century. Somewhat later coins of Metapontum of thicker fabric, and belonging to the early years of the fifth century, are restruck on coins of Corinth of the third type, bearing the head of Athena.[2] This evidence is, however, indefinite; it only shows the coins of Corinth in each case to be older than the Metapontine restriking; but does not tell us how much older.

I should modify Mr. Head's dates, which in any case are too precise, in the following way:

[1] Von Fritze, *Zeitschr. f. Numism.*, xx. p. 143.

[2] Babelon, *Traité*, ii. 1, p. 1405.

Class 1	(about)	650–600 B.C.
Class 2	,,	600–550 ,,
Class 3	,,	550– ,,

As we have no reason for connecting a change of fabric with any special events in the history of Corinth, any attempt at great accuracy cannot be successful.

There is however one indication, that of weight, which Mr. Head does not seem to have used. If we compare the coins of Class 2 with those of Class 3 we shall find that the latter are distinctly the heavier. From the collection in the British Museum, which contains only coins in good condition, we reach the following results:

Of 21 staters of Class 2 the average weight is 127 grains.

Of 28 staters of Class 3 the average weight is 132 grains. That proves that at about the time when Class 3 came in, the standard of the stater was raised by about five grains. A precisely similar rise in the standard from 130 grains to 135 × 2 grains took place at Athens in the time of Peisistratus, as I shall presently try to prove. I conjecture that the occasion of raising the standard at Athens was the acquisition by Peisistratus of the silver mines on the Strymon and at Laurium. Corinth seems to have followed the lead of Athens, probably because she could not help herself. This little investigation of weights strongly confirms the fixing of the middle of the sixth century at Corinth as the time of the introduction of the head of Athena as reverse type. One may even suspect that the type itself was borrowed from the fine coinage of Peisistratus.

To go back. It is safe to attribute the origin of coinage at Corinth to Cypselus. Generally speaking, we find the wealthy and art-loving tyrants of Greece responsible for such innovations. We have next to consider the monetary standard, and the reason for selecting it.

The Corinthian stater of 130 grains is of the weight of the Daric or gold shekel of Persia, and of pre-Persian times. Like the people of Euboea, those of Corinth transferred a gold standard directly to silver, as the people of Phocaea had transferred it to electrum. But they did so with a difference. The Euboeans, as we have seen, took the stater as a didrachm, and divided it into two drachms of sixty-five grains or twelve obols of eleven grains. They thus completely Europeanized it, following the system of Pheidon. The Corinthians retained the Asiatic system of division by three. They divided their stater into three drachms of forty-three grains, and eighteen obols of seven grains. This fact was already known from the statements of ancient metrologists, and received final confirmation when inscriptions on the coins were read as marks of value,[1] Δ or ΔIO standing for diobol, TPIH for trihemiobol, and H for hemiobol. As the weights of these diobols, trihemiobols, and hemiobols are just what they should be when the drachm weighs forty-three grains, the proof that this was the standard is beyond doubt.

If we seek a reason for this system, one may easily be found. The object of Cypselus seems to have been to make terms with the two systems of weight in use in Greece, the Euboic[2] and the Aeginetan. The Corinthian stater of 130 grains would pass not only as an Euboic stater, but as two-thirds of the Aeginetan stater of 192 grains. The Corinthian drachm of forty-three grains would be equivalent to two-thirds of the Euboic drachm of sixty-five grains, and four-ninths of the Aeginetan drachm of ninety-six grains. Mr. Head[3] has suggested that the Corinthian drachms may have been regarded as practically the equivalent of an Aeginetan hemidrachm of forty-eight grains. It is, however, difficult to believe that the drachm when equated with Aeginetan currency would pass at a higher rate than the stater or tridrachm; and this is implied in Mr. Head's view. It is, however, quite probable that in some places in later periods of Greek history, the Corinthian drachm and the Aeginetan hemidrachm

[1] First by myself, in *Num. Chron.*, 1871.

[2] The coins of Cypselus seem to be earlier than any extant coins of Euboea; but we may well suppose the Euboic standard to have been already in existence.

[3] *Hist. Num.*, ed. 2, p. 399.

were equated. The fact is that we know very little indeed as to the way in which Greek coins of various systems were related in value on the tables of the money-changers: there may have been a fixed convention in the matter, or there may have been continual fluctuations according to demand and supply. This is a matter for further investigation.

The trinal division of the Corinthian stater is valuable to the numismatist, as it enables him to discern, in the Greek colonies of Italy, Sicily, and Chalcidice in Macedonia, the influence of Corinthian commerce. There is a natural presumption that when cities which adhere to the Attic standard divide their stater of 135 grains by two they belong to the sphere of Euboean or Athenian commerce; when they divide it by three, they seem rather to be under Corinthian influence. This reasonable view, however, has not been accepted by Dr. Imhoof-Blumer, who sees in the trinal division of the stater in Chalcidice a trace of Asiatic influence. The point is a fine one, but not unimportant. I prefer to consider the actual facts of exchange and commerce as more important to the people of Chalcidice than mere traditions of Asiatic procedure. That some of the cities of Chalcidice and of South Italy use a drachm of 43–45 grains is therefore an important fact in the history of commerce. We shall later return to this subject of investigation.

§ 2. Corcyra.

In the case of Corcyra also there is an interesting clashing between the Aeginetan, the Corinthian, and the Euboic systems. We might naturally have expected the city, when it first issued coins, to take as its model the Corinthian coinage, which was then in existence. But the relations of Corcyra to the mother-city were never from the first cordial; and the first issue of coin probably took place at the time when the people of Corcyra asserted their independence about 585 B.C., after the death of Periander. (Pl. II. 13.) The type of the obverse, a cow suckling a calf, seems to refer to the early settlement of the island from Euboea, that being an ordinary type of Carystus, and referring probably to the worship of the Mother-Goddess.[1] The reverse type, a stellar pattern, is unlike anything in Greece proper, and bears a nearer likeness to devices used in Ionia. The weight is the Aeginetan, but somewhat light; probably through the influence of the Corinthian standard, which was in use at Anactorium and about the mouth of the Corinthian gulf. The Corinthian drachm, it must be remembered, 43-45 grains, is distinctly lighter than the Aeginetan hemidrachm of forty-eight grains. The coins of Corcyra do not from the beginning exceed 180 grains (grm. 11·66) for the stater, and 90 grains (grm. 5·83) for the drachm. If the above conjecture is correct, these would pass as four and two drachms of Corinth.[2] As the coinage of Corinth was closely copied by the cities of Acarnania, Anactorium, Leucas, and the rest, so the cities founded by Corcyra in the north, on the coast of the Adriatic, notably Dyrrhachium and Apollonia, closely copied the coins of Corcyra, from which their money only differs in virtue of the inscriptions which it bears. The coins give us a vivid impression of the clear geographical line which separated the commercial sphere of Corcyra from that of Corinth. That the Corcyrean standard had no influence in Italy or Sicily, but only in the Adriatic is an important fact, indicating that the course of Corcyrean trade ran northwards only.

It has been suggested [3] that the coin-standard of Corcyra might not be connected with that of Aegina, but directly derived from some of the cities of Asia, Miletus, or Camirus. But all likelihood is taken from this conjecture by the fact that it does not correspond with any Asiatic standard. It is too heavy for the official standard of Persia; too light for that of Miletus. It is therefore better to derive it

[1] *B. M. Cat. Thessaly to Aetolia*, p. xlvii. There are, however, doubts whether this story of Euboean colonization is historic.

[2] I have established this equation in *B. M. Cat. Thessaly, &c.*, p. xv of the Introduction.

[3] *Hist. Num.*, ed. 2, p. 326.

from the Pheidonian standard which had course in all Greece Proper, from Thessaly to Sparta.

It is possible, as I have suggested in a later chapter, that the lowness of the Corcyrean standard may have some relation to the silver standard in use in Etruria and central Italy.[1]

[1] Below, Ch. XI.

CHAPTER VIII

EARLY COINS OF ATHENS

There is no subject in Greek Numismatics which has been so fully discussed as the earliest coinage of Athens; and there are few subjects in regard to which a greater variety of opinion prevails. The discussion has not been confined to numismatists, but has been taken up by philologists and historians. Without going into all the by-ways of the subject, I shall try briefly to portray its main features.

§ 1. The Earliest Coinage.

There are three views as to what were the earliest coins of Athens. If we could settle this question, which is a purely numismatic one, we could with more confidence approach the other questions, philological, economic, and historic, which are involved.

The first claimants are certain coins of electrum, small pieces of the weight of about twenty-one grains, having on one side an owl, and on the other side an incuse. These we have already discussed and shown that they lie outside the regular Athenian coinage.

The next claimant is the silver coins of various types, the so-called *Wappenmünzen*, of the weight of 130 grains, which are found in Euboea, Attica, and Boeotia. I have spoken of them already under Euboea, and claimed them mostly for Chalcis, Eretria, and other cities of that island. But it is probable that some of them may belong to Athens, and that Athens, early in the sixth century, may have issued coin closely like that of the cities of Euboea.

As we have seen, the coins of this class which can best

claim Athenian parentage are those of the type of the owl. M. Babelon mentions[1] the following examples:

Didrachms 124·1 grains (8·04 grm.), British Museum.
130·8 „ (8·47 „), De Luynes.
130 „ (8·42 „), „
Obols 11–9·6 grains (0·72 to 0·60 grm.). Several examples.

The best indication whether early uninscribed coins belong to a city is to be found by comparing the types with those of the later and recognized coins of that city. As the acknowledged coins of Athens are stamped with an owl, we may claim the uninscribed coins with that type for Athenian. As the later tetradrachms of Athens have an amphora, on which the owl stands, for type, and many weights have an amphora as type, we may fairly claim for Athens also the uninscribed coins stamped with an amphora.

While we may attribute the owl coins and the amphora coins to Athens, I should stop there. I think M. Babelon's[2] attempts to find mythological justification for the assignment of such types as the horse and the wheel to Athens are fanciful. The bull's-head type, which some writers would assign to Athens, is so closely connected with the Gorgon-head, which almost certainly belongs to Eretria, that we must refuse it to Athens.

Some numismatists attach value to the statement of Plutarch that Theseus struck coins bearing the type of a bull. Pollux also says that the didrachm was of old the coin of the Athenians, and was called a bull, because it had a bull stamped on it.[3] In consequence of these statements, those coins have been attributed to Athens which have as type a bull's head. It is, however, very probable that the statements arose from a misunderstanding of the laws of Draco, in which fines were stated in oxen. Later writers fancied that by oxen Draco must have meant some kind of coin, knowing that the coins of Aegina were called tortoises, those of Corinth horses, and those of Athens owls.

[1] *Traité*, ii. 1, p. 701. [2] *Traité*, ii. 1, p. 707. [3] ix. 60.

But we know that Draco was speaking of real oxen. And it may be added that the head of an ox is a very different thing from an ox.

The earliest coins, then, of Athens, appear to be silver didrachms of Euboic weight, bearing as type the owl or the amphora. These may be safely given to the time of Solon, and connected with his reforms. The tetradrachms bearing the head of Athena were almost certainly, as I shall try to show, first issued in the time of Peisistratus. Thus the coinage of Athens, during the first half of the sixth century, seems to exhibit the city as closely related to Eretria in Euboea, and a member of a monetary union including a group of cities in the region. The fact is not uninstructive. In the time of Solon, Athens was still struggling with Megara for the possession of Salamis, and dreams of the headship of Hellas, whether in letters, in commerce, or in arms, had not yet risen above the horizon. It was the legislation of Solon, and still more the ambition of Peisistratus, which turned Athens from a small city into a great one.

§ 2. The Reforms of Solon.

The question of the Solonic reform of the Athenian coinage is one which has aroused more controversy than any other in Greek numismatic history. Numismatists used to think that they had a satisfactory account of the matter in a passage of Androtion (probably from his Ἀτθίς) quoted by Plutarch in his *Life of Solon* (xv). But certain statements in Aristotle's *Constitution of Athens*, since brought to light, have been held to be quite irreconcilable with those of Androtion. Some writers, such as W. Christ,[1] still regard Androtion as the preferable authority, thinking an archaeologist more likely to be accurate in such matters than a philosopher. But the great majority of the commentators on the work of Aristotle[2] maintain that his authority is

[1] *Münchener Sitzungsber.*, 1900, 118.

[2] The literature of the subject, which is extensive, is given in Head's *Historia Numorum*, ed. 2, p. 365.

final. In my opinion it is possible to reconcile the statements of the two authorities, except in one or two points. This I shall proceed to do.

The text of Plutarch runs as follows: *Καίτοι τινὲς ἔγραψαν, ὧν ἐστιν Ἀνδροτίων, οὐκ ἀποκοπῇ χρεῶν, ἀλλὰ τόκων μετριότητι κουφισθέντας ἀγαπῆσαι τοὺς πένητας, καὶ σεισάχθειαν ὀνομάσαι τὸ φιλανθρώπευμα τοῦτο, καὶ τὴν ἅμα τούτῳ γενομένην τῶν τε μέτρων ἐπαύξησιν καὶ τοῦ νομίσματος τιμήν. Ἑκατὸν γὰρ ἐποίησε δραχμῶν τὴν μνᾶν πρότερον ἑβδομήκοντα καὶ τριῶν οὖσαν· ὥστ' ἀριθμῷ μὲν ἴσον, δυνάμει δ' ἔλαττον ἀποδιδόντων ὠφελεῖσθαι μὲν τοὺς ἐκτίνοντας μεγάλα, μηδὲν δὲ βλάπτεσθαι τοὺς κομιζομένους.*

According to Androtion, then, the alteration in the coinage was part of Solon's *Seisachtheia* or relief of debtors. Solon, says Androtion, did not cancel the debts but moderated the interest. He caused the mina, which before had been of the weight of 73 drachms, to be equivalent to 100, so that debtors paid the same number of drachms which they had borrowed, but in drachms of less weight; thus those who had sums to pay were gainers, while those who received them were no losers. It was this operation which gained for Solon and his friends the name of *χρεωκοπίδαι* or debt-cutters. Androtion, however, adds that at the same time Solon made an increase of measures, that is, no doubt, measures of capacity. Apart from this phrase, to which we will return later, the passage seems quite clear. As the proportion of 73 to 100 is nearly the proportion in weight between the mina and drachm of the Athenian coinage and those of Aegina, numismatists naturally concluded that the Aeginetan standard was before Solon's time in use at Athens, and that he lowered the standard from Aeginetan to what may be called Solonic or Attic level, in order that debtors should save 27 per cent. in their repayments. To say that the creditors would lose nothing is of course absurd: whatever the debtors would gain they would lose; but it is very natural that Solon should not have realized this fact. M. Babelon has no difficulty in showing that the measure attributed to Solon was financially unsound;[1] but that is scarcely to the point. It is quite certain that, all through the course of history, coinage has been debased in order to accommodate debtors or to relieve the financial straits of governments; and we have no reason to think that Solon would be too wise to attempt such things.

We must next turn to the passage bearing on the question in the recently discovered work by Aristotle on *The Constitution of Athens.*

The text of Aristotle, as determined by Blass and Kenyon, runs[2]: *Ἐν μὲν οὖν τοῖς νόμοις ταῦτα δοκεῖ θεῖναι δημοτικά, πρὸ δὲ τῆς νομοθεσίας ποιῆσα[ι] τὴν τῶν χ[ρ]εῶ[ν ἀπο]κοπήν, καὶ μετὰ ταῦτα τήν τε τῶν μέτρων καὶ σταθμῶν καὶ τὴν τοῦ νομίσματος αὔξησιν. ἐπ' ἐκείνου γὰρ ἐγένετο καὶ τὰ μέτρα μείζω τῶν Φειδωνείων καὶ ἡ μνᾶ πρότερον [ἄγο]υσα στα[θμ]ὸν ἑβδομήκοντα δραχμὰς ἀνεπληρώθη ταῖς ἑκατόν. ἦν δ' ὁ ἀρχαῖος χαρακτὴρ δίδραχμον. ἐποίησε δὲ καὶ σταθμὰ πρὸς τ[ὸ] νόμισμα τ[ρ]εῖς καὶ ἑξήκοντα μνᾶς τὸ τάλαντον ἀγούσας, καὶ ἐπιδιενεμήθησαν [αἱ τ]ρεῖς μναῖ τῷ στατῆρι καὶ τοῖς ἄλλοις σταθμοῖς.*

The only serious question as to the reading arises over the phrase beginning *τήν τε τῶν μέτρων* with the repetition of the article *τήν* before *τοῦ νομίσματος*. Hill had already remarked on the oddness of the phrase, and suggested as a possible emendation *τήν τε τῶν μέτρων καὶ σταθμῶν ⟨αὔξησιν⟩, καὶ τὴν τοῦ νομίσματος ⟨μείωσιν⟩*. This may be the original reading; but in any case the word *αὔξησις* if applied to coin need not mean its increase in weight, but may, as some commentators have pointed out, only imply a greater abundance. I shall presently, however, suggest a better explanation, namely, that Aristotle somewhat misread his authority.

Let me, however, give a paraphrase to show how I would interpret the passage:

Such were the democratic features of his lawgiving;

[1] *Journ. Intern. de Numism.*, vii. 228.

[2] Quoted from Hill in *Num. Chron.*, 1897, 285, Ἀθ. Πολ. c. 10. I have not thought it necessary to mark the editors' restorations where they are certain.

before which he arranged (1) the cutting-down[1] of the debts; and after it (2) the increase in weights and measures and the multiplication[2] of the coins. For under him the measures became greater than those of Pheidon; (3) and the mina which formerly weighed seventy drachms was filled up with the hundred drachms. (4) The early stater was a didrachm. (5) He made also weights to go with the coinage, a talent weighing 63 minae, which extra three minae were distributed over the stater and other weights.

I am not at all convinced that Aristotle means to say anything very different from what Androtion says. If we put the two sets of statements in parallel columns there will appear a remarkable likeness between them.

Androtion.	*Aristotle.*
(1) He favoured the poor and lightened their burden, not by cutting down the debts, but by moderating the interest: this benevolence they called *Seisachtheia*.	He arranged the cutting down of the debts;
(2) It was accompanied by an increase of the measures, and a change in the value of the coins.	after that, an increase in weights and measures, and increase (?) of coin, the measures becoming greater than those of Pheidon.
(3) He made the mina which before had contained 73 drachms consist of 100 drachms, so that, when men repaid coins equal in number but less in weight, they were greatly advantaged, while those who received were not injured.	The mina which formerly weighed 70 drachms was filled up with the hundred drachms.
(4)	The early stater was a didrachm.

[1] ἀποκοπή means mutilation rather than destruction.

[2] Or decrease, μείωσιν, as above suggested.

(5)	He also made weights to go with the coinage, a talent weighing 63 minae, which extra 3 minae were distributed over the stater and other weights.

In passage (1) no doubt there seems a formal contradiction between the authorities; but it is not deep, since the proceeding of Solon might be regarded equally well in either aspect, as a diminution of the debt, or as a lightening of the interest. A reduction in the value of the coin would serve both purposes, since interest as well as principal would be paid in the reduced coinage. (2) Here both authorities are confused. Both are clear that the measures of capacity were increased, so as to become, as Aristotle says, larger than those of Pheidon, but as to what happened to the coin they are less explicit. The phrase in Plutarch is *γενομένην τῶν τε μέτρων ἐπαύξησιν καὶ τοῦ νομίσματος τιμήν*. The phrase in Aristotle is *τήν τε τῶν μέτρων καὶ σταθμῶν καὶ τὴν τοῦ νομίσματος αὔξησιν*. The phrases sound as if the writers were following the same authority, but did not understand precisely what happened to the coins. But Plutarch (or Androtion) goes on to show clearly what he supposed to have taken place, and we have no reason for thinking that Aristotle would have rejected his explanation, which obviously implies that the value of the coins was lessened. (3) Commentators have commonly supposed that here there is no real conflict of the two authorities, but that while Aristotle uses the round number 70, Plutarch gives the more precise figure of 73. But the difference is in my view important. The proportion between 70 and 100 is nearly that between the *Euboic* mina and the Aeginetan; the proportion between 73 and 100 is nearly that between the *Attic* mina and the Aeginetan.[1] Metro-

[1] As we have seen above (p. 124), the Euboic drachm weighed 65 grains (4·21 grm.); the Attic, 67·5 grains (4·37 grm.). The difference between them is 3·6 per cent. Taking the Aeginetan drachm at 94 grains (6.09 grm.), a mina weighing 70 such drachms would give 100 drachms weighing 65·8 grains, and a mina weighing 73 such drachms 100 drachms of 68·6 grains.

logists have not usually distinguished between the Euboic and the Attic mina, calling it the Euboic-Attic. But if we discriminate between the two, as I think we are bound by undeniable facts to do, then we must consider Aristotle's statement as the more correct. It is very natural that Plutarch's authority, writing at a time when the Attic standard was in universal use, should have supposed that it was that which was introduced by Solon. But we have in Aristotle a valuable record of the real facts of the case: if we may believe him, it was not the later Attic standard which Solon introduced, but the real Euboic, which was appreciably lighter. The coins bear out this view.

Turning to the coins themselves, as the only safe test where authorities differ, we are justified in saying that there were at Athens none at all before the time of Solon. The fines in the laws of Draco are given in oxen; and as in the time of Draco the coins of Aegina were widely circulated, we may be sure that Athens was dilatory in the introduction of coinage. As we are expressly told that the measures which Solon introduced superseded the Pheidonian, we may fairly assume the same in regard to the coins, and conclude that the Aeginetan mina and drachm were in use at Athens in 600 B.C. For the current didrachms of Aegina, Solon substituted coins weighing 130 grains, that is staters of the Euboic standard, which was already accepted at Chalcis and Eretria, and (with a different system of division) at Corinth. The whole question then narrows itself down to this, were these staters, as Androtion asserted, didrachms intended to pass in place of the heavier Aeginetan didrachms, or were they drachms, as Aristotle is supposed by some recent authorities, such as Six, Head, Hill, Babelon, and others to assert? They suppose that for some reason Solon introduced a mina not of the Euboic weight, but of double that weight, which mina was again lowered by the half by Hippias. They allow that at the end of the sixth century a coin of 130 (or 135) grains was a didrachm, but they think that for the first three-quarters of that century it was called a drachm.

Their reasons are twofold. In the first place, they insist on interpreting the word *αὔξησις* as implying an addition to the weight of the coins. In the second place, they appeal to the testimony of extant Athenian weights.[1] They cite one of archaic style, bearing the inscription *ἥμισυ ἱερὸν δημόσιον Ἀθηναίων*, weighing 426·6 grammes (6,585 grains), which yields a mina of 13,170 grains and a drachm of 131 grains, and another inscribed *δεκαστάτηρον*, weighing 177·52 grammes (2,738 grains), yielding a stater (or didrachm?) of 273 grains. The second of these, however, proves little, as the familiar tetradrachm of Athens of the usual type, and weighing 270 grains, might well be called a stater. And the first in fact only confirms what we knew before, that there was in use at Athens, for some unknown purposes, a mina and drachm of double the weight of those ordinarily used for coins. But the use of this double mina was by no means confined to the period between Solon and Hippias, as it should be to give it any value in the present connexion. On the contrary, it was used contemporaneously with the ordinary Solonic weights in the fifth and fourth centuries.[2] It can, therefore, have had nothing to do with the Solonic reform of the coinage.

There is then no argument to be drawn from existing coins or weights to overthrow the view which I read in our ancient authorities. Let us next turn to the historic probabilities of the case.

These seem to me entirely on the side of the reduction of weight. Solon was essentially a moderate, wishing to destroy neither rich nor poor, but to find for them a way of living together. But the poor were overwhelmed with debt, and had largely mortgaged their land. In such a case, to reduce the debt without abolishing it would be the natural plan for a mediator. And although Solon was, doubtless, a very great and wise man, I cannot see why he should not have thought that he could most fairly accom-

[1] *Num. Chron.*, 1895, 177; 1897, 288; Pernice, *Griech. Gewichte*, pp. 81, 82.

[2] Murray, *Greek Weights*, in *Num. Chron.*, 1868, 68, 69; cf. article *Pondera* in Smith's *Dict. of Antiquities*.

plish this by reducing the weight of the coinage. It is a process which has been resorted to by financial reformers in all ages, until the English pound in silver weighs a third of a pound, while the French *livre* weighs but a fraction of an ounce. We have no reason to think that Solon's wisdom lifted him above all the ways of thought of the time.

On the other hand, it is hard to imagine any reason which Solon could have had for raising the standard of the coin. The only suggestion I find as to a motive is given by M. Babelon, who observes[1] that he would by this means give an advantage to Athenian coin, and promote its circulation. This will scarcely stand. In the first place, in the time of Solon the Athenians had not discovered the mines of Laurium, which were first worked in the time of Peisistratus, and so had no particular motive for pushing their coin. In the second place, if the Athenians were prepared to exchange their own coin of 130 grains for the Aeginetan drachm of 96 grains they must have been very bad men of business. A slight addition to the weight of the drachm would bring the coinage of Athens into request; but an addition of 40 per cent. would not have had this effect at all: it would be simply introducing a new monetary standard without any visible reason.

We come now to statement No. 4, that the old standard coin was a didrachm. I have translated χαρακτήρ by 'standard coin'; for, though the word properly means the type stamped on a coin, it may also stand for the coin which bore the type. Six, Babelon, and Hill have taken the phrase as proving that the early Athenian tetradrachms really passed as didrachms. But if in Solon's time, as I have maintained, only didrachms of the ordinary Euboic weight of 130 grains were issued, then Aristotle's assertion exactly corresponds with the fact. Indeed, it entirely confirms my contention.

We return to paragraph No. 2, in which we have again a valuable historic record which modern commentators have

[1] *Journ. Int. de Num.*, vii. 226.

misunderstood. We can scarcely suppose the statement of Aristotle that Solon increased the measures and weights of Pheidon to be quite baseless. This is in itself unlikely, and is rendered less so by the fact that even Androtion also speaks of an enlargement of measures, at the same time that he speaks of the lightening of the coinage. Aristotle calls the enlargement of the measures a democratic measure, and it is clear that from the point of view of the man in the street the enlargement of measures was as much in his favour as the depreciation of the coin, in which he had to pay for such measures.[1]

The measures and weights of Pheidon being in use at Athens at the time, it would seem that Solon somewhat augmented them at the same time that he lowered the weight of the coins. That Pheidonian weights for goods were in use in later times we already knew; but Solon, perhaps temporarily, raised them in a small degree.

The probable nature of his proceeding is made clear by comparison with an Attic decree of some centuries later (*C. I. G.* i. 123, *I. G.* ii. 476) which runs as follows: 'The mina of commerce shall weigh 138 drachms of the Stephanephoros' (i.e. Attic drachms, and so be of the Pheidonian standard), 'and there shall be added (thrown in) 12 drachms.' It goes on to say that in every 5 minae, one mina shall be thrown in in like manner, and in every talent 5 minae. Thus in case of the talent, by this extraordinary decree, every seller was bound to add $\frac{1}{12}$, in case of 5 minae $\frac{1}{5}$, in case of a mina $\frac{1}{12}$. The date of the decree is the second or first century B.C.

Though it is difficult to understand the procedure in case of the 5 mina weight, which seems exceptional, it is impossible to regard this decree as anything but a deliberate attempt to make the sellers in the market give more than full weight. Probably a custom had arisen of adding a little beyond the exact weight, as indeed often happens among ourselves, and this is made compulsory, by a really

[1] This has already been pointed out by Prof. v. Wilamowitz-Möllendorff, *Aristoteles und Athen*, i. p. 48.

democratic law, a law which would have satisfied Shakespeare's Jack Cade. Of course it was futile; but the mere fact that it was passed throws a remarkable light on the nature of the later democracy of Athens. If such laws could be made in the Hellenistic age, after centuries of successful Athenian trading, we can scarcely be surprised that in the simple and unpractised sixth century B.C., even a wise lawgiver who wished to conciliate the people should legislate to a similar effect, and ordain that the seller should give the buyer full weight and a little more.

And this may explain a fact which I have elsewhere [1] noted, that it is quite usual in the case of Greek weights, and especially in the case of the numerous Athenian weights which have come down to us, that they should be appreciably heavier than the standard. A people so fond of bargaining as the Greeks, whether ancient or modern, would greatly appreciate a liberal measure; and by using such weights and measures a dealer in the market would be sure to increase his *clientèle.* We must not hastily apply modern scientific notions on such subjects in the case of the ancient world.

All through the course of history the tendency of coins is to deteriorate in weight and quality, unless when some fully organized State with a commercial instinct makes it a part of its policy to keep up the standard, and in so doing perhaps to keep up the standard of its neighbours. But the tendency in weights and measures for goods is quite different; competition keeps them up or even raises them. This may explain how it was that Solon, while he increased the measures and the commercial weights, lowered the standard of the coin. Formerly I supposed that his standard was slightly heavier than the Euboic, 67·5 grains for the drachm, in place of 65. But I am now convinced that this slight increase in the weight came in the time, not of Solon, but of Peisistratus, as shall be presently shown.

Paragraph (5) is made somewhat obscure by the addition

[1] Article *Pondera*, in Smith's *Dict. of Antiquities.*

of the phrase πρὸς τὸ νόμισμα. Apart from that, we might naturally have supposed that it gives one the exact percentage by which the Pheidonian weights were increased, namely three minae to the talent, or 5 per cent. And this must, in spite of the additional words, be what is meant. We must therefore take the phrase πρὸς τὸ νόμισμα to imply not that the coin-weights were raised, which is clearly not the fact, but that the weight of commodities which were bought and sold for money was raised. It seems to me that these interpretations give us for the first time a reasonable and probable view of the monetary reform of Solon.

§ 3. The Coinage of Peisistratus.

The date of the first issue of the well-known tetradrachms of Athens, which bear on one side the head of Athena, on the other an owl and an olive-twig, has been much disputed. The opinion of Mr. Head, an opinion always entitled to great weight, assigns this issue to the early years of the sixth century, and to the reform of Solon. He observes that[1] 'among them are the oldest and rudest examples of a human head on any ancient coins . . . and I take these to be quite the earliest Greek coins which were struck with both obverse and reverse types'. (Pl. II. 9–11.)

On the other hand, Dr. Imhoof-Blumer and M. J. P. Six regard it as impossible that coins with two types on obverse and reverse should make their appearance so early. These excellent authorities think that this coinage did not arise until the time of Hippias, 520–514 B.C. The coins which appear to Head so rude, and which are indeed of very careless and primitive style, are regarded by them as barbarous copies, or coins issued at a time of stress, and not really very archaic. Imhoof regards them as struck during the democracy which followed the fall of Hippias: Six prefers to suppose that they were struck when Hippias was besieged in the Acropolis.

[1] *Hist. Num.*, ed. 2, p. 369.

I have no hesitation in a partial acceptance of this view. It seems to me clear that a great proportion of the extant early tetradrachms is really of barbarous and imitative character. Such coins are Babelon Pl. XXXIV, Nos. 2–11; *B. M. Cat*, Pl. I, 3, 5, 6; and (our Pl. II. 11). These must be distinguished from the really fine archaic coins of Athens, which certainly preceded them. The fabric of the two classes of coins is very different; in the one case we have fine and careful work, in the other great carelessness and irregularity.

It is to be observed that the theta with crossed bar ⊕, which is a really archaic form, is found, so far as I am aware, only on coins of the finer and more careful type,[1] which I regard as struck at Athens itself. The other form of ⊙ is found invariably on the ruder coins, which may be barbarous copies. Although archaic forms of letters often reappear at a time when one would suppose them obsolete, and so are not a very trustworthy guide in the assignment of dates by inscriptions, yet the facts which I have noted fall in rather with the theory that these rude coins are late in date than with the view that they belong to the time of Solon.

The barbarous class may very possibly have been struck by the Persian army when in Greece. The troops of Xerxes would need silver money as well as the gold darics to pay for such necessaries as they could not procure without payment. And this view is actually confirmed by the discovery of coins of the class in the canal of Xerxes by Mount Athos,[2] and on the Acropolis itself between the Erechtheum and the northern wall, where were also heaped up the remains of the Persian destruction.[3] This theory had already occurred to Beulé and F. Lenormant. Such coins as I am considering may then fairly be given to the end of the sixth or the beginning of the fifth century.

[1] Such as *B. M. Cat.*, Pl. II, 5–7; Babelon, *Traité*, Pl. XXXIV, 15–17. This ⊕ is found in the very early inscriptions of Athens, down to the time of Euphronius. See Droysen, *Preuss. Akad. der Wiss., Sitzungsber.*, 1882, p. 8.

[2] Babelon, *Traité*, ii. 1, p. 765.

[3] Babelon, Pl. XXXIV, 2–8, 10, 11.

But what is the date of the really earliest coins of Athena type, those pieces of fine archaic type the style of which is so distinctive that we can venture with confidence to give them a date? I refer to such coins as Babelon Pl. XXXIV, 14–18; XXXV, 1, 2; *B. M. Cat.* Pl. I, 11, Pl. II, 2, 7; and our Pl. II, 9, 10. We must briefly consider their fabric and style. In regard to fabric, the most noteworthy fact is that they have a reverse—as well as an obverse—type. This is a rare phenomenon in the sixth century, east of the Adriatic. But double types were in use in Italy at the middle of the sixth century; and some coins of Samos, which must be given to the same date, have a reverse type enclosed in an incuse square.[1] But we know of no coins earlier than about 550 B.C. which have two types. In regard to style, we have a great range of Athenian sculpture in the sixth century for comparison. The coins do not exhibit the so-called island style, notable in the case of the dedicated Corae; but they may well be set beside the head of Athena from the pedimental Gigantomachy, which may date from about 530–520 B.C., the head of the Calf-bearer, and the heads of the bronze statuettes of Athena from the early strata.

I therefore accept the view of several authorities, perhaps best defended by von Fritze,[2] that the earliest tetradrachms of Athens belong to the middle of the sixth century Von Fritze shows that the head of Athena on them is about contemporary with that on the coins of Corinth of 550–500 B.C.[3] There can I think be little doubt that this coinage was initiated by Peisistratus. That Tyrant had, as every one knows, a special cult of Athena. He obtained possession of extensive mines of silver, both at Laurium and in the valley of the Strymon,[4] and required large issues of silver for the payment of his mercenaries. He filled Athens with artists, brought from Ionia and the Islands, and employed them on great works. He made the Panathenaic festival more splendid. In short, he was precisely

1 Gardner, *Samos*, Pl. I, 8–12.

2 *Zeitschr. f. Num.*, xx. 143. So also Perrot, Babelon, and Lermann.

3 See above, p. 136.

4 Hdt. i. 64.

the man to initiate a great coinage. It is possible that a great celebration of the Panathenaea by Peisistratus was the occasion of its first appearance.

The Athena coinage of Athens, from its first appearance, is regulated by a standard somewhat heavier than the Euboic—drachm 67·5 grains (grm. 4·37), instead of 65 grains (grm. 4·20). This is easily explicable if they were issued by a tyrant of magnificent ideas, anxious to make his city, his temple, his coins, the best in the world. The coins were of fine silver, almost without alloy; and they very speedily gained a reputation which they never lost. They seem to have given rise, almost at once, to barbarous imitations; and barbarous imitations existed until Hellenistic times, when the mint of Athens took careful measures to exclude such. Indeed, they were remarkably easy to copy; and there was no reason why they should not be copied by any tyrant or state which wished to put silver into circulation.

The raising of the monetary standard by Peisistratus is one of the landmarks of the early coinage of Hellas. We have seen, in dealing with coins of Euboea, Corinth, and other cities, that the action of Athens compelled them also to raise the weight of their coins, which otherwise would have stood in an unfavourable position in the neutral markets. And thus we are furnished with a date in arranging the early series of coins which is as valuable for the money of the sixth century as is the introduction of the Chian or Rhodian standard for the classification of the money of the early fourth century. Numismatists generally have missed this clue, because they have identified the Euboic and Attic standards, whereas the evidence of the coins themselves proves them to have been perceptibly different.

The standard introduced by Peisistratus was used in the earliest times of coinage, the sixth or even the seventh century, at Samos or some neighbouring city, for electrum and for silver.[1] It was also used at Cyrene for silver from

[1] Head, *Num. Chron.*, 1875, 273; *Cat. Ionia*, pp. xxiii, xli.

600 B.C. It appears to have been derived from Egypt, where a *kedet* of the weight of 135–140 grains (grm. 8·74–9·07) was in use in the Delta. Through Naucratis this weight spread in one direction to Cyrene, in another to Samos. Peisistratus adopted it partly perhaps with a view to trade with Egypt. It is a suggestive fact that large numbers of early Athenian tetradrachms have been found in Egypt, on the site of Naucratis and elsewhere.

Another explanation of the raising of the standard by Peisistratus may be found in the fact of his working mines of silver in Thrace. We see in examining the coins of Thasos and the neighbouring coast, that the stater in ordinary use there in the sixth century weighed from 140 grains (grm. 9·07) upwards. Whence this standard was derived is uncertain; but the source may very possibly be Egyptian.

Whencesoever Peisistratus derived his coin-standard, it is certain that its adoption at Athens was the beginning and foundation of Attic commercial supremacy. Thenceforward the Attic silver coin dominated more and more the trade of the Aegean. The pure and heavy coins of Athens tended to drive out inferior issues. When the reign of the tyrants at Athens gave way to that of the democracy, the determination of the people to force the circulation of their money grew stronger. Recently published inscriptions have proved to what a degree the Athenian Demos hindered and prohibited the issue of coins by the subject allies in the time of the Delian League.[1] In a well-known passage in the *Frogs* (405 B.C.) Aristophanes speaks of the Athenian coinage as everywhere dominant, received both by Greeks and barbarians. Even after the political fall of Athens, Xenophon could write [2] that foreign merchants who carried away from Athens not goods but the silver owls did good business, for they could anywhere part with them at a premium.

[1] Weil, in *Zeitschr. f. Numism.*, xxv. p. 52. Below, Ch. XIV.

[2] *De Vectigal.* iii. 2.

The roots of the flourishing Athenian Empire were fed largely by the silver of Laurium. The Peisistratid coinage presents a striking contrast to the modest issues of Solon, scarcely to be distinguished from those of Euboea. It marks what Shakespeare calls 'the tide in the affairs of men, which taken at the flood leads on to fortune'. None of the triumphs of the Athenian tetradrachms was greater than that which they won when the powerful tyrants of Sicily, Gelon and Hieron and Theron accepted their lead and initiated the splendid coinage of Sicily, consisting mainly of tetradrachms of Attic weight.

In the time of the Tyrant Hippias (527–511 B.C.) a fresh crisis took place in the Athenian coinage, if we may trust an obscure passage in the *Oeconomica* attributed to Aristotle, which runs 'he made the current money of Athens no longer legal tender, and fixing a rate of purchase ordered the people to bring it in to him, but when they were assembled in expectation of the issue of a new type he gave back the same money'.[1]

The natural way of taking this passage is as a statement that Hippias called in the current money, valuing it at a certain rate of discount, and crediting at that rate those who brought it in; but afterwards he paid these persons not in a new and full-weighted coinage, but in the old currency. This, of course, is a procedure the first part of which has been followed from time to time in all countries, when a coinage has become outworn or debased, though more usually in modern times it is the state and not the individual which bears the loss. But there are difficulties in supposing that this is the meaning of the writer, or at all events in supposing that this really took place at Athens. For the early money of Athens is of full weight and great purity, so that there could be no excuse for calling it in as debased, and it is difficult to see what could have been the motive of the Tyrant.

[1] *Τό τε νόμισμα τὸ ὂν Ἀθηναίοις ἀδόκιμον ἐποίησε, τάξας δὲ τιμὴν ἐκέλευσε πρὸς αὐτὸν ἀνακομίζειν· συνελθόντων δὲ ἐπὶ τῷ κόψαι ἕτερον χαρακτῆρα, ἐξέδωκε τὸ αὐτὸ ἀργύριον*, Oecon. ii. 4.

M. Six, followed by Mr. Hill, has supposed that though Hippias gave back the same coin, he did not give it back at the same rate; but that he reduced the standard of the drachm from the earlier level of 135 grains to the later level of 67·5 grains, thus halving its weight; and while he had accepted the ordinary Athena and owl coins as didrachms he returned them as tetradrachms, thus making a gain of 50 per cent.[1] We have, however, seen that there is no valid reason for supposing the drachm between the times of Solon and Hippias to have been of double the weight of the later Athenian drachm: the view of M. Six therefore lacks foundation.

Mr. Head has suggested[2] that Hippias may have improved and modernized the types of the coinage; although to the people who were expecting something quite different it might well seem the same coin over again. Perhaps this suggestion is the best. If we are to accept the statement of the *Oeconomica* as historic, the best plan is to take it quite literally and simply. Hippias, on some pretext, called in the money of the Athenians at a discount, and then, instead of issuing an entirely fresh coinage, gave out coins of the old types at full value. A possibility which occurs to us is that his object may have been to exclude from the coinage the barbarous imitations which seem to have been so abundant. In any case the extant coins sufficiently prove that no great change took place at that time in the Athenian issues.

M. Babelon and M. Six have been successful in showing that the fortunes of the house of Peisistratus have left decided traces on the coinage of Athens. The alliances and projects of the Tyrants are reflected in it.

They cite the following coins[3]:

[1] *Num. Chron.*, 1895, p. 178; cf. *Num. Chron.*, 1897, p. 292. So M. Babelon, *Traité*, p. 742.

[2] *Num. Chron.*, 1893, p. 249.

[3] I cannot accept the reading of Mr. Seltman, who finds the inscription ΠΙ on an early tetradrachm of Athens (*Num. Chron.*, 1908, p. 278). The supposed letters seem to me to be accidental marks, and the omission of the

1. Helmeted head of Athena. *Rev.* HIΠ. Owl and ear of corn (*Corolla Num.*, p. 1). Obol. Weight grm. 0·65 (10 grains).
2. Janiform heads, both beardless. *Rev.* ΑΘΕ. Head of Athena helmeted to r. *B. M. Cat.* II. 10; Babelon, *Traité*, Pl. XXXIV, 19; Trihemiobol.
3. Head of Athena r. helmeted. *Rev.* ΑΘΕ. Female head l. hair turned up behind. *B. M. Cat.* II. 9; Babelon, *Traité*, XXXIV. 20; Trihemiobol.

Of these coins the first, bearing the name of Hip(pias), must almost certainly have been issued by the Tyrant, on some occasion. As the name of Athens is absent, one may with great probability conjecture that it was struck not in that city, but at some other place in which the Tyrant took refuge. If it were a city of the Persian Empire, the Great King might well allow Hippias to place his name on the coin, as he allowed Themistocles to do at Magnesia, half a century later. The city of Sigeium has the best claim from the historic point of view; since Hippias certainly repaired to that place, and from thence conspired against Athens. M. Babelon, however, observes[1] that the later coins of Sigeium never have an ear of corn as type, but the purely Athenian types of the head of Athena and the owl. He is therefore disposed rather to think of the Thracian Chersonese, where the ear of corn is frequent on the coins, although the historians do not inform us that Hippias had partisans in that district, which was in the power of Miltiades. The mint of the coin must therefore be left doubtful.

No. 2 is by M. Six[2] regarded as a memorial of the alliance between Hippias and Hippolochus, Tyrant of Lampsacus, and a favourite of Darius, whose son Aeantides took in marriage a daughter of Hippias; and this conjecture has numismatic probability, as the janiform head is a frequent feature of the early coins of Lampsacus, and scarcely

aspirate cannot be explained. The coin is very rude—probably a barbarous imitation.

[1] *Corolla Num.*, p. 5.

[2] *Num. Chron.*, 1895, p. 172.

of other places. We have a coin of Lampsacus of Attic weight, perhaps struck on the same occasion (see p. 174).

No. 3 is of more doubtful assignment. M. Six compares with the female head of the reverse that of Hera on coins of Heraea, and thinks that the coin may be a memorial of the alliance of Hippias with the Spartans; the Spartans having no coinage, Hippias might regard that of Heraea as the most characteristically Peloponnesian. This, however, is fanciful. Unless the alliance was under the special patronage of Hera, her effigy would scarcely be borrowed for the coin; we might rather expect on the coin under the circumstances the head or figure of the Zeus of Olympia. M. Babelon is disposed[1] rather to regard the head on the coin as that of the Nymph Larissa, and to consider it as a record of an alliance of Hippias with the powerful Aleuadae of Larissa. In fact, a Thessalian alliance of the Tyrant is mentioned by Herodotus (v. 63), the Thessalians sending him a force of 1,000 horse.

There is perhaps a weak point in these conjectures in the fact that coins (2) and (3) are both trihemiobols, that is, coins of an unusual denomination; and for such denominations at Athens special types were chosen.[2] Nor is there any inscription on them to indicate that they are other than usual coins of Athens.

§ 4. The Olive-Wreath of Athena.

On the earliest tetradrachms of Athens the helmet of the goddess bears no wreath. But the later archaic types (**Pl. II. 12**) regularly have the wreath. The question naturally arises, on what occasion the change was made, and what it means. To this question a fairly satisfactory answer can be given. The suggestion was made by M. Six[3] that it has reference to the victory of Marathon, in 490 B.C.,

[1] *Traité*, ii. 1, p. 757.
[2] See below, Ch. XIV.
[3] *Num. Chron.*, 1895, p. 176.

and M. Babelon[1] has been able to contribute numismatic evidence which seems almost conclusive in favour of that view.

About 1839 there was found in the canal of Xerxes at Mount Athos a treasure of 300 darics and 100 Athenian tetradrachms.[2] This treasure was almost certainly buried at the time of the Persian invasion in 480 B.C. One of the tetradrachms has been figured. It is of barbarous fabric, probably an imitation, but the helmet of the goddess bears a wreath, thus conclusively proving that the wreath was introduced on the coins some time before 480 B.C.

In 1886 there was found on the Acropolis of Athens, between the outer wall and the Erechtheum, just where the dedicated Corae were discovered, a treasure of Athenian coins, consisting of 35 tetradrachms, 2 drachms and 23 obols. These coins[3] were probably buried about 480 B.C. They are nearly all of barbarous fabric, and without the wreath. One only (which seems not to belong to the find[4]) is of careful work, and has the wreath. Thus it would seem that it was very shortly before 480 B.C. that the olive-wreath made its appearance.

Among the earliest in type of the coins which bear it are the great Athenian decadrachms. These are rare and exceptional coins. It seems almost certain that they are contemporary with the Damareteia of ten drachms struck in Sicily by Gelon after his defeat of the Carthaginians. As to the date and occasion of these latter there is no dispute.

Thus the victory of Marathon seems to have left its mark, not only in great dedications at Delphi and works of art at Athens, but also on the issues of the Athenian mint. Henceforward Athena bears constantly on the coins the olive-wreath of victory. Decadrachms seem in Greece only to

[1] *Traité*, ii. 1, p. 765.

[2] Beulé, *Monn. d'Athènes*, p. 44.

[3] Some of them in Babelon's *Traité*, Pl. XXXIV, 2–11.

[4] Mr. Kampanes has proved (*Bull. Corr. Hell.*, 1906, p. 89) that the coin with the olive-wreath is a later insertion in the find.

have been issued on the occasion of some great national triumph.[1]

If we may synchronize the decadrachm with Marathon, we obtain a valuable fixed point in the Athenian series. For the decadrachm is the latest of the true archaic coins, and the type thus fixed is perpetuated on the tetradrachms for a century. It is true that the stereotyping of the style is not complete. We may trace first an excessive and lifeless convention in the copying, and then, in the fourth century, greater irregularity and carelessness. But speaking generally, the type of the normal Athenian coinage during the greatness of Athens is thus given. Just as the victory of Marathon fixed for the future the Athenian ideas of patriotism and glory, so the coinage of Marathon fixed for the future the character of the Athenian coin.

[1] The only decadrachms issued in Greece were the following:

Syracuse—after Gelon's victory.
Athens—after Marathon.
Syracuse—after the defeat of the Athenians.
Agrigentum—after the defeat of the Athenians.
Alexander the Great—after his victories.

CHAPTER IX

EARLY SILVER OF ASIA

§ 1. Earliest Issues.

It appears that the silver coins issued by Croesus and the Persians were the earliest silver issues of Asia of wide circulation. But they were certainly not the very earliest in use. Silver coins of primitive aspect, with rough incuse reverses, had already been struck by some of the Greek cities of the coast and the islands. This we may conclude on various grounds.

(1) A few silver coins of Asia are of extremely early fabric, and closely resemble the Ionian electrum. I would take as examples the following:

(A) *Obv.* Rude female head. *Rev.* Two incuse squares, one much larger than the other. Weight 153·1 (grm. 9·92). Much worn and reduced in weight. Brit. Mus. (**B. T. XVIII. 9.**) The coin is probably of Aeginetan standard. It is attributed with probability to Cnidus.

(B) Coin of Cos (British Museum). *Obv.* Crab. *Rev.* Two incuse squares, one much smaller than the other. Weight 189·5 (grm. 12·33). **Pl. III. 1.** Stater of Aeginetan standard.

(2) The coins of Phocaea appear to cease (for a long while) after the abandonment of the city by its inhabitants about 544 B.C. There are known many small silver coins of Phocaea which must have been struck before this time. (See Babelon, *Traité* ii. 1, pp. 323–330.) The standard of these coins is uncertain, but there exist, as we shall presently see, larger coins of Phocaea of Aeginetan weight, which also precede the migration. The coinage of Phocaea is further discussed under South Italy (Ch. XI).

The people of Teos also migrated about 544 B.C. to Abdera on the Thracian coast. The coinage of the city is not however in this case brought to an end, but continues. The earliest coins (type, griffin with one paw raised) (**B. M. II. 24**) follow the Aeginetan standard, and are certainly earlier than the migration to Abdera.

(3) Definite evidence of the issue of silver coins in Asia Minor, and of the source whence the suggestion of them came, is furnished by the important Island finds of staters, mostly of Aeginetan weight, which have been already discussed in Chapter V. In these finds the great mass of the coins was from the mint of Aegina. But there were many coins, of Aeginetan weight, and similar in type and appearance to Aeginetan coins, which were struck at other islands of the Aegean. In describing these finds I observed that some of the coins seemed to belong to the earliest issues in silver of the cities of Ionia and the islands of the Ionian and Carian coasts. This observation requires expansion and comment.

The coins in question, almost all from the Island finds, are as follows:

1. **Cyme in Aeolis.**
   Obv. Fore-part of horse, to r. or l. *Rev.* Two incuse squares, one large and one small, enclosing patterns. Weight, 181–6 grains (grm. 11·70–12·04). (**B. T. XIII. 22–24.**)

2. **Miletus.**
   Obv. Fore-part of lion looking back, with paw. *Rev.* Square incuse, sometimes enclosing a pattern. Weight, 181–6 grains (grm. 11·70–12·04). (**B. T. XIX. 11–14.**)

3. **Chios.**
   Obv. Sphinx seated, body nearly parallel to ground. *Rev.* Incuse square, beside which a smaller incuse. Weight, 184–92 grains (grm. 11·97–12·44). Babelon, *Traité*, ii. 1, p. 630.

4. **Teos.**
   Obv. Griffin seated with curled wing, l. fore-paw raised. *Rev.* Rough incuse square. Weight, 90·4 grains (grm. 5·85). (**B. T. XIII. 2.**)

5. **Phocaea.**

Obv. Fore-part of griffin. *Rev.* Incuse square in four compartments. Weight, 96 grains (grm. 6·26). Babelon, *Traité*, ii. 1, p. 327.

6. **Iasus.**

Obv. Youth riding on dolphin. *Rev.* Incuse square. Weight, 92 grains (grm. 5·98). (**B. T. XVIII. 1–2.**)

7. **Lindus in Rhodes.**

Obv. Head of lion, mouth open. *Rev.* Incuse square, divided into four. Weight, 167–72 grains (grm. 10·80–11·10). (**B. T. XX. 16–18.**)

8. **Poseidion in Carpathos.**

Obv. Two dolphins passing one another. *Rev.* Incuse square in eight sections, as on the earliest coins of Aegina. Weight, 188–93 grains (grm. 12·18–12·50). (**B. T. LXII. 16–17.**)

9. **Cos.**

Obv. Crab. *Rev.* Larger and smaller incuses, the larger divided into triangles. Weight, 188–90 grains (grm. 12·15–12·33). (**B. T. XIX. 1.**)

These coins require a few comments.

(1) **Cyme.** M. J. P. Six has proposed for these coins the attribution to Mylasa in Caria, partly on the ground of fabric, and partly because a stater of electrum with the type of a half-horse is of the Milesian class, and should belong to the south of Asia Minor. This electrum stater, however, belongs to the Ionian Revolt, and may very probably have been struck at Cyme. The silver also are best attributed to that city, which was near to Smyrna.

(2) **Miletus.** The chief difficulty in assigning these coins to Miletus is the inscription ΟVΛ which occurs on some of them, and has hitherto defied interpretation. But the type is practically identical with that in use in Miletus at a later time (lion looking back at a star), and the Milesian origin is most probable. It seems very unlikely that Miletus, being at the height of her power in the sixth century, would not issue silver coins.

(3) **Chios.** No silver coins of Asia are more archaic in appearance than some which bear the type of the sphinx, and have usually been attributed to Chios. A recent excellent paper on the coins of Chios, by Mr. J. Mavrogordato,[1] enables us satisfactorily to deal with these coins.

1. The earliest class consists of didrachms of Aeginetan standard:

Obv. Archaic sphinx seated, body almost parallel to ground. *Rev.* Incuse square, beside which smaller incuse. Weight, 184–92 grains (grm. 11·97–12·44). **(Pl. III. 3.)**

2. Next comes a rare didrachm of Euboic weight:

Obv. Sphinx in form similar, but a little more advanced; in front rosette. *Rev.* Incuse square, quartered. Weight, 130 grains (grm. 8·42).

3. Next are didrachms of a lighter weight:

Obv. Sphinx resembling the last, with separate lock falling from head, but the body slopes more. *Rev.* Incuse square, quartered. Weight, 113–20 grains (grm. 7·32–7·78). One weighs 105 grains (grm. 6·80, but this is quite exceptional).

Three specimens of No. 1 were found in a hoard containing mostly coins of the islands of the Aegean Sea.[2] Some writers, without adequate reasons, have regarded it as improbable that this coin is of Chios. The rare Chian coin of Euboic or Attic weight must have been struck on the occasion of some convention with Athens or Euboea. After this come the didrachms of the ordinary Chian standard, though at first they are somewhat light.

(4) It is noteworthy that at Teos, Iasus, and Phocaea the drachm, and not the didrachm, of Aeginetan weight is in use.

(5) The Aeginetan standard of this coin, as well as its mint, seems certain. But the coin of Phocaea, which succeeds it,

Obv. Griffin walking, raising fore-foot. *Rev.* Incuse square quartered. Weight, 193 grains (grm. 12·51),

[1] *Num. Chron.*, 1915, p. 1.

[2] Greenwell in *Num. Chron.*, 1890, p. 18.

is somewhat later in fabric. Mr. Head[1] observes that it has lost 20 grains through corrosion; it must therefore follow the Phoenician standard, rather than the Aeginetan.

(7 and 8) The authorities have been greatly exercised as to the attribution of these coins. No. 7 they have given to a great variety of places: no. 8 to Argos, Delos, and Thera. The whole difficulty has arisen because numismatists did not observe that shortly after coinage was started at Aegina many of the cities of Asia Minor and the islands of the coast issued money on the same standard; and then before long gave up the Aeginetan for Asiatic standards, retaining the types. If this is borne in mind, it will be most natural to regard the lion's head coin, (no. 7) as belonging to Lindus, since the type is almost identical with that of later coins of Lindus, and the coin with the dolphins (no. 8) as belonging to Carpathos, which city is naturally indicated by the type.

10. Dardanus in Troas (?)

Obv. Cock l. *Rev.* Incuse formed of eight triangles. Weight, 190 grains (grm. 12·31). Montagu Collection. (**B. T. XVI. 10.**)

This coin also belonged to the Santorin find. The attribution to Dardanus was suggested by Mr. Head;[2] but here again the evidence of the electrum points in another direction. There are many early electrum coins with the type of the cock, some of them found by Mr. Hogarth[3] on the site of the temple of Artemis at Ephesus, and belonging almost certainly to Southern Ionia. The electrum stater of the time of the Ionian revolt, bearing the cock as type, is of uncertain attribution; but Miletus has as good a claim to it as any city. As we have seen, Miletus did, in all probability, strike silver staters of Aeginetan weight; and it is possible that the coin above mentioned may belong to Miletus. The best plan is to leave its place of mint undetermined.

[1] *B. M. Cat. Coins Ionia*, p. 214. [2] *B. M. Cat. Ionia*, p. xxxiii.
[3] *Excavations at Ephesus*, p. 81.

The dominance of the Aeginetan coinage is conspicuous. It seems even to have been used at Athens till the time of Solon. Westwards it did not spread; for it is a mistake to regard as of Aeginetan standard either the staters of Corcyra or the earliest issues of Sicily at Naxos and Himera. In both these cases the standard was really that of Corinth: the Corcyrean staters being tetradrachms of that standard, and the early coins of Sicily didrachms. But on all shores of the Aegean and the Euxine the Aeginetan standard was victorious. It was not only that the Aeginetan was the earliest silver coinage, and held for a time a monopoly, but that the Aeginetans were the most successful and wealthiest of merchants, though they founded no colonies.

The invasion of Ionia by the Aeginetan standard is a very interesting phenomenon. How coins minted on this standard fitted in with the electrum issues which were there in possession, we have no means of knowing. All these coins are very early, earlier than the time of Croesus. And it would seem that as soon as the state issues of Croesus and Cyrus in pure gold made their appearance, and the Ionian electrum was superseded, most of the cities which had for a time adopted the Aeginetan standard gave it up for some silver standard (Phoenician or Persian) more in accord with the Croesean and daric currency.

There were, however, three districts in which the Aeginetan standard was retained after the time of Croesus. The first is the cities of S.W. Asia Minor, Cnidus, Iasus, Cos, Camirus. The Carian cities had a Dorian origin, and probably retained a connexion with Peloponnesus. They had an union centring in the temple of Apollo Triopius near Cnidus. Herodotus[1] gives the names of the cities belonging to the league as Cnidus, Halicarnassus, Cos, and the three Rhodian cities, Lindus, Ialysus, and Camirus. It is interesting to observe that this religious league does not include all the Carian cities which used the Aeginetan standard; but five of the cities above mentioned, Cnidus, Halicarnassus, Cos, Lindus, and Camirus, used this standard.

[1] i. 144.

So did Chersonesus, that is the Tripolis of Chersonesus[1] in the immediate neighbourhood of Cnidus, and Iasus farther to the north.

Some of the most noteworthy coins of the Carian district in the latter part of the sixth century are—

Cnidus.

Obv. Fore-part of lion. *Rev.* ΚΝΙΔΙΟΝ (usually abbreviated) Archaic head of Aphrodite. Weight, 94–9 grains (grm. 6·10–6·46). (**Pl. III. 6.**)

Cos.

Obv. Crab. *Rev.* Incuse squares. Weight, 189·5 grains (grm. 12·28). British Museum. (**Pl. III. 1.**)

Camirus in Rhodes.

Obv. Fig-leaf. *Rev.* Incuse divided by band. Weight, 183–86 grains (grm. 11·89–12·03). (**Pl. III. 7.**)

Chersonesus of Caria.

Obv. Fore-part of lion, with paw. *Rev.* ΧΕΡ Fore-part of bull. Weight, 183 grains (grm. 11·83). (**Pl. III. 5.**)

Iasus in Caria.

Obv. Youth riding on dolphin. *Rev.* Incuse square. Weight, 92–3 grains (grm. 5·97–5·99). (**B. T. XVIII. 1, 2.**)

It is noteworthy that the cities of this district of Asia Minor are cut off by mountains from the interior, so that island influence would, in their case, be considerable.

The second group consists of a single Ionian city, Teos, which kept to the Aeginetan weight when the other cities of Ionia gave it up. The reason for this anomaly may probably be found in the fact that the Aeginetan standard for silver coin was dominant in the Black Sea, and the relations between Teos and the Black Sea are indicated by the foundation of Phanagoria on the Asiatic side by the people of Teos.

It was the Phoenician standard, not the Aeginetan, which the people of Teos carried with them to their new home at Abdera in Thrace. Phocaea, as we have seen, seems to have issued a few coins on the Aeginetan standard. But

[1] See Babelon, *Traité*, ii. 1, p. 433.

in the case of Phocaea, as in that of Teos, it was not the Aeginetan standard but an Asiatic standard which the people who emigrated took with them to their new home. The base silver issued by Phocaea is discussed later.

The third group comprises some cities on the Black Sea, of which Sinope and Panticapaeum struck money before 500 B.C. These, it is probable, in the great time of Miletus used the Milesian electrum. They seem to have been unaffected by the coinages of Croesus and the Persians. After the fall of Miletus there came a time when the trade of the Black Sea fell partially into the hands of the Aeginetans. Xerxes at the Hellespont[1] saw ships sailing out of the Euxine laden with corn for Aegina and Peloponnese. The silver coinage of Sinope[2] begins just at this time, and it seems to follow the Aeginetan standard, only issuing the drachm instead of the didrachm. The earliest coins of Sinope are very heavy.

Sinope.

Obv. Eagle's head: beneath, dolphin. *Rev.* Incuse square in four compartments. Weight, 100–92 grains (grm. 6·45–5·98). (**B. T. XVII. 1–8.**)

Panticapaeum.

Obv. Lion's scalp, facing. *Rev.* Rough incuse square. Weight, 91 grains (grm. 5·89). (**B. T. XVII. 9.**)

The facts thus put together seem to indicate that the Aeginetan standard was an exotic in Pontus, but that several cities and districts passed on to it from the Milesian standard. The Milesian stater only weighing 222 grains (grm. 14·40), the fall to the Aeginetan stater of 192 grains (grm. 12·44) was not great, and may have been gradual. Nevertheless the adoption of the Aeginetan stater marks not only a slight lowering of standard, but also the introduction of the drachm in place of the trinal division, the adoption of silver instead of electrum as the standard, and

[1] Hdt. vii. 147. Though the speech of Xerxes on this occasion may be an invention, we may accept the testimony of Herodotus as to facts of commerce.

[2] Six and Wroth (*B. M. Cat.*) give it to the time after 480 B.C.

the passing over to an essentially European way of reckoning. And the change must have taken place early in the sixth century, certainly before the destruction of Miletus by the Persians.

There is another region, that of Cilicia and Cyprus, in which early coins of Aeginetan standard are usually supposed to have been struck. But this opinion appears to be erroneous.

M. Babelon gives the following attributions:

Celenderis in Cilicia.

Obv. Goat kneeling. *Rev.* Rude incuse. Weight, 93–90 grains (grm. 6·05–5·85). (**B. T. XXV. 1–3.**)

Mallus in Cilicia.

Obv. Winged figure running. *Rev.* Conical stone in rude incuse. Weight, 185–178 grains (grm. 11·98–11·50). (**B. T. XXV. 5–17.**)

Both of these assignments are more than doubtful. The coin given to Celenderis probably belongs to the island of Andros. The coin given to Mallus was assigned to that city by the high authority of Dr. Imhoof-Blumer; but the latter has since retracted his attribution.[1] He now gives the coin to Aphrodisias in Cilicia; but there does not appear to be any better reason in this case than in the other. In the absence of any other coins of Aeginetan weight belonging to cities on this part of the coast, we may best regard the coin as belonging to some other region. The weight would best suit Caria. It has commonly been supposed—and the view is even accepted by Head—that the archaic coins of Cyprus follow the Aeginetan standard; but Mr. Hill in the *B. M. Cat. Cilicia*[2] states the matter exactly. 'For all practical purposes the coins (of Cyprus) were of the Persic standard.' I do not think that there are any grounds for holding that the Aeginetan standard gained even theoretic sway in Cyprus.

It is interesting to see that the Aeginetan silver standard,

[1] *Kleinasiat. Münzen*, ii. p. 435. [2] p. xxii.

like the power of the Athenian Empire, does not extend as far west as Cilicia and Cyprus.

§ 2. The Attic Standard.

There are very few certain examples of silver coins being minted in Asia at this period on the Euboic, Corinthian, or Attic standards. The coins commonly given to Samos, and regarded as of Attic weight, with types of the fore-part of a bull, and a lion's head facing, have already been considered in Chapter I, where it is suggested that they follow a standard different from the Euboic and of earlier origin than the Attic. The archaic coin bearing as type a lyre, attributed to Colophon in the *Historia Numorum* (ed. 1), is withdrawn from that city in the *British Museum Catalogue of Ionia*, and assigned, in the second edition of the *Historia*, to Delos. The remarkable archaic coin (*Obv.* Lion tearing prey: *Rev.* Forepart of winged boar in incuse: Weight, 266 grains (grm. 17·23): (**B. M. II. 23**)) was formerly attributed to Clazomenae, but is now reckoned among the uncertain. The weight is certainly Attic (or Cyrenaic), not Euboic. It seems very improbable that it can belong to Ionia. A few of the coins of Chios, as we have seen, were minted on the Euboic standard; but it soon gives way to the standard called Chian. There remains only the beautiful coin of Methymna, which is certainly of Attic weight:

> *Obv.* ΜΑΘΥΜΝΑΙΟΣ. Boar to r. scratching himself. *Rev.* Inscr. repeated. Head of Athena r., Pegasus on her helmet. Weight, 132–126 grains (grm. 8·55–8·15). (Pl. **VI. 11.**)

M. Six[1] assigns it to the period 523–513 B.C., between the death of Polycrates and the institution of Coes as ruler of Lesbos by the Persians. I do not think that it can be so early, and I would assign it to the period 480–460 B.C. It must have been struck on the occasion of some alliance or understanding with Athens. An alliance with Athens

[1] *Num. Chron.*, 1895, 191.

suggests itself in the case of a coin struck probably at Lampsacus[1]:

Obv. Fore-part of winged horse. *Rev.* Incuse square, quartered. Weight, 33 grains (grm. 2·16).

This is clearly a hemidrachm of Attic standard: in fabric it is earlier than the silver of Lampsacus struck at the time of the Ionian Revolt. It may well be a memorial of an alliance between Lampsacus and Hippias of Athens, as M. Six has suggested.[2]

We have above (p. 167) met with a coin of Chios of Attic weight, perhaps recording a similar alliance.

§ 3. Phoenician Standard.

Although the Asiatic cities in the half-century preceding 480 B.C., setting aside the exceptions which I have mentioned, are usually said to have issued silver money on either the Babylonic (Persian) or the Phoenician (Graeco-Asiatic) standard, yet as a matter of fact there prevails a great irregularity in the weights of such coins. Strictly speaking, every city seems to have used a standard of its own, which (a remarkable fact) seems, when once fairly established, to have held its own for long periods. We can, however, distinguish a heavier standard with a stater of about 240 grains (grm. 15·50), or the half of this, 120 grains (grm. 7·75), and a lighter standard with a stater of about 216 grains (grm. 14), or the half of this, 108 grains (grm. 7), and we can distinguish between the heavier Persian standard, with a stater of about 168 grains (grm. 10·88), or its half, 84 grains (grm. 5·44), and the lighter Babylonic standard with a stater of 152–142 grains (grm. 9·84–9·20).

We have seen, in treating of the electrum coins of Asia, that cities to the north of Smyrna and the Hermus valley,

[1] Babelon, *Traité*, ii. 1, p. 378.

[2] Babelon in *Corolla Numismatica*, p. 3.

such cities as Lampsacus, Cyzicus, and Phocaea, minted electrum on the Phocaean standard, which is the same as that above called heavy Phoenician. At the same period, the cities to the south of the Hermus, such as Miletus and Ephesus, used the Milesian standard, which is identical with that above called the light Phoenician. The same division applies in the case of the silver coin. The cities to the north of the Hermus still use the heavier, and those to the south of the Hermus the lighter standard. We may well then retain the names Phocaean and Milesian standards in preference to the more cumbrous names of heavy and light Phoenician or Graeco-Asiatic.

We begin with the cities which struck silver on the Phocaean standard:

Phocaea.

Obv. Seal. *Rev.* Incuse square. Weight, 57–60 grains (grm. 3·68–3·85). (**B. T. XIII. 12.**)

Tenedos.

Obv. Janiform heads, male and female. *Rev.* ΤΕΝΕΔΙΟΝ. Bipennis; amphora attached to it. Weight, 239–43 grains (grm. 15·48–15·73). (**Pl. III. 8; B. M. II. 19.**) Also the half of this: the didrachm.[1]

Parium.

Obv. Gorgon head. *Rev.* Pattern in incuse square. Weight, 50–61 grains (grm. 3·24–3·95). (**B. T. XVI. 22, 23.**) Also the half and the quarter.

The attribution to Parium of these coins is probable but not certain. It is notable that Tenedos and Parium are close to the Hellespont, and in the line of commerce.

Chios also may be classed as using the Phocaean standard, though some of its coins, up to 122 grains (grm. 7·90) (**B. T. XII**), exceed the limit usual with this standard. We shall see in a later chapter[2] that in the fifth century the

[1] Babelon, *Traité*, ii. 1, p. 367.

[2] Ch. XIV.

Chian tetradrachm was regarded as a fortieth of the mina of Aegina; and it is quite possible that from the beginning it had a recognized relation to the island coinage. In that case the Chians, after beginning, as we have seen, with a stater which was a fiftieth part of the Aeginetan mina (p. 167), went on to a stater which was the fortieth part of that mina.

Some cities, Phocaea, Mytilene, and Cyzicus, also issued, on the Phocaean standard, coins of base quality, bearing the same relation to silver which electrum bears to gold. At a later period, as we know from the excellent testimony of an inscription, Phocaea and Mytilene made a convention by which they issued alternately hectae of electrum struck on the Phocaean standard, hectae of poor quality of metal, though good as works of art. The base silver issued earlier by Phocaea and Mytilene is of metal called billon, being silver adulterated with copper and lead. It is interesting to observe that the chief cities which issued electrum also struck in base silver. Mr. Head long ago conjectured that whereas the Milesian electrum was intended to pass as a special metal, the Phocaean electrum was intended to pass as gold[1]; and we may best accept this view. The Phocaean electrum contains, according to the experiments of Mr. Head, from 51 to 64 per cent. of gold; the billon of Mytilene, according to Lenormant, contains about 40 per cent. of pure silver.[2] It may be suggested that the people of Cyzicus, Phocaea, and Lesbos, having found their issues of electrum exceedingly profitable, tried a similar experiment with silver. There is no pure silver at Mytilene contemporary with the billon. The billon begins about 550 B.C. and continues till about 440. Silver begins at Mytilene about 440.[3] The exceptional silver coin issued at Methymna about 480 B.C. conforms, as we have seen, to the Attic standard.

[1] *Cat. Gr. Coins, Ionia*, p. xxvi; above, p. 81.

[2] *Cat. Troas*, &c., p. lxiv.

[3] *Ibid.*

The principal early coins in billon are the following (all ıave incuse reverse):

Lesbos.	Weight. grm.	grains.	Babelon.		
. Four-leaf device (on shield)	15·24–15·30	235–6	p. 344	Pl. XIV.	1
. Head of lion to l.	15·10–15·19	233–4	p. 345	,,	2
. Lion's scalp facing	14·85	229	,,	,,	3
. Gorgon-mask	14·28–14.45	220–3	,,	,,	5
. Fore-part of boar	6·85	106	p. 347	,,	6
. Two calves' heads	10·50–11.22	162–73	p. 359	Pl. XV.	14
. Calf's head	5·40–5·52	84–5	,,	,,	17
. Calf kneeling; above, cock	3.88	60[1]			
Cyzicus.					
. Head and tail of tunny	14.22–14·70	220–7	p. 390	Pl. XVI.	25

The coins of Parium, above described as being of silver, ,re not of quite pure metal.

A quantity of smaller divisions was issued; but, as ɺ. Babelon observes, they are not to be trusted for the letermination of standards; they vary considerably in veight, and a little added or subtracted takes them over ,pparently from one standard to another.

If we examine the above-mentioned larger coins, they ɔresent simple phenomena. M. Babelon, losing as I think he wood in the trees, assigns the base silver coins of ?hocaea and Mytilene to a number of standards, the Euboic, ɩeginetan, Persian, and Phocaean. All, however, except ; and 7, may be reasonably assigned to the standard which ve may call Phocaean, with a tetradrachm of 236 grains grm. 15·30) and a didrachm of 118 grains (grm. 7·65). ɺumbers 6 and 7 of the list, however, follow the Persian tandard. They are certainly later than the others, and it vould be natural to assign them to the period of the ıxpeditions of Darius and Xerxes.

The principal issues of silver, according to the lighter ᵓhoenician or Milesian standard, in the latter part of the ixth century, are:

ıamos.

Obv. Lion's scalp, facing. *Rev.* ΣA. Fore-part of bull. Weight, 198–202 grains (grm. 12·80–13·05). **(Pl. III. 10; B. T. XI. 23–30.)**

[1] *Num. Chron.*, 1899, p. 276.

Ephesus.

Obv. Bee. *Rev.* Incuse square, quartered. Weight, 50–56 grains (grm. 3·20–3·60). (**Pl. III. 9; B. T. XI. 13–16.**)

Poseidion in Carpathos.

Obv. Two dolphins passing one another; beneath, a smaller dolphin; in square. *Rev.* Incuse square divided by band. Weight, 209–214 grains (grm. 13·50–13·90). (**Pl. III. 11; B. M. III. 22; B. T. XIX. 8–10.**)

Ialysus in Rhodes.

Obv. Fore-part of winged boar. *Rev.* ΙΕΛΥΣΙΟΝ. Eagle's head; in square. Weight, 223–30 grains (grm. 14·42–14·86). (**Pl. III. 12; B. M. III. 31; B. T. XX. 14.**)

Lindus in Rhodes.

Obv. Lion's head. *Rev.* Inscr. Incuse square divided by band; sometimes inscr. ΛΙΝΔΙ. Weight, 210–213 grains (grm. 13·60–13·80). (**B. T. XX. 16–20.**)

It will be observed that the standards of these coins vary notably.

A coin of Milesian weight has been, in the *B. M. Cat. Troas* (no. 1, p. 42), given to Cebren—

Obv. Head of ram r. *Rev.* Quadripartite incuse square. Weight, 217 grains (grm. 14·06).

Here again we may follow the lead of the electrum coins on which a ram and a ram's head are frequent devices;[1] but in all cases they are of Milesian weight and South Ionian character. It seems clear that the coin we are considering cannot belong to the Troad. Clazomenae has been suggested as an alternative, and to this there is not the same objection.

Other silver coins of Milesian weight, mostly didrachms, struck at Lampsacus, Erythrae, Clazomenae, Miletus, and Chios, at the time of the Ionian Revolt, have been discussed already in Ch. III.

It is noteworthy that, whereas the electrum of Ionia is divided into thirds, sixths, and twelfths, the silver coinage of the cities of Asia from the first divides by two and four

[1] Babelon, *Traité*, ii. 1, p. 80.

We have the tetradrachm, the drachm, the obol, and their divisions and multiples. We must suppose that it was the influence of Hellas, and mainly of Aegina, which introduced into Asia the drachmal division. But this division, while thoroughly adopted by the Greek cities, does not seem to have passed into the state coinage of Persia. The silver coin there is properly the siglos or shekel; and if it is sometimes spoken of as the Persian drachm, this way of speaking is only derived; nor does the shekel divide in currency: there are no Persian state hemidrachms or obols of silver; only among the later issues we find thirds of the shekel, which might, no doubt, be called diobols.[1]

If there were a serious attempt to keep the silver coins in a certain ratio of value to the gold, it might seem to account for considerable fluctuations in their standard. When or where gold was at a premium, the silver standard might rise, as at Chios, to 240 grains: where gold was at a discount the silver standard might fall, as at Ephesus and Samos, to near 200 grains. This explanation, however, does not satisfactorily account for the varieties of the Ionian silver standards, and there remains to be accounted for the fact that when once a silver standard has gained acceptance in a city, it remains fixed there for centuries. Gold could not be permanently at a lower value in the northern cities of Ionia than in the southern, distant only a few hours' sail. This view must therefore be definitely rejected.

§ 4. Persian Standard.

It was on this standard that the main currency of Asia in early times was based. The Persian silver sigli or shekels of 86 grains (grm. 5·57) circulated in immense quantities in the interior of Asia Minor and are now found in hoards. A great proportion of them bear countermarks, small devices stamped upon them, probably by the collectors of the king's taxes, or by the local authorities in the different satrapies[2]

[1] Babelon, *Traité*, ii. 2; Pl. lxxxvii. 5, 13.

[2] See *Num. Chron.*, 1916, p. 1.

The countermarks may have been intended to guarantee them for currency in particular districts. The sigli do not appear, however, to have been the normal currency in all parts of Asia Minor. In the south of that region they were dominant, and the Greek cities of Pamphylia, Cilicia, and Cyprus conformed the coins of their civic issues to this standard. In the cities of the Ionian and Mysian coast, on the other hand, the Persian sigli were less frequent, and the standard used for the civic issues was, as we have seen, usually some variety of the Phoenician.

As I have already observed, in the civic coinages which followed the Persian standard, the weight of the siglos was treated as a drachm, and multiplied or divided after the manner of the Greek silver coinage.

Didrachms of this standard, 172–176 grains (grm. 11·14–10·50) were minted at many cities of the south coast as early as or earlier than 500. But in no case can they be given to an earlier date than the Persian Conquest.

Among these cities are:

Phaselis.

Obv. Prow of galley in the form of a boar's head. *Rev.* So times inscr. Incuse square; or stern of ship in incuse. Weight, 167–172 grains (grm. 10·80–11·15). (**Pl. III. 13; B. M. III. 36; B. T. XXIII.**)

Aspendus and Selge.

Obv. Warrior advancing. *Rev.* Inscr. Triquetra of legs. Weight, 164–170 grains (grm. 10·60–11). (**B. T. XXIII.**)

Side.

Obv. Pomegranate. *Rev.* Head of Athena. Weight, 158–172 grains (grm. 10·20–11·10). (**B. T. XXIV. 6–9.**)

These cities lie near together in Pamphylia on the southern shore of Asia Minor. Opposite is the island of Cyprus, where most of the cities used the same standard, Salamis, Citium, Idalium, and Paphos. Outside this region we cannot find cities which have used it. The cities of Cilicia would no doubt have used it, had they struck coins in the sixth century. But this does not seem to have been the case; and other coins of the Persian standard, given to the sixth century and to Asia Minor mints, seem to be wrongly assigned.

J. P. Six,[1] followed with much hesitation by M. Babelon, proposes to give to the Cilician city of Issus a series of archaic coins having on the obverse the head of a roaring lion with paw advanced, on the reverse an incuse square made up of four triangles. Weight 168–158 grains (grm. 10·86–10·23). For this attribution, however, the only evidence is a very doubtful reading by M. Six of IΣΣAIΟN on a satrapal coin at The Hague which bears on the obverse a lion's head and two paws. The legend certainly cannot be read on a photograph of the coin,[2] and M. Babelon rejects it. Mr. Hill is disposed to give these coins to Selge[3] in Pamphylia.

There is a very remarkable stater given to the island of Calymnos:[4]

Obv. Rude head of warrior in a crested helmet. *Rev.* Seven-stringed lyre fitted into an incuse. Curious flat fabric. Weight, 162–156 grains (grm. 10·50–10·10). (**Pl. III. 14; B. M. III. 29.**)

The coin is carefully struck: it is quite a mistake to suppose the exaggerated and absurd features of the head of the obverse to be the result of clumsy archaism: they are intentionally made so. Nor is the fitting of the reverse-type into the incuse really archaic. Almost the nearest parallel is to be found on the early coins of Parium and of Zancle in Sicily; also on a coin of Eretria in Euboea,[5] where the sepia on the reverse is similarly fitted into an incuse. This coin of Eretria is given in the *B. M. Catalogue* to 480–445 B.C.; I do not think that the coin before us is much earlier. Closely similar also are the earliest coins of Tyre, of about 450 B.C., bearing on the reverse an

[1] *Num. Chron.*, 1888, p. 115; cf. Babelon, *Traité*, ii. 1, p. 567.
[2] *Traité*, Pl. xxv. 20.
[3] *B. M. Cat. Lycia*, p. cxv.
[4] *B. M. Cat. Caria*, Pl. xxix. 8; *Traité*, Pl. xviii. 22.
[5] *B. M. Cat. Central Greece*, p. 121, 25; Pl. xxiii. 4.

owl fitted into an incuse (*B. M. Cat. Phoenicia*, Pl. XXVIII. 9). It is true that the two types of a helmeted head and a lyre are found together on later coins of Calymnos. Yet the fabric of our coin, which is quite different from that of Caria, and the weight, which is unknown west of Lycia, make us hesitate to give the coin to Calymnos, and we must certainly withdraw it from the very early period.

Several Greek cities on the Asiatic side, situated near the entrance to the Euxine, or on the shores of the Propontis, struck coins on the Persian standard before or during the Persian wars.

Antandros.

Obv. Fore-part of lion. *Rev.* Goat and pine-tree. Weight, 171 grains (grm. 11·10). Didrachm. (**B. T. CLXIII. 1.**)

Abydos.

Obv. ΑΒΥΔΗΝΟΝ. Eagle. *Rev.* Gorgon-head. Weight, 84–80 grains (grm. 5·41–5·21). Drachm. (**B. T. CLXVII. 29.**)

Lampsacus.

Obv. Janiform female head. *Rev.* Head of Athena. Weight, 85–72 grains (grm. 5·50–4·65). (**B. T. XVI. 18.**)

Astacus.

Obv. Lobster. *Rev.* ΑΣ. Head of Nymph. Weight, 76 grains (grm. 4·90). (**B. T. CLXXXI. 1–5.**)

It is to be observed that M. Babelon gives these coins of Antandros, Abydos, and Astacus to the time after 480 B.C. It is rather on the ground of historic probability than on any other ground that I place them earlier.

It is noteworthy that there is no corresponding coinage of Persian weight before 480 B.C. on the European side. Cardia in the Thracian Chersonese issued, as we have seen, money on the Attic standard. The coins of Salymbria are almost undistinguishable from those of Dicaea, and follow, like them, the standard of Abdera.

The coins of the Lycian cities certainly do not follow the royal Persian standard, but one 20 grains lighter.

The Lycian coins struck before 480 B.C. seem to have the following weights: [1]

Stater	148–136 grains . . (some lighter)	grm. 9·60–8·80
Third or tetrobol . .	46–38 grains . .	grm. 3 –2·46
Sixth or diobol . . .	22–18 grains . .	grm. 1·40–1·16

The only other district which struck on a similar standard is that of the minting tribes of the Thraco-Macedonian coast. But their stater is half a gramme heavier, and they divide it by two and do not strike any coin equivalent to the Lycian thirds.

This standard is difficult to explain. It cannot be the Attic, being decidedly too heavy. What is clear is that it is a system of thirds and sixths like that of the electrum coins or that of Corinth, and that the weight of the coins varies in a remarkable and inexplicable way (see p. 188).

Six and Head have called it Babylonic. But it cannot be the silver standard adopted by the Persians from Babylon. If we could with any confidence accept the statement of Herodotus that there was a talent in use for silver in the Persian Empire equal to 70 Euboic minae,[2] this would about give us the required weight. But Mommsen, with the general approval of numismatists, has corrected Herodotus's 70 to 78; and it is certain that if the Lydian and royal Persian silver coinage was minted on the Babylonic standard, 78 : 60 rather than 70 : 60 represents the true proportion of that standard to the Euboic. The fact that the stater in Lycia is divided into thirds and sixths, not into halves, is a strong reason for supposing that, whencesoever the standard may be derived, it is of Asiatic character.

The natural supposition would be that the heavier coins were the earlier, and that the lighter coins, which are practically of Attic standard, were struck towards the

[1] *B. M. Cat. Lycia*, pp. 1–10.

[2] Hdt. iii. 89. Julius Pollux (*Onom.* ix. 85) gives the same proportion as Herodotus. It is uncertain whether Herodotus is his authority or not.

middle of the fifth century, in the time of the Athenian Empire. Such an effect seems to have been produced in Thrace towards 440 B.C., by the spread of the Athenian sea-power, on the coins of Thasos and Neapolis.[1] But the misfortune is that the fabric of the Lycian coins does not bear out the theory. Coins of less than 140 grains weight were issued in the sixth century; indeed, some of the earliest we have are among the light specimens:

Obv. Fore-part of boar. *Rev.* Rude incuse square (Brit. Mus.). Weights, 136·2 grains (grm. 8·83), 143 grains (grm. 9·26). (B. T. XXI. 1.)

Thus the Lycian standard does not appear to have been originally the same as that of Persia; but it is exceptional.

It may be well briefly to sum up the conclusions of this chapter. Silver coinage appears in Asia at some of the Greek cities in the sixth century. The weight of it, the Aeginetan, and the drachmal system according to which it is divided, alike indicate an European influence; silver coinage seems to have spread from the Cyclades to the cities of the mainland. After the introduction of the gold staters of Croesus and the darics, these dominated the silver issues of Asia, and the Aeginetan weights survived only in a few districts, as stated above. The electrum coinage of the coast disappears; and in place of it the Greek cities strike silver coins on the two systems which work in with the daric and the gold bars or pellets of 130 grains (grm. 8·42) which preceded the daric, the systems called Persian and Phoenician. The properly European systems, the Euboic, Corinthian and Attic, get no footing in Asia. Whether any silver coins of Asia are earlier than the time of Croesus, excepting only those of Aeginetan weight, is improbable. It would simplify matters, from the historical point of view, if we could make the silver issues of the Asiatic standards subsequent in every case to the electrum issues; but we are scarcely at present able to affirm this with confidence.

[1] See Ch. XIV.

The districts dominated by the four systems, heavy Phoenician, light Phoenician, heavy Persian, and light Persian, may be mapped out clearly. Heavy Phoenician (Phocaean) dominates the coast north of the Hermus river, light Phoenician (Milesian) from the Hermus southward to Caria. Caria, with the Pontic region, retains the Aeginetan standard. The light Persian system prevails in Lycia, and the heavy Persian in Pamphylia and Cyprus. Thus what seems at first sight to be a chaos of weights is reduced by a careful scrutiny to a reasonable system. The wild assertion of Lenormant that Greek cities regulated the weight of their coins without regard to any external authority, or the customs even of their neighbours, turns out to be as inconsistent with the facts of the surviving coins as it is contrary to probability and reason. They were guided, as we should be, by considerations of commercial utility; though no doubt the force of tradition was stronger with them than with us.

CHAPTER X

EARLY COINS OF THRACE AND MACEDON

THE region comprising Southern Thrace and Eastern Macedon [1] must be regarded as one from the numismatic point of view. It was a region in which various streams of influence contended for the mastery, with the result that the variations of standard are many and frequent. It may be regarded as a meeting-point of European and Asiatic influences, the latter being in early times more powerful. We may discern five lines upon which various influences moved:

(1) The island of Thasos was a great source of precious metals, especially gold; and the neighbouring coast of Thrace, which was unequalled for richness in the precious metals, was much under its hegemony.

(2) The region of Chalcidice, including Mount Athos, was from a very early period fringed with colonies from Hellas, sent out principally from the great colonizing cities of Chalcis in Euboea and Corinth. Athens was also active in this district, and Neapolis, somewhat farther to the east, was regarded as a colony of Athens.

(3) The cities farther to the east, notably Abdera and Maronea, were colonized, not by the Greeks of Europe, but by those of Asia, and their relations were rather with Ionia than with Europe.

(4) The Kingdom of Macedon had a powerful inland influence. The Kings of Macedon boasted of Argive descent, and imported some Greek culture into the mountain valleys to the west of the Strymon, where the mass of the people were of Thracian and Paeonian descent.

[1] I use the current names: Mr. Svoronos, with some reason, suggests Paeonia as a more satisfactory name.

From 500 B.C. onwards the power of the kings gradually extended eastward. It is their coins, bearing the names of kings and so to be dated, which enable us to reduce to some order the mass of coins struck in the silver-producing districts of Mounts Pangaeus and Bertiscus.

(5) In the days of Darius and Xerxes Persian armies crossed the Hellespont, and made their way along the Thracian coast. These armies needed abundant supplies, and must have increased the demand for a coinage.

I. Thasian Standard.

The coins of Thasos must be regarded as giving the key to the coinages of the neighbouring districts of Thrace. Thasos was in very early times used by the Phoenicians as a source of gold. At some early but unassigned period they were succeeded by colonists from Paros, who are said by Herodotus[1] to have made a great revenue from gold mines on the island and on the neighbouring coast shortly before the invasion of Xerxes. We have, however, with the doubtful exception of rare coins in electrum,[2] no early gold coins of Thasos. But the produce of the silver mines on the coast adjoining Thasos and under Thasian dominion was issued as coin during most of the sixth century—abundant silver coins, notable for their type and style. The type is a satyr carrying off a woman. (**Pl. IV. 1; B. M. IV. 3.**) The style is so massive and vigorous, though somewhat rude, that Brunn made it one of the corner-stones to support his theory of a north Greek style of art mainly Ionic in tendency. We may distinguish a rounder and more lumpish fabric which belongs to the earlier part, from a flat fabric which belongs to the later part, of the sixth century.

It was doubtless in imitation of the coins of Thasos that certain of the tribes of the mainland took to minting. The influence of Thasos may be observed alike in the monetary standard used and in the types chosen. The latter are taken from the circle of Dionysus, a satyr pursuing or

[1] VI. 46. [2] See Ch. IV.

carrying a nymph, or a centaur bearing a woman in his arms. Sometimes the type is a horseman beside his horse. In the Pangaean district the moneying tribes were the Orrescii and Zaeelii: we know hardly anything about them; not even their exact geographical location. In the Emathian district coins of the same weight and types were issued by the Letaei.

It has been the custom to suppose that these tribes were in a very backward state of civilization, and that their comparatively early entry into the list of peoples who issued coins must be attributed partly to the abundance of silver in their country, and partly to the influence of Hellenic cities founded on the coast. But in a remarkable article [1] Mr. Svoronos has claimed for them a higher state of culture; and certainly, so far as the coins go, they testify to the existence of a robust and vigorous, if somewhat coarse, school of art in the district.

Whether the coins of the same class, and usually attributed to the cities of Aegae and Ichnae in Macedon, really belong to those cities is not certain. Dr. Svoronos maintains that in Macedon coinage was only issued by the kings; that the coins given to Aegae are wrongly attributed, and that the Ichnae which struck coins was not the city in Macedon, but one farther to the west on the river Angites.

The standard on which the Thasian coins were issued is noteworthy. The staters weigh 152–140 grains (grm. 9·84–9·07), and sometimes nearly reach 160 grains; the drachms are of rather lower standard, not exceeding 70 grains (grm. 4·53); there are also obols (type two dolphins) weighing 10–7 grains (grm. 0·65–0·45), and half obols (type one dolphin) weighing 5 grains (grm. 0·32).[2] This standard has been by numismatists regarded as a light variety of the Perso-Babylonic standard, of which the drachm weighs

[1] *Numismatique de la Péonie et de la Macédoine* (*Journ. Internat. de Numism. archéol.*, vol. xv).

[2] We should naturally expect the coin with two dolphins for type to be a diobol, and the coin with one dolphin to be the obol. But an obol of only 5 grains is unknown.

86 grains (grm. 5·57), which was adopted by Croesus and the Persians. It seems, however, absurd to suppose that a Thasian drachm of a gramme less weight would be in currency accepted as the equivalent of the Persian siglos: we know that provincial issues in relation to standard coins were tariffed not above, but below, their metal value. Thus it seems best to speak of the Thasian standard as one apart. The remarkable fluctuations in the weight of the coins is also difficult to explain. It is indeed probable that the coins of Thasos issued at the time of Athenian supremacy (465–424 B.C.) were adapted to the Attic standard, since they fall to its level. But in the case of earlier coins it does not seem possible to find any reasonable explanation for their variation. A similar problem met us in Lycia.[1] But though the Lycian stater in weight approximates to that of Thasos, it is divided not into drachms but into thirds, which seems to show that the two standards cannot be identical.

In the field, on the coins of the Letaei, there appear often a number of globules or pellets, which should, one would think, be marks of value.

Before 500 B.C.

Didrachm, six pellets, three pellets. (**B. M. IV. 4; B. T. L.**)

Diobol, three pellets.

After 500 B.C.

Didrachm, three pellets.

Diobol, two pellets.

On some coins of each kind the number of pellets is smaller; but it is in such cases impossible to be sure that some pellets cut in the die were not outside the area of the coin as struck. It seems impossible to recover the meaning of these pellets. Apparently they would give an unit of 25 grains (grm. 1·62), afterwards raised (not lowered) to 50 grains (grm 3·24). This unit cannot be the pound of

[1] Ch. IX, p. 183.

bronze or copper, as bronze was not a measure of value in this region.

The early coins bearing as type a Gorgon's head (**Pl. IV. 5**; **B. M. IV. 6**), and corresponding in weight and fabric to those of Thasos, have usually been attributed to Neapolis, which is described in the Athenian tribute-lists as situated *παρ' Ἀντισάραν*. It is not certain that Neapolis was a colony of Athens, though at a later time it was closely connected with that city.[1] Svoronos,[2] however, tries to show that the Gorgon-head coins, some of which are marked with the letter Α and some with Σ, were issued by the two cities of Scabala and Antisara, both on the sea-coast of the rich district belonging to Daton, and not far from Thasos. Theopompus[3] mentions Scabala as a place belonging to the Eretrians, which would account for the Gorgon type, since the Gorgon is on the early coins of Eretria. Neapolis was apparently a later foundation.

II. Abderite Standard.

We can date back the beginning of the coinage of Abdera to the time of the foundation of the city about 544 B.C. For before that time the people of Teos, the mother-city of Abdera, had issued coins, with the same type as that used at Abdera, the griffin, but of a different weight, the Aeginetan. The colonists who settled at Abdera carried with them the type of the griffin, probably Apolline, but did not preserve the monetary standard. It is in fact only by considering the standard used that we can distinguish the early coins of Teos from those of Abdera.

This change of standard is a very remarkable fact, and one requiring explanation. When Abdera was founded, few coins were struck in Thrace or Macedon, except in Chalcidice. We may, however, assign to this early age the earliest coins of Thasos and those of the neighbouring mainland, of thick and rounded fabric, which follow the

[1] See an inscription of 356 B.C.: Schöne, *Griech. Reliefs*, No. 48, p. 23.

[2] *l. c.*, p. 232.

[3] Quoted by Stephanus, *s. v.* Σκάβαλα.

Thasian standard. The large coins of the tribes of the valley of the Strymon were certainly later, and in all probability took their standard from Abdera, as did in later times the Macedonian Kings. Thus there was not, so far as we know, any precedent for the Abderite standard to be found in Thrace. It would be most natural to seek for a commercial reason for it. The reason which naturally suggests itself is that on leaving their city and settling in Thrace, the people of Teos found themselves in a different commercial connexion. The Aeginetan standard, which they had hitherto used, was isolated in the midst of Ionia, though both in Pontus and in Caria it was in general vogue: at least this was the case after such cities as Cyme, Miletus, and Chios had given up their early sixth-century issues on the Aeginetan standard. Why the Abderites chose the particular variety of standard, which as a matter of fact they did select, is less evident. We should have expected them to adopt either the standard of Thasos, the wealthiest city of Thrace; or if they preferred an Ionian connexion, to adopt the North Ionian standard of Phocaea, or the South Ionian standard of Miletus. The people who remained at Teos still kept to the Aeginetan standard: we may well suppose that there was a sharp collision between the conservatives who were willing to submit to Persian rule and the more nationalist and freedom-loving citizens who preferred expatriation to submission.

The standard which the Abderites actually adopted, and fully naturalized in Thrace, was half-way between the Phocaean and Milesian. The stater weighed about 230 grains (grm. 14·90), and most nearly corresponds to the coins issued at a later time in Phoenicia. We can, however, scarcely regard its introduction as a proof of Phoenician influence, since it was the domination of Persia and the Phoenician allies of Persia which the people of Abdera were most anxious to avoid.

The Abderite coin-standard, whencesoever derived, being thus planted on the Thracian coast, spread both towards the east and towards the west. On the east it was used by the cities of Dicaea and Maronea in the sixth century. Dicaea in Thrace, which must be distinguished from the Dicaea in Chalcidice, a colony of Eretria, is called in the Athenian tribute-lists Dicaea near Abdera. To this city are given very early coins with a head of Heracles on the obverse and an incuse on the reverse, of Thasian weight, 150 grains, or the double[1] (grm. 9·72 or 19·40). These are succeeded by coins with a very similar head of Heracles on one side, and on the other the letters ΔIK and the head and shoulders of an ox, in an incuse: weight 112–110 grains (grm. 7·25–7·12). These coins are of Abderite weight. Mr. Head[2] gives them to the time of Darius: I think them somewhat earlier. The type of the reverse seems to be taken from the coins of Samos, which island was about 530–520 B.C. at the height of its power under Polycrates. The Samians at this time were predominant on the north shore of the Propontis, where were their colonies Perinthus and Bisanthe. It is therefore reasonable to regard Samos as probably in close relations with Abdera and Dicaea. Very possibly indeed Dicaea may have been a Samian colony. Some of the late coins of Perinthus have as type a head of Heracles with the inscriptions TON KTICTHN IΩNΩN on the obverse, and ΠΕΡΙΝΘΙΩΝ ΔΙC ΝΕΩΚΟΡΩΝ· Heracles then may have been regarded as oekist alike at Perinthus and Dicaea; and his head on coins of the latter city would be quite in place.

The coinage of Maronea, which was almost certainly an Ionian colony, follows the same lines as that of Dicaea. Before the middle of the sixth century Maronea also used the Thasian weight, and afterwards went over to that of Abdera. We have staters of 150–132 grains (grm. 9·72–8·54) and obols of 14·5 grains (grm. 0·94). Coins of later fabric, and bearing the name of the city, weigh, for the stater, 118–114 grains (grm. 7·63–7·36), and for the half-stater 56–50 grains (grm. 3·62–3·24). There was a tradition, cited

[1] Head, *H. N.*, ed. 2, p. 252. This is the only known tetradrachm of this standard.

[2] *B. M. Cat. Thrace*, p. 115.

by Scymnus, of a Chian colony about 540 B.C.; and this might account for the somewhat high weight of the staters of Maronea, as the standard of Chios is nearer to the Phocaean than to the Abderite weight.

It is clear that in the early days of Persian dominion the southern shore of Thrace served as a place of refuge for the Ionians who would not accept the Persian yoke, and thus it became in all respects largely Ionized.

We have next to trace the westward course of the standard of Abdera. It was not adopted at Thasos nor at Lete. But of the mining tribes, the Orrescii appear to have adopted it. Their earliest coins, of lumpy fabric, are on the Thasian standard: the later and larger coins, of flat fabric with a neat incuse square on the reverse, are of Abderite weight.[1] Whether the latter weight wholly superseded the former, or whether the tribes used both standards at once, is not an easy question to settle: in any case there must have been some recognized connexion between the coins struck on the two standards. To this question I will return.

About 500 B.C. there appear on the southern shore of Thrace a number of coins of great size, almost the largest which have come down to us. It is reasonable to think that these coins were the result of Persian influence, and issued at the time when the great Persian armies of Darius and Xerxes passed that way. War, even in those days, necessitated a great store of specie; and if the tribes of Paeonia had to pay tribute to the Persians, or to buy supplies of food for their armies, they would greatly need an abundance of coin. It is to be observed that the issues of decadrachms by Gelon at Syracuse, and by the Athenians, took place about 480 B.C., also as a result of Persian or Carthaginian invasion.

Notable among these great coins are those of the Derrones. They bear the inscription *Δερρονικός* or *Δερρονικόν*, and were formerly attributed to a king called Derronikos. But

[1] *B. M. Cat. Macedon*, pp. 145–9.

Gaebler[1] has shown that the inscription is an ethnic. What was the seat of the Derrones is somewhat doubtful; but the coins come from Istip near the river Axius:

Obv. Draped personage seated in a car drawn by an ox: above, helmet; beneath, flower. *Rev.* Triquetra of legs, and acanthus ornaments. Weight, 624 grains (grm. 40·43). Brit. Mus. (**B. M. V. 17.**)

On another coin of similar type, weight 610 grains (grm. 39·48), Mr. Svoronos[2] has read the legend Euergetes, the name probably of a Paeonian chief. With these coins go others issued by the Laeaei of similar type and weight,[3] but with a figure of Pegasus on the reverse.

Of lesser size and weight are the coins issued at the same period by other tribes, the Bisaltae, Edoni, Orrescii, Ichnaei, and Sapaei. A type adopted by the Bisaltae was a herdsman accompanying two bulls (**B. M. V. 16; Pl. IV. 7**): that adopted by the Edoni was the same; on the coins appear the name of the King Getas. The Orrescii and Bisaltae adopted the type of a spearman walking beside a horse. (**Pl. IV. 8.**) The weight of all these coins is 420–440 grains (grm. 27·20–28·50). There can be little doubt that as the coins of the Derrones were 12 drachm pieces of Abderite standard, so these are 8 drachm pieces of that standard.

A fixed landmark in the history of the early coins of Thrace is given us by the earliest of the money of Alexander I, King of Macedon, which bears his name, and can be definitely assigned to him.

Obv. Warrior carrying two spears standing on the farther side of a bridled horse r. *Rev.* ΑΛΕΞΑΝΔΡΟ round a shallow incuse square, within which a raised linear square. Weight, 450–400 grains (grm. 29–26). (**Pl. IV. 9.**)

This coin, alike in type and in weight, is almost identical with the coins of the Bisaltae: one was found in Egypt

[1] *Zeitschr. f. Num.*, xx. 289. [2] *Journ. Intern.*, xv, p. 200.
[3] *B. M. Cat. Macedon*, p. 151.

with early coins of Terone and the Bisaltae. When Alexander acquired the territory of the Bisaltae, which he did shortly after the Persian wars, he continued the coinage in his own name, maintaining the same types and standard. His coins are, however, somewhat more advanced in style than those of the Bisaltae, the incuse of the reverse being surrounded with an inscription. The weight is clearly Abderite.

The early silver coins of Thasian standard are so irregular in weight that it is almost impossible to determine what amount of silver they were intended to contain. They seem to grow lighter with time until they approximate to the Attic standard, about 450 B.C.

There must have been some means of relating one to the other the coins of the Abderite and Thasian standards. The Orrescii struck on both standards, and if the two issues were not actually contemporary, they were so nearly contemporary that there must have been some understanding as to their respective values. According to Brandis the coins of the Babylonic and Phoenician standards stood thus related:

Babylonic stater $= \frac{1}{10}$ gold Daric.
Phoenician stater $= \frac{1}{15}$ two Darics.
Babylonic : Phoenician : : $7\frac{1}{2}$: 10 : : 3 : 4.

But this applies to the Babylonic stater weighing 168 grains: in Thrace the Thasian standard is ten or more grains lighter than the Babylonic, whereas the Abderite standard is on a level with the Phoenician. Thus two-thirds would be much nearer to the actual proportion of value between the staters than three-fourths. And that this relation held in practice seems to be indicated by the facts of some of the coinages. The Bisaltae, for example, issue at the same time coins of 440–445 grains (grm. 28·50–28·30) and coins of 61–68 grains (grm. 4–4·40). The larger coins may well be octadrachms of Abderite weight. The smaller coins can scarcely be drachms of that weight; but must rather be drachms or half-staters of Thasian weight, and must have passed as octobols or sixths of the octadrachm of Abderite weight. Thus the octadrachms of Abderite weight struck by the Bisaltae are very nearly of thrice the weight of the Thasian staters issued by the same tribe. The relations between the standards being thus simple, coins struck on either might well circulate together, just as did the coins of Corinth and Athens, which bore a similarly simple relation to one another.

A few words must be added in regard to M. Svoronos' important paper already cited. This writer, in opposition to Head and other numismatists, denies that there was any clashing of monetary standards in the Thraco-Macedonian district, which he calls Paeonia. He regards all the coins as belonging to a standard which he calls Paeonian.

8 drachms	40·80 grm.	630 grains.
6 "	30·60 "	472 "
2 "	10·20 "	158 "
1 "	5·10 "	79 "

Such a view might seem plausible, if we left out of account the influence of Abdera, which was certainly great in those parts. At Abdera, in the sixth century, besides the tetradrachm of 230 grains (grm. 14·90), there were current coins of double the weight, 460 grains (grm. 29·80); and these must certainly have passed as octadrachms of the local standard. When then we find that the Bisaltae, Orrescii, Edoni, Ichnaei, and Sapaei issued coins of exactly this weight, it is scarcely possible to disconnect them from the influence of Abdera.

Mr. Svoronos makes an exception from his Paeonian standard for one set of coins, having the type of Pegasus (**B. M. IV. 12, 13**), which he gives conjecturally to the Crestonians.[1] These coins are found at Salonica, and weigh 14·30 grm. (220 grains) or less. Svoronos and Babelon call the standard the Milesian, but it must clearly be that of Abdera. And if these coins are of Abderite weight, it is reasonable to think that other coins of the region follow the same standard. Abdera clearly set the

[1] Babelon, *Traité*, p. 1239, Pl. LVIII; p. 803, Pl. XXXVI.

fashion in striking coins of unusual size; and the other cities or tribes, in following that fashion, kept the Abderite weight.

III. Chalcidice.

The cities of Chalcidice, such as Acanthus, Terone, Olynthus, Scione, Mende, Potidaea, Dicaea, Aeneia, all follow the same course. They strike tetradrachms according to the Attic standard (270 grains; grm. 17·50); but the divisions are not Attic drachms, but Corinthian, of 45–38 grains (grm. 2·91–2·46). Mr. Head in the *Historia Numorum* calls these latter tetrobols; and of course they would pass as tetrobols of Attic standard. But proof that they were intended rather for drachms is not wanting. At Olynthus[1] was struck a coin of double the weight (86·3 grains); and Mr. Head consistently calls it an octobol; but since the type is a horseman leading a second horse, which in Sicily is the usual type for the didrachm, it is fair to judge that it at Olynthus also indicates the didrachm (Corinthian). Thus the ordinary coins of half this weight, bearing as type a single horseman, would be Corinthian drachms. Hemidrachms of Corinthian weight occur at Acanthus and Potidaea, and in the case of the latter city again the type suggests that the coin is not an Attic diobol but a Corinthian hemidrachm; it is a naked horseman on the *fore-part* of a prancing horse.[2] These facts indicate that, whereas the stater was intended to pass as equivalent to the ordinary silver tetradrachm of Athens, the divisions follow the Corinthian standard. Probably the chief seat of Corinthian influence was Potidaea. We know that that city was a Corinthian colony, and received yearly magistrates called epidamiurgi from Corinth.

I know of only one set of coins attributed to a city of Chalcidice which is of the weight of an Attic drachm. This is given to Acanthus.

[1] *Hist. Num.*, ed. 2, p. 208.

[2] *Hist. Num.*, ed. 2, p. 212.

Obv. Bull kneeling, head turned back; above or in exergue, flower. *Rev.* Incuse square. *Hist. Num.*, ed. 2, 205. Weight, 62 grains (grm. 4).

This coin, however, is not inscribed, and its attribution is very doubtful. It must be placed among the uncertain coins of Macedon, and probably is a light example of a drachm of Thasian standard.

The standard, then, in use in Chalcidice is the Attic, with Corinthian divisions. It would be natural to expect the Euboic weight in any coins issued before 550 B.C., when in the time of Peisistratus the true Attic standard first appears at Athens, and influences the issues of Euboea and Corinth. We have therefore to consider the question whether all the extant coins of the district are later than that date. Those of Acanthus, Terone, Aeneia, and most of the cities certainly are. The fabric at Acanthus and Terone is flat and akin to that of the coins of Lete and Thasos in their second, not their earliest form. The date of this fabric is given us by the coins of Alexander I of Macedon as belonging to about 500 B.C. But there are coins of the district of an earlier style, such as:

Potidaea.

Obv. Poseidon on horse. *Rev.* Incuse square.
Weight, 266–271 grains (grm. 17·20–17·57).

Mende.

Obv. Ass standing, crow perched on his back. *Rev.* Incuse of eight triangles.
Weight, 262 grains (grm. 16·97). Brussels.

Scione.

Obv. Helmet. *Rev.* Incuse of eight triangles.
Weight, 263–262 grains (grm. 17–16·97). Paris.[1] (B. T. LII. I.)

Olynthus.

Obv. Quadriga facing. *Rev.* Incuse of eight triangles.
Weight, 259 grains (grm. 16·78). Sandeman Collection.

[1] B. M. IV. 8. Of the same period is an early drachm of Mende (*Num. Chron.*, 1900, p. 6): weight, 42 grains (grm. 2·72).

These certainly precede in date the coins of flat fabric, but not by many years. They do not appear to be in any case earlier than the coins of Abdera, which cannot precede 543 B.C. There is, therefore, no reason why they should not be of later date than the Peisistratid tetradrachms of Athens, which began about 560 B.C. At the same time the standard used by Peisistratus does occur earlier at Samos, Cyrene, and other places. (See Chaps. I, XIII.)

IV. The Thracian Chersonese.

The Thracian Chersonese stands by itself in regard to coinage. The early money of the district consists of tetradrachms and smaller denominations of Attic weight, with Corinthian sub-divisions, as in Chalcidice.

Obv. Lion advancing to r., head turned to l., paw raised. *Rev.* XEP (sometimes). Head of Athena in incuse square. Weight, 264 grains (grm. 17·10).

Obv. Fore-part of lion looking back, paw raised. *Rev.* Incuse square divided into four. Weight, 43–38 grains (2·75–2·40) [1]: also the half of this.

This district, as is well known, was a hereditary kingdom or appanage under the rule of the wealthy Athenian family of the Philaidae. Miltiades I, son of Cypselus, was the first ruler, about 550 B.C.: he founded a colony at Cardia, and cut off the Chersonese from the incursions of the Thracian barbarians by a wall, thus making it almost an island. The type of Athena has reference to the native city of Miltiades: the lion type probably belongs to Miletus, for somewhat earlier the Chersonese had been within the circle of Milesian influence. It is, however, only the type of the coin which reminds us of Miletus. The weight of the stater, and the manner of its division, corresponds to the coinage of Chalcidice. We have seen that the smaller coin in that district must be a Corinthian drachm rather than an Attic tetrobol. It is therefore

[1] Babelon, *Traité*, ii. 1, p. 1228, Pl. LVII, 15, 16.

probable that the conditions of trade were the same in Chalcidice and in the Chersonesus. On the map, the Corintho-Attic standard looks out of place among the Babylonic and Abderite weights of Southern Thrace. But the Chersonese of Thrace was on the high road from Athens, Aegina, and Corinth to the Pontus, whence those thickly populated cities obtained their supplies of dried fish, corn, hides, timber, and other necessaries of life and materials for manufacture.

It is natural that each city of Greece should have its special port of call at the entrance to the Pontus. Aegina appears to have had some connexion with Sinope. Megara was the mother city of Byzantium and Chalcedon, and doubtless kept up a connexion with them: neither of them struck coins until late in the fifth century. Cardia in the Thracian Chersonese would be the natural entrepôt of Athens, as its ruler was an Athenian citizen. Sigeum was also a stronghold of Athens. The distant Panticapaeum in the Crimea appears like Sinope in its early issues of coins to adhere to the Aeginetan standard.[1]

To sum up: the key to the coin-standards of Southern Thrace is to be found in the action and counter-action of the commercial influences radiating from Thasos on one side and Abdera on the other. Chalcidice stands apart, and with it goes the Thrasian Chersonese. The influence of the expeditions of Darius and Xerxes does not seem to have resulted in a change of standard, but it may be conjectured in the issue of coins of unusually large denomination.

[1] Babelon, *Traité*, ii. 1, p. 401.

CHAPTER XI

COINS OF SOUTH ITALY, 600–480 B.C.

The earliest Greek coins struck in Italy are those issued by several cities, of uniform flat fabric, bearing on one side as type the arms of the city, and on the other side the same type reversed and incuse. The cities and types are as follows:

Tarentum. Apollo kneeling; Taras on dolphin. (**B. M. VII. 3, 4.**)

Metapontum. Ear of barley. (**B. M. VII. 10.**)

Siris and Pyxus. Bull with head turned back. (**B. M. VIII. 14.**)

Sybaris. Bull with head turned back. (**B. M. VIII. 15.**)

Laüs. Man-headed bull looking back. (**B. M. VII. 8.**)

Poseidonia. Poseidon thrusting with trident. (**B. M. VII. 12.**)

Croton. Tripod. (**B. M. VIII. 19.**)

Caulonia. Apollo with winged genius on arm, and stag before him. (**B. M. VIII. 17; Pl. V. 1.**)

Rhegium. Man-headed bull, kneeling.

Zancle in Sicily. Dolphin in harbour.

Only a few years later we find at some cities a variety, the incuse device of the reverse becomes different from the type of the obverse. Thus at Tarentum we have as obverse type Apollo kneeling; as reverse type, Taras on dolphin. (**Pl. V. 2.**) Later still, but before 480, we have two types in relief, Taras on dolphin; hippocamp. (**Pl. V. 3.**) At Metapontum we have as obverse, ear of barley; as reverse, bucranium (sixths of stater only). At Croton we have as obverse, tripod; as reverse, flying eagle.

These coins are by no means of rude or primitive make, but, on the contrary, of careful and masterly work; and the types are some of the finest examples we possess of fully-formed Greek archaic art. Thus it would seem that coinage was introduced into Italy fully developed; and many questions are suggested as to the occasion when it was introduced, the reasons for the peculiar fabric, the meaning of the uniformity, and the like. We will consider in regard to this whole class of coins (1) date, (2) fabric and the reasons for it, (3) monetary standards.

(1) The date of the earliest Greek coins of Italy can be only approximately determined. Siris issued coins before its destruction by the people of Metapontum, Croton, and Sybaris; but the date of this destruction is unknown to us, except that obviously it must precede the destruction of Sybaris. Fynes Clinton, on reasonable evidence, fixes the date of the foundation of Sybaris to 720 B.C., and its destruction to 510 B.C. The coins of Sybaris show some development in style, and are found in abundance; their beginning therefore can scarcely be placed later than 550 B.C.

The same date is suggested by the facts of the coinage of Zancle in Sicily. Zancle, with its close neighbour Rhegium, forms a group apart, transitional between the coins of Italy and those of Sicily, at some periods more closely conforming to the Italian type of coin, at other periods to the Sicilian. Before 500 B.C. the Italian influences prevail, and the coinage at Zancle is of the peculiar fabric introduced in Italy. Sir A. Evans, discussing a find of coins at Zancle,[1] points out that previous to 494 B.C. there were several successive issues of coins there, passing from the types above mentioned to the type in relief on the reverse, a succession implying a period of at least half a century.

Valuable evidence as to the date of the early incuse issues of Italy is furnished by the restrikings of coins at Metapontum. For some unknown reason that city appears to have been especially addicted to the custom of using the coins of other cities as blanks, whereon to impress her own types. Coins of this class are sometimes restruck on pieces

[1] *Num. Chron.*, 1896, p. 105.

of Corinth which have a mill-sail incuse on the reverse (Pl. V. 5), a class of money which precedes the introduction of the head of Athena, and must be dated as early as 550 B.C. And it must be observed that this coin of Metapontum is not of the earliest flat fabric: this may, however, be the result of using a Corinthian coin as a blank. Metapontine incuse coins of the later and thicker class are restruck on pieces of Syracuse of the time of Hiero I (obverse, head of Persephone amid dolphins; reverse, horseman) and on pieces of Gela of the same date (obverse, head of river-god; reverse, horseman) and of Agrigentum.[1]

Thus it would seem that at Metapontum the issue of the incuse series of coins lasted more than half a century, until 470 B.C. or later. At some other cities it cannot have come down to so late a date. At Rhegium and Zancle, for instance, it is superseded by coins with an ordinary type on both sides before the arrival of the Samian exiles about 494. As regards Tarentum Sir A. Evans writes[2]: 'At Tarentum the issue of the incuse pieces must have been of but short duration. From the evidence of finds there can be but little doubt that the first Tarentine coins of double relief, those, namely, which exhibit a wheel on one side, were in existence some years before the destruction of Sybaris in 510, and that the first issues of the succeeding class on which a hippocamp appears must have been more or less contemporary with that event' (Pl. V. 3). Evans adds in regard to other cities, 'In the Cittanova finds, buried at latest before the end of the sixth century, we find the relief coinage of Kroton, Kaulonia, and Laos already beginning.' At Sybaris down to the time of its destruction none but incuse coin was issued, if we except some obols which have on the reverse the letters MY. Thus it would appear that the incuse coinage of South Italy begins about 550 B.C., continuing at most cities until the end of the century, and at Metapontum for thirty years later.

[1] As to these restrikings see *B. M. Cat. Italy*, pp. 239–40; Babelon, *Traité*, ii. 1, 1403-6, Pl. LXVI.

[2] *The Horsemen of Tarentum*, p. 2, where the evidence of finds is set forth.

(2) The fabric and its meaning. As a matter of development, the prototype of the coins of Italy would seem to be the early coins of Corinth, having on the obverse an archaic Pegasus, and on the reverse an incuse maeander pattern or swastika. These latter belong to the first half of the sixth century. In fabric they are flat and spread, offering a remarkable contrast to the contemporary coins of Athens, Euboea, and Aegina; beyond doubt they furnished in great part the currency of South Italy in the middle of the sixth century: some of the coins of Metapontum, as we have seen, were restruck on them; and they are of the same weight (Euboic not Attic) as the earliest Italian coins.

But the peculiar arrangement of placing on the reverse the same type as on the obverse, only incuse and retrograde, is the invention of some notable Greek of South Italy. Probably he was merely imitating the repoussé bronze work which was at the time largely used for the decoration of the person, chests, tripods and the like,[1] and which seems to have been distinctive of Argos and Corinth. The peculiar pattern, called a cable border, with which the type is encircled on the coins, is characteristic of this bronze work. A Corinthian bronze mould in the Ashmolean Museum[2] presents us with a whole series of figures cut in it which might almost have served as the dies for coins: all that would be necessary would be to make a punch to fit roughly into such die; then a thin round blank would be placed between the two and stamped.

It has been suggested as a reason for the introduction of the fabric that it would make forgery more difficult. But a little consideration will make us reject this notion. The fabric was usual in the case of decorative bronze plates: it was in fact more in use for bronze than for silver, and nothing would be easier than by this method to produce coins of bronze, and then to wash them with silver. A considerable number of the specimens in our museums are

[1] See De Ridder, *De ectypis aeneis*.

[2] *Journ. Hell. Stud.*, xvi, p. 323.

bronze coins thus washed. Thus the fabric in fact offered unusual facilities to forgers. Some other reason must be sought for its introduction: at present I have none to suggest, except the above-mentioned commonness of repoussé work.

By degrees the coins of South Italy grow thicker and less spread. Then at some cities, as we have seen, comes a transitional stage, in which the incuse fabric is retained, but the reverse type is different from that of the obverse. At other cities the change of reverse type from incuse to relief takes place without this intermediate stage.

Some writers have seen in the uniformity of the fabric of South Italian coins proofs of the existence of an alliance, not merely monetary but political; and much has been written as to the efficacy of the working of Pythagoras and his followers in the formation of a close federation among Greek cities in Italy. This, however, is play of imagination. Pythagoras does appear to have founded something like an order, and through his followers he exercised great influence at Croton; but his working was not in the direction of politics. The date of his migration to Italy, moreover, not earlier than 540 B.C., is too late to affect the earliest Italian coinage. That there were in early times frequent conventions of a monetary kind between Greek cities of Italy probably indicating political co-operation, we know from the inscriptions of extant coins. We have money struck in common by Croton and Sybaris, by Siris and Pyxus, by Sybaris and Poseidonia, by Metapontum and Poseidonia, by Croton and Pandosia, by Croton and Temesa, by Croton and Zancle. We may with probability conjecture that the occasions of these alliances were usually offered by the necessity to make head against the warlike tribes of the interior, Samnites and others, the same pressure which in later times caused the Greek cities to call in the Epirote Alexander, son of Neoptolemus. But the very existence of these more special alliances disproves the existence of any general federation of the Greek cities. Very probably the occasion of the issue was mere commercial convenience, especially in the case where Croton and Zancle strike in conjunction.

(3) In Southern Italy, during the period 550–480 B.C., Corinthian influence is predominant. The great majority of the Greek cities, Laüs, Terina, Caulonia, Croton, Sybaris, Metapontum, all in early times struck coins on a system, in which the stater weighed 128 grains (grm. 8·29) or somewhat less, and the chief lesser coin, the third of this, 42–40 grains (grm. 2·72–2·59). There can be no doubt that these lesser coins were reckoned as drachms: the proof of this is to be found in the marks of value on certain coins of Croton and Metapontum.

Croton.

Obv. ϘPO (retrogr.). Tripod-lebes. *Rev.* OO. Fore-part of Pegasus flying l. Weight, 12·7 grains (grm. 0·82). *B. M. Cat.*, 348, 58.

Obv. ϘP. Tripod-lebes; in field ivy leaf. *Rev.* O over O. Hare r. Weight, 10·2 grains (grm. 0·66); another, 11·9 grains (grm. 0·76). *Ibid.* 60–61.

Metapontum.

Obv. OO. Ear of barley. *Rev.* OO. Barleycorn, incuse. Weight, 12·2 grains (grm. 0·80). *B. M. Cat.*, 242, 44.

These coins are clearly diobols, and being such must be of Corinthian standard. The hemidrachm of 20 grains, and the obol of 6–7 grains occur at several of these cities.

The difference between the system of Chalcidice and that of Greek Italy is that in the latter country not only the divisions but also the staters follow the Corinthian standard. The stater in South Italy is somewhat low in weight, below the level even of the Euboic standard. It by no means rises to the level of the Sicilian coinages. The reason of this must be local, in the equation to the bronze litrae of Italy.

It is noteworthy that whereas Sybaris stood, as Herodotus tells us, in the closest relations with Miletus, the coinage of Sybaris shows no trace of such connexion, but is uniform with that of the neighbouring cities.

In discussing the coins of Corinth, I have shown that there takes place at that city, about 550 B.C., a raising of the monetary standard, following the example of Athens, from 127 to 132 grains (grm. 8·22 to 8·55), that is, in effect, from Euboic to Attic weight. This change does not take place in Italy; but the lower standard of 127 grains or thereabouts is retained, and in fact the coinage soon falls almost everywhere to a lower level still.

In regard to Tarentum, Sir A. Evans[1] observes that in the incuse coinage the silver stater alone was issued. In the earliest coinage with double relief, fractions were indeed struck, but 'on a different system from that of the other cities. Whilst in the Achaean colonies the monetary unit was divided on the Corinthian system into thirds and sixths, the early Tarentine divisions are by halves and again by fifths, combining thus the Attic drachm and the Syracusan litra.' The Syracusan litra equated with the tenth of the Attic didrachm or Corinthian tridrachm, seems to have been current in South Italy as well as in Sicily, possibly as far north as Cumae, though later in Campania the heavier Romano-Oscan libra was the standard.[2] The types of the early litrae of Tarentum are, obverse, cockle-shell; reverse, wheel. Weights 12·5–11 grains (grm. 0·8–0·7).

There are two cities which we should expect to be among the earliest to strike coins, but they do not appear in the list above given. These are Cumae, founded from Euboea at a very early time; and Velia or Hyele, which was a Phocaean colony of the middle of the sixth century.

It is certainly remarkable that Cumae, the great source of Greek influence in Central Italy, should have struck no very early coins. Of those which have come down to us, the earliest, struck about 500 B.C., in the time of the tyrant Aristodemus, resemble the coins of Sicily rather than those of South Italy. They are as follows:

1. *Obv.* Head of Nymph, hair in archaic style. *Rev.* KYMAION

[1] *Horsemen of Tarentum*, p. 11.
[2] Haeberlin; cf. Hill, *Historical Roman Coins*, p. 5.

(retrograde). Mussel-shell; above it, drinking cup. Weight, 130 grains (grm. 8·42).[1]

2. *Obv.* Lion's scalp between two boars' heads. *Rev.* KYME. Mussel. Weight, 84 grains (grm. 5·42).[2]
3. *Obv.* Lion's scalp between two boars' heads. *Rev.* KYMAION. Mussel. Weight, 62 grains (grm. 4·02).[3]

The weights of these coins are remarkable and suggestive. We have the Attic didrachm, or Corinthian tridrachm, the Attic octobol or Corinthian didrachm, and the Attic drachm or Corinthian drachm and a half. There thus appears at Cumae, as in Chalcidice and in South Italy generally, a wavering between Attic and Corinthian standards. The second coin cited appears, like coins of the same weight in Sicily,[4] to be intended for a Corinthian didrachm; while the third is primarily Attic. The second coin connects Cumae closely with the Chalcidic cities of the straits of Messina, Rhegium, and Zancle, which also issued Corinthian didrachms at this time, and indicates that the line of its commerce passed directly by them. Later, about 480 B.C., Cumae adopted the so-called Campanian standard.

An unique phenomenon in the coinage of Italy is the striking at Cumae, about 480 B.C., of certain small coins of gold:

1. *Obv.* Archaic female head wearing sphendone. *Rev.* KYME. Mussel-shell. Weight, 22 grains (grm. 1·43). Paris.
2. *Obv.* Corinthian helmet. *Rev.* KYME. Mussel-shell. Weight, 5·5 grains (grm. 0·35). Brit. Mus.

The authenticity of these coins has been disputed, but is maintained by the officials of the museums to which they respectively belong. If genuine, the first will be a diobol and the second a hemiobol of Attic weight. M. Babelon[5]

[1] Santangelo Coll. Naples: another example, much oxidized, 8·10 grm. See Sambon, *Monn. Ant. de l'Italie*, p. 152, pl. II. 252; also *Num. Chron.*, 1896, p. 1.

[2] Paris, Sambon, p. 150, no. 244.

[3] Sambon, p. 150, no. 245, Berlin.

[4] See next chapter.

[5] *Traité*, ii. 1, 1439.

observes that the second coin is of later date than the first: he assigns it to about 470 B.C., while the first belongs to about 490 B.C. They present a perfectly unique phenomenon in the history of Italian coinage. Mr. Head[1] attempts to account for the striking of no. 2 by observing that, if gold be reckoned at fifteen times the value of silver, it would be the equivalent of the silver coins of the time which weigh 84 grains, and which he regards as Aeginetan drachms. But these silver coins appear to have been in fact Corinthian didrachms or Attic octobols. This equivalence then (gold hemiobol = 8 silver obols) would give a relation between gold and silver of 16 to 1, which is higher than any ratio of which we have evidence. If, therefore, these gold coins are really antique, they must have been struck on some quite unusual occasion, when a supply of gold was available, under some such circumstances as produced the gold coins of Agrigentum about 406 B.C., or those of Pisa near Elis about 364 B.C.

A certain amount of confusion has arisen from the notion that the foundation of Cumae was a joint enterprise of the Chalcidians of Euboea and the Aeolians of Cyme in Asia Minor. But the participation of the latter rests only on a statement of Ephorus, who, being a native of Cyme, was anxious to give the city all the credit he could. Most modern writers think that if any Cyme had a share in the settling of Cumae it was the small town of Cyme in Euboea (a place the existence of which is not well attested). We must therefore regard Cumae as exclusively Euboean, and be still more surprised at the appearance there of gold coins, which were not ever issued in Euboea in early times.

The earliest coins of Velia are not of Italian fabric, but resemble rather the coins of Asia Minor; indeed it has been thought by some numismatists that they were struck in Asia, and brought to Velia by the colonists who came from Phocaea about 544 B.C.

[1] *Hist. Num.*, ed. 2, p. 36.

1. *Obv.* Phoca or seal. *Rev.* Incuse square. Weight, 15·4 grains (grm. 1).
2. *Obv.* Fore-part of lion tearing the prey. *Rev.* Incuse square divided into four. Weight, 60–58 graius (grm. 3·88–3·75); division, 18 grains (grm. 1·16) or less: the half and smaller fractions of this were also struck.

Coins of this class were found in numbers in the hoard discovered at Auriol near Marseille,[1] together with a hemi-obol of Aegina, and a large number of small coins bearing as types griffin, half winged horse, winged boar, lion's head, calf's head, boar's head, dog's head, ram's head, head of Heracles, female head, and other types. Of these, some are of barbarous work; some are of excellent early fabric: nearly all have an incuse square on the reverse.

The weights of these coins being irregular and puzzling, it is hard to draw inferences from the smaller ones, which may be of almost any standard. Of the larger coins—

Types.	*Grains.*	*Grammes.*
Half winged horse,[2] weigh	43–42	2·78–2·73
Lion's head and head of Heracles, weigh .	42–41	2·73–2·65

Barbarous copies of these coins are of the same or slightly greater weight.

Most numismatists have regarded the standard of these coins as being that of Phocaea.[3] The standard of Phocaea both for electrum and silver coins is practically the Euboic, though the coins are a little below the Euboic standard, the drachm not usually exceeding 60 grains, and the hecte 40 grains. Mommsen, however, regarded the Phocaean standard imported into Italy as a form of the Phoenician. The standard on which the staters used at Velia, and the small coins of the Auriol find, were struck seems to be almost identical with that used by the Achaean cities of South

[1] See Babelon, *Traité*, ii. 1, p. 1571.

[2] M. Babelon, *Traité*, ii. 1, p. 1587, calls this a hippocamp. It is the regular type of Lampsacus; and in the *B. M. Cat.* it is rightly described as merely the fore-part of a winged horse, both wings showing, in archaic fashion.

[3] See Babelon, *l. c.*

Italy, with a drachm of 42 grains, which I have above called Corinthian. And a Phocaean third or trite was nearly equivalent to a Corinthian drachm. But there is an appreciable difference in weight between the coins of Velia which succeed those above cited and the coins of the Achaean cities.[1] The stater of the latter weighs up to 128 grains (grm. 8·30), the stater of Velia only up to 118 grains (grm. 7·64). And this lighter standard is used at Cumae after 480, and at Poseidonia from the beginning in 550 B.C. onwards.

The ordinary view, accepted by Head,[2] is that the Phocaean standard spread from Velia to Poseidonia and Cumae and afterwards to other cities, being in fact what is later called the Campanian standard. The difficulty is that the earliest coins of Velia and Cumae are not regulated by it; but only those after 480 B.C. But if the origin of the Campanian standard be doubtful, its existence and prevalence is certain.

In regard to Rhegium we shall have more to say in the next chapter.

[1] One coin of Velia, however, weighs 126 grains (grm. 8·16); it is early, contemporary with coins of the same weight struck at Cumae (see above).

[2] *Hist. Num.*, ed. 2, p. 86.

CHAPTER XII

COINS OF SICILY, 550–480 B.C.

In the earliest coinages of the cities of Sicily, as in those of the Italian cities, we may trace the influence of the coinage of Corinth.

The earliest of all appear to be the coins of Zancle of exactly the same fabric as those of the Italian cities, that is, with the type of the obverse incuse on the reverse, namely a dolphin within sickle-shaped harbour. These were published by Sir A. Evans[1] from a hoard found near Messina. He rightly observes that as there were two or three later series in the coinage before Zancle in 494 B.C. changed its name to Messana, the coins in question cannot be much later than the middle of the sixth century B.C., and must be contemporary with the Italian coins which they so closely resemble. Their weight is 90–79 grains (grm. 5·83–5·12). There are coins of this weight, not quite so early, at Himera and Naxos.

Zancle.

Obv. DANKVE. Dolphin within sickle-shaped bar of harbour. *Rev.* Same type incuse; or *Rev.* Dolphin incuse; or *Rev.* Scallop-shell in relief, in the midst of an incuse pattern. (Pl. V. 6.) Weights, 90 grains (grm. 5·83), 16 grains (grm. 1·02), 11·5 grains (grm. 0·75).

Himera.

Obv. HI. Cock. *Rev.* Flat incuse square, with eight compartments, four in relief. Weights, 90 grains (grm. 5·83) (B. M. IX. 27), 13·5 grains (grm. 0·87).

Naxos.

Obv. Head of Dionysus with ivy wreath. *Rev.* NAXION.

[1] *Num. Chron.*, 1896, pl. VIII. 1, 2, p. 104.

Bunch of grapes. Weights, 90 grains (grm. 5·83) (B. M. IX. 31), 13 grains (grm. 0·87), 12 grains (grm. 0·78).

With these coins we may class for weight the coin of Cumae above cited, and the coins of Rhegium,—RECINON retrograde: Bull with human head: *Rev.* Same type incuse. Weight, 87 grains (grm. 5·63). This coinage seems to have been imitated from that of Rhegium by the neighbouring Zancle. The Rhegine coin is of the same fabric as prevails in other Italian cities, though the standard of weight is different. The coins of Zancle are of the same weight and the same period, 550–500 B.C.

The standard (90 grains) on which these coins are struck is remarkable. Head calls it Aeginetan. But historically it is improbable that the Aeginetan standard would find its way to Sicily. It has been suggested that this standard may have come to the Sicilian Naxos from the Aegean island of that name, whence the Sicilian city was founded. But in fabric the coins show the influence not of Aegina but of Corinth. And the standard makes its first appearance, not at Naxos, but in the cities on either side of the straits of Messina, Rhegium, and Zancle.

The coins of Macedonian Chalcidice give us a hint. At Olynthus coins of 90 grains were issued which can be shown to be Corinthian didrachms.[1] And at other cities of Chalcidice we find Corinthian drachms and half-drachms. On this analogy we should naturally suppose the early coins of Rhegium and the Chalcidian cities of Sicily also to be of Corinthian standard, in fact didrachms and diobols. It is not, however, easy to explain why the curious weight of the didrachm was chosen, while all the other cities of Italy issued the Corinthian tridrachm of 130 grains, which was also (nearly) the Attic didrachm.

These 90-grain coins would pass naturally as thirds of the Attic tetradrachm of 270 grains; and early Attic tetradrachms were no doubt current in great quantities in Italy and Sicily at the time. But they were not contemporary

[1] Above, Chap. X.

with the Sicilian tetradrachms of later style and Attic weight, as they ceased to be issued when the regular Sicilian coinage of Attic weight came into existence.

It is a good rule, speaking generally, not to insist on the testimony of the small divisions of silver money as regards the standard employed, since they are far more irregular in weight than larger coins, and were probably little more than money of account, struck for local use. But sometimes it is necessary to make exceptions to the rule. Small coins were issued at the same time as the larger ones under consideration, and they must help us to decide whether the standard was really Aeginetan or Corinthian. If it were Aeginetan, they should be obols of the weight of 16 grains (grm. 1·03) or 15 grains at least. But among all the early coins of the class belonging to Naxos, Himera, and Zancle, published by M. Babelon, or appearing in the British Museum Catalogue, only one (of Zancle) weighs 16 grains; the rest vary from 13·6 to 11 grains (grm. 0·88–0·72). They seem thus not to be Aeginetan obols nor Corinthian diobols, which would be of nearly the same weight, but litrae of Sicilian standard. This issue of the litra, or equivalent of the pound of bronze beside the drachm and its fractions, is common in Sicily in the fifth century: it is interesting to be able to trace it back into the sixth century. Curiously the litra, the normal weight of which is 13·5 grains, is no exact part of the Corinthian didrachm, but $\frac{3}{20}$ of it, being $\frac{1}{10}$ of the tridrachm or Corinthian stater. There was thus evidently an attempt to conform the coinage to a variety of needs. The litra seems also to have been struck at Zancle under its new name of Messana about 490 B.C.: *Obv.* lion's scalp; *Rev.* MES; weight, 14 grains (grm. 0·90).[1]

The earliest Sicilian tetradrachms of Attic weight are those of Syracuse, bearing the type of a chariot, but without the figure of Victory floating over it; on the reverse is an incuse or a female head in an incuse. (**Pl. V. 9; B. M. IX. 34.**) These coins were by Mr. Head given to the Geomori, magis-

[1] Evans regards this as an Aeginetan obol, *Num. Chron.*, 1896, p. 112.

trates who governed at Syracuse until about 500 B.C.:[1] some other writers have preferred to give them to the democracy which succeeded the expulsion of the Geomori. This last view is rendered improbable by the fact that we have two successive issues of these tetradrachms, in one of which the reverse is occupied only by an incuse square, whereas in the other there is a female head also: it is difficult to suppose that both of these issues were struck in the brief period which intervened between the expulsion of the Geomori and the conquest of Syracuse by Gelon, Tyrant of Gela. The coinage of Syracuse must have begun at least as early as 520 B.C. With Gelon comes the Victory which hovers over the chariot, as a result of the victory at Olympia in the chariot-race won by Gelon in 488 B.C. (**Pl. V. 10; B. M. IX. 35**): it appears not only on the coins of Syracuse but also on those of Gela and Leontini, which cities were under the rule of Gelon. (**B. M. IX. 26, 28.**) A little later the well-known decadrachms, the Damareteia (**Pl. V. 11; B. M. XVII. 33**), give us a fixed point in chronology (479 B.C.); and the great superiority of the style of the Damareteia over the earlier coins of Gelon proves that art was in a rapidly progressive stage at the time, so that we need not put back the very earliest issues of Syracuse far into the sixth century.

It is noteworthy that while the cities of the east coast of Sicily, Syracuse, Leontini, Catana, and Gela made the tetradrachm of Attic standard their chief coin, the cities of the west, Selinus, Segesta, Agrigentum, Himera, struck instead the Attic didrachm or Corinthian tridrachm. The weight of this stater is considerably greater than that of the contemporary coins of the cities of Magna Graecia. Nevertheless we are probably justified in seeing here Corinthian influence, the cities being Doric. And we may fairly account for the inferiority in weight in the issues of the cities of South Italy as compared with those of Western Sicily by supposing that the Italian cities took as their model the

[1] The time of their supersession is uncertain.

early Corinthian tridrachms of Euboic weight (130 grains, grm. 8·42), while the Sicilian cities took as their model the later Corinthian tridrachms of Attic weight (135 grains, grm. 8·74).

In the early coinage of Syracuse there is, as in Magna Graecia, an adaptation of the silver coinage of Greek type to the value of the litra or pound of bronze which was probably the standard of value among the native inhabitants of Sicily, as well as in South Italy. A litra in silver was issued at Syracuse; it is distinguished from the obol not only by its greater weight but by the type. The type of the obol is the sepia; that of the litra is the wheel. The silver litra is of the weight of 13·5 grains (grm. 0·87). If the weight of the litra in bronze was 3,375 grains (grm. 218·6),[1] this gives a proportion between the values of silver and bronze of 250 to 1.

But here we come to a considerable difficulty. Haeberlin[2] has maintained that in the third century B.C. the proportional value of silver to bronze was 120 to 1, and the majority of archaeologists agree with him. And we have already seen (Chap. V) that such a proportion well suits the facts of the early Aeginetan coinage. But it is scarcely possible that silver should have been in Sicily twice as valuable in proportion to bronze as in Greece and Italy. The question is a vexed one, and I cannot here attempt its solution: it is important rather in connexion with the heavy bronze issues of Rome in the third century than in connexion with earlier Greek coinage.

The Corinthian stater (the *δεκάλιτρος στατήρ*) was equivalent to ten pounds of bronze, and the Syracusan tetradrachm to twenty. We have already seen that the Tarentines also issued a litra in silver with the type of a wheel.

Another fixed date in the early coinage of Sicily is fur-

[1] This is the weight generally accepted for the litra. See Head, *Coinage of Syracuse*, p. 12. It is just half the weight of the Attic mina; but it is hard to say whether this proves derivation or merely adaptation.

[2] *Systematik des ält. röm. Münzwesens*, 1905. Compare Hill, *Historical Roman Coins*, p. 30.

nished us by the change of name of the city Zancle, which took the name Messana soon after 494 B.C. The earliest coins bearing that name are—

Obv. Lion's head facing. *Rev.* MESSENION. Calf's head (Attic tetradrachm). (Pl. V. 8; B. M. IX. 30.)

Obv. Lion's head facing. *Rev.* MES in incuse circle (litra).

These coins bear the types of Samos, and there can be no reasonable doubt that their occasion was the arrival in Sicily of Samian fugitives, after the collapse of the Ionian revolt. As regards the history of these fugitives, their connexion with Anaxilaus, and their final settlement, there are many historic difficulties [1]; but the broad fact that Zancle took a new name, and issued coins with Samian types and of Attic weight on their arrival, seems to be beyond dispute. Valuable historical evidence is furnished by a small hoard of coins [2] found at Messana and containing some twenty archaic tetradrachms of Athens, four tetradrachms of Acanthus in Macedonia, coins of Rhegium and Messene with the above-mentioned types, and some coins of Attic weight (Pl. V. 7) bearing the thoroughly Samian types of a lion's scalp on one side and the prow of a galley on the other, but without inscription. It has been suggested that by these coins we seem to be able to trace the course of the Samian immigrants. They started bearing with them, as it would seem, coins with their native types but specially struck on the Attic standard; they tarried at Acanthus, possibly also at Athens; and the Rhegine and Messanian coins of the hoard show the result of their arrival in Sicily. These are the chief landmarks in the coinage of Sicily before the time of the Persian wars.

[1] Discussed by Mr. C. H. Dodd in *Journ. Hell. Stud.*, xxviii, p. 56.

[2] *Zeitschr. f. Numismatik*, iii. 135, v. 103. Cf. also Babelon, *Traité*, ii. 1, p. 1489.

CHAPTER XIII

COINS OF CYRENE, 630–480 B.C.

THE archaic coinage of Cyrene is remarkably varied and abundant.[1] The richness of the country, and the trade in wool and silphium which Cyrene carried on with Greece and with Egypt, will fully account for this. The coinage must have begun soon after the foundation of the city about 630 B.C., and become abundant in the prosperous reign of Battus the Fortunate, about the middle of the sixth century. Coins of Cyrene were in the remarkable find at Myt-Rahineh[2] in Egypt, a hoard of coins from several parts of the Greek world. Arcesilas III, king about 528 B.C., had to fly from his kingdom to Samos, whence he returned with an army of Samians to re-establish his power. It has been held that at this time the remarkable tetradrachm in the British Museum was issued—

> *Obv.* Lion's head in profile; silphium plant and seed. *Rev.* Eagle's head, holding serpent in beak. Weight, 266 grains (grm. 17·23).

If we could insist on this date, it would be a valuable asset to us. But, unfortunately, it is anything but certain. The lion's head in profile and the eagle's head remind us of the types of Lindus and Ialysus in Rhodes. The lion's head in profile has been set down as a Samian type (which at the time it is not); and it has been assumed (without warrant) that Rhodians as well as Samians took part in the expedition which replaced Arcesilas on the throne. But when it is recognized that there is no trace of Samian influence on the coin, and that Arcesilas had no connexion with Rhodes,[3]

[1] See Babelon, *Traité*, ii. 1, pp. 1335–64; also a paper by Mr. E. S. G. Robinson in *Num. Chron.*, 1915, p. 53.

[2] Longpérier in *Rev. Num.*, 1861, pl. XVIII. See below

[3] Hdt. iv. 163.

the occasion of the striking of the coin becomes quite uncertain. Its style points rather to the end of the sixth century than to 528 B.C. Probably, however, the coin was struck at Cyrene.

A very noteworthy fact is that, from the first, Cyrenaean coins are issued on a standard of which the full weight is as much as 17·23 grammes, 266 grains: M. Babelon calls this the Euboic standard, but the Euboic standard, as we have seen, does not rise above 260 grains. The standard at Cyrene is the same as the Attic, according to which the tetradrachm weighs up to 270 grains (grm. 17·50). But the Attic standard did not come into use at Athens until the time of Peisistratus, and the earliest coins of Cyrene are of so archaic a character that they must be given to the beginning of the sixth century. Nor does there appear any reason why the people of Cyrene should have adopted the Attic standard. It was not in use in the islands of the Aegean and of the Asiatic coast, with which Cyrene, as we know from the history of Arcesilas III, was in closest relations.

It is clear that we have here an interesting historic problem. It would seem that the people of Cyrene and those of Athens independently adopted the standard, the former as early as 600 B.C., the latter half a century later. We are taken some distance towards the solution of it by the facts of the find at Myt-Rahineh,[1] which may have been a silversmith's hoard, consisting partly of bars of silver, partly of very archaic Greek coins, none apparently later than 550 B.C. Many of these coins were broken. Amongst them were coins of the Thracian coast (Lete, Maroneia) and of the coast of Asia Minor (Ephesus, Chios, Naxos, Cos). It is noteworthy that there were no coins of Athens of the Athena type; and since the early tetradrachms of Athens have been found in numbers in Egypt, this seems to furnish a proof that they were not yet circulated at the time of the burial of the hoard. Coins of Corinth were present, one weighing 129·5 grains (grm. 8·40), the other weighing 137·5 grains (grm. 8·90); but M. Longpérier observes that

[1] *Revue Numism.*, 1861, p. 425, pl. XVIII. Article by Longpérier.

the latter was considerably oxidized and had gained in weight. We may therefore assume that these coins were of the ordinary early Corinthian standard of 130 grains. Coins of Cyrene also were present, but so much broken up that their original weight could not be ascertained; but they doubtless followed the ordinary standard of Cyrene. It seems clear, first, that the standard of Cyrene was not that of Corinth (or the Euboic); and second, that coins of Cyrene were well known in Egypt at a very early time. In fact, the geographical position of the countries is such that there must always have been communication between them. History confirms this inference: we read of interference by the kings of Egypt in the affairs of Cyrene from the days of Apries and Amasis at the beginning of the sixth century to those of the Ptolemies.

We may, therefore, fairly look to Egypt for the source of the standard of Cyrene; and we find it at once. The *kedet*[1] of Egypt seems to have been of various weights at different times and in different parts of the country. A large number of weights attributed to this standard were found at Naucratis, and have been published by Prof. Petrie.[2] They give a unit of 136·8–153 grains (grm. 8·85–9·91). On the next page Prof. Petrie gives a list of weights also from Naucratis of Attic drachm standard giving 127·80–148·8 grains (grm. 8·27–9·63) for the didrachm. As all these weights are uninscribed, there is difficulty in determining to which series they really belong; but supposing Petrie to be right in his attributions, it is evident that the Attic didrachm is equivalent to a light kedet weight. Petrie shows[3] that the kedet at Heliopolis in Egypt was of a somewhat low standard, of 139 grains (grm. 9·0). There is, he observes, a well-known weight inscribed '5 Kat of Heliopolis', which gives this standard, and it is confirmed by other weights found in the locality. Thus we come still nearer to the ordinary Attic weight. Heliopolis was one of the cities of Egypt most readily

[1] This word is spelt in a great variety of ways.

[2] *Naukratis*, i. pp. 75–6. Compare *Encycl. Brit*, ed. 11, xxviii. 485.

[3] *Ibid.*, p. 84.

accessible to the Greeks, lying in the south of the Delta, and it was to Heliopolis that Herodotus and Plato repaired for information from the learned priests of the temple of the Sun-god. The kedet of Heliopolis is of almost exactly the weight of the standard of Cyrene. There can be little doubt but that the people of Cyrene adopted the weight not later than the days of Apries and Amasis, when the relations between Egypt and Cyrene were intimate. The latter king made a durable peace with Battus of Cyrene, and even married a lady of his family. The adoption of the same standard at Athens was somewhat later. We have, however, traces of its use at Samos and elsewhere for electrum coins, as early as at Cyrene (Chap. I).

Concurrently with the money struck on this standard at Cyrene, we find, towards the end of the sixth century, coins weighing approximately 52 and 26 grains (grm. 3·36 and 1·68).[1] These can be nothing but drachms and hemidrachms of the Phoenician (or Milesian) standard. The drachms must have borne some relation to the tetradrachms of the ordinary standard, and it is natural to suppose that that relation would be 1 to 5. We should thus have a decimal and a duodecimal coinage concurrently at Cyrene. It is noteworthy that Mr. Head takes these coins as drachms of the Phoenician, and M. Babelon as pentoboli of the Attic standard.[2] Situated between Egypt and Carthage, both of which used the Phoenician standard for silver, Cyrene must have come to terms with it; while for trade with Sicily, with Athens, and with Corinth, and the places within the spheres of their influence, the Attic standard would be most useful.

The issue of money at the other cities of Cyrenaica, Barce, and Euesperides, does not begin so early as at Cyrene; but it begins in the sixth century. It follows the same standards.

The monetary types of Cyrene are mostly derived from the silphium plant, which was in all the Mediterranean world regarded as a most valuable medicine, and which grew in the district of Cyrene.

[1] *Num. Chron.*, 1915, p. 61.

[2] Head, *Hist. Num.*, ed. 2, p. 867. Babelon, *Traité*, ii. 1, p. 1347.

CHAPTER XIV

COINS OF THE ATHENIAN EMPIRE

I. ATHENS, SILVER.

THE ordinary silver coinage of Athens from 480 to 400 B.C. is almost unvaried. By the former date a head of Athena and an owl of fixed and conventional archaic type had been adopted for the coin. The olive-wreath which adorns the helmet of the goddess seems to have been adopted during the glow of triumph after Marathon. At the end of the century there were certain issues of gold coins, of which we shall speak later. But the great mass of the coinage was in silver. The Athenians obtained silver in abundance from the mines of Laurium and those of Thrace, and it was part of Athenian policy to circulate the coins as widely as possible, and to make them the standard currency of the Aegean. Silver was to Athens what gold was to Persia, the backbone of the finance of the state, and, together of course with the tribute of the allies, the source whence came the plentiful wealth which Athens used for great building-works at home and for expeditions abroad. The early silver coins of Athens are found on many shores, in Egypt, in Italy, in Sicily, in Greece and Asia. There is a well-known passage in the *Frogs* of Aristophanes in which their vogue is described.[1] Aristophanes speaks of the Athenian staters as not alloyed, as the most beautiful of coins, the only ones rightly struck, and ringing truly, accepted among Greeks and barbarians everywhere. The poet is somewhat carried away by patriotic fervour. The coins are indeed of pure metal, but their beauty is to say the least somewhat antiquated, and their striking careless. If we

[1] *Frogs*, line 780.

want to see what dies bearing the head of Athena could be produced by Athenian artists in the fifth century, we must turn to the money of the Athenian colony of Thurium, where most beautiful heads of the goddess make their appearance. Several writers have dwelt on the artistic influence exercised in Italy and Sicily by the die-cutters of Thurium.[1] This is, however, a subject on which we cannot here dwell: it is more in place in speaking of the coins of Italy.

Why the Athenians should in this case have taken a line so much opposed to all their artistic instincts it is not hard to see. The reason was commercial convenience. It is a familiar fact to all students of the history of coins that when a particular type of money has taken root, and gained a wide commercial vogue, it becomes stereotyped and no longer varies. Thus the coins bearing the name and types of Alexander the Great were widely current in Greece and Asia until the middle of the second century. The staters of Cyzicus retained the archaic incuse on the reverse until they ceased to be issued. Among ourselves the retention of Pistrucci's type of George and the Dragon for the reverse of the sovereign is in part at least the result of a similar conservatism. But other Greek cities, such as Corinth and Sicyon, while they kept to their early types, modified the style of their coins in response to the growth of art.

It might well seem that nothing could be easier than to copy the Athenian silver of the fifth century. It bore no magistrates' names and had no subsidiary devices, and it was rudely struck. Probably, however, the mere archaism of the types made them hard to copy in an age of astonishing vitality in art. And it is certain that the Athenians would keep a sharp eye on all attempts at forgery. Imitations of the money were, as I have already shown, abundant down to 480 B.C. From that time until 400 they are scarcely to be found.

In the time of the Second Empire, about 393 B.C., the

[1] Poole in *Num. Chron.*, 1883; Furtwängler, *Masterpieces*, p. 104; Evans, *Num. Chron.*, 1912, p. 21, and elsewhere.

Athenians modified the types of their coins. The money struck between that year and the date of Alexander betrays, as Mr. Head observes,[1] an 'endeavour on the part of the engraver to cast off the trammels of archaism, which is manifested chiefly in the more correct treatment of the eye of the goddess, which is henceforth shown in profile'. The dies, however, are executed in a careless way, and so ill adapted to the blanks used that often both of the types are only partly to be found on the coins. This coinage seems to have been continued until the days of Alexander, or later. Perhaps some of the worst examples may be money struck in military camps or in other cities.

In the last years of the Empire, when in great need, the Athenians did begin a coinage both in gold and in bronze. Of this we shall speak later. They also used money of electrum for dealings with Asia. But in Greece and the Aegean, and to the west in Italy and Sicily, it is only silver coin which comes in. The Athenians issued coins of all sizes and all denominations, slightly varying the types to indicate value.

Denomination	Noof drac ms	B. M. Cat.	Reverse-type	Weight	
				Grains	G1
1. Decadrachm . .	10	Pl. III. 1	Owl facing: olive twig	675	43
2. Tetradrachm . . .	4	Pl. III. 2–8	Owl to r.: ,,	270	17
3. Didrachm . . .	2	Pl. IV. 4	,, ,,	135	8
4. Drachm	1	Pl. IV. 5, 6	,, ,,	67·5	4
5. Triobol	1/2	Pl. IV. 7, 8	Owl facing: two olive twigs	33·7	2
6. Diobol . .	1/3	Pl. IV. 9	Two owls: olive twig	22·5	1
7. ,, ...	1/3	Pl. V. 16	Two owls with one head	22·5	1
8. Trihemiobol . .	1/4	Pl. IV. 10	Owl facing: olive twig	16·8	1
9. Obol	1/6	Pl. IV. 11	Owl to r.: ,,	11·2	
10. ,, ...	1/6	Pl. V. 17	Four crescents	11·2	
11. Tritartemorion . .	1/8	Pl. V. 18	Three crescents	8·4	
12. Hemiobol	1/12	Pl. IV. 12, 13	Owl to r.: olive twig	5·6	
13. Trihemitartemorion	1/16	Pl. V. 20	Calathos	4·2	
14. Tetartemorion . .	1/24	Pl. V. 21	Crescent	2·8	
15. Hemitetartemorion	1/48	Pl. V. 22	Owl facing: two olive twigs	1·4	

These coins are probably not all of the same time. In the *B. M. Cat.*, as will be seen from the references given above, Mr. Head assigns coins 1–6, 8, 9, 12 to a period before

[1] *B. M. Cat. Attica*, p. xxiii, pl. V.

430 B.C.: coins 7, 10, 11, 13–15 to a period after that date. It is difficult to judge of the style of the head of Athena, which is our only means of assigning period, on coins so small. But in general I should be willing to accept Mr. Head's assignment of date. The didrachm is of extreme rarity, and, as M. Babelon observes,[1] was only struck about 480 B.C. The reason for this procedure is unknown. The Corinthian staters would fill the gap; but considering the hostility between Athens and Corinth there is not likely to have been an understanding between the two cities as to the use of their respective coins.

Some confusion has been introduced into the silver coinage of Athens by mixing up those coins which bear a head of Athena of the fixed type, wearing Attic helmet adorned with olive-wreath, with some pieces of distinctly later style, in which the goddess wears a helmet without olive-wreath and of another character, and even with coins of the fourth century in which she wears a helmet of Corinthian form. These coins may be thus described:

On obverse, Head of Athena, in helmet without olive-leaves.

Tetrobol: *Rev.* Two owls: 45 grains (grm. 2·91) (*B. M. Cat.*, Pl. V. 12).

Triobol: *Rev.* Owl facing: 33·5 grains (grm. 2·18) (*B. M. Cat.*, Pl. V. 15).

The former of these coins fits in with the Corinthian system: the tetrobol being the equivalent of the Corinthian drachm. This gives us a clue: the coins may well belong to the time of the Corinthian alliance of Athens 394 B.C. Later there is a *Pentobol*, on obverse Head of Athena, in Corinthian helmet: on rev. Owl to r. with wings open; in front, an amphora: weight, 56·2 grains (grm. 3·64) (*B. M. Cat.*, Pl. V. 11). This coin is certainly later than the middle of the fourth century.

The careful discrimination of denominations is characteristic alike of the love of the Athenians for their silver coins —the γλαῦκες Λαυριωτικαί of which Aristophanes speaks so

[1] *Traité*, ii. 3, p. 77.

fondly[1]—and of the fine perfection of their intellectual faculties. A dull-witted people could never have used or invented such a coinage, which stands in history as unique as the drama or the sculpture of Athens.

A good reason for the fondness of the people for small coins of silver, at a time when in some places, as in Sicily, a beautiful bronze coinage was coming in, is to be found in the Athenian custom of carrying small change in the mouth. Occasionally, no doubt, these minute coins were swallowed; but this risk weighed less heavily than the unpleasantness of the taste of bronze in the mouth.

The smaller coins do not appear to have had much circula tion outside Athens: they were merely local small change. Many of the cities of Asia, as we shall see, while they used the silver staters of Athens, or the Cyzicenes, for larger payments, struck small coins of their own for the local markets. It is to be observed that the didrachm at Athens is of great rarity, and even the drachm scarce, in contrast to the immense abundance of the tetradrachm.

Some time after 480 B.C. Athens begins to exercise a policy which remains fixed with her until the fall of her empire, the policy of prohibiting the issue of silver coin by any city which might come fully under her power. This policy had already been suspected by numismatists in consequence of the non-appearance of money in the Athenian colonies and wherever Athens was dominant. It is conclusively proved to have prevailed by certain inscriptions put together, in the *Inscriptiones Maris Aegaei*, by Hiller von Gärtringen.[2] They are two copies of an Athenian decree of the fifth century, one from Siphnos, the other copied by Baumeister at Smyrna in 1855.[3] They mention a decree, which was proposed by one Clearchus, by which the Athenians definitely

[1] *Birds*, 1106.

[2] *I. G.* xii. 5, No. 480, p. 123; R. Weil, *Münzmonopol Athens im ersten attischen Seebund* in the *Zeitschrift für Numismatik*, xxv. p. 52.

[3] The editor of the *Corpus* writes 'fuit inter marmora Arundeliana sicut chronicon Parium'. But certainly this marble was never among the Arundel marbles, which have been at Oxford since 1667, including the Parian Chronicle.

forbid in the cities subject to them the use of any silver money save the Attic, as well as any other weights and measures than Attic.

It appears that this decree was not in all cases obeyed; for it is further ordered by a second decree that a copy of it shall be set up in the agora of each city. A second copy is to be set up before the mint of each city. In case of non-compliance a heavy penalty of 10,000 drachms is threatened. The sending of a herald (κῆρυξ) or commissioner from Athens is also threatened. The people are ordered to bring to the civic mints foreign coins and those locally issued: these are to be recorded in a public register, and presumably (for here the fragments come to an end) Attic coin will be issued in exchange.

It is noteworthy that the decrees relate not only to the use of Athenian coin, but also to the use of Athenian weights and measures, no doubt with the object of facilitating commercial intercourse. The editor of the *Corpus* cites the passage in the *Birds* of Aristophanes (line 1040) which runs, with the emendations of Cobet and Bergk, as follows: χρῆσθαι Νεφελοκοκκυγιᾶς τοῖς αὐτοῖς μέτροισι καὶ σταθμοῖσι καὶ νομίσμασι καθάπερ Ὀλοφύξιοι.[1]

Aristophanes puts this proclamation in the mouth of a hawker of decrees, and is clearly alluding to the passing of the very decrees under discussion. The date of the *Birds* is 414 B.C.: that of the decrees would be earlier; they appear to express a policy on which the Athenians had been acting at all events since the transfer of the Delian Fund to Athens in 454 B.C.

Weil observes also that, whereas in the Treasurer's lists at Athens of 434 B.C. we have separate mention of silver coins of Boeotia, Chalcis, and Phocis, after 418 foreign silver is reckoned only by weight, in talents and fractions, indicating that it was regarded only as material to be melted down and re-issued; thus the only silver coin regarded as legal tender at Athens is the owl coinage.

[1] Olophyxus was a small town in Chalcidice. Why it is chosen for the present context is unknown.

It would be very satisfactory, if it were possible, to fix precisely the date of these two decrees. The most probable view is that of Weil that the earlier decree is before, and the later decree after, the expedition to Syracuse.

Looking broadly at the numismatic evidence, it would seem that the policy of Athens in the matter was fixed from the earlier days of the Delian League, at all events after the middle of the fifth century, but insistence upon it became more and more stringent as difficulties arose with the allied cities.

It is difficult to over-estimate the importance of the discovery of these decrees in regard to the monetary and financial history of Greece. It definitely proves that some Greek cities made deliberate efforts to spread their systems of weights and measures as well as the vogue of their coins. To numismatists it is quite a revelation; for they have been accustomed to think that the kind of weights and measures and of coins used by a city was a purely internal concern. They have accepted the great variety which prevailed in this matter as a pathless morass. M. Babelon[1] doubts whether even the King of Persia tried to control the gold issues of Greek cities within his dominions. And the ablest writers on coins think it sufficient to label issues of money with the name 'Babylonic Standard' or 'Aeginetan Standard', or 'Attic Standard', and to accept the weights as ultimate facts. But we want explanations of these facts. No city can have altered its standards without good reason, political and commercial. The business relations of Greek cities spread like a network over the lands, and dictated the customs of coinage. The new decrees encourage us to hope that, with time and patience, we may be able to unravel the whole twisted skein, and to give some kind of reason for all the varieties of standard.

In regard to the history of the Athenian Empire, in particular, great use can be made of coins. The cessation of intermission of coinage by a city belonging to the

[1] *Traité*, ii. 2, p. 18.

Athenian confederacy becomes *prima facie* evidence that the power of Athens over that city is being more severely exerted, and the numismatic data must be carefully compared with another great series of records, the inscriptions [1] which state the tribute levied year by year on the members of the Delian Confederacy, which tribute after about 454 B.C. was laid up in the Acropolis of Athens. These inscriptions cover the period Ol. 81, 3 to 88, 4: 454–425 B.C. We have to compare the data which they give us with the testimony of the coins.

How necessary to the maintenance of the Athenian Empire an ample supply of coined silver was, we may judge from the well-known speech of Pericles in Thucydides ii. 13. He reminds the Athenians that not only do they receive 600 talents a year from the allies, but they also have 6,000 talents of coined silver laid up in the Acropolis, besides all the gold and silver offerings in the temples, and the resources in private hands. Cavaignac [2] gives a budget of the receipts and expenditure of Athens in the fifth century. The expenses were very great: the pay of the jurors in the law courts, the provision of theatre-money, and contributions towards the splendid temples then rising on the Acropolis were a constant drain. But a greater drain occurred in connexion with the military expeditions on a great scale, which were constantly taking place. It seems that from the time of Pericles, the troops, even though consisting of Athenian citizens, were paid, at first a drachm a day, out of which the soldier provided his own food, and later three obols, besides his food.

The revenue came mainly from three sources, the tribute of the allies, customs duties, and the mines of Laurium and Thrace, in addition to the voluntary contributions of the wealthy. It was not until the last years of the Peloponnesian War that the city was in actual straits

[1] *I. G.*, vol. i; U. Köhler, *Delisch-attischer Bund*; Cavaignac, *Hist. financière d'Athènes*.

[2] *Op. cit.*, pp. 49 and foll.

for want of money: the reserve of a thousand talents of silver was not used until the revolt of Chios.

From the financial point of view the policy of Athens in regard to the coinage raises interesting questions. Cavaignac suggests that difficulties of exchange were the cause which made Athens forbid moneying in subject cities: 'Les matelots n'acceptaient comme solde que des pièces ayant un cours international, et réclamèrent de plus en plus exclusivement des chouettes d'Athènes. L'autorité fédérale dut donc chercher tout de suite à décourager les monnayages locaux, au moins ceux qui n'étaient pas étalonnés suivant le système attique.'[1] This explanation does not seem to me sufficient. The Greek bankers must at all times have been accustomed to deal with a great variety of coins, struck on many standards. If the sailors wanted their pay in Attic money, there could not be at any time any difficulty in finding it for them. But that does not account for the unwillingness of the Athenians to allow money other than their own to pass in the markets of the allied states.

It is clear that we must take together the prohibition of coinage and the prohibition of using other weights and measures than the Attic, since both prohibitions are mentioned in the same decrees. It seems very likely that in this fashion the Athenians meant to gain a commercial advantage. We know from the facts of modern commerce that trade is facilitated when the trading countries have the same monetary standard and the same measures. And, of course, the Athenians may have estimated this advantage at a higher rate than actual experience would justify.

This notion of gaining a commercial advantage certainly in other cases inspired Athenian policy. There exists an inscription of the time of the second league, whereby the export of ruddle from Ceos to any other place than Athens is forbidden.[2] The best ruddle came from Ceos, and it was necessary for the manufacture of Athenian pottery, the

[1] Cavaignac, p. 184.

[2] *C. I.* ii. 546.

bright red surface of which was regarded as one of its chief attractions. Pottery was one of the chief exports of Athens in the fifth century, and even in the earlier part of the fourth. If another city could imitate this pleasing appearance by securing the proper ruddle, it might interfere with Athenian trade.

It must of course have been impossible for Athens to force her money into circulation at a fictitious value. This could only have been done by securing a monopoly of silver; and this in the case of so common a metal as silver would have been impossible. The Greek cities which minted silver had no difficulty in procuring the metal; and the owls of Athens could only hold their own by means of the purity of their composition.

We may suspect that after all it was mainly a matter of national pride. Athens was fond of dictating to the subject allies whenever she could. She made them bring their legal cases to Athens for settlement, partly to find work for Athenian dicasts, and partly out of arrogance. We have only to consider the policy of states at the present day to see how great a force national pride may exert in public politics. When nations make war, other motives than those of mere commercial advantage are usually involved. And it is well known how strong motives pride and the love of dominance were at Athens.

Another difficult financial question is why the Athenians, when in possession of the rich gold mines of the Pangaean district, did not themselves issue gold coin. It is probable that they might have done so had they been earlier in possession of the mines. But by the time, 463 B.C., when they wrested them from Thasos, their policy was already fixed and their silver in possession of the field. Hence the Thracian gold was kept in bars, or carried to Cyzicus to be minted as electrum coin.

In the last days of the Empire, when Deceleia was occupied by the Spartans, the winning of silver from Laurium was partly interrupted.[1] Many of the slaves who worked

[1] Thuc. vii. 91.

there made their escape. At the same time Athenian power in Thrace was greatly diminished. These causes, with the disastrous results of the Sicilian expedition, led to that impoverishment of Athens which is marked by an issue of gold coins of necessity, of which we shall speak later.

As I shall have, in the following pages, frequently to mention the standards of weight for coins in cities belonging to the Athenian League, it may be convenient to give in concise form the ordinary weights of denominations under the principal standards.

Attic standard. See above.

Chian (Phocaean) standard.
Tetradrachm (stater): 240 grains (grm. 15·55).
Drachm: 60 grains (grm. 3·88).

Persian standard.
Drachm (siglos): 86 grains (grm. 5·57).

Aeginetan standard.
Drachm: 96 grains (grm. 6·22).

Standard of Thasos and Erythrae.
Didrachm (stater): 144 grains (grm. 9·32).

Milesian standard (Samos, &c.).
Tetradrachm (stater): 204 grains (grm. 13·21).

Phoenician standard (Melos and Abdera).
Tetradrachm (stater): 224 grains (grm. 14·50).

II. Electrum of Asia Minor.

But though her *owls* were everything to Athens, she could not at a stroke substitute in Asia her silver for the gold and electrum coins to which the people of the coasts of Asia Minor had been accustomed for centuries. Gold came largely from the eastern shores of the Black Sea, from Colchis and the Crimea. The gold, for which the Arimaspians waged a constant war with griffins, filtered down to the Greek cities of the coast, in exchange for manufactured goods, and the corn and timber of the Pontic region had to be purchused with gold. In this region the Athenians had to provide a substitute for their silver. And there can be no doubt as to what the substitute was: it was the electrum money of Cyzicus, Lampsacus, Phocaea, and Mytilene.

The standard of weight adopted for these coins is that of Phocaea:

Stater, 254–248 grains (grm. 16·45–16).
Hecte, 42–40 grains (grm. 2·72–2·59).
Half hecte, 21–20 grains (grm. 1·36–1·29).

The staters and hectae of Cyzicus may be regarded as a continuation or revival of the electrum coinage issued by cities of Ionia during the Ionian revolt of 500 B.C. The coinage would seem to have begun afresh with the formation of the Delian Confederacy, and to have been from the first an international or federal issue. It is noteworthy that it never bears the name of Cyzicus; only the tunny, the well-known type of the city, serves to mark the place of mintage. For a century and a half it represented Hellas, as the daric represented Persia, on the Ionian and Pontic coasts, and only came to an end with the establishment of Macedonian supremacy, when the gold Philips and Alexanders ousted it.

In determining the periods of issue of these coins, three kinds of consideration have to be taken into account: (1) historic probability, (2) the evidence of ancient historians and inscriptions, and (3) the evidence of the coins themselves.

(1) The indications of historic probability are clear. If the King of Persia jealously guarded his monopoly of the issue of gold coin, and if he, in accordance with the general view of antiquity, regarded electrum as a species of gold, then it is improbable that he would permit any of the cities of Asia under his immediate lordship to begin an issue of electrum coins. Such issues must almost necessarily have begun at a time when the Persian power on the coast was destroyed, or at least greatly weakened. Now it is well known that Persian lordship did thus suffer a check in the days following the repulse of Xerxes from Greece. The Greek victory of Mycale in 479 did much to drive back the Persian

power. Herodotus (ix. 106) tells us that immediately the people of Samos, Chios, Lesbos, and other islands joined the Greek league, and after Cimon had in 466 won the great battle on the Eurymedon, Persia was still further repulsed. Whether this battle was followed by a peace humiliating to Persia is a matter much discussed by historians. But in any case it is certain that the result of it was to secure autonomy to the Hellenic cities of Asia. And we learn on excellent authority that there was a definite agreement that Persian war-fleets should not appear in the Aegean. From this time, for a while, the Greek cities suffered little interference from Persia. At first they were subject to Athens; but after the disaster in Sicily the power of Sparta also largely prevailed on the Asiatic coast.

That Cyzicus and the other cities began their issues of electrum after Mycale and under Athenian protection seems very probable. The Cyzicene staters, as we know, were largely used by the Athenians, especially for their trade in the Black Sea. But the date of their cessation is less easy to determine; the evidence of the coins themselves must decide. We can, however, easily suppose that the Persian king might be willing to allow in the fourth century the continuance of what had by the end of the fifth century become quite an institution.

(2) Let us next make a brief survey of the inscriptional and literary evidence.

Various writers have given a list of the mentions in inscriptions of Cyzicene electrum staters.[1] One of the earliest appears to be in the Lygdamis inscription found by Sir C. Newton at Halicarnassus, and dated about 445 B.C. The mention here, however, is only of *staters*, and the staters need not have been Cyzicene. Cyzicene staters occur in a fragment of the building-records of the Parthenon of the years 447 B.C. onwards (twenty-seven staters and one hecte); and as the same sum recurs year after year, we may conclude

[1] *Num. Chron.*, 1876, 295 (Head); Lenormant, *Revue Numismatique*, 1867. Recently Mr. Woodward has gone carefully into the matter. *J. H. S.*, xxxiv. p. 276.

that they could not well be used for current expenses.[1] During the Peloponnesian War Cyzicenes were used with Attic coins for official payments in the years 418, 416, 415, and down to the taking of Athens. That they are spoken of as gold is an important point, as it seems to show that the mercantile world was accustomed to regard them as coins of a special variety of gold rather than of mixed metal.

Lysias in his orations against Eratosthenes (403 B.C.) and Diogeiton at the end of the fifth century speak of them in a way which shows that at that time they constituted, with the darics, the main gold coinage of Greece. Cyrus the younger promised his mercenaries a Cyzicene stater a month as pay. The gold tetradrachm (*sic*) preserved in the Parthenon, and mentioned in the inventories of Ol. 89, 3 and subsequent years (*C. I.*, i, p. 74), was doubtless a double stater of Cyzicus or Lampsacus. Its weight was 7 drachms 2½ obols Attic, that is 500 grains (grm. 32·40).

At a considerably later time, just in the middle of the fourth century, we learn from the oration of Demosthenes against Phormio[2] that then Cyzicene staters were current coin on the shores of the Black Sea. This does not, however, positively prove that they were then issued, for they might naturally continue in use in remote districts even when the mint was closed.

Lampsacene staters (70 in number) are mentioned in an Attic inscription of 434, and in other inscriptions of the same period. These may be with certainty identified as electrum staters of Lampsacus, not the gold coins issued from that mint, as we shall see, at a somewhat later time.

The staters and hectae of Phocaea are mentioned in several Attic inscriptions dating from 429–384 B.C.[3] Staters of Phocaea are also mentioned by Thucydides (iv. 52 *δισχιλίους στατῆρας Φωκαΐτας*, of the year 424 B.C.) and by Demosthenes,[4] who speaks of a sum of 300 Phocaic

[1] *J. H. S.*, 1914, p. 277.
[2] p. 914.
[3] *C. I. A.*, i. 196, 649, 660.
[4] Πρὸς Βοιωτόν, 1019.

staters as procured at Mytilene. The text of a remarkable convention between Phocaea and Mytilene for the common issue of electrum, dating from about the end of the fifth century, was published by Sir C. Newton.[1] The two cities were in alternate years to undertake the minting of the coins; and if the mint-master debases the coin beyond a certain point, the penalty of death is assigned. It is remarkable that so important a detail should be decided, not by the city, but by a single official.

(3) Turning from the literary and inscriptional evidence to that of the coins themselves, we have much material to deal with. And first of Cyzicus.

Every one accustomed to study the coins of the ancient world is astonished at the abundance, the variety, and the artistic beauty of the Cyzicene staters[2] (**Pl. VI. 2**). 172 different types were mentioned by Mr. Greenwell in 1887; and more are now known. The inscriptional and literary evidence makes it clear that the staters of Cyzicus, together with the darics, constituted the main gold coinage of the Greek world from the time of Thucydides to that of Demosthenes. Yet Cyzicus does not seem to have been a great or wealthy city. It belonged to the Satrapy of which the chief resided at Dascylium. It had great natural advantages, being built on a peninsula, united with the mainland of Mysia only by a narrow neck of land,[3] and having two good harbours. But we are told by Thucydides (viii. 107) that as late as 411 B.C. the city was unfortified, and was occupied almost without resistance by the Athenian fleet. It seems to have been in the Roman age that it grew, and covered much ground. Why a city comparatively unimportant should have possessed so remarkable a privilege presents an interesting historic problem. In my

[1] *Roy. Soc. Lit.*, viii. 549. Michel, *Recueil*, No. 8.

[2] *Num. Chron.*, 1887: a more complete account by von Fritze, *Nomisma*, Part VII.

[3] Originally it seems to have been an island, but the passage between it and the mainland was silted up by the time of Alexander the Great, who cut a fresh canal across the isthmus. Plans of the site are given in *Journ. Hell. Stud.*, 1902, pl. XI; 1904, pl. VI.

opinion the secret must be the patronage of Athens, which was at the height of its power in the time of Cimon, and down to the disaster in Sicily. Some of the types of the staters of Cyzicus, the Tyrannicides Harmodius and Aristogeiton, Cecrops, Ge holding the young Erichthonius, Triptolemus in his winged car, are quite Attic. One, the young Heracles strangling serpents, commemorates the victory of Conon over the Spartans in 394 B.C., and cannot have been struck much later than that year.

As regards the dates of the Cyzicene coins, numismatic authorities are not altogether agreed. Mr. Greenwell, on the evidence of style, gives them to the period 500–360 B.C. Mr. Head in 1876 was disposed to think that their issue ceased early in the fourth century. French and German numismatists[1] had, on the other hand, brought the latest of them down to the time of Alexander the Great (331). In the *Historia Numorum* Mr. Head accepts the date 500–350. And in the *British Museum Catalogue of Mysia* the latest date is fixed at 350, the cessation of the Cyzicenes being regarded as the result of the great issues of gold coin by Philip of Macedon.

One of the latest of the staters of Cyzicus is a coin published by Millingen,[2] bearing the inscription ΕΛΕΥΘΕΡΙΑ, which has been regarded as a reference to Alexander's victory at the Granicus. It is, however, more than doubtful whether the people of Cyzicus, who had already enjoyed freedom, would look on the Macedonian conquest in this light. Mr. Head suggests that the reference is rather to the victory of Conon at Cnidus in 394 B.C., and he finds nothing in the style of the coin to conflict with the supposition.[3] But a far more suitable occasion for the boast of freedom is suggested by the assertion of Marquardt[4]

[1] F. Lenormant, in *Revue Numismatique*, 1864, 1867; Brandis, p. 177.
[2] *Anc. Greek Coins*, pl. V. 11.
[3] Head, in *Num. Chron.*, 1876, p. 292.
[4] *Kyzikos und sein Gebiet*, p. 65.

that the people of Cyzicus expelled the Persian garrison in 365, twenty-two years after the peace of Antalcidas. Marquardt's ancient authorities[1] only say that Timotheus liberated Cyzicus when besieged; but the inference of Marquardt that until the city had expelled the Persians it could hardly have been besieged by them seems a reasonable one. It was after this time that Cyzicus possessed an important arsenal, and two hundred ship-sheds. As the Cyzicenes repulsed Memnon, the Rhodian general of Darius, they seem to have preserved their autonomy until the time of Alexander. As the Cyzicene staters were a common currency till beyond the middle of the fourth century, there does not appear to be any reason why we should suppose that their issue ceased before Alexander's time, or at all events before the taking of Athens by Philip.

The fifth-century electrum staters of Lampsacus, the obverses of which bear the type of half a winged horse (Pl. VI. 1), are far rarer than those of Cyzicus, and belong to a briefer period. What that period was seems to be decided alike by the style of the coins, and by the fact that several of them were found with a number of Cyzicene staters which are neither archaic nor late in style.[2] We have seen that Lampsacene staters are mentioned in Attic inscriptions from 447 B.C. on, and this date admirably suits the extant examples of the coinage.

The small hectae or sixths issued by Mytilene and Phocaea in conjunction, in accordance with the above-mentioned treaty, the text of which has come down to us, are extant in great abundance. There is but one stater of Mytilene known, and as yet none of Phocaea. We have, however, seen that staters and hectae of Phocaea are frequently mentioned in Attic inscriptions.

Some of the hectae of Phocaea are distinctly archaic in style. M. Babelon[3] does not hesitate to attribute them

[1] Diodorus, xv. 80; Cornelius Nepos, *Timotheus*, 1.

[2] This find is published in the *Numismatic Chronicle*, 1876, p. 277.

[3] *Revue Numismatique*, 1895, p. 12.

to a time before the Persian War. Mr. Head gives them to the end of the sixth century.[1] But the weakness of the city at that time is shown by the fact that it contributed only three ships to the Ionian fleet. Most of the inhabitants had abandoned the city to sail to the west. It is unlikely that at such a time it would begin an issue of electrum coins. I should therefore regard them as issued just after 480 B.C. And Mr. Wroth gives the corresponding coins of Lesbos to 480–350 B.C., in the *B. M. Cat. Troas, &c.*

The only existing electrum stater of Chios of a period later than the Persian wars is at Berlin (B. T. VIII. 9). Its fabric is like that of the Cyzicene staters, and the type, the Sphinx, is enclosed in a vine-wreath, just like that on the already mentioned staters of Lampsacus. There can be little doubt that it is contemporary with these latter, dating from the time of the Peloponnesian War.[2]

Such are our data. What are the historic results to be drawn from them?

It seems abundantly clear that at some date not long after 480 B.C. three or four of the cities of the coast resumed their issues of electrum. The chief of these cities were Cyzicus, Mytilene, and Phocaea; Lampsacus and Chios joining them about the middle of the fifth century. It is impossible to tell with certainty when the issues of Cyzicus, Lesbos, and Phocaea began, since we have only the evidence of style to go by. But the incuse reverses of the earliest examples are distinctly later than those of the group of coins which I have given to 500–494 B.C. The incuses of Cyzicus and Phocaea are of mill-sail type; those of Lesbos are in the form of a second type. Thus the examination of the coins themselves confirms the view which is in itself far the most probable, that these issues of electrum were not sanctioned by Persia, but were begun

[1] *Cat. Ionia*, p. xxii.

[2] I leave this paragraph as I published it in 1913: it is satisfactory to find that Mr. Mavrogordato (*Num. Chron.*, 1915, p. 367) accepts this date.

at the time after the battles of Plataea and Mycale, when Greek fleets sailed the Aegean, and the power of Persia was being driven steadily westward by the arms of Athens. They are a sign of the Ionic independence of Persia which had been lost for half a century, except during the stormy years of the Ionian revolt.

It would be natural to expect that in the early years of the fourth century, when the mutual hostilities of Sparta and Athens had allowed the Persian power to reassert itself on the shores of the Aegean, and especially after the peace of Antalcidas had acknowledged the suzerainty of the Persian king over the Ionian cities, the electrum issues of Cyzicus and the other cities would come to an end. This appears, from the evidence of the coins and of the orations of Demosthenes, not to have been the case. For some reason or other the Great King allowed the invasion of his prerogative of issuing gold coin to go on. Why he did so we cannot with certainty say. We must, however, remember that though the power of Persia seemed to be increasing in the early part of the fourth century it was less centralized. The Satraps of Asia Minor were often in revolt, and maintained something like independence. And the long reign of Artaxerxes Mnemon, 405–359 B.C., was not one in which the privileges of royalty were strongly asserted.

The electrum issues seem to have persisted at Cyzicus until the appearance of the gold coins of Alexander the Great. Mr. Head has suggested as a reason for their ceasing the abundant issues of gold coins by Philip II of Macedon. This, however, appears to be a less likely occasion. Philip had little authority on the Asiatic side of the Bosporus; and one does not see why the cities of Asia should forgo their own commercial advantage in order to further the circulation of his money. It seems likely that the popularity of the gold Philippi would rather decrease the volume of the issue of electrum than bring it to an end.

We have next to consider how the Cyzicene stater was related in value to other current coins. No doubt in Greece, as in the modern world, there would usually be an *agio*, and the rate of exchange would fluctuate accordingly as gold, electrum or silver was in greater demand in the market. Yet there would probably be a normal equivalence.

This Mr. Woodward has tried to fix by means of Attic inscriptions;[1] but unfortunately these are so imperfect in preservation that they do not give him the means to solve the problem with certainty. He shows, however, that electrum staters of Cyzicus were used at Athens in 418–414 B.C. in payment to strategi. The ratio to the Attic drachm is fixed approximately to 24 to 1 by possible restorations of the inscriptions.

It is almost certain that the Cyzicene and the daric were regarded as equivalent. This I have tried to show elsewhere, by three or four lines of argument.[2] Mercenaries in Asia were sometimes paid a daric a month, and sometimes a Cyzicene a month. The soldiers of Cyrus the younger received a daric a month, which pay, in consideration of the serious nature of his expedition, he increased to a daric and a half.[3] Later on, the same troops are promised by Timasion a Cyzicene a month;[4] and Seuthes of Thrace promises them the same pay.[5] And the equivalence is confirmed by analysis. A fair average proportion of gold and silver in a Cyzicene of 254 grains is 117 grains of gold and 137 of silver, the latter being equal to 10 more grains of gold. Thus the whole coin is about of the value of 127 grains of gold, and 127 grains is just the weight of the daric, which is almost pure gold. Further, it is noteworthy that the silver coins of Cyzicus, dating from 400 B.C., are struck on the Phoenician standard of about 232 grains: of these pieces 15 at the rate of 1 : 13⅓ are the equivalent of two darics. The system of silver is clearly adapted to a currency of darics; but we must also in reason believe that it was also adapted to a

[1] *J. H. S.*, 1914, p. 278.
[2] *Num. Chron.*, 1887, p. 185.
[3] *Anab.* i. 8. 21.
[4] *Anab.* v. 6. 23.
[5] *Anab.* vii. 3. 10.

currency of electrum staters; that is, that the daric and the electrum stater were equivalent.

The daric, we know, was equivalent to 20 Persian sigli or shekels; and as the value of the Persian siglos was in Xenophon's time regarded in Asia as equal to 7½ Attic obols, or 1¼ Attic drachms,[1] the daric must have been there equivalent to 25 Attic silver drachms. We have, it is true, another statement in Hesychius, that the Persian siglos was equivalent to 8 Attic obols, and therefore the daric to 26⅔ Attic drachms; and this value may have held in some places; but the statement of Xenophon, based on his personal experience in Asia, is to be preferred.

With regard to the value of the Cyzicene in Attic silver, we have a number of conflicting statements. It is probable that 24–25 drachms was the ordinary or standard value. But in the works of the great orators, whose testimony is apt to be warped by the interests of their clients, there is considerable divergency. Very instructive is the oration against Phormio by Demosthenes. The question raised in it is, whether Phormio has or has not paid to one Lampis in Bosporus a debt of 2,600 Attic drachms. Phormio declares that he has paid it with 120 Cyzicene staters, to which Demosthenes replies that this is on the face of the thing absurd, since a Cyzicene stater is worth 28 drachms, and so 120 staters are worth 3,360 drachms, and not 2,600. Thus Phormio reckoned the value of a Cyzicene at 21⅔ Attic drachms, and Demosthenes at 28. We have no means of deciding between them; but if we regard the two valuations as representing the extreme fluctuations of value, 25 drachms is just midway between them. All these distinct lines of reasoning seem to point to a normal or ideal equivalence of the daric and the Cyzicene.

The value in currency of the hectae of Phocaea is not easy to fix definitely. They weigh about 40 grains (grm. 2·60) and their pale colour suggests that they contain but a small proportion of gold, a suspicion which analysis has

[1] *Anab.* i. 5. 6.

confirmed. J. Hammer has submitted the composition of the hectae of Phocaea and Mytilene to a careful examination.[1] The result is to show that they are regular and uniform in mixture. They contain 40 per cent. of gold, 52 of silver, and 8 of copper; they are thus rather less than half of pure gold in value. This would give us 16 grains of gold and 21 grains of silver for the hecté. If then gold were to silver as 14 to 1, we should have a value of grm. 15·87, 245 grains of silver; if of 13 to 1 of grm. 14·83, 229 grains of silver; if of 12 to 1 of grm. 13·80, 213 grains of silver. A natural supposition would be that they passed as the equivalent of a Cyzicene silver tetradrachm (232 grains); but the only mention of them in literature scarcely confirms this equivalence. Crates, the Athenian comic poet, is quoted by Julius Pollux[2] as saying in his *Lamia* that a half-hecté of gold was equivalent to eight obols (of silver). One would naturally suppose that Crates was speaking of Attic obols; in which case he would equate the hecté of gold (electrum) with 16 obols, 2⅔ drachms, 180 grains of silver (11·66 grm.). As Hesychius gives the value of a Persian silver siglos or shekel as eight Attic obols, the hecté would seem to have been equivalent to two shekels. The difficulty is that this fixes the value of electrum so very low, at only four and a half times the value of silver; and we are accustomed to higher exchange values for electrum.

III. The Islands.

In the Introduction to the British Museum *Catalogue of Coins of the Aegean Islands*, Mr. Wroth observes,[3] 'The troubles of the Persian Wars, and the long period during which the Aegean Islands were in more or less complete subjection to Athens, seem to have been unfavourable to the appearance of currencies in the islands, and coins

[1] *Zeit. f. Num.* 26, p. 47.

[2] *Onomasticon*, ix. 62. The half-hecté mentioned must be of Mytilene or of Cyzicus.

[3] p. xliv.

belonging to the fifth century, and, in a less degree, to the earlier part of the fourth, are rare.' But the rarity or abundance of such coins is less to our present purpose than the concession or withholding by the Athenians of the right to strike money at all. As a general rule the issue of coins by Aegean Islands, which had been a marked feature of the sixth century,[1] entirely ceases at the Persian wars.

Dr. R. Weil has, however, published an important paper, in the *Zeitschrift für Numismatik* for 1910, in which he tries to show that at first Athens did not interfere much with the island issues; but that as her hold on members of the Confederacy tightened, one island after another ceased to issue money; but a contributing cause was the impoverishment of the island world in the fifth century. The large island of Naxos certainly issued no coins for a long time after the island was conquered by the Athenians in 470 B.C. and a colony settled there. We must briefly consider the island coinages which persisted into the fifth century. Notable among them is the money of Peparethus, dealt with by Mr. Wroth.[2] Mr. Wroth thinks that the most striking specimens belong to the beginning of the fifth century; he adds, 'Between *circ.* 470 and 400 B.C. there is a broad gap in the coinage of Peparethus'.

More important, and coming down to a later time, is the coinage of Melos. Melos is said to have been peopled by Minyae from Lemnos and Imbros; but for practical purposes it was Dorian. Already, in the sixth century, Melos struck coins on a different standard from that of most of the other islands of the Aegean, the stater weighing about 224 grains (grm. 14·50). Certain coins of the Santorin find (p. 122) are not of Aeginetan but of this Phoenician weight. Their types are—head and tail of fish, head of boar, head of satyr with pointed ear: in each case the reverse bears an incuse square without definite divisions. These coins can hardly be assigned to cities by their types; and they are

[1] See especially *Num. Chron.*, 1884, Pl. XII, p. 269.

[2] *Journ. Hell. Stud.*, 1907.

uninscribed. But some of them at all events may belong to a group of islands which use from the first the Phoenician standard: the southern Cyclades, including Melos Thera and Carpathos. Though the coins of these places are mostly later than the find of Santorin, they begin in the sixth century. Among the earliest issues are the following:

Melos.

Obv. ΜΑΛΙ (archaic). Ewer. *Rev.* Incuse square, divided into four by two diagonals. Weight, 228 grains (grm. 14·45). (B. T. LXII. 8, 9.)

Poseidion in Carpathos.

Obv. Two dolphins passing one another within a linear square. *Rev.* Incuse square divided by a bar into two oblongs. Weight, 217–210 grains (grm. 14·06–13·60). (B. T. XIX. 8–10.)

If one looks at the map of the Aegean,[1] the facts may almost be said to 'leap to the eyes'. Melos belongs to a line of Dorian islands running across the sea from Laconia to Caria: Melos, Thera, Astypalaea, Carpathos, Rhodes. The cities of Poseidion in Carpathos, and Ialysus and Lindus in Rhodes, use the same standard; whereas Cos, and Camirus in Rhodes, like Cnidus and the cities of the mainland of Caria, use the Aeginetan standard. There was at Melos a tradition of a Phoenician colony from Byblus; and it is likely that the monetary standard of this kindred group of cities was in origin Phoenician. Some of the letters of the Melian alphabet are also strikingly like those of Phoenicia. The Laconian settlement was very early; but it does not seem to have brought with it the Pheidonian weights; whereas the islands to the north of Melos—Paros, Naxos, Siphnos, and the rest—strike staters of Aeginetan weight freely in the sixth century, Melos, Carpathos, and Rhodes adhere to the Phoenician standard. In this connexion it is important to observe that the finds in Rhodes belonging to the archaic period contain many objects of Phoenician character.

[1] Kiepert's *Formae Orbis antiqui* Pl. XII.

This coinage was continued at Melos into the fift century. Recent finds show that it was abundant an marked with a great variety of types on the reverse, th obverse being occupied by the pomegranate, inscription rendering the attribution certain (Pl. VI. 3, 4). Amon the reverse types we may note a triquetra, a wheel, a flowe three dolphins, a crescent, a ram's head, a helmeted head, &c. This is the only important coinage of the Aegean in th time of the Delian League. Its existence helps us t understand the bitter feelings towards the Melians in th minds of the people of Athens, which led to the massac of 416 B.C. Until 425 B.C., the year of the deepest humilia tion of Sparta and the greatest triumph of Athens, Melo does not figure in the Athenian tribute lists, but in th list of increased payments, *τάξις φόρου*, of that year Melo is assessed at 15 talents, the same as Andros and Naxos Whether this tribute was ever actually paid we cannot tell But Thucydides tells us that the demand made to th Melians in 427 that they should accede to the League o Delos was rejected by the islanders, and that Nicias faile in his attempt to coerce them, though he sailed to Melo with a fleet of 60 triremes and ravaged it. Thucydide adds that in fact the Melians had never been allies o Athens. The importance of their issues of coins show that the island was wealthy and prosperous. Unfortunatel we cannot venture to decide whether these issues cease in 425 or 416.

After the fall of Athens, a remnant of the Melians wer restored to their island by Lysander. They recommence a coinage on the Chian or Rhodian standard, which in th early years of the fourth century was rapidly making way.

The group of islands to the south of Delos, comprisin Paros and Siphnos, seems to have passed through simila vicissitudes. Paros and Siphnos continued into the fiftl century their early coinage of Aeginetan weight. Thi coinage may have lasted until 450 B.C., up to which tim

[1] See *Hist. Num.*, ed. 2, p. 486; *Rev. Num.*, 1908, pp. 301 and foll. and 1909 *Traité*, ii. 3, Pl. CCXLI–II.

the three islands do not appear in the Attic tribute lists. After that year they pay heavy tribute, and cease to strike coins until the end of the fifth century, when Naxos and Paros resume the issue of money on the Chian standard. Of the three islands, Siphnos is nearest to Attica, and hence we are not surprised to find there more traces of the influence of Athenian commerce. The stater in the early fifth century is of Aeginetic weight (186·4 grains) (**Pl. VI. 5**), but it is divided into three drachms of Attic standard, 60–61 grains (grm. 3·88–3·95). (See Chap. XVIII.)

Coming next to the islands close to Attica we find, as we should expect, clear traces of the Athenian monopoly. Aegina became tributary to Athens in 456 B.C.;[1] and it is probable that after that date the coinage of Aegina ceases, though M. Babelon attributes some small coins (drachms and obols) to a later date. At any rate we must regard the coinage as coming to an end in 431 B.C., when the island was finally conquered and the people ejected. After the conquest of Athens by Lysander, the inhabitants of Aegina were reinstated, and resumed their coinage on the old standard.

In the island of Euboea, Athenian dominance makes a clear breach in the coinage. Mr. Head observes that after the Persian wars the coinage of Euboea undergoes three changes: (1) the coins become thinner, and flatter; (2) reverse types appear; (3) inscriptions come in. Such coins are issued at Chalcis (types, flying eagle with serpent in beak; wheel) (**B. T. XXXI. 1–6**);[2] at Eretria (types, cow scratching itself; and sepia) (**B. T. XXXII. 1–6**); and at Carystus (types, cow suckling calf; and cock) (**B. T. XXXII. 14–15**). How long these issues lasted we cannot be sure; but they would certainly cease in 445 B.C., when the island was conquered by Pericles. After the Sicilian disaster in 411 B.C., Euboea recovered her autonomy.

[1] *Hist. Num.*, ed. 2, p. 397; cf. *Rev. Num.*, 1913, p. 470.

[2] *Cat. Central Greece*, p. lv.

IV. Ionia and Caria.

As regards the cessation of coinage in the cities of Asia, our evidence is of course negative. We know that we have no coins of certain cities at given periods; but at any time a fresh find may furnish us with the missing coins. Also, it is not easy, in the absence of definite evidence, to assign an exact date to the issues of many of the cities of Asia Minor.

The facts, however, appear to be these: The three great islands of the Ionian coast, Chios, Samos, and Lesbos, which were admitted to the Delian League on terms of equality with Athens, seem to have issued coins almost uninterruptedly during the fifth century; but with differences. We will begin with Samos, the history of which island is well known to us.[1] After the suppression of the Ionian Revolt, during which Samos had issued electrum staters, the city struck an abundant coinage in silver on a standard used also at Ephesus and other Ionian cities, which I call the standard of Miletus, and which is generally regarded as a light variety of the Phoenician standard. The stater or tetradrachm weighs about 204 grains (grm. 13·22). It is noteworthy that three Attic drachms would be almost equivalent, 202·5 grains (grm. 13·12). The results at Samos of the revolt and the Athenian conquest of 439 B. C. are very apparent. For a short time the Milesian standard is abandoned for the Attic, tetradrachms and drachms of Attic weight being issued. The style of these coins is different from, and superior to, that of the Samian issues, so that the die was probably made by an Athenian artist.[2] Afterwards, when the coinage of Milesian weight is resumed, the olive-branch of Athens regularly takes its place on the coin behind the half-bull, thus testifying to Athenian supremacy.[3] The Samians, however, were not expelled, nor were their lands given to Athenian settlers: they were only compelled

[1] I have written a treatise on Samos and its coinage: *Samos and Samian Coins*, Macmillan, 1882. (Reprint from the *Numismatic Chronicle*.)

[2] *Samos and Samian Coins*, Pl. II, 1, 2.

[3] *Ibid.*, Pls. II, III.

to surrender their fleet and raze their fortifications: they still remained, at least in name, allies rather than subjects. It is satisfactory to find an instance of clemency after conquest by Athens, and in fact after conquest long and painfully delayed, to set against the well-known examples of Athenian harshness in the cases of Mytilene and Melos. The reason of the difference may be the nearness in blood between Athens and Samos.

The metrological relief from Samos, in the Ashmolean Museum,[1] is also an interesting monument of the Athenian conquest. It records the measures of the foot and the fathom used at Samos at just the period in question, and those measures are, as Michaelis has proved, the Attic. This fact is very interesting, as we have already seen from the decrees that Athens was anxious to impose her weights and measures on the subject states: the relief confirms this, being evidently a standard set up by authority. And it proves that the policy of Athens was fixed at least as early as 439 B.C.

What happened at Samos between 439 and the end of the century is not easily to be made out. Doubtless the Athenians set up a democracy in the island; and since we read in Thucydides[2] of Samian exiles at Anaea on the coast of Asia opposite Samos, who in the earlier years of the Peloponnesian War sided with the Spartans, we may be sure that these exiles were of the aristocratic party. But curiously, when the island again emerges into the light of history in 412 B.C., we are told by Thucydides that the party in power was the aristocratic, that of the *gamori* or landowners. Against these, in 412, the demos revolted, and being victorious, with the help of some Athenian ships, was accepted by Athens as an equal ally. Thucydides's[3] phrase is *Ἀθηναίων τε σφίσιν αὐτονομίαν μετὰ ταῦτα ὡς βεβαίοις ἤδη ψηφισαμένων, τὰ λοιπὰ διῴκουν τὴν πόλιν*. This implies that whereas, until 412, the rule at Samos had been aristocratic, and the Athenians had kept

[1] *J. H. S.*, iv. 335 (Michaelis).
[2] iv. 75.
[3] viii. 21.

the island in dependence, after that date they felt sure of it and allowed it full liberty. But on what occasion did the aristocratic party gain the upper hand? and why did Athens allow them to do so?

The coins from 439 onwards fall into two classes: first, the rare coins of Attic weight (Pl. VI. 6); second, the coins of Samian weight, bearing an olive-twig as the mark of Athenian supremacy. These are usually marked in the field with a letter of the alphabet, the earliest being B and the latest Ξ (Pl. VI. 7). If these letters mark successive years, they imply a space of fourteen years. We may suppose that Athens prohibited coinage, save on the Attic standard, for some years after 439; but that the aristocratic party, coming into power about 428, at the time, we may suppose, of the revolt of Lesbos, issued coins for fourteen years or more on the old Samian standard, but retaining the olive-branch as a mark of loyalty.

A remarkable and quite exceptional silver tetradrachm of Athens (B. T. CLXXXVII. 7) has in the field of the obverse a bull's head. It has been reasonably supposed that this coin records some conjunction between Athens and Samos, of which island the bull's head is a frequent type. The coin seems to be in style too late for the time of the Athenian conquest: it seems more reasonable, with Koehler, to assign it to the time of Alcibiades, when the Athenian fleet had its head-quarters at Samos.

The silver coinage of the island of Chios is fairly continuous from 480 B.C. to the time of Alexander,[1] for Chios was never, like Samos and Lesbos, completely conquered by Athens. The type was a sphinx and an amphora, above which are grapes (Pl. VI. 8): in these we may find an allusion to the wine of Chios, which has always been celebrated. The stater or tetradrachm weighed 240 grains (grm. 15·55) and the more usual didrachm 120 grains (grm. 7·77). This is clearly the old standard of Phocaea, used for

[1] See Mavrogordato in *Num. Chron.*, 1915, p. 364.

gold and electrum from a very early time. I shall have to dwell on the importance of the Chian standard in the fifth century, an importance which hitherto no one has recognized.

At the time of the Ionian Revolt the silver stater was divided into six, and coins of about 40 grains (grm. 2·60) were struck.[1] Later the more truly Hellenic division by four came in, and drachms of 60 grains (grm. 3·90) or less made their appearance. Such a collision between the customs of dividing by 3 and multiples, and dividing by multiples of 2, meets us elsewhere, in Chalcidice of Macedonia and in South Italy. There it seems to result from a collision of Attic and Corinthian influences. At Chios, however, we should probably regard the trinal division as the old Asiatic custom, and the dual division as the result of the rapidly growing Athenian influence of the fifth century.

Fortunately for us, the Chian staters are mentioned both by Thucydides and Xenophon in a way which gives us valuable information, though this testimony has been usually misunderstood. At the end of the Peloponnesian war, the Spartan admiral Mindarus, sailing from Chios, in 411 B.C., procured as pay for each of his men three Chian fortieths, *τρεῖς τεσσαρακοστὰς Χίας*.[2] Since the tetradrachms of Chios, reckoned at 240 grains, were exactly one-fortieth of the Aeginetan mina of 9,600 grains, and as it was quite natural for the sailors of Peloponnese to look at them in relation to the standard to which they were accustomed, this statement exactly fits in with our knowledge. What each sailor received was clearly three Chian silver tetradrachms.[3] Xenophon,[4] speaking of a time a little later, 406 B.C., narrates that Callicratidas, the Spartan admiral, procured for each of his sailors from Chios a *pentadrachmia*. Reading this statement in close relation with the last, we may conclude that each soldier received two Chian tetradrachms, which together were the exact equiva-

[1] *J. H. S.*, 1911, p. 158; 1913, p. 105.
[2] Thuc. viii. 101.
[3] Hultsch rightly identified these fortieths: *Metrologie*, p. 554.
[4] *Hellen.* i. 6. 12.

lent of five Aeginetan drachms of 96 grains. M. Babelon[1] and Mr. Head[2] are, I think, mistaken in supposing that the Chian coin is equated by Xenophon with five 'south Ionian' drachms of 48 grains, a species of coin which I do not recognize. Xenophon, it is to be observed, avoids the word πεντάδραχμον, which would imply that he was speaking of coins each singly of the value of five drachms, and uses the vaguer term πενταδραχμία, which need not bear that meaning. If, however, we prefer to regard the πενταδραχμία as a coin, the Chian silver stater of the time is nearly equivalent to five drachms of Corinth, which are of about the same weight as Aeginetan hemidrachms. The view of M. Six, who regarded the Chian pentadrachms as electrum coins, has not persuaded numismatists; nor are there electrum staters of Chios of this period.

From such testimony we see that the Chians in the regulation of their coinage had regard, not only to the old Phocaean standard, but also to that of Aegina. The Chian drachm was regarded as five-eighths of the value of an Aeginetan drachm; the evidence that this was the accepted valuation is conclusive. Here again we have a numismatic and indeed a political fact of the greatest importance. The Aeginetan standard had been before the Persian wars dominant in the Aegean; but the growing predominance of Athens, and her determination that her dependent allies should use her measures, weights, and coins, had swept it aside. But with the Chian revolt of 412 B.C., and the appearance of Laconian fleets in the Aegean, the balance of power was altered. We learn from Thucydides viii with what a tempest of despair and rage the Athenians heard of the revolt of Chios and her allies. They at once repealed the law which punished with death any one who proposed to encroach on the reserve of 1,000 talents set aside to be used only in case of dire necessity. It was the beginning of the end. It was at that time that Chios evidently made an effort to come to terms with the

[1] Babelon, *Traité*, ii. 2, p. 1134. [2] Head, *Hist. Num.*, ed. 2, p. 600.

Aeginetan standard, which was still of universal use in Greece south of the Isthmus and west of Attica.

The fortunes of Lesbos were more varied. The Lesbians, like the people of Samos and Chios, did not pay tribute to Athens, but contributed ships to the navy. Athens could have no claim to proscribe their coinage, though she doubtless had a convention with them in regard to the hectae of electrum. But in 428 B.C. Mytilene and the other cities, except Methymna, revolted against Athens. Every reader of Thucydides will remember how after a siege the people of Mytilene were obliged to surrender; and how the inhabitants of Lesbos by a very narrow margin escaped a general massacre. As it was, a thousand of the most distinguished inhabitants were put to death, and the lands of all the cities except Methymna were divided among Athenian proprietors. I say *proprietors* rather than *settlers*, because it is doubtful how many Athenians really settled in the island and how many were absentee landlords.

We next turn to the extant coinage of Lesbos. The earlier coins were of base metal, billon, struck on the standard of Phocaea (above, p. 177). About 480 B.C. begins the issue of hectae of electrum, with a few staters, by the mints of Mytilene and Phocaea in common, of which I have already spoken. It lasted, according to Mr. Head and other authorities, until about 350 B.C.

To the period shortly after 480 B.C. I would assign the remarkable coin of Methymna, already mentioned (p. 173), with the types of the boar and the head of Athena. This coin must have been struck on the occasion of some alliance or understanding with Athens, with which city Methymna always remained on good terms.

We cannot of course assign to the coins a date so exact that we can tell whether the events of 429–427 B.C., so disastrous for the people of Mytilene, caused an interruption of these issues. M. Babelon[1] observes that it is from

[1] *Traité*, ii. 2, p. 1194.

about 400 onwards that they become most abundant. The hectae struck at Phocaea bear the mint mark of the seal (phoca), and it has been observed first by Mr. Wroth[1] that the obverse types of the Lesbian sixths are almost invariably turned to the right, while the types of the Phocaean sixths face to the left.

Towards the middle of the fifth century a few silver coins make their appearance at Mytilene and Methymna:

Mytilene.

Obv. Head of Apollo, laureate. *Rev.* MYTIΛHNAON. Head of Sappho, in incuse. Weight, 3·94 grm. (61 grains). (**B. T. CLXII.** 8.)

Obv. Head of Sappho or nymph, three-quarter face. *Rev.* MYTI. Lion's head in incuse. Weight, 0·96 grm. (15 grains). (**B. T. CLXII.** 4.)

Obv. Head of Apollo, laureate. *Rev.* MYTI. Head of bull in incuse. Weight, 1·97 grm. (31 grains). (**B. T. CLXII.** 2.)

Methymna.

Obv. Head of Athena. *Rev.* MA⊗YMNAION. Lyre on a square field in excuse. Weight, 6·43 grm. (99 grains). (**B. T. CLXII.** 30).

Obv. Head of Athena. *Rev.* MAΘ. Kantharos in incuse. Weight, 3·18 grm. (49 grains). (**B. T. CLXII.** 31.)

Obv. Head of Athena. *Rev.* MA. Lion's face in incuse. Weight, 1·57 grm. (24 grains). (**B. T. CLXII.** 28.)

It is clear that these two neighbouring cities struck on different standards; and this is readily to be understood. Methymna was democratically governed, and in close connexion with Athens; Mytilene was an aristocracy sometimes hostile to Athens. The standard in use at Mytilene is clearly the old Phocaean standard, still in use at Chios, Cyzicus, and elsewhere. The standard in use at Methymna is of doubtful origin. Babelon calls it the Samian, with the weight of which it certainly nearly agrees. 'Samos, colonie Athénienne,' he writes, 'était en rapports constants avec Méthymne.'[2] This explanation is not altogether satis-

[1] *B. M. Cat. Troas, &c.*, p. xviii.

[2] *Traité*, ii. 2, p. 1241.

factory, since, if my account of the Samian coinage be correct, the use of the old standard in the island is rather a sign of disaffection towards Athens than of loyalty to her. What we might *a priori* have expected would be that Methymna would strike, after, as before 480, on the Attic standard.

It is not probable that any coins were struck in Lesbos between the Athenian conquest in 427 B.C. and the end of the Athenian Empire.

The coinage of the large islands of Caria, Cos and Rhodes, offers interesting phenomena. They were not, like the great islands of Ionia, admitted to the League on terms of equality; nevertheless their size and power might seem to entitle them to preferential treatment. Such treatment Cos received.

Previous to the Persian wars the island had issued coins on the Aeginetan standard. After them it strikes on the Attic standard, issuing tetradrachms between 479 and 400. The type is on one side a Discobulus and a prize tripod, on the other a crab (Pl. VI. 10). As the successive issues of these coins bear first the legend ΚΟΣ, then ΚΩΣ, and finally ΚΩΙΟΝ, it would seem that the right of coinage was exercised continuously, and the use of the Attic standard seems to testify to a special understanding with Athens. The types of the coins probably refer to the festival of Apollo held on the Triopian promontory: they may have been struck only on the occasion of the festival, as seems to have been the case at Elis: this would give the Athenians a reason for exceptional treatment.

Rhodes was less favoured. But we must observe that, until the foundation of the city of Rhodes in 409, Rhodes does not appear to have been under a single or even a federal government; and so it was easily dealt with. The three chief cities all issued silver coins before the Persian wars, but not on the same standard. Camirus had issued abundant didrachms and drachms on the Aeginetan standard. These ceased when, after the battle of the Eurymedon in

465 B.C., the Persian power gave way to that of Athens: after that Camirus issued no more money. Lindus struck in the sixth century staters of Phoenician weight: under the Attic supremacy she issued only what seem to be hemidrachms and obols of Attic weight.

Obv. Fore-part of horse. *Rev.* Lion's head.[1] Weight, 32·2–31·6 (grm. 2·15–2·05); 7·9 (grm. 0·50). (**B. T. CXLVI. 34.**)

Ialysus struck in the sixth century also on the Phoenician standard. It is doubtful whether any of the staters extant are later than 465: their style is quite early, their inscription ΙΑΛΥΣΙΟΝ. Head and Babelon give some of them to a later time; but analogy is against this view. Thus the coinage of the island during the time of the Athenian Empire is very small.

Of the Greek cities in Western Asia Minor, none issued coins uninterruptedly during the fifth century. Some intermitted their coinage during the time of the Delian confederacy: some issued a few coins of Attic weight; but most of these struck only small denominations: some, as we shall presently see, adopted the standard of Chios, which was clearly a rival of that of Athens.

Coins of the Attic standard are after, as before, 480 B.C. exceptional in Asia. Themistocles, while tyrant of Magnesia, about 465 to 450 B.C., struck remarkable didrachms of Attic weight, having as obverse type a standing Apollo, as reverse type a flying eagle. Their weight is 8·56–8·59 grm. (132–133 grains). (**Pl. VI. 11.**) Even in exile Themistocles regards Athens as his mother city, or else wishes to remain on terms with the Attic coinage. It is one of the revenges of time that Themistocles should appear in our coin-cabinets only as a vassal of Persia. Another point to be noted is that of the few coins of Themistocles which have come down to us, two are only plated with silver; and it

[1] M. Babelon calls these coins Aeginetan diobols, Mr. Head Phoenician tetrobols. The analogy of Cos would lead us rather to regard them as coins of Attic weight, used only for small currency.

is very probable that these debased specimens were issued from the mint with the others, for we have definite evidence that the issue of a proportion of plated coins among those of full value was a proceeding known to some ancient mints, notably that of Rome. And we suspect that the dangerous cleverness of Themistocles might dispose him to adopt such a plan.

The cities of Ionia seem during the fifth century to have almost universally ceased to issue money. An exception is Miletus, which issued small coins on the Attic standard, probably intended to pass locally as fractions of the Attic stater:

Obv. Lion to right. *Rev.* Stellar pattern in incuse. Weight, 32 grains (grm. 2·10). Attic triobol.

Obv. Head and paw of lion. *Rev.* Stellar pattern in incuse. Weight, 19·3–16·3 grains (grm. 1·25–1·05). (**B. T. CXLIX. 1–4.**)

M. Babelon[1] sets down these last coins as diobols of the old Milesian standard; and in fact they do more nearly conform to that standard than to that of Attica. They are in fact a continuation or revival of an issue of the sixth century.

Of Ephesus Mr. Head remarks, 'whether coins continued to be struck during the Athenian hegemony 469–415 B.C. is doubtful'. There are in fact no coins of Ephesus which can be safely given to this period. But about 415 the city revolted, and apparently went over to the Persians. In 408 the Athenian general Thrasylus made an attempt to reduce it, but he was driven off by the troops of the city, who were aided by Tissaphernes the Persian and the Syracusans.[2] It must have been about this time that the Ephesians resumed their interrupted coinage. And it is noteworthy that the standard which they use is that of Chios: didrachm 116–118 grains (grm. 7·51–7·64). M. Babelon[3]

[1] *Traité*, ii. 2, p. 1050.

[2] Xenophon, *Hellen.* i. 2; cf. Head, *Coinage of Ephesus*, p. 21.

[3] *Rev. Num.*, 1913, p. 474.

thinks that probably some of the staters of Ephesus belong to the period of Attic domination; he also allows staters of Teos. At Clazomenae there is a noteworthy break in the silver coinage, after the time of the Ionian Revolt, until the early part of the fourth century. There are, however, a few small coins of Attic standard, which Mr. Head attributes to this period:

Obv. Fore-part of winged boar. *Rev.* Gorgon-head in incuse square. Weight, 30 grains (grm. 1·94); 18 grains (grm. 1·16).

It seems to me not improbable that these coins may precede the Persian wars; if not, they would belong to the time immediately after. Coinage is also intermitted at Phocaea, Teos, and Cyme in Aeolis. Of Priene we have no early coins. The coinage of Colophon and Erythrae will be presently considered; it is probable that, at all events in the former city, the issue of coin in the latter half of the fifth century was due to Persian preponderance.

In two of the Carian cities which paid tribute to Athens, Cnidus and Astyra, we find a notable cessation of coin in the middle and end of the fifth century. Cnidus, however, in the opinion of M. Babelon, struck drachms and diobols during Athenian domination. The city resumed silver coinage after 412. The earliest known coin of Iasus is of the time of the Cnidian league, 394 B.C. We find, however, at Idyma a few coins which seem to belong to the latter half of the fifth century:

Obv. Head of Pan facing. *Rev.* IΔYMION Fig-leaf. Weight, 58–50 grains (grm. 3·75–3·25). (**B. T. CXLVI. 8–10.**)

In 445 B.C. Idyma was ruled by a tyrant named Pactyes.[1] It does not appear in the tribute lists after 440 B.C. It is therefore highly probable that the coins were struck at a time when Persian influence prevailed. They are of the Chian standard.

On the Persian standard was of course issued the official

[1] *B. M. Cat. Caria*, p. lxi.

coinage of the Persian Empire, the silver sigli. It does not, however, appear that these ever circulated freely beyond the limits of Asia Minor, within which they have been usually found. Even the gold darics were limited in their range. Indeed, the people of the interior even of Asia Minor, as well as those of Persia and Mesopotamia, used coins but little, and continued to use bars of the precious metals in exchange. It is true that when Alexander captured the great cities of Persia, such as Ecbatana and Susa, he found in them great hoards of darics, as well as of uncoined gold and silver; but this does not prove that the darics circulated in those cities. They may have come as tribute from the west. The chief use of the Persian coins was for payment of mercenaries in military expeditions in Asia Minor; and it appears that it was only on the occasion of military expeditions that the satraps of the Great King issued coins from the mints of Greek cities, bearing their own names.

Among the old cities of Ionia, only one keeps to the Persian standard during the time of the Athenian Empire:

Colophon: Inscription, ΚΟΛΟΦΩΝΙΩΝ or -ΟΝ.

Obv. Head of Apollo. *Rev.* Lyre in incuse square. Drachm. Weight, 84–3 grains (grm. 5.45–5.35). (Pl. VI. 12.)

Also hemiobols of 7.5–6.5 grains (0.49–0.40 grm.) and tetartemoria of 4.5–3.5 grains (0.29–0.23 grm.).[1] These coins can scarcely be so late as the Peloponnesian War: the style is archaic or transitional.

There must be reasons for the unusual course taken by this city. We learn from Thucydides[2] that at the beginning of the Peloponnesian war, the Persians gained possession of Colophon; while in the harbour-city of Colophon, Notium, two miles distant from it, the party opposed to the Persians, having gained the upper hand through the help of Paches,

[1] These coins bear marks of value HM and TE (half and quarter obol). This fact is important as proving that the coins are really of Persian weight. The obol they give is somewhat heavy in proportion to the drachm.

[2] iii. 34.

the Athenian admiral, set up a hostile power. How lon this division between Colophon and Notium lasted we d not know. In the Athenian tribute lists after this Colophoı which had previously paid three talents and then one an a half, only makes the nominal payment of 500 drachms, the twelfth of a talent. It seems likely that this tribut was from Notium, not from old Colophon.

These events, it is true, do not directly account for the us of the Persian standard at Colophon, since that standar comes into use early in the fifth century. But they sugges that Colophon, which was not exactly on the coast, wa more under Persian influence than the cities which coul be directly reached by the Athenian fleet.

Another Ionian city which is usually regarded as havin struck coins on the Persian standard is *Erythrae*.

Obv. Horseman running beside his horse. *Rev*. ΕΡΥΘ Flowe Weight, 72–67 grains (grm. 4·69–4·35); 17–13 grain (grm. 1·10–0·80). (B. T. CLIV. 24–31.)

Obv. Pegasus flying. *Rev*. ΕΡΥΘ Flower. Weight, 22–1 grains (grm. 1·40–0·80). (B. T. CLV. 4.)

This weight offers us a difficult problem. Babelo suggests that it is Persian, and observes that if the smalle coin of the first series is an obol, it will give a drachm o 5·40 grm. (84 grains). But it is more likely that the smalle coin is a fourth of the larger: the only safe plan is to g by the weight of the larger coins of a city, for the weigh of small denominations varies greatly, and cannot be relie on. We must therefore regard the normal weight of th drachm of Erythrae as 72 grains (grm. 4·69).

Before 480 B.C. Erythrae had issued coins on the Milesia standard, while Chios, her powerful neighbour, had adhere to the standard of Phocaea. This makes one suspect tha the relations of the two states were not cordial, althoug Herodotus tells us that they were of kindred race and spok the same dialect;[2] and in fact we know that they were a war in the seventh century.[3] Indeed, nearness of blood wa

[1] Koehler, *Del.-attisch. Bund*, p. 156. [2] Hdt. i. 142. [3] Hdt. i. 18.

no conclusive reason why neighbouring Greek cities should agree together. So it is not surprising that after 480 B.C., while Chios adhered to her standard, Erythrae should adopt a different one. We may judge that the mere fact that Erythrae struck coins at all was the result of an anti-Athenian tendency. An inscription[1] proves that in the middle of the fifth century there was a Persian party at Erythrae: it is likely that that party became dominant, and that the issue of coins was the result of such domination. But what is the standard?

The same standard recurs about 450 B.C. at Termera in Caria, in the unique coin of the British Museum, issued by the Tyrant Tymnes.

Obv. ΤVΜΝΟ. Bearded Herakles kneeling. *Rev.* ΤΕΡΜΕΡΙΚΟΝ. Head of lion. Weight, 72·4 grains (grm. 4·68). (Pl. VII. 1.)

This coin is given by Babelon to the period about 500 B.C.: I agree with Mr. Head in assigning it to a later time. Tymnes was probably a tyrant owing allegiance to Persia; and his coin may have been struck at a time when the city was free from the yoke of Athens.

The weight of the drachm of Erythrae requires some explanation. That its adoption shows Persian and anti-Athenian influence seems clear. At first sight it would seem that a city on a peninsula lying opposite to the island of Chios and connected with the mainland of Asia only by a narrow neck of land, must follow the fortunes of the islands of the Aegean, and be closely under the dominion of Athens. But if we look again at the district in the map we note the strength of Asiatic influence in the neighbourhood. Erythrae is quite near to Sardes, a centre of Persian power. Smyrna, after it had been destroyed by Sadyattes of Lydia, was not allowed for 400 years to rise again, in spite of a splendid commercial position. Colophon was largely in Persian hands, and Ephesus was the most fully Oriental in religion and manners of the cities of Ionia.

[1] *C. I.* i. 9-11.

Clazomenae was friendly to Athens; but it was an island-city, and the inhabitants were mainly people of Cleonae and Phlius, of Peloponnesian stock. One of the most remarkable clauses of the treaty of Antalcidas was that which secured to the King of Persia 'The islands of Clazomenae and Cyprus'. The juxtaposition of the great island of Cyprus and the tiny islet of Clazomenae is almost ludicrous; but it certainly shows that the king attached great importance to his predominance in the coast district between the mouths of the Hermus and the Cayster.

It is, however, almost impossible to suppose that drachms of 72 grains can have passed as equivalents of the Persian drachm or siglos of 86 grains; or of such coins on the Persian standard as those of Colophon: there is a difference of almost a gramme between the two; and small local issues were tariffed rather below than above their true value in international currencies.

The drachm of 72 grains was, however, normal in the fifth century at Thasos and other cities of Thrace, and we find it, as will presently be seen, at several cities of the Propontis—Selymbria, Cyzicus, Lampsacus, Astacus, Abydus, and Dardanus. This coincidence can scarcely be accidental: we will return to the subject.

Passing farther to the East we reach a region where Persian power was never seriously shaken, and the Athenian tribute was not exacted.

The cities of Cilicia—Issus, Nagidus, Mallus, Soli and others—adhere from their first issues to the Persian standard. As the expeditions of the Persian admirals were mostly fitted out in the harbours of Cilicia, this is not to be wondered at.

The district of Lycia and the island of Cyprus do not show in the weight of their coins any Athenian influence: they go on uninterruptedly until the age of Alexander. Phaselis only, a Greek city on the Lycian coast, paid tribute to Athens, and intermitted its coinage after 470 B.C.

V. Pontus and Propontis.

The cities of the next group, that of the Euxine Sea, adhere through the fifth and fourth centuries to the Aeginetan drachm. Sinope, Trapezus, Amisus, and Heraclea, retain this standard, though the weight of the drachm slowly falls. We may conjecture that the obstinacy with which Sinope adheres to her numismatic customs is due to the fact that the barbarous tribes, Scythians and others with whom she dealt, could not easily be persuaded to recognize another kind of money.

The cities to the south and east of the Black Sea were, when not autonomous, mostly under Persian domination. Shortly after 440 B.C. Pericles led an Athenian armament to Sinope. The Tyrant Timesilaus who bore rule there was expelled, and the estates of his followers made over to a body of 600 Athenian colonists. But this interference led to little result: Sinope never paid tribute to Athens. That city continued down to the time of Alexander to issue coins on its original standard, drachms seldom exceeding 94 grains (grm. 6·10). It is hard to see how these can have been reckoned except as equivalent to Persian drachms, though they usually decidedly exceed them in weight. We find at Panticapaeum a parallel fact. The gold money there issued in the middle of the fourth century weighs as much as 140·5 grains (grm. 9·10); but must have passed as gold didrachms of Attic standard (135 grains; grm. 8·42). It is not unnatural that remote places where the precious metals are abundant should make their issues acceptable, by slightly over-weighting them.

A new type is introduced at Sinope, probably, as M. Babelon suggests, at the time of the Athenian expedition, and the institution of democracy.

Obv. Head of the Nymph Sinope. *Rev.* Sea eagle standing on dolphin. Weight, 93–80 grains (grm. 6·02–5.18). (Pl. VII. 2.)

Historically it would be probable that the heavy weight

of the Aeginetan standard at Sinope arose originally because it was inherited from the somewhat heavier Milesian standard, which had earlier been current, when Miletus was dominant on the Euxine.

Generally speaking, we may trace in the region of the Euxine a gradual fall in the weight of the drachm from Aeginetan to Persian. Probably the cities of the coast, finding that their money was tariffed at the Persian rate, did not see any advantage to be gained by greatly exceeding the Persian standard. At the same time it must be allowed that there is no regular and uniform decline in weight, some of the coins of the fourth century being heavier than some which are quite archaic. In fact, the irregularity of the weights of the coins of Sinope, when they are of uniform type and general appearance, is a remarkable phenomenon, for which it is not easy to account.

Of the same irregular weight as the coins of Sinope, and of similar type, are the drachms of Istrus, on the European side of the Black Sea. Somewhat lighter in weight, but probably of the same standard, are the drachms of Trapezus.

Amisus, at the time of Pericles' expedition to Sinope, also received Athenian colonists, and the name Peiraeus appears upon its coins, drachms similar to those of Sinope, but bearing the Athenian type of an owl standing on a shield, in place of the eagle standing on a fish (**Pl. VII. 3**).

Coming from the Pontus to the Propontis, we reach the region of Athenian domination, or rather of the clashing of Persian and Athenian power. We have already seen, in the Introduction, that the Pontic region was more important than any other to Greek trade, as all Greece depended upon it for the supply of food, and for the materials for shipbuilding. Athens was constantly on the watch to dominate the gate of the Euxine between Byzantium and Calchedon. Byzantium at one period paid a tribute of more than twenty talents, and Calchedon as much as nine talents. At two periods, 411–405 and 390–387 B.C., Athens endeavoured to occupy the gate herself, and to compel ships passing through to pay a tribute of ten per cent. This right of demanding toll was exercised by the people of Byzantium from time to time. We cannot therefore be surprised to find that in the whole region from Byzantium to Abydos no large or abundant coinage can be traced at the time of the Athenian Empire. But at the same time the Persian satraps at Dascylium, on the southern shore of the Propontis, near Cyzicus, were very powerful, alike by means of arms and through control of resources. The Persian standard would therefore be likely to come in importance next to that of Athens. From the monetary point of view the most important cities of this district were Cyzicus and Lampsacus, whose coinage of electrum may almost be regarded as the official money of Athens for Pontic trade.[1] Of silver at Cyzicus before 405 B.C. there is very little; M. Babelon, however, attributes to the city small pieces, sometimes marked with the letter K, a drachm of 75 grains (grm. 4·83) and smaller divisions.[2] We may be almost sure that there was a monetary convention, according to which Athens supplied silver coin, except perhaps small divisions, and Cyzicus staters and hectae of electrum. With Lampsacus also Athens had probably a similar arrangement. During the first half of the fourth century Lampsacus gave up her issues of electrum and began a beautiful series of gold staters, others being at the same time struck at Abydos; and these coins also seem to have been meant for Athens and Athenian trade. But silver drachms seem to have been freely issued at Lampsacus in the fifth and fourth centuries. The types are

Obv. Janiform female head. *Rev.* Head of Athena. Weight, 72 grains (grm. 4·66). (B. T. CLXX. 25.)

We have then at these two important cities a coinage in silver which conforms to the standard of Thasos, commonly called Babylonian and sometimes Persian, but which is really distinct from both. We have already met this

[1] As to this see above, p. 232.

[2] Babelon, *Traité*, ii. 2, p. 1458. Types, Fore-part of boar; Lion's head.

standard at Erythrae, and decided that in that city it seems a sign of Persian influence.

Other cities of the Propontic region, however, strike on a standard which seems nearer to the ordinary Persian weight.

The following are of the period 480–450:

Cardia (Thracian Chersonese).

Obv. Fore-part of lion with head reverted. *Rev.* Incuse square, two sections deeper and two shallower. Weight, 36–40 grains (grm. 2·33–2·60).

Astacus.

Obv. Lobster. *Rev.* Head of Nymph. Weight, 76 grains (grm. 4·90); 23·5 grains (grm. 1·52). (**B. T. CLXXXI. 4–6.**)

Abydos.

Obv. ΑΒΥΔΗΝΟΝ. Eagle standing. *Rev.* Gorgoneion. Weight, 79–84 grains (grm. 5·12–5·41); 48 grains (grm. 3·08). (**B. T. CLXVII. 9–33.**)

Dardanus.

Obv. Horseman. *Rev.* ΔΑΡ. Cock. Weight, 72–75 grains (grm. 4·65–4·86). (**Pl. VII. 4.**)

It will be observed that these coins are all of small denomination, drachms, hemidrachms, tetrobols, and triobols: all the mints except Astacus are on the Hellespont.

In other cities of the same region we find a different standard at the same period:

Parium.

Obv. Gorgoneion. *Rev.* Incuse square, within which a pattern. Weight, 47–60 grains (grm. 3–3·88); 25–26 grains (grm. 1·62–1·68). (**B. T. XVI. 22–23.**)

Assos.

Obv. Griffin lying. *Rev.* Lion's head in incuse. Weight, 55·8 grains (grm. 3·59–5·78); 24 grains (grm. 1·55). (**B. T. CLXIII. 25–27.**)

In these examples, while the drachm appears to follow the Chian standard, the smaller coin is of the same weight as the smaller coin at Astacus. Evidently we have to do with issues of small coins to meet local needs.

At a somewhat later time, other cities come in on what seems to be the Chian standard.

450–400 B.C.

Antandros.

Obv. Head of Artemis. *Rev.* ANTAN. Goat standing. Weight, 50–58 grains (grm. 3·23–3·67). (**B. T. CLXIII. 3–5.**)

Gargara.

Obv. Head of Apollo. *Rev.* ΓΑΡΓ. Bull feeding. Weight, 42–49 grains (grm. 2·74–3·14). (**B. T. CLXIII. 13–15.**)

Obv. Head of Apollo. *Rev.* ΓΑΡ. Horse galloping. Weight, 22 grains (grm. 1·44).

Lamponeia.

Obv. Head of bearded Dionysus. *Rev.* ΛΑΜ. Bull's head. Weights, 53–59 grains (grm. 3·41–3·81); 27–29 grains (grm. 1·72–1·88). (**B. T. CLXIII. 22–24.**)

Neandria.

Obv. Head of Apollo. *Rev.* NEAN. Altar, horse or ram. Weight, 29 grains (grm. 1·85–1·86). (**B. T. CLXVI. 1–4.**)

Proconnesus.

Obv. Female head. *Rev.* ΠΡΟΚΟΝ. Oenochoe. Weight, 38·8 grains (grm. 2·50). (**B. T. CLXXIX. 18.**)

All these small coins seem to follow the Chian standard, of which they are mostly drachms or half-drachms.

Scepsis is somewhat exceptional. Being an inland town, on the head-waters of the Scamander, it was less completely at the mercy of the Athenians than other cities of Troas. It paid from time to time a tribute of a talent. Its coinage, however, is fairly continuous, and evidently of some importance. It follows the Chian standard, didrachm 118 grains (7·68 grm.) and drachm 59 grains (3·84 grm.). Types, Half galloping horse; Fir-tree.

It is noteworthy that the city of Sigeium, at the entrance to the Propontis, a city connected with Athens from the time of Solon downwards, issued no coins in the fifth century, using doubtless those of Athens. When Sigeium does issue coins, in the fourth century, her types are thoroughly Athenian, the head of Athena and the owl.

The coinage of Byzantium and Calchedon belongs mainly to the fourth century, but a few coins of both cities are of the fifth century. Both Byzantium and Calchedon paid heavy tribute to Athens. The money of Calchedon, of which I speak, consists of drachms of 61 grains (grm. 3·95) and hemidrachms of 30 grains (grm. 1·94). These appear to follow the standard of Chios:

Obv. Bearded male head. *Rev.* Wheel. Weight, 37·5–30 grains (grm. 2·42–1·94). (Pl. VII. 5.)

Obv. Same head. *Rev.* ΚΑΛΧ. Wheel. Weight, 61–58 grains (grm. 3·95–3·78). (B. T. CLXXXI. 7–13.)

Obv. Beardless head. *Rev.* ΚΑΛ. Wheel. Weight, 33–30 grains (grm. 2·10–1·97).

Obv. Round shield. *Rev.* Same. Weight, 16 grains (grm. 1·05).

Their date is not much later than the middle of the fifth century. Perhaps they were intended as fractions of the electrum staters of Cyzicus and the hectae of Mytilene.

At Byzantium drachms of Persian weight were issued (84 grains, grm. 5·44) with the type of a bull standing on a dolphin, and a somewhat primitive incuse on the reverse. It is hard to determine their date on stylistic grounds, as the incuse is obviously a mere survival, as it is at Cyzicus and Cardia; but I think that Mr. Head, in assigning it to 415 B.C., comes down too late. The date of the coins being doubtful, and the history of Byzantium full of vicissitudes, it is impossible to assign them to any particular phase of the history of the city. They seem to have continued for a considerable time, and to be the most noteworthy sign of Persian influence in the region. After the fall of Athens, or possibly before it, Byzantium and Calchedon both issued tetradrachms on the standard of Chios.

On the coins of Selymbria, a city on the European shore

of the Propontis, we can trace with unusual distinctness the progress of Athenian domination in the fifth century. Early in that century, the city had issued coins on that Thasian standard which was in use in Thrace:

Obv. ΣΑ. Cock. *Rev.* Incuse square. Weight, 76·4 grains (grm. 4·96) (Br. Mus.).

After 450 B.C. she strikes rare coins on the Attic standard.

Obv. Cock. *Rev.* ΣΑΛΥ. Ear of corn (Berlin). Weight, 67 grains (grm. 4·34).

Obv. Head of Heracles. *Rev.* Cock in incuse. Weight, 57 grains (grm. 3·70).

This is a clear example of the process which at this time was going on along the Thracian coast.[1]

A city on the west coast of the Euxine, which seems to have belonged to the Propontic group, is Apollonia, a Milesian colony near Mount Haemus. It is supposed to have struck [2] about 450–400 B.C.

Obv. Anchor with crayfish. *Rev.* Gorgoneion. Weight, 58–44 grains (grm. 3·75–2·85).

VI. Thrace and Macedon.

The changes in monetary standard in Thrace and Macedon during the period 480–400 B.C. are many, and not always easy to explain. The less explicable they seem the more important they become, as showing the working of tendencies and forces not at present understood. In science it is to residuary phenomena that we look for clues.

At the time of the Persian Wars there were three standards in ordinary use in the district. Starting from Thasos, a standard commonly called Babylonic, with a stater

[1] *Hist. Num.*, ed. 2, p. 271.

[2] Reasons for this attribution are given by Tacchella (*Rev. Num.*, 1898, p. 210); the alternative attribution to Apollonia ad Rhyndacum in Mysia, once held by Imhoof-Blumer (*B. M. Cat. Mysia*, p. 8) and J. Six, is now given up. See *Hist. Num.*, ed. 2, p. 278.

of 144–152 grains (grm. 9·33–9·84), had spread to the Thracian mining tribes through the seaport of Neapolis, opposite Thasos. Concurrently the so-called Phoenician standard had spread westward from Abdera, and been adopted by many tribes, as well as by the Kings of Macedon. The coins of Chalcidice used from the first the Attic standard, combined with the Corinthian divisions of the stater. (See above, p. 186.)

When we realize the standing policy of Athens as regards coins, the fixed determination to monopolize the silver currency of the Aegean, we understand the great importance which she attached to the possession of the southern shore of Thrace. For the silver mines of the Pangaean Mountains and that district were the most important source of silver in the Aegean, together with the mines of Laurium. In days before the Persian Wars the local tribes had issued silver coin in great abundance, long before it could have been expected of such rude peoples. The inhabitants of Thasos had acquired riches and importance by their possession of mines on the mainland opposite, as well as in their own island. Herodotus,[1] as is natural, speaks more of their gold mines than of those of silver: the more valuable metal naturally attracting most attention. But the gold of Thrace and Thasos seems never to have been in any considerable quantity turned into coin on the spot until the days of Philip of Macedon. The silver from very early times had been so struck, and the Athenians might well hope that if they secured this rich source of silver they might almost make a *corner* in the metal, and control the market for it. Hence, the Athenians were determined to gain the mastery of Thasos. They fell out with the islanders over the continental mines; and in 465 an Athenian armament under Cimon first shut up the Thasians into their city, then reduced them by siege, and compelled them to surrender their ships and their continental possessions. The successive foundations by the Athenians at the Nine Ways

[1] vi. 46.

and at Amphipolis show with what determination they adhered to the control of the district, which they regarded as the citadel of their power.

To turn to the coins. The coinage of the local tribes, the Letaei, Bisaltae, Orreskii and the rest, seems not to have lasted after the Persian Wars. These tribes were pressed on all sides. The powerful and wealthy city of Thasos was close to them for attack, but being on an island was not liable to counter-attacks. The power of the Kings of Macedon, who boasted of a certain Hellenic culture, was steadily growing. And the rich coinage of Abdera shows the dominant position which that city assumed in regard to the trade of Thrace. The appearance of the names of magistrates on the coins of Abdera from a very early time seems to show that the city was under a more compact and aristocratic rule than most Greek cities. Thus it is natural that the weaker tribes who worshipped Dionysus on the Pangaean mountains were deprived alike of their wealth and their independence. But the Thasian domination soon came to an end, and the Athenian took its place. After the expedition of Cimon, Neapolis, which was then the Athenian factory, ceased to issue coin until 421. And the Thasians struck but little coin in the second half of the century, that which they did strike following the standard of Athens, and later that of Chios, which was usual in the district after the time of Brasidas.

Coins of Thasos.

1. *Obv.* Satyr carrying nymph. *Rev.* Incuse square. Weight, 135–130 grains (grm. 8·74–8·42). **(Pl. VII. 6.)**
2. *Obv.* Head of bearded Dionysus. *Rev.* ΘΑΣΙΟΝ. Heracles shooting arrow, in incuse. Weight, 230 grains (gr. 14·90). **(Pl. VII. 7.)**

Coins of class 1 belong mostly to the first half of the fifth century: those of class 2 to the time after Brasidas.

Coins of Neapolis.

1. *Obv.* Gorgon head. *Rev.* Incuse square. Weight, 150-140 grains (grm. 9·72–9·07).

2. *Obv.* Gorgon head. *Rev.* ΝΕΟΠ. Head of Nike.[1] Weigh
58–55 grains (grm. 3·75–3·56).

In the time of Brasidas a change of standard takes plac
see below.

Although, however, the coinage of the Thracian trib
disappears, we have a few coins struck by Thracian dynas
in the time of the Athenian Empire. The Odrysae, i
particular, under their king Sitalces, dominated a gre
region, from Abdera to the Euxine Sea, at the time
the Peloponnesian War; and that dominion lasted in pa
until the time of Philip of Macedon. The Thracian chie
do not appear to have issued coins except at Greek citie
which, from time to time they either occupied or controlle
Some of the most notable of these coins are as follows:

Sparadocus, brother of Sitalces.

Obv. Horseman bearing spears. *Rev.* ΣΠΑΡΑΔΟΚΟ. Eag
devouring serpent, in incuse. Attic tetradrachm.

Drachms and diobols of the same ruler are known. Th
types and the weight alike seem suitable to Olynthus, an
Head[2] conjectures that the coins were struck in that city
but it is scarcely possible to suppose that the power
Sparadocus spread so far to the west: Aenus is far mo
probable.

Seuthes I, son of Sparadocus.

Obv. Armed horseman. *Rev.* ΣΕΥΘΑ ΚΟΜΜΑ or ΣΕΥΘ
ΑΡΓΥΡΙΟΝ. No type. Attic didrachm and drachm.

The mint of these coins cannot be determined.

Eminacus.

Obv. ΕΜΙΝΑΚΟ. Heracles kneeling, stringing his bow. *Re*
Wheel, around which dolphins, in incuse. Weight, 18
grains (grm. 11·73).

In the time of the Peloponnesian War the Aegineta
standard was used at Abdera. Eminacus, a person unknow

[1] So *B. M. Cat.* Parthenos is a better identification. Cf. Schöne, *Grie
Reliefs*, Pl. VII, where Parthenos appears as the representative of Neapolis.

[2] *Hist. Num.*, ed. 2, p. 282.

to history, would seem at that time to have adopted it. The coin was found near Olbia.[1]

Bergaeus.

Obv. Silenus carrying Nymph. *Rev.* ΒΕΡΓΑΙΟΥ; incuse square. Weight, 50 grains (grm. 3·24).

This is obviously an imitation of the coins of Thasos.

It is not easy to explain the facts in regard to the Thasian tribute to Athens. From 454 to 447 the island is entered in the lists as paying only three talents, after that year the quota is raised to thirty talents. Historians have supposed that the higher rate of contribution was consequent on the retrocession of the control of the mines by Athens to Thasos. This is a plausible conjecture, but it does not seem to be supported by definite evidence. Undoubtedly the raising of the tax was often an arbitrary proceeding on the part of the Athenian democracy.

The most important coinage in the middle of the fifth century, besides that of Thasos, is that of Abdera:

1. *Obv.* Griffin rampant. *Rev.* ἐπί with name of magistrate in incuse. Weight, 230–236 grains (grm. 14·90–15·30).
2. *Obv.* Griffin of later style. *Rev.* Magistrate's name round type. Weight, 215–216 grains (grm. 13·93–14). (**Pl. VII. 8.**)
3. *Obv.* Similar griffin. *Rev.* Magistrate's name and type. Weight, 193–198 grains (grm. 12·50–12·80).
4. *Obv.* Magistrate's name; Griffin recumbent or rearing. *Rev.* Head of Apollo, laureate. Weight, 170–175 grains (grm. 11–11·33).

To the question of the weights of these coins we will soon return. Coin No. 1 follows the old Abderite standard, while No. 2 shows a reduced weight which is also found at Maroneia at this time.

Obv. Prancing horse. *Rev.* ἐπί, with magistrate's name, round vine. Weight, 210–220 grains (grm. 13·60–14·25).

The crucial point in the history of the coins of Thrace

[1] Head, *Hist. Num.*, ed. 2, p. 283.

and Macedon is to be found in the expedition of Brasidas, 424 B.C., together with the peace of Nicias, which followed the death of Brasidas and Cleon in 421.

During the hegemony of Athens, 465–424 B.C., the coins of so-called Babylonic standard, struck at Thasos and Neapolis, do not in fact exceed the Attic weight, or very slightly exceed it.[1] If Attic coin were at the time largely current in the markets of Thrace, as is almost certain, and if the coins of Thasian standard were regarded only as equivalent to Attic didrachms, there would be a valid reason for gradually reducing their weight. To maintain it would have been a sheer waste of silver.

Thus in the middle of the fifth century, the standards in use were in effect but two, the Attic and the Abderite. And the Attic was encroaching. Aenus, which began to strike money about 460 B.C., used the Attic standard, in a rather light form (**Pl. VII. 9**): an exactly similar standard comes in for a time, probably just before the time of Brasidas, at Maroneia.[2] Afterwards, towards the end of the century, these two cities take divergent courses. At Aenus the Chian standard comes in; whereas Maroneia, no doubt under the influence of her powerful neighbour Abdera, accepts the Persian standard.

With the Thracian campaign of Brasidas the whole matter becomes far more complicated. The sway of Athens on the Thracian coast, which had long been almost unquestioned, and which was strongly confirmed by the foundation of Amphipolis in 437 B.C., was greatly shaken, and thenceforward most of the cities became autonomous. It does not appear that the cities of Thrace had, like those of Ionia and the Cyclades, generally given up the issue of coins during the time of Athenian preponderance; but it is noteworthy that we have no coin that we can with confidence give to Eïon on the Strymon in the middle of the fifth century, and that Amphipolis struck no coins until its autonomy was secured after 421 B.C. And further, at certain cities, such

[1] Cf. *B. M. Cat. Thrace*, p. 218.

[2] *Hist. Num.*, ed. 2, p. 250.

as Acanthus, Aeneia, Mende, and Terone in Chalcidice, there appears to be a decided break between the coinage of the early fifth century and that of the time after Brasidas. Even the Kings of Macedon, who of course did not renounce coinage rights in favour of Athens, issued very little coin. The money of Alexander I is abundant; but of his successor Perdiccas II, who reigned about 454–413 B.C., we have only rare diobols and tetrobols: at least these are the only coins bearing his name. In the early part of his reign Perdiccas was on very friendly terms with the Athenians, but later he fell out with them. Archelaus, who succeeded in 413, struck money on the Persian standard, which, as we shall see later, came in at Abdera and elsewhere towards the end of the fifth century.

After 421 B.C. there is a great outbreak of coinage on the part of the cities of Thrace and Macedon, and in nearly every case they strike not on the Attic standard but on the 'Phoenician' standard hitherto in use at Abdera. Among these cities are Amphipolis, the cities of Chalcidice, and Neapolis. The weight of the stater is about 230–220 grains (grm. 14·90–14·25). It is practically at this period identical with the Rhodian standard, which had become of almost universal use in Asia Minor.

Strange to say, Abdera seems to choose this very time for altering her own standard. For some time during the last quarter of the fifth century she gives up the 'Phoenician' standard which she had used since the foundation of the city, and adopts another of which the stater weighs about 196 grains (grm. 12·75). Mr. Head calls this standard the Aeginetic, but observes that probably the change in weight was gradual rather than sudden.[1] I must, however, dispute the latter view.

Mr. Head,[2] taking the coinage of Abdera in an isolated way, suggests that the changes of standard, which are so noteworthy in that city, may result from a constant striving after bimetallism, that is to say, an attempt to secure the

[1] *Hist. Num.*, ed. 2, pp. 254–5. [2] *Ibid.*, ed. 2, p. xliii.

equivalence of a round number of silver staters with a gold unit, which would naturally be the daric. I very seldom find myself at issue with Mr. Head, but on this occasion I am driven to this attitude. And the controversy is important, as the coinage of Abdera may well give the key to that of all the Thracian cities.

At Abdera, he writes, 'between the Persian wars and the time of Philip, when its autonomous coinage came to an end, the tetradrachm or stater falls in weight, successively, from 240 to 224 grains, then from 198 to 190 grains, and lastly from 176 to 160 grains or less. It is hard to account for these reductions, usually regarded as inexplicable changes of standard, from (1) Rhodian[1] to (2) Phoenician, from Phoenician to (3) Aeginetic, and from Aeginetic to Persic (4), except on the theory that the rapid fall of the silver value of gold, which we know took place in Europe between 500 and 356 B.C., influenced the silver coinage. In other words, Abdera, though it is not known to have struck gold, seems to have been striving after a bimetallic system of exchange. . . . The gold unit from first to last would be equivalent to eight silver staters, the weight of which, as time went on, would be reduced as follows:

128 grains	of gold at	15 to 1	= 8 silver staters of 240 grains (cl. 1).
„	„	$14\frac{1}{2}$ to 1	= 8 of 232 grains (cl. 1).
„	„	14 to 1	= 8 of 228 grains (cl. 2).
„	„	13 to 1	= 8 of 208 grains (cl. 2).
„	„	12 to 1	= 8 of 192 grains (cl. 3).
„	„	11 to 1	= 8 of 176 grains (cl. 3).
„	„	10 to 1	= 8 of 160 grains (cl. 4).'

Mr. Head then thinks that the changes in standard were gradual rather than sudden; and that the legal change registered a fact that had taken place rather than produced a cataclysm. Mr. Head's argument is plausible, and it is

[1] This is a slip: naturally the Rhodian standard did not exist in the fifth century, before the city of Rhodes was founded. It is really the standard of Phocaea and Chios that Mr. Head means.

necessary to examine it with care, as, if established, it will have far-reaching consequences.

We ought to begin by fixing the date of the actual changes of standard, though this can only be done approximately. Mr. Head places the transition to the Aeginetic standard (3) about 430 B.C. and to the Persian standard (4) about 408 B.C. The last date must be not far from right, though a few years too early; for the transition to the Persian standard was probably the result of the fall of Athens, and took place in the neighbouring kingdom of Macedon in the reign of Archelaus I, 413–399 B.C. (**Pl. VII. 10**). The former date is less easily fixed; and in the absence of knowledge of the history of Abdera must remain doubtful, as well as the meaning of the modification of standard which then took place. The really important landmark is, of course, the expedition of Brasidas. Von Fritze's dates, after a most minute examination of the coinage (*Nomisma*, No. 3), are 425 B.C. for the first change of standard, and 400 for the second.

Two preliminary objections to Head's view occur. In the first place, his theory assumes that Abdera acted in the issue of coins quite independently of the other cities of Thrace and Ionia, which is exceedingly improbable. In the second place, it assumes that the commerce of the district was dominated by the gold darics of Persia, whereas in fact it was dominated by the silver coinage of Athens. It is to be observed that when the Thracian cities of Thasos, Aenus, Maroneia, and Amphipolis strike gold coins, as they do occasionally between 411 B.C. and 356 B.C., they follow the standard, not of the daric, but of the somewhat heavier gold coinage of Athens. But apart from these objections, I do not think that Mr. Head accurately states the facts. It does not appear to me that the coinage falls gradually from 240 to 224 grains, from 198 to 190, and so on; but that the heavier coins in each series are in many cases later than the light ones. This may easily be seen on consulting the British Museum catalogue. The coins are there arranged in chronological order as indicated by style, and the weights vary, within the limits of the standard, upwards and downwards. The two tetradrachms put in that catalogue in the first place as the most archaic, dating from the sixth century, weigh 224 and 228·5 grains respectively: coins 24 to 26, dating from the middle of the fifth century, weigh 230·4, 236·7, 224·7 grains respectively. There can thus be no question of a gradual fall of standard, down to the time of Brasidas. Also of the coins following the supposed Aeginetan standard the weight does not fall in any marked or distinct way with time.

Moreover, the dates of the reductions of the exchange value of gold do not correspond with the changes of standard at Abdera. The fall from fourteen to one to twelve to one should, according to Mr. Head's table, take place about 430. In fact it does not occur until the end of the fifth century; perhaps, as M. T. Reinach suggests, in consequence of the influx of darics into Greece. 'Cette proportion de 14:1', writes M. Reinach,[1] 'se maintint probablement en Grèce jusque dans les dernières années de la guerre du Péloponnèse.'

Thus, while we do find at Abdera an unusual number of changes of standard, and the weight of the coins does fall, there does not seem to be any ground for supposing that the motive of those changes was a pursuit of a bimetallic standard. And since Abdera is the example most favourable to such an explanation, we may fairly dismiss it as fanciful in the case of other cities. The early issues of Asia were based upon a desire to make a certain number of coins of silver or of electrum equivalent to one or two gold staters. But this plan was never adopted at Athens, where, as Xenophon implies,[2] and as clearly appears from inscriptions, silver was the standard of value, and gold was regarded only as an article of commerce. Nor was it adopted in any cities of European Greece. We have, however, evidence, as will appear below, that the cities of Sicily resorted to bimetallism for a few years before 400 B.C.

We have still to consider the curious and unexpected

[1] *L'Histoire par les monnaies*, p. 50. [2] *De Vectig.* iv. 10.

appearance of the Aeginetan standard at Abdera. That it is the Aeginetan, though the coins in some cases slightly exceed that weight, seems to be undeniable; for the weight suits no other standard. This phenomenon may best be accounted for on political rather than financial grounds. After the disaster at Syracuse we know that many of the allies of Athens revolted. We have an indication that Abdera was among these in a passage of Diodorus. Describing the events of the year 408 B.C., he writes,[1] 'After this' Thrasybulus, with fifteen Attic ships 'sailed to Abdera, and brought over the city, which was then one of the most powerful cities of Thrace'. That so much was accomplished by so small a force need not surprise us, if we remember that in most of these Greek cities political power was divided between the partisans of Athens and those of Sparta, and a small armament might turn the scale. But the passage definitely indicates that at the time Abdera had fallen away from Athens. At such a time we can scarcely be surprised if she tried to introduce a coinage of Peloponnesian weight. The Spartan fleets were constantly in that region, and the sailors reckoned, as we can prove from the dealings of the Peloponnesian admirals with Chios, by the Peloponnesian standard. But the attempt of Abdera can scarcely have been successful or of long duration. Very soon it was abandoned, and the Persian standard took its place.

The Editor of the Berlin *Corpus* of coins of Thrace[2] has pointed out that while the people of Abdera were issuing staters of full Aeginetan weight, they were also issuing hemidrachms on a different standard. While the didrachm weighs 196 grains or thereabouts (grm. 12·70), half drachms bearing the same names of magistrates, and so certainly contemporary, weigh only 44 grains or less (grm. 2·85). These smaller coins already seem to follow the Persian standard, which at the end of the fifth century comes in also

[1] xiii. 72.

[2] *Die ant. Münzen N. Griechenlands*, ii. 36. This writer (Dr. M. L. Strack) does not call the standard of these coins the Aeginetan.

for the staters. We are of course used to the phenomenon that small and fractional coins, intended for use only in the home market, are often not struck of full weight. But the weight of the hemidrachms under discussion is so uniform that it would seem to be purposeful. Dr. Strack thinks that this issue of coins indicates that the Persian standard was in the last half of the fifth century coming in on certain lines of trade, especially the trade with Cardia, and the cities of the Hellespont; and that this line of trade became more important about 400, so as then to conquer the whole coinage of Abdera.

Amphipolis does not issue any coin before the time of Brasidas: after that, the city strikes most beautiful coins on the Abderite standard. (**Pl. VII. 11.**) But the type of these coins is a full-face head of Apollo, which we can scarcely venture to place earlier than the full-face head of Arethusa at Syracuse by Kimon. This latter head is attributed by Sir A. Evans [1] to 409 B.C.; the coinage of Amphipolis must therefore be given to the very last years of the fifth century.

The coins of the district of Chalcidice furnish interesting phenomena. The largest city of the region, Acanthus, appears to have issued coins uninterruptedly during the period of Athenian hegemony: until the time of Brasidas (424 B.C.) they were struck on the Attic standard (**Pl. VII. 12**); after Brasidas on the Abderite standard. That there was no interval between the latest coins of the former class and the earliest coins of the latter class may be seen from a comparison of Nos. 6 and 22 in the *Brit. Mus. Cat. of Macedon*, the reverses of which are almost identical, though the standard is changed. Mende also seems to have struck tetradrachms of Attic standard about the middle of the fifth century. Potidaea does not appear to have issued any silver money after the Athenian siege of 432; and in fact all the extant silver seems to belong to a time before the middle of the fifth century. Other cities of Chalcidice either intermit

[1] *Syracusan Medallions*, p. 70

coinage altogether between 450 and 424, or else strike only coins of small denominations, usually the Attic tetrobol or Corinthian drachm, for local use. This is the case with Olynthus, Dicaea, Terone, and other cities.

We may observe that Acanthus, being a wealthy and powerful city, situated not actually on any of the rocky peninsulas, but with access to the interior, was almost in the same position in regard to Athens as Abdera and Maroneia. The smaller cities, situate among the mountains of the promontories, were at the mercy of an Athenian fleet, and in much the same position as the islanders. Hence Athenian pressure would be more likely to bear upon them than upon Acanthus.

In an important paper published in the American *Classical Philology* for 1914[1] Mr. Allen B. West gives reasons for thinking that the Chalcidian League was not founded, as has been supposed, in 394 B.C.; but had existed as early as the time of Xerxes, and was organized on a closer footing in 432 B.C.[2] Mr. West suggests that some of the coins inscribed *Χαλκιδέων*, and struck at Olynthus, belong to the latter part of the fifth century. The weight, that of Abdera, is quite suitable for the time after Brasidas. It is most probable that the gold staters of the class (*Obv.* Head of Apollo, *Rev.* Lyre and name of magistrate) (**B. M. XXI. 9**) were issued soon after 394, following the lead of Athens. Some of the silver coins, being of a somewhat severe style, and showing remains of an incuse square (**B.M. XXI. 10**), may well have been struck before 400 B.C. The striking of civic staters in silver by the cities of Chalcidice, except Acanthus, which did not belong to the League, would probably cease at the same time; but some cities, such as Terone and Aeneia, seem to have continued their issues of smaller coins on the standard of Abdera.

Terone.

Obv. Naked Satyr looking into an oenochoe. *Rev.* TE. Goat in incuse. Tetrobol. Weight, 36 grains (grm. 2·33).

[1] pp. 24–34. [2] Compare Thucyd. i. 58.

Aeneia.

Obv. Head of Athena. *Rev.* Bull looking back in incuse Tetrobol. Weight, 36 grains (grm. 2·33).

Contemporary with these are the coins of Olynthus.

Obv. ΟΛΥΝΘ. Head of Apollo. *Rev.* ΧΑΛΚΙΔΕΩΝ. Lyre in incuse. Weight, 35 grains (grm. 2·26).

Mr. West has not cited one coin which tells strongly in favour of his view.

Obv. Free horse cantering. *Rev.* XALK. Eagle carrying serpent in incuse square.[1] Weight, 41 grains (grm. 2·65).

As this coin is precisely similar, save for the inscription to one of Olynthus,[2] we must suppose it struck in that city But it bears the inscription *Χαλκ* . . . in decidedly archaic letters, and must have been issued by Chalcidian moneyers before the end of the fifth century.

VII. Italy and Sicily.

The cities of Italy and Sicily at no time formed part of the Athenian Empire. In fact it was the attempt of Athens to extend the bounds of her empire in this direction which was the cause of her fall. But it may be well, in the present connexion, to consider what are the results of Athenian influence to be traced on the coins of Italy and Sicily. The Athenians had a claim, the exact nature of which is doubtful, on the territory of Siris, a city of Italy destroyed by its neighbours after the middle of the sixth century. This may have been a reason for the choice of the site of Sybaris, near by, as a place for the foundation of an Athenian colony by Pericles, about 443 B.C. This colony by no means consisted entirely of Athenians, it included the descendants of the old inhabitants of Sybaris destroyed about 510 B.C., as well as a number of people from Peloponnese, North Greece, and the Islands. This colony

[1] *Hist. Num.*, ed. 2, p. 208. Compare *Num. Chron.*, 1897, p. 276.
[2] *B. M. Cat. Macedon*, p. 87, 2.

is interesting to lovers of Greek literature, because among the colonists were Herodotus and Lysias the orator. And it is interesting to the numismatist, because the coins of the new colony, in their types, give us information as to the history of the colony. On the earliest coins we find the name, not of Thurii but of Sybaris, and the olive with which the helmet of Athena is bound seems to indicate an Athenian connexion.

Obv. Head of Athena, helmet bound with olive.
Rev. ΣΥΒΑΡΙ. Bull with head reverted or lowered. Weight, 42–40 grains (grm. 2·72–2·60).
Rev. ΣΥΒΑ. Same type. Weight, 18–16 grains (grm. 1·16–1·03).
Rev. ΣΥΒΑ. Head of bull. Weight, 6 grains (grm. 0·38).

The attempt to combine the old inhabitants of Sybaris with the new colonists was not successful. The former expected to take the lead;[1] and being frustrated, withdrew to a settlement apart. Some authorities would attribute to this separate town the coins above cited; others think that the colony at first bore the name Sybaris. Before long the old Sybarites were destroyed; and it cannot in any case have been long after the foundation that the regular issue of coins in the name of Thurii began.

Obv. Head of Athena, helmet bound with olive wreath. *Rev.* ΘΟΥΡΙΩΝ. Bull butting. Weight, 230 grains (grm. 14·90); 123–119 grains (grm. 7·97–7·71); 40 grains (grm. 2·59); 18–16 grains (grm. 1·16–1·03).

But Thurii was never a dependent ally of Athens. The people were a mixed race, as we have seen. In the war between Athens and Syracuse Thurii was, as a rule, neutral. Only the head of Athena seems to bear witness to Athenian influence; and even there the figure of Scylla, which the helmet of the goddess after the first usually bears, shows that it was rather as a local deity than as a protrectress of

[1] Diodorus, xii. 11.

Athens that Athena was chosen for the obverse of the coins.

The artistic influence of the Athenian settlers of Thurii in Italy and Sicily appears to have been considerable. This subject was first treated by R. S. Poole,[1] whose views have been accepted and expanded by Furtwängler,[2] Evans, and other writers.

But this artistic influence seems the only kind of influence in Italy that the foundation of Thurii brought to Athens. We cannot doubt that Athens had intended by the foundation to acquire political and commercial power; and here she was foiled. A crucial test lies in the consideration that the coins of Thurii were not minted on the Attic standard, but on that of other cities of South Italy, such as Croton and Metapontum. This standard, being almost exactly the same as the Chian, would favour the coinage of Aeginetan rather than that of Attic weight. At the same time we may observe that the issue of the tetradrachm in place of the didrachm, almost universal in South Italy at the time, may be a result of Athenian traditions.

The figure of Athena is also prominent on certain coins of Camarina in Sicily. She appears in a quadriga on coins of the middle and latter part of the fifth century. As about 427 B.C. we find Camarina allied with Leontini and Athens against Syracuse,[3] we might be at first disposed to see a phil-Attic allusion on these coins. But Camarina soon gave up her alliance with Athens, and since the early coins of the city also bear a figure of Athena, we may best suppose the type to be purely local.

We may therefore say with confidence that the influence of Athens is scarcely to be traced on the coins of Italy and Sicily in the fifth century, save as regards art.

[1] *Num. Chron.*, 1883, p. 269.
[2] *Meisterwerke*, p. 143.
[3] Thuc. iii. 86.

VIII. Historic Results.

We proceed to consider how the data thus gained from a study of the coins fit in with received notions as to the history of Athens and her allies during the seventy years of Athenian domination. We took our start from the claim of Athens to a complete monopoly of the issue of coins where she was strong enough to enforce it. She certainly succeeded in enforcing it firstly in the case of her own colonies, secondly in the case of the Aegean Islands (at all events in the period after 450 B.C.), and thirdly at most of the cities of Asia Minor excluding the great islands of Chios, Samos, Lesbos, and Cos.

Negative evidence is proverbially untrustworthy. The fact that we have no coins of a city during a certain period does not prove that no coins were struck there. But when city after city is drawn blank, and that at a time when commerce was very active, we cannot escape from a conclusion. Nor is it only the gaps in the coinages of the islands and the cities of Ionia which testify to the dominance of the Athenian owls, but other indications may be cited.[1] The fact that at Naucratis in Egypt out of ninety-seven coins of early period found on the site eighty-six were Athenian tetradrachms, in the great majority of cases dating from the period 480–394 B.C., is sufficient proof that Athens served the Greeks in Egypt as their mint. In the same way, that the Messenians settled at Naupactus by the Athenians, 460 B.C., did not issue any coins on their own account, must be regarded as a proof that they used the Athenian money.

In some of the cities where Athens was not able to impose her own coinage she caused a change to the Attic standard in the currency. This is the case in Samos and in Rhodes, where however the supremacy of the Athenian standard was very brief. At Cos it for many years replaced the Aeginetan standard.

[1] *Naukratis*, i, p. 63.

In some cities of Asia, while Athens appears to have supplied the bulk of the coin, there were local issues of small denominations. At Miletus these fractions were of Attic weight. But in the district of the Propontis they were often of the standard of Chios or of Persia. At Cardia, Abydus, and Dardanus they were of Persian weight; at Parium and Assos they were of Chian weight.

In 500–480 B.C. the influence of Aegina had been marked by the use of the Aeginetan standard in Pontus, at Teos in Ionia, and more especially on the southern shores of Asia Minor, in Cos, Cnidus, and Camirus. It is instructive to see how, as Aegina sinks beneath the yoke of Athens, the Aeginetan monetary standard drops away in the cities of Asia. At Cos it gives way to the Attic standard. At Cnidus and Teos coinage seems entirely to have intermitted. In the district of Pontus the weight of the drachm falls from Aeginetan to Persian level. The Aeginetan standard holds its own in Greece Proper, and in the large island of Crete; elsewhere it is everywhere recessive.

In Thrace, Thasos, and Lycia, where the 'Babylonic' drachm was in use, it shows towards the middle of the fifth century a marked tendency to fall in weight, and to conform to the Attic standard. In Thrace especially this result is completely reached by the time when Amphipolis was founded. Aenus, which began to issue coins about 460 B.C., starts with the Attic standard.

The rivals in Asia of the Attic standard were those of Persia and of Chios. It seems that the spread and the recession of these standards is sometimes a reflection of the advance or retrogression of the influence of the states to which the standards respectively belong.

In districts to the east of the Bosporus and Rhodes, the power of Persia seems steadily to increase during the latter part of the fifth century in the Greek cities. The hold of Persia on the cities of the coast tightens; and we are prepared for the revival of Persian preponderance which is so marked a feature of the early fourth century. On the other hand there is but one city of the Ionian coast,

Colophon, which actually uses the Persian standard, though in other cities, such as Erythrae and Termera, we find a weight scarcely to be distinguished from it.

One of the most remarkable features of the coinage of Asia Minor in the fifth century is the tenacity with which the Chian standard kept its place, and, towards the end of the century, rapidly extended its influence. This was the old standard originally used for dark electrum (or gold) coins of the northern part of the west coast of Asia Minor. It was applied to silver in the sixth century at Tenedos, Parium, and Chios; and to billon or base metal at Mytilene, Phocaea, and Cyzicus.

At the time of the Ionian revolt, though the people of Chios were foremost in the rebellion against Persia and at the battle of Lade, Miletus remained the head-quarters of the Ionian League; and the coins of electrum and of silver issued by the cities of the League were minted on the standard of Miletus.

After the suppression of the revolt, Miletus suffers eclipse. The Chians, though they had to suffer the rigours of Persian conquest, probably remained the most powerful state of the Ionian coast. They did not issue electrum or gold; but the striking of silver on the old North Ionian standard went on. About the middle of the fifth century this standard was adopted at Parium and Assos. Towards the end of the Athenian domination, it spread from Chios to several cities of the Propontis. Towards the end of the century it was adopted at Byzantium, Antandros, Scepsis, Lamponeia, and Apollonia and Mesembria on the Euxine. But its chief success was at the newly founded city of Rhodes, about 400 B.C. The Chian standard after that spreads in the early part of the fourth century all along the coast of Asia Minor.

By the choice between the Attic and the Chian standards by the cities which issued coins late in the fifth century, we may perhaps judge whether they preferred the alliance of Athens or that of Sparta, though the slight difference of the standards in normal weight makes the test difficult to apply practically. When dealing with the coinage of Chios, I have shown that there was a well-known and acknowledged relation between the coinage of Chios and that of Peloponnese. The Chian tetradrachm was regarded as the fortieth of the Aeginetan mina, or as equivalent to two and a half Aeginetan drachms. The Chian drachm was thus one hundred and sixtieth of the Aeginetan mina or five-eighths of the Aeginetan drachm. This was an official tariff; and the sailors and soldiers of the Peloponnesian fleet were paid in Chian money at this rate. It is clear that we must connect these facts, so clearly established, with the spread of the Chian standard at the very time when Peloponnesian fleets preponderated in the Aegean, and in the very district which they made their head-quarters.

The political importance of this fact seems to me to be considerable, and it has not been hitherto appreciated by numismatists. The mere facts recorded by Thucydides and Xenophon show that the Peloponnesian fleets looked to Chios for their resources in money, as the Athenians looked to the silver mines of Thrace and Laurium. But the study of the coins carries us further. For it proves that, precisely at this time, the standard or coin-weight of Chios began to spread rapidly among the cities of the coast. I think that most numismatists have missed this clue, because they have been accustomed to regard this standard as belonging to the island of Rhodes, and its spread as due to the commerce of Rhodes. In fact Rhodes merely adopted it from Chios, and was by no means the earliest city of Asia to do so, although no doubt its rapid spread in the fourth century was favoured by the rise of Rhodian commerce.

The misfortunes of Athens, even before the capture of the city by Lysander, had greatly shaken the Athenian Empire; and the people of Asia Minor, especially those of the Bosporic region, were no longer under any necessity to accept the Athenian weights and the Athenian coins. Persia had not yet fully used the opportunity to recover predominance on the coast of the Aegean. Thus there was an open field; and at the time Chios was probably the wealthiest and most powerful state on the coast. At the same time, as we have seen, the Chian money was on recognized terms with that of Peloponnesus.

It appears also to have had a recognized relation to the silver coinage of Persia. For the Chian drachm of 56 to 60 grains (grm. 3·62–3·88) was almost exactly of the weight of two-thirds of the Persian drachm of 84–86 grains (grm. 5·44–5·57). It is to be observed that at this time several cities of north Asia Minor issued drachms of the weight of 3·60 grammes, which probably belonged equally to the Chian and the Persian standard.

It would be a gain of great historic importance if we could trace chronologically the spread of the Chian standard. Unfortunately, we can at present only do so tentatively: with time we may attain to more complete knowledge.

Perhaps the most archaic in appearance of the coins on the Chian standard, save those of Chios itself, are those of Ephesus:

Obv. ΕΦ. Bee. *Rev.* Incuse square, quartered by two broad or narrow bands. (Head, *Ephesus*, Pl. I, 15–21.)

The tetradrachm of this series, inscribed with the name ΜΕΝΤΩΡ,[1] seems to have disappeared and its weight is not recorded. Two didrachms in the British Museum weigh 116–117 grains (grm. 7·51–7·58): one bears the name of Timarchus. Smaller coins in the same Museum weigh 42–47 grains (grm. 2·72–3·04): one bears the name Timesianax.[2]

These coins are certainly earlier than the coins of the Cnidian League at Ephesus, 394 B.C.: therefore the name Mentor cannot be that of the well-known Satrap of the time of Philip of Macedon. Mr. Head assigns the coins to 415–394 B.C. As Ephesus had become by 410 B.C. not only

[1] Mionnet, *Suppl.* vi, No. 183.

[2] There are also published gold coins of similar fabric and Attic weight: according to Mr. Head they are forgeries. (*Ephesus*, p. 22.)

detached from Athens, but even the head-quarters of the anti-Athenian party in Ionia, it is reasonable to suppose that the issue of these coins marked the defection from Athens about 415; and the use of the Chian weight is instructive: the old standard at Ephesus had been quite different.

The coins of Calchedon of which I have spoken as of Chian weight are certainly early, not later than 420 B.C.; and if it seem at first sight uncertain that their weight is Chian rather than Attic, this is rendered at least very probable by comparison with the coins of Mesembria and of Apollonia on the western shore of the Euxine. These cities certainly struck on the Chian standard considerably before 400 B.C. The same holds of Parium, Assos, and Scepsis, all cities near the Sea of Marmora.

It was about the time of the fall of Athens that the Chian standard became rapidly more widely diffused. It is, however, impossible from the coins to trace the course of its diffusion so exactly as to determine what was due to the political events of the end of the fifth century, and what was due to the rapid growth of Rhodian commerce and wealth at the beginning of the fourth century. It will be better therefore to avoid here any further discussion of the matter.

Thucydides[1] records an interesting fact in regard to the comparative vogue of the Athenian and Aeginetan standards in Peloponnese. When in 420 Athens concluded an alliance with Argos, Elis, and Mantinea, it was arranged that the foot-soldiers in the service of the league should receive half an Aeginetan drachm a day, and the horse-soldiers a whole Aeginetan drachm. It is clear that the soldiery of Peloponnesus always adhered to the native standard.

IX. Gold at Athens.

Gold coins were first struck at Athens, as has been conclusively shown by Dr. U. Köhler,[2] in 407 B.C. It was a

[1] v. 47.

[2] *Att. Goldprägung; Z. f. N.* 1898.

time of great need: the Athenian fleet had been defeated at Notium, and the city was nerving itself for a final effort which, as every one knows, only led to the decisive defeat at Aegospotami. The golden Victories of the Acropolis were melted down, and from the proceeds coins were struck in gold. These gold coins are apparently alluded to in the *Frogs* of Aristophanes exhibited in 405 B.C., where he contrasts the good old-fashioned citizens of Athens with the new favourites of the people, likening the former to the old silver, not alloyed, the most beautiful and well-struck of coins, received everywhere among Greeks and barbarians, and to the gold coins recently struck (*τὸ καινὸν χρυσίον*); while he compares the latter to base copper coins (*πονηρὰ χαλκία*) lately struck in clumsy fashion.[1]

This passage in Aristophanes is very difficult, and has been much discussed. I am disposed to accept the interpretation of it above given, which is due to M. Six. But a further consideration of it is unnecessary for our present purpose. Its chief importance for us is that it has elicited definite statements by the Scholiast as to the dates of the first issues of gold and bronze money. The Scholiast gives the authority of Hellanicus for the assertion that gold was issued in the archonship of Antigenes (407 B.C.) and the authority of Philochorus for the assertion that the gold was procured by melting down the golden Victories. He also says that the bronze coin was issued in the next year, that of the archonship of Callias.

These gold coins have been satisfactorily identified by Köhler.

1. *Obv.* Head of Athena, early style. *Rev.* AΘE. Incuse square, in which owl on olive branch: behind, olive-spray. Drachm.
2. *Obv.* The same. *Rev.* AΘE. Incuse circle, in which owl to front, wings closed, in an olive-wreath. Hemidrachm.
3. *Obv.* The same. *Rev.* AΘE. Incuse square, in which two owls face to face: olive-branch between them. Diobol.
4. *Obv.* The same. *Rev.* AΘE. Incuse square, in which owl r. on olive-branch. Obol. (B. T. CLXXXIX. 1–8.)

[1] *Frogs*, line 730 and foll. and Scholiast.

The types of 2 and 3 are the same as those on silver coins of the same denominations, an important fact, as showing that this coinage was meant only to be subsidiary to, or in place of, the ordinary money.

This issue of gold coin had far-reaching effects. Hitherto the only coins of pure gold in use in the world had been the Persian darics. But there were struck at just this time a few small coins of Agrigentum (issued just before the destruction in 406), of Camarina and of Gela (issued just before 405), and of Syracuse (about 413 B.C.)—all of which coins seem to have been money of necessity, struck from golden images and dedications melted down during great stress. The weights of these Sicilian coins are 27, 20, 18, 13, and 9 grains. According to Mr. Head, the ratio given by these coins between gold and silver is fifteen to one; in which case the coin of 18 grains would be equivalent to a tetradrachm in silver. But this cannot be regarded as by any means a certainty. It is, however, in any case probable that the gold was regulated in weight so as to pass for a certain number of litrae in silver or bronze: in a word it was bimetallic.

But the Athenian issue of gold marks a great and important new departure in the matter of finance; the same weight was used for gold and silver; and the silver being the standard coin, the value of the gold conformed to it. The weights of the gold coins make one feel sure that at the time at Athens gold was tariffed at twelve to one; in which case the four denominations issued would be valued as follows:

Gold drachm	=	12 silver drachms.
„ hemidrachm	=	6 „ „
„ third	=	4 „ „
„ sixth	=	2 „ „

If this were so, the accident that the relation of the metals at the time stood at twelve to one would bridge the chasm between a monometallic and a bimetallic system.

At a later time the Athenians issued didrachms, hemidrachms, and diobols in gold, bearing a head of Athena executed in a later style. The weight of the stater or didrachm does not exceed 133 grains (grm. 8·60) (Pl. X. 7). In regard to these Head writes,[1] 'At what precise date Athens was again compelled to have recourse to an issue of gold coin is doubtful. One point is, however, quite clear, and that is that the gold coins of the second issue are identical in style and fabric with the tetradrachms issued from 393 onwards' (Pl. X. 8).[2] To the time immediately after 394 I would boldly give them. This view conflicts with that of Köhler, who thinks that the gold coins in question were issued in the time of stress of 339 B.C., when Philip was marching on Athens. Köhler points out that, according to the Attic inscriptions, great dedications of gold figures of Victory and of vessels were made in the years 334–330 B.C., which suggests that these dedications had been melted down shortly before.

However, a decisive proof that the Athenian gold coins of the second issue must be given to an earlier time than the middle of the fourth century is furnished by Köhler himself.[3] He cites an Attic inscription of 'about the beginning of the fourth century' in which mention is made of Attic staters, and, as appears from the context, Attic gold staters. Now no staters are known of the issue of 407 B.C., but only drachms and lesser denominations. Of course, it does not follow that because at present no didrachms are known, none were struck. We can reach only probability, not certainty. But in archaeology we can seldom reach complete certainty: we have to walk by the light which we possess.

A further proof of this view is furnished by an Attic inscription published by Mr. Woodward,[4] which records

[1] *Hist. Num.*, ed. 2, p. 375.

[2] Mr. Head's date for this class of tetradrachms is confirmed by the occurrence of an example in the Cilician find, buried about 380, published by Mr. Newell in the *Num. Chron.*, 1914.

[3] *Z.f.N.*, 1898 (p. 13 of reprint), *I.G.* ii. 843. The inscription cannot, unfortunately, be exactly dated. Mr. Woodward (*J.H.S.*, 1914, p. 280) thinks it possible that it may be earlier than 400.

[4] *J.H.S.*, xxix (1909), p. 172. Cf. *Num. Chron.*, 1911. The reading τοὺς

the dedication of certain dies which had been used for gold coin—*οἱ χαρακτῆρες καὶ ἀκμονίσκοι, οἷς τοὺς χρυσοῦς ἔκοπτον*. The inscription dates from between 385 and 375 B.C. Mr. Woodward supposes that the dies had been used for the first issue of gold coin in 407. But this interpretation will not stand, as the χρυσοῖ must be *staters* of gold, not drachms, which might be χρυσία, but could not be χρυσοῖ. This proves that an issue of staters or didrachms must have taken place before 375 B.C.[1]

It is in some measure a confirmation of these views that Conon, when he died in Cyprus in 389 B.C., bequeathed to Athena at Athens and Apollo at Delphi a sum of 5,000 staters.[2] As the nature of the staters is not mentioned, it may be disputed of what kind they were. M. T. Reinach[3] thinks that they were Lampsacene or Daric staters; but it seems far more probable that they were of the new Athenian issues. M. Reinach shows the stater mentioned to have been worth 24–22 silver drachms; there can, I think, be little doubt that 24 drachms was at the time the normal value.

This dating is satisfactory and removes difficulties. The first issue of small denominations was a money of necessity struck at the time of deepest need. The second issue is of another character, more plentiful and varied, and deliberately intended for currency. The monopoly of the Attic silver having departed, and its place in the commerce of the Aegean being taken by the darics and the staters of Cyzicus, there was no longer any reason to abstain from issuing gold, in competition with these.

The first abundant issue of gold coin by Athens comes naturally at a time when the great victory of Conon at

χρυσοῦς (or τὸς χρυσοῦς) is conjectural; but it seems to be fairly certain, as the number of letters fills a gap.

[1] Mr. Woodward (*l. c.*), while allowing the force of my remarks as to the use of the word χρυσοῖ, yet thinks that a dedication was much more likely in the case of dies used at a time of necessity and then thrown aside. If it be so, yet I think my argument more weighty than a mere probability.

[2] Lysias, *De bonis Aristophanis*, c. 39.

[3] *L'Hist. par les Monnaies* p. 50.

Cnidus had laid the foundation for a new period of expansion and empire. The staters became the models on which were framed the issues of Thebes and Olynthus and many cities in Asia, of Tarentum in the west, and Cyrene in the south. This subject I further discuss in my account of the gold coinage of Asia.

X. Bronze at Athens.

As regards the date of the earliest issues of bronze coins at Athens we have definite information. The Scholiast on Aristophanes' *Frogs* (l. 730) says that bronze was first struck in the archonship of Callias (406 B.C.). And in the *Ecclesiazusae*, Aristophanes narrates how they were demonetized in 393 B.C. The town-crier announced (l. 821) that they were no longer to be current: ἀνέκραγ' ὁ κῆρυξ μὴ δέχεσθαι μηδένα χαλκοῦν τὸ λοιπόν, ἀργύρῳ γὰρ χρώμεθα. It seems that the unfortunates, who at that moment possessed the bronze coin, had to submit to the loss. The coins were thus current only for thirteen years. Clearly they were a money of necessity, struck at the time of Athens' deepest need, and withdrawn after the victory of Conon at Cnidus, when the gold staters began to be struck.

According to Mr. Earle Fox[1] they were only the following:

> *Obv.* Head of Athena to left of fine style, in close fitting helmet. *Rev.* ΑΘΗ. Owl facing, wings closed, standing on a grain of corn, between two olive-branches (*B. M. Cat.*, Pl. VI. 5). Also a smaller coin, on which the olive-branches are wanting.

The unusual character of the head of Athena and the Η in the inscription seem to me to be in conflict with the ascription of these coins to so early a date.

[1] *Num. Chron.*, 1905, p. 3, Pl. I.

I am disposed to regard as the coins mentioned by Aristophanes the following:

1. *Obv.* Head of Athena, helmet bound with olive. *Rev.* ΑΘ. Two owls within olive-wreath (*B. M. Cat.*, VI. 2).
2. *Obv.* Similar head. *Rev.* ΑΘΕ. Two owls with one head: olive spray on either side (*B. M. Cat.*, VI. 6).

The close resemblance of No. 1 to the silver tetrobols and of No. 2 to the silver diobols appears to show that these bronze coins were issued at a time of stress to take the place of the silver.

On the use of bronze coins, as money of necessity, in the place of silver of the same types, light is thrown by an interesting inscription of Thebes of the second century B.C.[1] This inscription shows that bronze coins of the same size and types as the silver drachms of the same period were issued at Thebes as legal tender, but in fact passed at 25 per cent. discount. The hipparch was, however, obliged to pay his soldiers in silver, which he had to buy at a premium.

Later in the fourth century there was no doubt a regular issue of bronze money. Julius Pollux[2] mentions bronze coins as in use in the time of Philemon, that is, the age of Alexander. They seem to have varied in value from three-quarters of an obol (six chalci) to the single chalcus. The fact that Aristophon, a poet of the Middle Comedy, living about the middle of the fourth century, speaks of a five chalcus piece,[3] seems to show that the issue of regular bronze money began in the time of the second Athenian Empire.

Another view has recently been set forth with much learning by Mr. Svoronos.[4] He maintains that the only bronze coin issued at Athens in the fifth century was the *κόλλυβος*, a small piece introduced by Demetrius surnamed *ὁ Χαλκός* about 430 B.C. Such small pieces of bronze have

[1] *Hermes*, 1874, p. 431; *C. I.* vii. 2426.
[2] *Onom.* ix. 65.
[3] Pollux, *l. c.*
[4] *Journal intern. d'archéologie numismatique*, 1912, p. 123.

long been known at Athens; Mr. Svoronos publishes a long list. I am by no means convinced by his arguments, but I have not space to discuss them. I adhere to the usual view that these pieces were not currency, but tesserae.

Bronze coins had before this been issued in many Greek cities, notably in those of Sicily. It was natural that their use should spread eastward from Italy and Sicily where in early times bronze was the standard of value, as was silver in Greece and gold in Asia.

CHAPTER XV

SILVER OF ASIA, 400–330 B.C.

§ 1. Spread of the Chian Standard.

In treating of the coinage of the Athenian Empire we have seen how the Chian standard of weight for coins spread from city to city, during the period after the disastrous Athenian expedition against Syracuse. After the taking of Athens by Lysander in 404 B.C., that spread became more marked. The tetradrachm of Chios, it will be remembered, weighed about 240 grains (grm. 15·55) and the didrachm 120 grains (grm. 7·77). The substitution of the Chian standard for that of Athens at any city would seem to mark a revolt against the influence of Athens. This course of matters is not surprising. The Aeginetan standard which was in use in victorious Peloponnesus had no longer any currency outside Greece proper, nor was there in Peloponnesus any important commercial city, if we except Corinth, which city had a standard of its own. We can therefore understand why the Aeginetan standard did not at this time spread to Asia.

We may also observe that the Chian standard worked in easily with those of Aegina and Persia. It has been shown by documentary evidence,[1] statements of Thucydides and Xenophon, that at the end of the fifth century the admirals of Sparta procured from Chios money for payment of their sailors, and that in such payments the tetradrachm of Chios was reckoned as equivalent to a fortieth of the Aeginetan mina (240 grains × 40 = 9,600 grains). There was also an easy *modus vivendi* between the Chian standard and that of Persia in the equation of the Chian drachm (56–60 grains,

[1] Above, Chap. XIV.

grm. 3·62–3·88) with the Persian tetrobol, or two-thirds of a drachm (56–58 grains, grm. 3·62–3·75). At many cities there were issued coins of about 56 grains (grm. 3·62) which served as either of these denominations.

But perhaps the event which most of all contributed to the spread of the Chian standard was its adoption by the rising commercial city of Rhodus. Attention has often been paid by numismatists to the rapid rise of Rhodes, and the vogue of its standard. Mr. Head,[1] however, rightly saw that the Rhodian standard was in fact that of Chios. When about 408 B.C. the ancient cities of the island of Rhodes, Lindus, Camirus, and Ialysus, combined to found the new city of Rhodus, the new foundation rose almost immediately to a great height of prosperity, and for centuries was a dominant factor in the commerce of the Aegean Sea. For a few years after the foundation Rhodus used the Attic standard, as was not wonderful, considering that until the fatal battle of Aegospotami Athens was very powerful on the coast of Asia Minor, and the Attic weight was used in the neighbouring island of Cos. These pieces of Attic standard are, however, very rare, and probably the issue of them ceased with the fall of Athens in 404. Rhodus then adopted the Chian standard, and, as we have already observed, helped greatly in its extension among the islands and cities of Asia and Thrace. The smaller islands on the Carian coast, Calymna and Megista, followed suit. Ephesus also took to the Chian weight before the end of the fifth century.

In tracing the spread of the Chian or Rhodian standard in the early fourth century, we may best begin with one of those fixed points which are of inestimable value to the historian of coinage.

M. Waddington first set forth the view of the establishment in Asia of a defensive league of cities, after the victory of the Athenian admiral Conon at Cnidus in 394 B.C. Some recent historians have preferred the date 387, which seems

[1] *Hist. Num.*, ed. 2, pp. 600, 604.

to me far less probable; that is rather the time of the end than of the beginning of the League. The cities known to have belonged to the league are Samos, Rhodus, Ephesus, Iasus, Cnidus, and Byzantium.[1] These cities issued an almost uniform coinage, of which the peculiarity is that each of the cities belonging to the alliance, while placing on one side of the coin its own device, places on the other the type of young Heracles strangling the serpents. This type is usually accompanied by the legend ΣΥΝ, which probably stands for *συνμαχικόν*, a word which is found on the coins issued by the federated cities of Sicily in the time of Timoleon. Only at Rhodes is this legend wanting.

Samos.

1. *Obv.* ΣΑ. Lion's scalp. *Rev.* ΣΥΝ. Young Heracles and serpents. Weights, 263 grains (grm. 17); 173–178 grains (grm. 11·20–11·55). **(Pl. VIII. 7.)**

Rhodus.

2. *Obv.* ΡΟ. Rose. *Rev.* Young Heracles and serpents. Weight, 175 grains (grm. 11·35). **(B. T. CXLVII. 5.)**

Ephesus.

3. *Obv.* ΕΦ. Bee. *Rev.* ΣΥΝ. Young Heracles and serpents. Weight, 172–177 grains (grm. 11·12–11·44). **(B. T. CLII. 23; B. M. XIX. 29.)**

Iasus.

4. *Obv.* ΙΑ. Head of Apollo. *Rev.* ΣΥΝ. Young Heracles and serpents. Weight, 166 grains (grm. 10·73). **(B. T. CXLVI. 25.)**

Cnidus.

5. *Obv.* ΚΝΙΔΙΩΝ. Head of Aphrodite: prow. *Rev.* ΣΥΝ. Young Heracles and serpents. Weight, 165–167 grains (grm. 10·67–10·83). **(B. T. CXLV. 20.)**

Byzantium.

6. *Obv.* ΒΥ. Cow on Dolphin. *Rev.* ΣΥΝ. Young Heracles and serpents. Weight, 174 grains (grm. 11·30).

[1] Byzantium, however, was not liberated by the Athenians until 389 B.C. *Zeit. f. Numism.*, xxv. 207.

The first coin in this list, that of Samos, weighing 263 grains, is restruck on a tetradrachm of Athens, which looks as if the allied cities hesitated at first what standard they should adopt; but they soon decided on that of Chios.

Other cities adopt the type, but not the weight, nor the inscription ΣΥΝ. Such are Lampsacus, Cyzicus, and even the distant Croton and Zacynthus. The type seems to be taken from the coinage of Thebes, where an infant Heracles strangling the serpents appears on the formation of an anti-Spartan alliance between Thebes, Athens, Corinth, and Argos in 395 B.C.[1] The political bearing of the type is indeed obvious; Heracles was the hero of Thebes, and his victory over the serpents is an emblem of the success for which the newly-arisen power of Thebes hoped in its struggle with the overmastering power of Sparta. Xenophon and Diodorus tell us that after the victory of Conon at Cnidus most of the cities of Asia and the islands threw off the Spartan yoke. The coins enable us to be sure that an actual alliance was concluded between some of the cities.

To what standard these coins belong is an interesting question. Mr. Head[2] has suggested that they are tridrachms of Chian or Rhodian standard, and it is to be observed that Cnidus issued at the same time what can scarcely be other than Rhodian drachms—*Obv.* Forepart of lion; *Rev.* Head of Aphrodite Euploia (weight, grm. 3·62–3·74; 56–58 grains). But why the allied cities should have issued tridrachms instead of tetradrachms, when the tetradrachm was the ordinary Rhodian coin, and was coming in at many points of the Ionian coast, has not been explained. It is to be observed that precisely the same combination of tridrachms of 170–180 grains and drachms of 56–58 grains had been usual in one island, Zacynthus, ever since coins were first struck there, early in the fifth century B.C., and Zacynthus adopted the type of Heracles and the serpents when it was introduced in Asia. In fact, the treatment of the subject on Zacynthian coins is closer to that usual in Asia than to that

[1] See Grote, Chap. 74.

[2] So also Six, and Holm, *Griech. Gesch.* iii. 55.

used at Thebes. Such is the fact, but we are inclined to regard the coincidence as fortuitous, for the weight of the tridrachms could not have been adopted in order to conform to a standard used in distant Zacynthus. No doubt these Rhodian tridrachms were also regarded as didrachms of Persian standard; and a hint is given that the allied cities were probably not without reliance upon Persian support against Sparta.

I have above pointed out that this League of the fourth century may fairly be regarded as an echo or temporary revival of the old Ionian League of 500 B.C., which was broken up after the battle of Lade.

At Athens at this time a relation of twelve to one existed between the value of gold and that of silver. If we suppose the same ratio to have held in Asia, the gold didrachm or stater of 133 grains (grm. 8·60) would be equivalent to 1,596 grains of silver (grm. 103·4), somewhat less than ten pieces of 170 grains (grm. 11·0). But if the old Asiatic relation of thirteen and a third to one still persisted, the gold didrachm would be equivalent to 1,800 grains of silver or rather more than ten of the new silver staters. And that it did persist we have good reason for thinking, since the weights of the Persian daric and siglos seem in some places to have persisted to the end of the Persian Empire, and one daric remained equal to twenty sigli. If this view be sound we have some interesting equivalences. It seems that the Chian or Rhodian drachm was regarded as the thirtieth part, alike of the daric and of the rare gold staters of the Greek cities, which thus were regarded as equivalent, though the daric is some three grains or a fifth of a gramme lighter.[1] And the Aeginetan mina of silver, which was, as we have seen, equal to 160 Rhodian drachms, would be equivalent to $5\frac{1}{3}$ Persian darics. Of course, these mutual values are all approximate and liable to vary in one direction or another according to the rate of exchange or *agio*; but they are not without importance.

[1] Harpocration definitely states this equivalence, s. v. Δαρεικός.

We can trace the adoption of the Chian or Rhodian standard for coin northwards along the coast of Asia. Its progress seems to be largely due to its acceptance by the powerful Satraps of Caria, Hecatomnus and Mausolus. As we can date the coins of these dynasts, the information which they give us is precise.

Hecatomnus, whose rule lasted from 395 to 377 B.C., struck coins of two different classes:

1. *Obv.* Zeus Stratius standing, holding the bipennis. *Rev.* ΕΚΑΤΟΜ. Lion to r. Weight, 221–234 grains (grm. 14·32–15·17). (**Pl. VIII. 8.**)
2. *Obv.* ΕΚΑ. Lion's head and paw. *Rev.* Starlike flower. Weight, 191·5 and 65 grains (grm. 12·40 and 4·20–4·25). (**B. T. LXXXIX. 17.**)

The capital of Hecatomnus was Mylasa, and it is probable that he there struck No. 1, the types of which combine the worship of the Carian Zeus, Osogo, with the lion, not specially connected with him, but rather with the Apollo of Miletus. Coin No. 2 was doubtless issued at Miletus. We have no historic record that Hecatomnus was ruler of Miletus; but if we consider the geographical situation of Mylasa, which lay in the high lands behind Miletus, we shall regard an extension of the power of this Satrap of Caria down to the coast as probable. Mausolus removed the seat of his power to Halicarnassus. His rule and influence were more widely extended than his father's, including not only Miletus, but also the island of Rhodes, which was in the power of his oligarchic partisans.[1]

The coins of Mausolus are of the same two classes as those of Hecatomnus:

1. *Obv.* Head of Apollo facing, laureate. *Rev.* ΜΑΥΣΣΩΛΛΟ. Zeus Stratius standing, with bipennis. Weights, 228–249 grains (grm. 14·75–16·13); 50–57 grains (grm. 3·21–3·72). (**Pl. VIII. 9.**)
2. *Obv.* ΜΑ. Lion's head and paw. *Rev.* Starlike flower. Weight, 196–202 grains (grm. 12·68–13·07). (**B. T. XC. 1.**)

[1] Demosthenes, *De Rhod. Lib.*, pp. 191, 198.

We will begin with considering the coins of class 1 of both rulers. Between the money of this class issued by Hecatomnus and that issued by Mausolus there is not only a change of type, but a distinct raising of the standard. In both these particulars we may trace the influence of Rhodes. The full-face head of Apollo on coins of Mausolus is a clear imitation of the Rhodian type. And the weight also is raised to conform to the Rhodian standard. Hecatomnus seems to have adhered to the (Phoenician or Milesian) standard used at Miletus. Mausolus, having moved his capital to the sea-coast opposite Cos, and entering fully into the sphere of Rhodian commerce, naturally raised the standard so that his coins should pass with those of that commercial city.

The sets of coins No. 2 under the two rulers bear the recognized types of Miletus, and were almost certainly struck in that city. Their weights are interesting and suggestive. The larger denomination, under both Hecatomnus and Mausolus, seems to be a tetradrachm of the old Milesian standard, which was used at Samos and Ephesus in the fifth century, but was there abandoned for the Chian or Rhodian late in the fifth or early in the fourth century. This would seem to be an example of the vitality of local coin standards, which often persist in an almost inexplicable way. Under Hecatomnus the third of this piece was also struck, weighing 65 grains (4·20 grm.). This must have passed as an Attic drachm, and we are reminded that, before this, hemidrachms and diobols of the Attic standard had been current at Miletus,[1] locally issued as fractions of the Athenian tetradrachms, which doubtless made up the main currency.

In 366 the people of Cos imitated those of Rhodes in forming a fresh city which they built at the eastern end of the island, and in migrating thither.[2] All the coins issued at this new capital are of Rhodian weight, which therefore was adopted at Cos in the lifetime of Mausolus.

[1] Chap. XIV, p. 257.

[2] Diodorus, xv. 76.

Quite as early as this it was accepted at Cnidus, where we have very fine tetradrachms, bearing on the obverse the head of Aphrodite. Previously, as we have seen, Cnidus kept to the standard of Aegina, as Cos had adhered to that of Athens.

At Samos the Rhodian (or Chian) standard must have found admission quite near the beginning of the fourth century. For we have a long series of coins struck in accordance with it, tetradrachms, drachms, hemidrachms and diobols, before the Samians were conquered and expelled from their island by the Athenians in 365 B.C.

At Ephesus the introduction of the Chian standard must have taken place earlier (Pl. VIII. 10). Mr. Head in his work on the coinage of Ephesus puts it at 415. But the coins of Ephesus are very hard to date, as we have only the style of the bee and the incuse square to go by. If we could be sure of the date 415, it would be a valuable fact, showing that Ephesus at that time fell away from the Athenian alliance. It is almost certain that Ephesus accepted the standard before Rhodes did, and before the end of the fifth century (see p. 257).

We possess also a tetradrachm of Chian standard struck at Smyrna about the middle of the fourth century.

> *Obv.* Head of Apollo, laureate. *Rev.* ΣΜΥΡΝΑΙΩΝ. Lyre in concave field. Weight, 232 grains (grm. 15·03).[1]

This coin seems to prove that, though we hear nothing of Smyrna between the destruction of the city by Alyattes and its rebuilding by Antigonus and Lysimachus, yet it existed in the interval.

A tetradrachm of Cnidus of the same standard was found by Gell on the site of the city.

> *Obv.* Head of Aphrodite. *Rev.* Fore-part of lion in incuse square, ΕΟΒΩΛΟΣ. Weight, 233 grains (grm. 15·09).[2] (Pl. VIII. 11.)

[1] *Hist. Num.*, ed. 2, p. 592; cf. *Corolla Numism.*, Pl. XV. 6, p. 299. M. Six thinks that the coin was minted at Colophon. Babelon omits it.

[2] *B. M. Cat. Caria*, p. 87.

To the time of Mausolus, if we may judge from the style belong some interesting coins of Miletus.

Obv. Head of Apollo, facing. *Rev.* ΕΠΙ ΔΙΔΥΜΩΝ ΙΕΡΗ. Lion looking back at star. Weight, 27 grains (grm. 1·70–1·76).

This is evidently a sacred coin struck on the occasion of a festival at the Didymaean temple. The word *ἱερή* is puzzling; but as the coin is evidently a hemidrachm of the Rhodian standard, we may supply *ἡμιδραχμία*, which seems a not impossible form, though *ἡμίδραχμον* would be more usual.

At Erythrae the Chian standard came in early in the fourth century. (Tetradrachm and drachm.)

Obv. Head of young Heracles. *Rev.* Club and bow in case.

These coins are given by M. Babelon[1] to the period of Alexander. But the character of the head of Heracles seems to me to indicate an earlier date, and the parallel coins of Samos and Ephesus date from the first half of the fourth century. At Colophon, early in the fourth century, we have tetradrachms, drachms, hemidrachms, and diobols of Chian weight:

Obv. Head of Apollo, laureate. *Rev.* Lyre, and name of magistrate. Weights, 200 grains (grm. 12·93), much used; 54–51 grains (grm. 3·50–3·30); 16 grains (grm. 1·03). (B. T. CLIII. 6–26.)

Obv. Same type. *Rev.* Tripod, and name of magistrate. Weight, 24 grains (grm. 1·55). Hemidrachm.

Passing farther to the north, we find the same monetary standard in use in the Troad and the Hellespont. We begin with Byzantium and Calchedon, cities which in the ordinary numismatic arrangement stand far apart, one being in Europe and the other in Asia, but which have a common history and were closely connected together, divided only by the narrow Bosporus. These cities in the fifth century used the Persian standard,[2] but they exchange it for that of Chios on the occasion of the formation of the

[1] *Traité*, ii. 2, p. 1045.

[2] Above, Chap. XIV, p. 268.

League of Cnidus. Byzantium begins with tridrachms in 394 B.C., but soon goes on to tetradrachms.

Byzantium, 411–394 B.C.

Obv. BY. Cow on dolphin. *Rev.* Mill-sail incuse. Weight, 80–84 grains (grm. 5·18–5·44). (Pl. VIII. 12.)

After 389 B.C.

Obv. BY. Cow on dolphin. *Rev.* Incuse square. Weights, 229–232 grains (grm. 14·84–15·03) (Pl. VIII. 13); 50–54 grains (grm. 3·24–3·50); 35–38 grains (grm. 2·26–2·46). Hemidrachm (Persian).

Obv. BY. Fore-part of cow. *Rev.* Incuse square. Weight, 22–26 grains (grm. 1·42–1·68). Hemidrachm (Chian).

Calchedon, 411–394 B.C.

Obv. ΚΑΛΧ. Cow on ear of corn. *Rev.* Mill-sail incuse. Weights, 81–2 grains (grm. 5·24–5·31); 35–40 grains (grm. 2·26–2·58); 16–18 grains (grm. 1·05–1·17). (B. T. CLXXXI. 14–22.)

After 394 B.C.

Obv. ΚΑΛΧ. Cow on ear of corn. *Rev.* Incuse square. Weight, 228–235 grains (grm. 14.75–15·23); 52–58 grains (grm. 3·40–3·79). (B. T. CLXXXI. 23–26.)

Obv. ΚΑΛ. Fore-part of cow. *Rev.* Three ears of corn. Weight, 28 grains (grm. 1·83). Hemidrachm. (B. T. CLXXXII. 5–7.)

Mesembria, a colony of Megara, on the west shore of the Euxine, issues about 380 B.C. coins of Chian weight.

Obv. Crested helmet. *Rev.* ΜΕΤΑ (ΜΕΣΣΑ) ΑΝΘΕΣΤΗΡΙΟΣ. Radiate wheel. Weights, 239 grains (grm. 15·48); 19 grains (grm. 1·23).

The magistrate's name is written at length, as on contemporary coins of Samos and Ephesus.

That the Persian standard should have made its way on the Bosporus when Athens declined is quite natural. It rules until 394 B.C. And at Byzantium at all events, after that date, Persian drachms and hemidrachms circulate concurrently with Rhodian denominations.

Byzantium and Calchedon are closely connected in their history. Both were early colonies of Megara. Mesembria was founded by them; and at the time of the Persian invasion their inhabitants took refuge in that city. The tetradrachm of Mesembria is cited by Mr. Head, and was in the Hirsch sale.[1] We can scarcely give it to an earlier period than about 400 B.C. The H in the name of Anthesterios shows a somewhat late date; the name seems to be Attic, and was probably that of a local tyrant. The same change of standard takes place at Abydos. This city as well as Assos and Cyzicus issues money on the Rhodian standard early in the fourth century.

Abydos.

Obv. Laureate head of Apollo. *Rev.* ABY. Eagle. Weight, 228–232 grains (grm. 14·79–15). (**B. T. CLXVIII. 3.**)

Assos.

Obv. Helmeted head of Athena. *Rev.* AΣΣION. Archaic statue of Athena. Weight, 231 grains (grm. 14·95). Paris. (**CLXIII. 28.**)

M. Babelon[2] gives the coin of Assos, on grounds of style, to 430–411 B.C. But a copy on coins of an archaic statue is scarcely possible in the fifth century. The style of the head of Athena is much like that of the head of Heracles at Cos already cited.

An abundant and important series of silver coins was issued in the fourth century at Cyzicus. This has been discussed in great detail by Dr. von Fritze,[3] and his views as to chronology are carefully worked out.

Obv. ΣΩTEIPA. Head of Cora, corn-crowned and veiled. *Rev.* KYZI or KYZIKHNΩN. Lion's head: beneath, tunny. Average weight, 229 grains (grm. 14·83); 72 grains (grm. 4·68); 48 grains (grm. 3·10). (**Pl. VIII. 14.**)

These coins Dr. von Fritze divides into two sets. The earlier group, put together on grounds of style, he gives

[1] *Hist. Num.*, ed. 2, p. 278; *Hirsch Sale Cat.*, Pl. VIII.

[2] *Traité*, ii. 2, 1269.

[3] *Nomisma*, Heft IX (1914).

to the period 405–363 B.C., when Cyzicus was sometimes under Spartan, and sometimes under Athenian influence. He raises the question whether the second Athenian domination was as fatal to the issue of an autonomous coinage in the subject cities as had been the first, at all events in its later years. But in any case, as the rule of Athens over the city was quite transient, we cannot expect to identify traces of it on the coins.

The second group von Fritze would give to the period 362 down to the days of the kingdom of Seleucus, when the seated Apollo comes in on the coins in the place of the lion's head.

I agree with the writer as to the time of commencement of this coinage. The adoption of the Chian standard could scarcely have taken place before the Athenian expedition against Syracuse, and may have first occurred after the fall of Athens. But I cannot think that the beautiful coins with the seated Apollo were contemporary with the early money of the Seleucidae, and think rather that the expedition of Alexander here put an end to the autonomous coinage. Von Fritze's second group, therefore, should be given to 362–330. The division of the stater into thirds as well as into four drachms is noteworthy, and may, perhaps, be accounted for by the custom long established at Cyzicus of dividing the electrum staters by three. These thirds, according to von Fritze, are issued only about 400 B.C.

It is a testimony to the force of Rhodian or Chian commerce that the Chian standard early in the fourth century comes into the coinages of some cities which had been very conservative of their own weight. Thus we have—

Teos in Ionia.

Obv. Griffin seated. *Rev.* Name of city and magistrate on the bars of an incuse square. Weight, 55 grains (grm. 3·56). (B. T. CLIV. 11.)

Teos had been very tenacious of the Aeginetan standard.

Tenedos.

Obv. Janiform male and female head. *Rev.* ΤΕΝΕΔΙΟΝ. Double axe. Weight, 218–226 grains (grm. 14·10–14·61); 50–56 grains (grm. 3·24–3·62). (**B. T. CLXVI. 22–24; B. M. XVIII. 20, 21.**)

The earliest coins of Tenedos follow the Phocaean standard. The coinage appears to cease during the time of the Athenian domination, and to be resumed on a slightly reduced scale, probably the Chian standard, in the later fifth or early fourth century.

To the east of Caria the Chian standard scarcely penetrates. Cilicia was fully in the power of the Great King; and the Persian Satraps who, as we shall see, minted there freely, naturally adhered to the Persian weight. But in the island of Cyprus we find some influence of the Chian weight. The great Evagoras I strikes his larger silver pieces on the Persian standard:

Obv. Head of Heracles. *Rev.* Goat lying. Weight, 171 grains (grm. 11·10);

but he seems, perhaps later in his reign, to have issued drachms of Rhodian weight:

Obv. Heracles seated. *Rev.* Goat lying to r. Weight, 51–48 grains (grm. 3·30–3·11).

His successor, Evagoras II, strikes didrachms on the same scale:

Obv. Bust of Athena. *Rev.* Bust of Aphrodite. Weight, 109–104 grains (grm. 7·10–6·73). (**B. T. CXXVIII. 10.**)

There are also didrachms of Rhodian weight conjecturally attributed to Amathus,[1] which weigh 103 to 96 grains (grm. 6·67–6·22). The relations of the silver of the Kings of Salamis to the gold coins which they issued will be considered in the next chapter.

There are certain staters of Rhodian weight struck by Persian satraps:

Obv. King, half-kneeling, holding spear and bow. *Rev.* Rough incuse.

[1] *B. M. Cat. Cyprus*, p. xxiii.

Sometimes these coins bear the name Pythagores; but who he may have been is uncertain:

Obv. King, half-kneeling, drawing bow. *Rev.* Satrap galloping, wielding spear.

These staters were probably struck in some city of south-western Asia Minor, as the Rhodian standard does not carry so far as Cilicia. Some specimens, however, bear (perhaps) Phoenician characters; and Head is disposed to regard them as money issued by some Persian commandant at a Phoenician mint.[1] Metrologically this is very unlikely.

§ 2. Attic Standard.

Early in the fourth century, in consequence of the misfortunes of Athens, the monetary standard of that city was recessive. In 394 B.C., however, after the victory of Conon at Cnidus, Attic power revived. We shall see in the next chapter how the gold coinage of staters, which appears then to have begun at Athens, was copied in several cities of Asia. In one city there seems to have been a contemporary coinage of silver on the Attic standard. That one city was Clazomenae. I have above observed that the special clause in the treaty of Antalcidas, which places Clazomenae under the Persian Empire, precludes us from giving the beautiful gold coins of Clazomenae to a time after 387 B.C. To the time 394–387 B.C. then belong also the silver staters of Attic weight:

Obv. Head of Apollo facing. *Rev.* ΚΛΑ or ΚΛΑΙΟ with magistrate's name. Swan. Weight, 250–262 grains (grm. 16·20–16·96); 55–63 grains (grm. 3·56–4·08). (**B.T. CLV. 22, 23; B. M. XIX. 25, 26.**)

M. Babelon gives these coins to the time after 374 B.C.; but M. Babelon does not think that the Persian king prohibited the issue of gold in Greek cities.

[1] *Hist. Num.*, ed. 2, p. 831.

§ 3. The Persian Region.

The standard of Chios did not spread to the east of Caria.[1] On the south coast of Asia Minor the Persian power was firmly established; and the Persian monetary standard, which followed the flag, had long been dominant.

In a few cities of the Ionian coast the Persian standard comes in, apparently towards the middle of the fourth century. At the same time that Cius issued gold staters[2] the city also struck drachms of Persian weight, 80–83 grains (grm. 5·20–5·33). Apparently contemporary are the coins of Mytilene:

> *Obv.* Head of Apollo. *Rev.* ΜΥΤΙ. Lyre. Weight, 161–168 grains (grm. 10·45–10·90). (**B. T. CLXII.** 17, 18.)

M. Babelon gives these coins to 350–300 B.C., which time their style well suits. At about the same time Lampsacus struck coins weighing 39–40 grains (grm. 2·52–2·58). They seem to be Persian hemidrachms.

> *Obv.* Janiform beardless head. *Rev.* ΛΑΜ. Head of Athena. (**B. T. CLXXII.** 10.)

M. Babelon calls these coins tetrobols, apparently of the Chian standard; and of course they may very well have passed as such. Contemporary are the coins of Parium of the same weight.

Seeing that the Persian standard was adopted at this time by Abdera and the kings of Macedon, it is not strange to find it in use exceptionally among the cities of North Ionia and the Propontis.

These coins are exceptional. But in the cities of the Pamphylian and Cilician coasts the Persian standard was normal. Phaselis, which paid tribute to Athens, seems to have intermitted coinage after 465 B.C. But the mints of Aspendus, Side, and Selge were active in the fifth and fourth centuries. Between Side in Pamphylia and Holmi in Cilicia in the fourth century, and probably earlier, there

[1] Except to Salamis in Cyprus.

[2] Discussed in the next chapter.

must have existed some monetary convention, indicated by an identity of type, the subsidiary symbol (a dolphin on the coins of Holmi and a pomegranate on those of Side) being distinctive of the two places.[1]

Mr. Head's dates for the beginnings of coinage on the Persian standard in cities of Cilicia are as follows: Celenderis, Soli, Tarsus, 450 B.C.; Mallus, 425 B.C.; Nagidus, 420 B.C.; Issus, 400 B.C. These dates, being based only on slight varieties of style, are not to be insisted upon. But we may fairly say that towards the end of the fifth century several of the more important cities of Cilicia were freely striking coins. There was nothing to prevent them; as the Persian king freely allowed the striking of silver by the Greek cities, and the arm of Athens could not reach so far.

With regard to the issues of coins by Persian Satraps in Cilicia, I largely follow M. Babelon, who has made a special study of them. He is in most cases responsible for the dates in the following paragraphs, which are only approximate.[2]

In 386–384 B.C. the Satrap of Sardes, Tiribazus, was placed at the head of the expedition organized against Evagoras, the revolted king of Salamis in Cyprus. In order to pay the mercenaries, and to buy munitions of war, he issued an abundant coinage in the cities of Cilicia. This coinage bears his name in Aramaic characters (Pl. IX. 1): the types are, Ormuzd, Baal of Tarsus, Heracles; and sometimes what appears to be an idealized portrait of himself. We can identify with certainty the mint of Issus, from the inscription IΣΣIKON, and with great probability the mints of Mallus (MAP), Soli (ΣO), Tarsus (T). All these coins are of full Persian weight, 164–159 grains (grm. 10·65–10·30).

Pharnabazus, the well-known Satrap of Dascylium, also struck fleet-money in Cilicia. The date of it can scarcely be fixed with certainty, as on three occasions he might well have issued it. In 398–394 B.C. he received from Artaxerxes Mnemon five hundred talents for the equipment of a fleet

[1] *B. M. Cat. Lycia*, p. lxxxi.

[2] *Perses Achéménides.* Also *Traité*, ii. 2.

to co-operate with the Athenian Conon.[1] Later, in 391–389 B.C., he prepared in concert with Abrocomas and Tithraustes an expedition against Egypt, then in revolt. And again, in 379–374 B.C., he equipped a fleet in conjunction with Datames, who succeeded him. It is probable that we must assign to the last of these periods the coins bearing the name of Pharnabazus, and struck at Nagidus, Tarsus, and elsewhere in Cilicia.[2] The most curious type of them is a full-face female head, evidently copied from the Arethusa of the coins of Syracuse of the end of the fifth century (Pl. IX. 2). The weight of these pieces is 165–155 grains (grm. 10·70–10·0), the full Persian weight. Divisions weighing 52–50 grains (grm. 3·37–3·25) and 13–11 grains (grm. 0·87–0·66) are evidently thirds of stater (tetrobols) and obols respectively.

Datames, 378–372 B.C., and Mazaeus, 361–334 B.C., continued this Cilician coinage, on the occasions when they had to raise troops or equip fleets. Thus we cannot be surprised that all the cities of the south of Asia Minor retained the Persian standard, Aspendus, Etenna, Side, Selge, Celenderis, Issus, Mallus, Nagidus, Soli, Tarsus. So did the cities of Cyprus, Citium, Marium, Paphos, and Salamis; all save, perhaps, Amathus. Mazaeus occupies an important place in the coinage of Asia in the fourth century.[3] M. Babelon divides his coins as follows:

1. Struck in Cilicia, 361–334 B.C.
2. Struck when he was Satrap of the Transeuphratic country and Cilicia, 351–334.
3. Struck when he governed Sidon, after 359.
4. Struck in Syria and Babylon, when he governed for Darius, 334–331.
5. Struck at Babylon, when he was Governor for Alexander, 331–328.

Coins of Class 5 are of the Attic standard: they still bear the Cilician types of Baal of Tarsus and the lion. There

[1] Diodorus, xiv. 39.

[2] Babelon, *Traité*, ii. 2, p. 394.

[3] Babelon, *Traité*, ii. 2, p. 443.

are also barbarous imitations of the coins of Athens and others which bear the name of Mazaeus.

It is remarkable that a man who occupies so small a place in history should be so dominant in relation to issues of coins.

Certain coins issued by Satraps or Dynasts, in north-west Asia Minor, appear to follow the Persian weight. The descendants of Damaratus, the exiled Spartan king, had a small principality which included the strong city of Pergamon. As the coins of Teuthrania and Pergamon, about 400 B.C., bear as type heads clad in the Persian tiara, it is probable that they were issued under rulers of this dynasty. And the name of Gorgion, another ruler of Greek extraction, is to be found on the contemporary coins of Gambrium in Mysia.[1] All these rulers issued the Persian third of a stater (grm. 3·38, grains 52) or half of this, which we may fairly call a Persian diobol, 25–23 grains (grm 1·60–1·50).[2] This is evidently a small coinage suited to go with the regal money of Persia. As these towns were not on the sea, they probably entered but little into the circle of Greek commerce.

There is another notable series of coins, apparently issued by Persian Satraps, or under their influence, which seems to combine the Chian (Rhodian) standard, used for the larger coins, with the Persian standard, the influence of which is to be traced in the lower denominations. The mints of these coins cannot be with certainty determined: but they are not Cilician; probably they were struck in the cities of north-west Asia Minor on some occasions when the influence of Persia was exceptionally strong.

The following are attributed by M. Babelon to Tissaphernes; but as they do not bear his name, the assignment is uncertain.

Obv. Head of a Satrap in Persian tiara. *Rev.* ΒΑΣΙΛΕΩΣ. The king advancing, holding bow and javelin: galley in

[1] Babelon, *Traité*, ii. 2, p. 94.

[2] These would, however, serve as Rhodian drachms and hemidrachms.

field. Weight, 230 grains (grm. 14·90). Rhodian tetradrachm. (**Pl. IX. 4.**)

Do. *Rev.* ΒΑΣΙ and the king, but no galley. Weight, 51 grains (grm. 3.30). Rhodian drachm?

Do. *Rev.* ΒΑ. The king, but no galley. Weight, 29 grains (grm. 1·85). Rhodian hemidrachm.

The place of issue of this money is uncertain; Babelon fixes on Caria (Iasus), Six on Aspendus. The coins can scarcely be earlier than the foundation of Rhodus, or even than the adoption of the Rhodian weight by Hecatomnus of Caria. The interesting point is that the two lesser denominations may just as well, or better, be considered as Persian tetrobols and diobols.

Orontes (362 B.C.) struck coins at Lampsacus bearing his name and his portrait: these were Persian tetrobols of 48 grains (grm. 3·13). He also issued coins at Clazomenae of the weight of 43 grains (grm. 2·78), which may possibly have been Persian hemidrachms. The very beautiful coin—

Obv. Head of a Satrap in Persian tiara. *Rev.* ΒΑΣΙΛ. Lyre. Weight, 232 grains (grm. 15). (**Pl. IX. 5.**)

is attributed by M. Babelon to Orontes, and to the mint of Colophon. As we have already seen, Persian influence was strong at Colophon; but it is exceptional that money bearing the portrait of a Satrap should be struck in a Greek city. Some Greek cities, it is true, Lampsacus, Phocaea, and others, issue coins bearing the portraits of Persians. These, however, mostly appear on gold or electrum money, which was a sort of international coinage, and very eclectic in its types: so that I should prefer to see in such cases a mere compliment paid to some neighbouring grandee, who was very probably elected to some magistracy in honorary fashion, as Antiochus IV of Syria was at Athens. There is a silver coin issued at Cyzicus by Pharnabazus and bearing his name:

Obv. ΦΑΡΝΑΒΑ. Head of Satrap in tiara. *Rev.* Prow and dolphins: beneath, tunny. Weight, 229 grains (grm. 12·84). (**B. T. CVIII. 1.**)

Here, again, since the weight conforms to that used by the people of Cyzicus after 400 B.C. (the Rhodian), I should be disposed to see a merely honorary intention.

There are Persian tetrobols, weight 45–38 grains (grm. 2·88–2·50), issued by Spithridates at Lampsacus:

Obv. Head of Persian Satrap in tiara. *Rev.* ΣΠΙΘΡΙ. Forepart of Pegasus. (**B. T. LXXXIX. 1–2.**)

Spithridates was Satrap of Sardis at the time of the Macedonian invasion.

The silver coinage of Cyprus, in the fifth and fourth centuries, runs on somewhat exceptional lines. The coins, excepting a few struck at Salamis and mentioned above, are all minted on the Persian standard; but the stater or didrachm is not divided by two into drachms: the denominations struck are the third or tetrobol, the sixth, and the twelfth.[1] I cannot here consider in detail the issues of the various cities, a subject still obscure, in spite of the admirable labours of M. Six, M. Babelon, and Mr. Hill.[2] In Mr. Hill's catalogue all that can be regarded as established in regard to it is set forth with excellent judgement.

§ 4. Pontus.

The drachms issued by Persian Satraps at Sinope conform to the standard, originally Aeginetan and always somewhat above the normal Persian weight, of the autonomous coins struck in that mint.

Issued by **Datames**, about 370 B.C.:

Obv. Head of the Nymph Sinope. *Rev.* ΔΑΤΑΜΑ. Eagle on dolphin. Weight, 93–91 grains (grm. 6·06–5·89). (**B. T. CX. 1.**)

Issued by **Abrocomas**, about 360 B.C.:

Same types with name of Abrocomas. Weight, 89–76 grains (grm. 5·72–4·90). (**B. T. CX. 4.**)

[1] *B. M. Cat. Cyprus*, p. xxiii.

[2] Six, *Revue Numism.*, 1883; Babelon, *Les Perses Achéménides*, 1893; Hill, *B. M. Cat. Cyprus*, 1904; Babelon, *Traité*, ii. 2, pp. 691–842.

Issued by **Ariarathes,** after 350 B.C. :

Same types with name of Ariarathes. Weight, 91–67 grains (grm. 5·87–4·38).

The name of Ariarathes also occurs on coins of Gaziura in Pontus:

Obv. Baal of Gaziura. *Rev.* Griffin devouring stag. Weight, 84–75 grains (grm. 5·42–4·87). (**B. T. CXI. 9.**)

At Panticapaeum, in the fourth century, we find Persian didrachms, weighing 182 grains (grm. 11·79), as well as coins weighing 52 grains (grm. 3·36). And this latter weight, 55–52 grains, is usual for the rather common coins of Cromna and Sesamus in the fourth century. We find this denomination of coin also in Cilicia and Mysia in the fourth century, and in Phoenicia. It seems to have been a Persian tetrobol (normal weight 56 grains; grm. 3·62) or a Rhodian drachm (normal weight 55–60 grains; grm. 3·56–3·88). It may be said that if the Persian standard were adopted for money in the district of Pontus by Sinope, Panticapaeum, and other cities, it would not be consistent to strike drachms of 94 grains and tetrobols of 56 grains at the same time; the latter should weigh 62 grains. But in fact the drachms of Sinope in the fourth century are very irregular in their weight, and seldom rise above 90 grains. The fractions also, being intended only for local circulation, were not obliged to reach the same standard as the drachms which had a wider circulation. And thus it is a general rule in the coins of Greece that the staters are heavier in proportion than the divisions.

The coinage of the Pontic Heracleia in Bithynia is abundant, and very important. As the city from 345 B.C. was governed by tyrants, who placed their names on the coins, we can date some of its issues within narrow limits.

The coinage begins early in the fourth century. The following seems to precede the time of the above-mentioned rulers:

Obv. Head of bearded Heracles. *Rev.* ΗΡΑΚΛΕΙΑ. Rushing bull. (**B. T. CLXXXIII.**)

An earlier issue weighs 74–76 grains (grm. 4·79–4·92): a later issue is more than ten grains lighter.

Later than these coins we have:

Obv. Head of young Heracles, slightly bearded. *Rev.* ΗΡΑΚΛΕΙΑ. Head of the city turreted. Weight, 171–181 grains (grm. 11·05–11·72).

There are also drachms of both these classes, the weight of which varies from 60 to 84 grains (grm. 3·88–5·44), and smaller divisions. The letters Κ and Σ, which are to be found on some of the smaller coins of the second type, may be the initials of the Tyrants Clearchus and Satyrus, who ruled 364–345 B.C.

The Tyrants Timotheus and Dionysius, who succeeded about 345 B.C., write their names on the coins at length:

Obv. Head of young Dionysus, ivy-crowned, with thyrsus. *Rev.* ΤΙΜΟΘΕΟΥ ΔΙΟΝΥΣΙΟΥ. Heracles erecting trophy.. Weight, 149–151 grains (grm. 9·65–9·80). Also the quarter (half-drachm).

The weights of the coins of Heracleia are very varied: they seem to fall gradually during the fourth century, but not in any regular way; and the staters keep their weight better than the smaller divisions. We must suppose that these divisions were in use only for local trade. The staters must have passed for two of the drachms of Sinope or Amisus. It has been observed, in a previous chapter (XIV), that this striking irregularity in weight is a feature of all the issues of the Pontic cities.

Istrus, a Milesian colony near the mouths of the Danube, began about 400 B.C. to issue coins of the same weight as those of Sinope.[1]

Obv. Two young male heads, one erect, one inverted. *Rev.* Eagle on dolphin. Inscr. ΙΣΤΡΙΗ. Weight, 109–73 grains (grm. 7·02–4·72).

According to Dr. Pick, all the coins of the earlier half of the fourth century exceed 100 grains in weight, and belong

[1] B. Pick, *Die antiken Münzen von Nord-Griechenland*, i, p. 177.

to the Phoenician standard, which standard the people about 350 B.C. give up for that of Aegina. There is, however, no satisfactory proof of any change of standard, and some quite late coins of the city are among the heaviest. We have in fact the same curious phenomena here as at Sinope: under this latter city we discuss them (Chap. XIV).

The Propontine region, with the neighbouring shores of the Euxine and the Aegean, is the most important of all districts in the history of Greek commerce, and in the matter of the clashing of Europe and Asia, of Greece and Persia. It may be well, therefore, to recapitulate the monetary history of the district in the successive periods of Greek history.

In the dawn of history, in the seventh and sixth centuries, the Ionic Miletus appears to have been dominant in the region of the Euxine. Many of the cities of the Propontis, such as Abydos, Cyzicus, Lampsacus, Parium; and cities of the Euxine, such as Sinope, Amisus, Panticapaeum, were regarded as Milesian colonies, though other Ionian cities such as Phocaea and Erythrae were said to have had a hand in them. The only serious rivals of the Ionians in the seventh century were the people of Megara, who founded, first Calchedon, then Byzantium, then the Pontic Heracleia. So far as I know, finds of the electrum coins of Ionia have not been made in the Euxine district.

In the sixth century, long before the fall of Miletus, some of the cities of the Euxine began to issue silver coins; the most notable of them being Sinope on the northern coast of Asia Minor, and Panticapaeum in the Tauric Chersonese. These cities follow the Aeginetan standard, though at Sinope the drachm sometimes rises as high as 100 grains. We know that the commerce of Aegina stretched to the Euxine, as Herodotus gives us the precious information that in the time of Xerxes Aeginetan ships laden with corn passed through the Straits. The Pontic cities adhere to this standard with greater tenacity than do most districts, but their adoption of it is quite according to precedent. We have seen (Chap. IX) how in Asia almost invariably the introduction of silver currency brings with it the use of the Aeginetan standard, however ill it may agree with the standards already in use.

About the time of the Persian wars, several cities of the Propontis, Abydos, Antandros, Astacus, and Lampsacus, issued drachms of Persian weight. This may well have taken place at the time of the passing of the Persian armies. There are three crossings from Asia to Europe—(1) across the Bosporus, from Calchedon to Byzantium; (2) across the Hellespont, from Lampsacus to Callipolis; (3) across the Hellespont, from Abydos to Sestos. The first of these ways was taken by Darius in his expedition against the Scythians; the third by Xerxes.

The above-mentioned coins of Persian weight were all, it will be observed, issued on the Asiatic side. The opposite shore of the Hellespont, the Thracian Chersonesus, struck, as we have seen, at that time on the Attic standard, no doubt in consequence of the influence of Miltiades.

In the time of the Athenian Empire, there can be no doubt but that the Athenian silver money, with the electrum of Cyzicus, Lampsacus, Phocaea, and Mytilene, constituted the bulk of the currency. But small coins for local circulation were struck on the Persian standard at Byzantium, at Cardia in the Thracian Chersonese, and on the Asiatic side at Astacus, Abydos, and Dardanus. There were small coins on the Chian standard before 450 B.C. at Parium and Assos; and after 450 at Calchedon, Antandros, Gargara, Lamponeia, Neandria, and Proconnesus. Scepsis, in the fifth century, issued didrachms on the Chian standard. Selymbria, on the Thracian shore of the Propontis, seems to have gone over from the Persian standard to the Attic about 450 B.C. Sinope and other Pontic cities continued their issues, but the weight had a tendency to fall from the standard of Aegina to that of Persia.

Early in the fourth century, Byzantium and Calchedon fully adopt the Chian standard, issuing an abundant coinage. The Persian Satraps who strike coins at Sinope adhere, no doubt for commercial reasons, to the Aeginetan standard.

But at Gaziura they use the Persian weight. At other cities, such as Cromna and Sesamus, coins are struck of about 56 grains, either Rhodian drachms or Persian tetrobols. The important Pontic Heracleia also at this time uses the Persian standard. Small silver coins were issued by the Sindi, a tribe who dwelt to the east of the Palus Maeotis, at their port of Sinde.

§ 5. THRACE AND MACEDON.

The Rhodian or Chian standard spread rapidly to the North in the later fifth and early fourth centuries. We have already seen it at Byzantium and Calchedon. Of the cities of the Thracian coast, Aenus seems to have adopted it before 400 B.C., the tetradrachms reaching a maximum of 240 grains (grm. 15·55). Thasos at the same time strikes very beautiful coins, already mentioned:

> *Obv.* Head of bearded Dionysus wearing ivy-wreath. *Rev.* ΘΑΣΙΟΝ. Heracles shooting. (Pl. VII. 7.)

These also rise to 236 grains (grm. 15·30), and the didrachm and drachm are struck as well as the tetradrachm. The cities of Chalcidice, notably Acanthus and Olynthus, at the same time go over to the standard of Abdera, which at this time is nearly the same as that of Chios, as does Amphipolis at the mouth of the Strymon. These changes one naturally associates with the changed political conditions which followed the expedition of Brasidas.[1]

We will follow the safe plan of beginning with the known, or at all events the ascertainable. The Kings of Macedon place their names on their coins, and their dates are approximately known; their coins then will serve as a clue for fixing the dates of coins of cities. With Archelaus, 413–399 B.C., the money of the Macedonian Kingdom ceased to be regulated by the old Abderite standard: in place of that we find, not the so-called Babylonic standard of Thasos, which at this time is scarcely to be distinguished from

[1] See above, Chap. XIV.

the Attic, but the Persian standard. The staters of Archelaus are:

1. *Obv.* Horseman. *Rev.* ΑΡΧΕΛΑΟ. Fore-part of goat. Weight, 160 grains (grm. 10·36).
2. *Obv.* Young male head (Apollo or Ares). *Rev.* Same inscr. Horse standing, with loose rein. Same weight. (Pl. VII. 10.)

He also issued diobols, obols, and hemiobols of Persian standard.

The successors of Archelaus, Aeropus, 396–392 B.C., and Pausanias, 390–389 B.C., issued staters of the same types as No. 2, together with smaller denominations. Under Amyntas III, 389–369 B.C., and Perdiccas III, 364–359 B.C., the type of the horse is retained, but the head of Heracles displaces that of Apollo on the obverse; the weight remains the same.

This brings us to the reign of Philip II, 359–336 B.C. (Chap. XXI).

It appears that in all their issues of money, the Kings of Macedon, who had little commerce to provide for, accepted the lead of the commercial Greek cities of the coast in their monetary issues: among these cities the most important was Abdera. It was from Abdera that Alexander I borrowed his monetary standard. At the time of the fall of Athens, late in the fifth century, the people of Abdera adopted the Persian standard. This is an interesting fact, but by no means inexplicable. With the fall of Athens the Athenian monetary system, imposed on the Athenian allies, fell also. And at the time the power of Persia was rapidly increasing. The generals of Sparta trusted largely to Persian subsidies. Great issues of money, consisting of didrachms of Persian weight, for supporting naval warfare, began to be made by the Satraps of the Great King, at first with the usual Persian types, later, in the fourth century, with their own names. Thus there can be no doubt that the staters of Archelaus and his successors were intended to pass as the equivalent of two sigli or the tenth of a daric.

Other cities of Thrace followed the lead of Abdera, notably Maroneia, which issued during the first half of the fourth century abundant coins weighing about 175 grains (grm. 11·33). Aenus, however, took another course and, like Byzantium and Thasos, accepted the rapidly spreading Chian standard. It is to be observed that Aenus is the furthest to the East of the cities of the Thracian coast.

The coinage of Philip of Macedon did not bring to an end the coinage of the kings who reigned in Paeonia, to the north of Macedon. We have a considerable coinage issued by Lycceius, who ruled about 359–340 B.C.

Obv. Head of Apollo.[1] *Rev.* ΛΥΚΚΕΙΟΥ. Heracles strangling lion. Weight, 214–188 grains (grm. 13·86–12·18).

His successor Patraüs issued money with another type.

Obv. Head of Apollo. *Rev.* ΠΑΤΡΑΟΥ. Horseman spearing foe. Weight, 200–188 grains (grm. 12·96–12·18).

The Kings of Paeonia notably depart from Macedonian precedents in their types: the Heracles type suggests Tarentum and Heracleia in Italy; the horseman type suggests Thessaly: but we are not justified in drawing any inference as regards the course of trade. The weight is regarded by Mr. Head as a degradation of the standard of Philip II of Macedon, 224 grains (grm. 14·51); but it seems scarcely possible that these coins can have passed as equivalent to those of Philip. On the other hand, it is a familiar fact that the barbarous imitations of standard coinages rapidly decline in weight. The Paeonian coins were in turn imitated by barbarous neighbours on the north and west.

The conquest by Philip, as a rule, marks the end of the autonomous coinage of the cities of Thrace and Macedon. Abdera, Aenus, Maroneia, and the island of Thasos cease their issues about 350 B.C. One city, however, Philippi,

[1] One of the staters of Lycceius has on the obverse the legend ΔΕΡΡΩΝΑΙΟΣ: this seems to be an epithet of Apollo, and it shows that the Derrones were near his dominions.

was allowed then to begin an autonomous coinage, striking gold staters, and silver coins, from the tetradrachm downwards, on the standards of Philip. They bear as types the head of Heracles and the Tripod.

Coins struck about 350 B.C. at Orthagoreia offer us a problem:

> *Obv.* Head of Artemis. *Rev.* ΟΡΘΑΓΟΡΕΩΝ. Macedonian helmet surmounted by star. Weight, 168 grains (grm. 10·88): also the quarter of this.

Orthagoreia is by one ancient authority stated to be a variant name of Stageira; but Pliny[1] says that it was an older name of Maroneia. The former of these statements is unsatisfactory, for it is extremely improbable that a city of Chalcidice, where Stageira was situated, would in the fourth century use the Persian standard. On the other hand, that standard is used at Maroneia: if that city about the middle of the fourth century took the name of Orthagoreia, it might have been allowed to make a temporary issue of coins.

The complexity and irregularity of the coin standards in use in Asia for silver in the fourth century appears on examination to be less than might appear at first sight. The Chian standard during the first years of the century rapidly makes its way, and is all but universally adopted, from Caria in the south to Byzantium and Aenus in the north, along the western shore of Asia Minor. The standard adopted by the people of Chalcidice, and from them by Philip of Macedon, is somewhat lighter than that of Chios, but not very different. It is either the old standard of Abdera, or may perhaps be an adaptation to the weight of the gold (Chap. XXI). The Attic standard is found only at Clazomenae, the Aeginetan only in the Pontic region.

[1] IV. 11, 18.

The Persian standard is altogether dominant to the east of Caria, and aggressive farther to the west. In some cities of the west coast of Asia Minor, and at Byzantium, it works in with the Chian. In Abdera it triumphs, and from Abdera passes to the Kings of Macedon, Archelaus and his successors until Philip. Even in Pontus the old-established standard of Aegina is modified and lowered by Persian influence.

CHAPTER XVI

GOLD OF ASIA MINOR, &c.

§ 1. 407–394 B.C.

I do not propose in this chapter to treat of the issues of electrum coins at Cyzicus, Lampsacus, Mytilene, and Phocaea, as I have already dealt with those issues in Chapter XIV, which treats of the coinage of the Athenian Empire. But there were important issues of pure gold in Asia and Thrace.

The earlier gold coins of Athens, which were contemporary with similar issues of gold by the cities of Sicily, when pressed by the Carthaginian invasion, seem to have been imitated by several cities of Thrace, of Cyprus, and other districts. These cities did not issue any higher denomination than the drachm: whereas in the period succeeding 394 B.C., and especially in the years between 394 and the peace of Antalcidas, 387 B.C., gold staters or didrachms make their appearance in several cities from Panticapaeum in the north to Cyprus and Cyrene in the south.

It is not claimed that all gold coins of smaller denominations belong to the period 407–394 B.C.: many of them belong to the middle of the fourth century. The claim is that in nearly all cases the issues of small gold coins are suggested by the Athenian issues of 407 B.C.; and that in nearly, if not quite, all cases the issues of gold staters are an echo of the Athenian striking of gold didrachms in 394. And this contention seems to be borne out by a consideration of the dates of the kings and dynasts who struck coins in the fourth century. Evidently the coins struck by kings can be more closely dated than those which bear the names of cities only.

We have the following approximate dates: Evagoras I of Salamis in Cyprus, 411–373; Nicocles, 371–361; Evagoras II, 361–351; Pnytagoras, 351–332; Nicocreon, 331–310; Melekiathon of Citium in Cyprus, 391–361; Pumiathon, 361–312; Pixodarus of Caria, 340–334; Philip II of Macedon, 359–336. Of these rulers, Evagoras I issued the half-drachm (31·4 grains, grm. 2·02) and smaller divisions; Nicocles two-thirds of the drachm (42·5 grains, grm. 2·75); Evagoras II, Pnytagoras, and Nicocreon didrachms or staters. Melekiathon and Pumiathon struck the drachm; Pixodarus the drachm; Philip of Macedon issued didrachms in abundance. All of these were of Attic standard. This list proves at least that, as we approach the middle of the fourth century, staters tend to take the place of smaller coins in gold.

In his *Catalogue of the Coins of Cyprus*,[1] Mr. Hill observes that Evagoras I in his coinage probably preserves the traditional relation of gold to silver at 13⅓ to 1, so that his half-drachm in gold would be equivalent to 2½ of his silver staters. The smaller denominations struck by Evagoras are in Mr. Hill's opinion tenths and twentieths of the stater of gold. This would be a novelty in coinage, as elsewhere the smaller gold coins follow the divisions into drachms and obols; and I am not sure that Mr. Hill is right, but his view has much in its favour.

The kings of Cyprus seem to stand in a separate class. Evagoras I was a ruler of great power and audacity, who by force of arms asserted his independence of the Great King, and was never subdued, but at last made a compact with him 'as a king with a king'. That this high-spirited monarch should have broken through the tradition, and issued gold coins on his own account, need not surprise us, nor that his standard should be rather that of the Athenian gold money than that of the daric. It is more remarkable that all his successors on the throne of Salamis should have continued the issues down to the time of Alexander the Great, and that the rival Phoenician kings of Citium should

[1] p. ciii.

have followed their example. Brandis suggests[1] that this must have been the result of special favour of the Persian king. In any case Cyprus is quite exceptional in thus coining gold all through the fourth century.

It is to be observed that the powerful Mausolus of Caria, who was almost an independent sovereign, issued no gold coin, though he struck abundant silver: only his successor Pixodarus at a later time, when the Persian Empire was obviously breaking up, struck a few small gold coins.

We take next the issues of small gold coins by some of the cities of Thrace and Macedon, on the Attic standard.

Aenus.

Obv. Head of Hermes. *Rev.* ΑΙΝΙΟΝ. Terminal figure of Hermes on throne. Weight, 32 grains (grm. 2·10). (**Pl. VIII. 1.**)

Maroneia.

Obv. Head of bearded Dionysus. *Rev.* ΜΑΡΩΝΙΤΕΩΝ. Vine. Weight, 62 grains (grm. 4·01).

Obv. Prancing horse. *Rev.* Same inscr. Vine. Weight, 48 grains (grm. 3·11).

Thasos.

Obv. Head of Dionysus, bearded or young. *Rev.* ΘΑΣΙΟΝ. Bearded Heracles kneeling, shooting with bow. Weight, 60 grains (grm. 3·88); 43 grains (grm. 2·78).

Amphipolis.

Obv. Young male head bound with taenia. *Rev.* ΑΜΦΙΠΟΛΙΤΕΩΝ. Torch. Weight, 63 grains (grm. 4·08).

The above coins are all rare, and seem to have been experimental.

These cities, while striking gold on the Attic system of weight, did not use that system for silver. But the mass of the currency in all the region at the time consisted of the silver coins of Athens. It seems, therefore, most likely that the gold coins were issued in reference to these rather than in reference to the autonomous silver coins of the

[1] *Münz-, Mass- und Gewichtswesen*, p. 256.

cities of Thrace. No doubt some terms would have to be made with the latter; and this would have been easy if on the coast of Thrace the old Asiatic relation of the two metals, $13\frac{1}{3}$ to 1, had persisted. Then a gold drachm of Attic weight would have been equivalent to five silver didrachms of Persian weight, or about fifteen Rhodian drachms. But it is far more likely that the Athenian proportion of 12 to 1 was accepted in Thrace, and that the gold coins were left to make their own terms with the contemporary civic issues.

With these coins of Thrace go small coins of Teos in Ionia, the mother-city of Abdera.[1]

> *Obv.* Griffin seated. *Rev.* Circular incuse, divided by a cross, on the limbs of which is inscribed THI and magistrate's name. Weight, 28·7 grains (grm. 1·85); 14·6 grains (grm. 0·94).

The weight of these coins is a difficulty. They are light for Attic triobols and trihemiobols: they are nearer to the weight of Aeginetan diobols and obols. And as Teos clings with great tenacity, almost alone among Ionian cities, to the Aeginetan weight for silver coins, at all events down to 394 (Head) or even later (Babelon), we may well suppose that, like Thebes, the city adopted it also for small pieces in gold. The gold or electrum coins of Thebes, and other cities of Greece proper, are considered in Chapter XVIII.

§ 2. 394–330 B.C.

The striking of gold staters or didrachms at Abydos, Rhodes, Lampsacus, and other cities was later; and what suggested them was probably not the Athenian money of necessity of 407, but the abundant issue of Athenian staters after 395. Mr. Wroth had already assigned the staters of Lampsacus to the time after 394, because one of the earliest of them bears the type of young Heracles

[1] *Hist. Num.*, ed. 2, p. 595. Babelon omits these coins, and their genuineness is not above suspicion.

strangling the serpents, the well-known device of the Cnidian League.[1] There are also small gold or electrum coins of Thebes, which can be dated to this time, bearing the same type.

It seems almost certain that the coins of Lampsacus, Abydos, and Clazomenae must all have been issued at the same period. But if we turn to the *British Museum Catalogue* we shall find considerable variety in their dating, which stands as follows: Lampsacus, 394–350; Abydos, 411–387; Clazomenae, 387–300. This loose and inconsistent dating has arisen from the fact that numismatists have considered each city separately—on its own merits, so to say—and have not taken up the general question why the cities in question should have struck gold at all, and why if they struck gold they should have minted it on that particular standard. In fact, they have made the mistake of detaching numismatics from the broad flow of history.

Cyzicus in the fourth century continues her electrum issues. But Lampsacus with the century begins to issue those very beautiful gold staters which have reached us in great variety (Pl. VIII. 2, 3). The type of their reverse is always the fore-part of a winged horse; but on the obverse are various types. Some of these types seem to have no special meaning,[2] but to be mere imitations of well-known coins or works of art. But a few convey more exact information. On one coin is the head of a Persian satrap: unfortunately he cannot be with any certainty identified. M. Babelon, following M. Six, takes him to be Orontes, and thinks that the coin belongs to the time, about 360 B.C., when Orontes was in revolt against the Great King. This identification, however, is very doubtful. Considering the imitative character of the coins, the appearance of the head of a Persian noble, very possibly

[1] *Cat. Mysia*, p. xxv.

[2] A list of thirty-one types in *B. M. Cat. Mysia*, pp. xxi–xxv. In the *Journal internat. d'Arch. numism.*, v, p. 1, Miss Agnes Baldwin increases the number to thirty-seven. It has since been still further increased.

copied from some silver satrapal coinage, cannot surprise us. A head of Pan on one coin is copied from the gold of Panticapaeum. Another interesting copy is a head of Athena, imitated from the silver money of Athens. The type of young Heracles strangling serpents is copied from the silver issued by the allied cities of Asia after the victory of Conon. We have seen that Lampsacus issued staters of electrum for a short period towards the middle of the fifth century. Why she should have resumed coinage about 394 B.C. we cannot of course tell without a more exact knowledge than we possess of the history of the city. But we must not forget the celebrity of the wine of the district, nor the position of the city on the Propontis near the stations of the Athenian and Spartan fleets, which might produce a need for a coinage.[1]

It is natural to think that the number of types on these staters (more than thirty-seven) indicates a considerable duration of the period during which they were struck. We should naturally suppose that the type would be changed once a year. And it is unlikely that we have recovered more than (at most) half of the varieties issued. In this case, if the coinage began about 394, it would have lasted down to the time of Alexander. This hypothesis of an annual change of type is not, however, a certainty. Mr. Head has made it probable that the type of the later coins of Athens was changed every year. But of the Cyzicene staters of electrum more than 170 types are actually known, and their issue can scarcely have lasted more than 150 years: at Cyzicus then there must have been more frequent changes. In any case it seems impossible to confine the varied staters of Lampsacus to the period before the Peace of Antalcidas: they must have gone on later.

The gold coins of Abydos are somewhat early in character: they seem to have been contemporary with the earliest of

[1] Mention of eighty-four gold staters of Lampsacus as contributed by the Byzantians to the cost of the war of the Boeotians with Phocis, 355–346 B.C. Dittenberger, *Syll.*, ed. 2, 120, 10.

the Lampsacene staters. One bears the types of Victory slaying a ram, and a standing eagle (Brit. Museum).

The gold coins of Rhodes (**B. M. XX. 37**) do not belong quite to the earliest issues of the city (409 B.C.). In the *B. M. Cat.* they are placed after 400 B.C. They are doubtless contemporary with the coins already mentioned. Their issue makes certain some easy and conventional relation between gold coins of Attic and silver coins of Rhodian standard.

It is a suggestive fact that Lampsacus and Abydos, as well as Cyzicus and Cius (of the coins of which last city I shall speak presently), are all on the Propontis in the direct line of the chief Athenian trade-route, that which led to the Black Sea. It would seem that the strength of Athens in this quarter, together with the influx of gold from Colchis and Scythia, produced abnormal conditions as regards the issue of gold coins.

It is necessary to consider the relations of these Greek cities to the Persian satraps in their neighbourhood. Almost in the midst of them was situated Dascyleium, the head-quarters of the Persian satrapy of Mysia. Xenophon [1] describes the city as a luxurious residence. 'Here', he says, 'was the palace of Pharnabazus with many villages round it, great and rich in resources: wild beasts for hunting abounded in the parks and the country round—a river flowed by full of fish of all sorts; and there were also abundant birds for such as had skill in fowling.' The description would be attractive to many an Englishman in India.

The view generally accepted by numismatists [2] is that the Persian satraps did not as such issue coins, but used the darics and sigli of the Empire. But on the occasion of military expeditions they sometimes issued silver coin at the Greek cities which they made their head-quarters. Thus Tiribazus, satrap of Western Armenia, struck silver money in some of the cities of Cilicia, Issus, and Mallus,

[1] *Hellen.* iv. 1, 15.

[2] Babelon, *Perses Achéménides*, Introd., p. xxiii.

on the occasion of the war with Evagoras.[1] Datames also issued silver coins in Cilicia at the time of an expedition against Egypt, about 378 B.C.[2] Tissaphernes issued silver coins, which are supposed to have been struck at the mint of Aspendus[3]; and other examples are cited in the last chapter.

Among the satraps who had head-quarters at Dascyleium, Pharnabazus, when in command of the Persian fleet, issued silver coins in Cilicia. He also seems on some unknown occasion to have issued silver coins at Cyzicus,[4] which we have already cited. Mr. Head is of opinion that a gold coin was also struck by Pharnabazus at Cyzicus; it is the following[5]:

> *Obv.* Persian king as an archer, kneeling. *Rev.* Prow of ship to left. Weight, 127·5 grains (grm. 8·25).

M. Babelon, however, attributes the coin to Darius III of Persia, and to some mint in Caria. M. Six gives it to Salmacis, and the time of Alexander the Great.[6] It is, in fact, of uncertain origin; and the reasons for attributing it to Pharnabazus are not strong enough to induce us to make this coin the one solitary gold issue by any Persian satrap. The continued loyalty of Pharnabazus to his master would make it very unlikely that he alone would infringe the royal prerogative.

It would seem then that so far as our evidence, which is certainly very fragmentary, goes, the satraps of Mysia had little to do with the issues of coins on the coast of the Propontis. No doubt they must have had frequent relations with these Greek cities. But if we adhere to the view that it was only on the occasion of military expeditions that the Persian satraps struck coins, we shall be slow in attributing to their influence coins so evidently commercial as the gold money of Lampsacus and Abydos. The available evidence,

[1] Babelon, *Perses Achéménides*, Introd., p. xxix.

[2] *Ibid.*, p. xxxix.

[3] *Ibid.*, p. xxxii.

[4] Babelon, *Perses*, p. 23, Pl. IV, 5. It is the presence of the tunny on the coins which makes the attribution to Cyzicus probable.

[5] *Ibid.*, p. 15, Pl. II, 22.

[6] *Num. Chron.*, 1890, p. 245.

then, seems to indicate that it was rather the influence of Athens than that of the Persian satraps of Mysia which gave rise to the gold coins of the shore of the Propontis in the early fourth century.

I may briefly summarize the historic situation as follows. It is very difficult to trace in detail the history of the Greek cities of the Propontis during the period 412–311 B.C., that is, between the Athenian disaster in Sicily and the rise of the Greek kingdom of Syria. They passed with bewildering rapidity from Athenian to Lacedaemonian hegemony and back again. Sometimes they seem to have had Persian garrisons and to have been subject to the king, sometimes they were in the hands of revolted satraps, sometimes they appear to have enjoyed almost complete independence. The facts are only to be occasionally gathered from slight references in surviving history. We are able, however, to discern three periods in the history of Asia Minor at this time—(1): 412–387. The constant hostilities between Sparta and Athens, of which the coast of Asia Minor was the cock-pit, caused constant commotion in the cities, until by the Peace of Antalcidas they were recognized by the Greeks as the property of the Great King. (2): 387–334. Under the incompetent rule of Artaxerxes Mnemon, there were perpetual revolts of satraps in Asia Minor, and of these satraps some achieved an almost unqualified independence. We know that they depended largely upon the help of Greek mercenaries; but in regard to their relations to the Greek cities we have scarcely any information. (3): 334–311. From the landing of Alexander to the establishment of the Seleucid dominion there was a time of great unrest, the military occupation of the country by the Macedonians not precluding the autonomy of the cities. It is to the first of these periods, even apart from the testimony of artistic style, that we should naturally attribute the origin of the gold coins of Lampsacus and Abydos. It is very improbable that any Greek cities would after the Peace of Antalcidas begin such issues. But the evidence seems to show that as Cyzicus continued her electrum issues down through the fourth century, so Lampsacus continued issues in gold. The reasons of this very exceptional privilege, which the Great King must at least have tolerated, can only be matter of conjecture.

Passing from the Propontis to the Ionian coast, we have to speak of the very exceptional issue of gold coins by Clazomenae.

The coin of Clazomenae—types, Facing head of Apollo and swan (**Pl. VIII. 4**)—is remarkable for its peculiar weight (grains 87·8; grm. 5·70). It is not a stater of the Attic standard, but exactly two-thirds of a stater. Clazomenae is almost alone among the cities of Asia at this period in using the Attic standard for silver. If the relation of value between gold and silver as accepted at Clazomenae was twelve to one, then this gold coin would be worth four of the tetradrachms of Attic standard, alike the tetradrachms of Clazomenae and those of Athens herself; this seems a natural relation. The gold of Clazomenae is very beautiful, bearing a full-face head of Apollo which may be compared with the head of the Sun-god on the coins of Rhodes, or that of Arethusa on the coins of Syracuse. The *British Museum Catalogue* gives for it the date 387–300 B.C., a wide date, which shows that Mr. Head did not feel sure of its exact time. But we must not overlook the remarkable fact that in the text of the king's peace, or the treaty of Antalcidas, as given by Xenophon, the Persian king expressly reserves to himself, besides the cities of the mainland, the islands of Clazomenae and Cyprus. To couple thus together the little island on which Clazomenae was built, and the great land of Cyprus, seems very strange; and it is to be observed that mention is not made of Cyzicus and other cities built on islands close to the coast. But since Clazomenae came definitely under Persian rule in 387, it would seem far more probable that the city struck its gold just before, and not after, that date. In the style of the coin there is nothing conflicting with this supposition; indeed the full-face head of a deity is as a coin type quite usual in the early years of the fourth century.

The ordinary opinion of numismatists in regard to the gold staters of Asiatic cities is that they were issued as rivals to the daric. As M. Babelon puts it, 'L'or des Grecs, sur le terrain commercial et économique, vient déclarer la guerre à l'or des Perses; la lampsacène est créée pour lutter contre la darique.'[1] And on this ground numismatists have tried to explain the fact that these gold pieces are heavier than the daric. They suppose that this extra weight was introduced purposely in order to force them into circulation. What the cities would gain by such a course no one has explained. When Germany introduced its new gold coinage, it made the standard not heavier but somewhat lighter than that of the English sovereign, and the German traders have greatly profited, by assuming the English sovereign and their own twenty-mark piece to be equivalent.

Athens used the same standard for her gold coins which she had long used for silver. And the reason seems obvious. If the gold and silver coins had the same weight, then, whatever proportion in value gold had to silver, at that rate the gold and silver coins would exchange. That is to say, wherever the silver money of Athens was used as the regular medium of exchange, gold minted on the same standard would pass with ease and convenience.

But we know from the well-known lines of the *Frogs*,[2] as well as from the testimony of finds, that about the year 400 B.C., even after the fall of Athens, Athenian silver was the regular currency of the shores of the Aegean, as well as largely current as far as Sicily and Egypt: received, as Aristophanes says, everywhere alike by Greeks and barbarians.

It seems then that the readiest way of explaining the adoption of the Attic standard for gold by the cities of Asia is to suppose that it was not minted in rivalry of the darics, but with direct reference to the monetary issues of Athens. Athens set the fashion as regards both metal and standard, and several cities of Asia followed it.

[1] *Perses Achéménides*, p. lxxiii.

[2] 720 and foll.

There are in existence gold coins bearing the types of Ephesus,[1] which, if genuine, would be contemporary with those of Lampsacus and Abydos. They are the stater, drachm, and diobol, having on the obverse the type of the bee and the name of the city, and on the reverse a quartered incuse. If they be genuine they will belong to 394–387. But their genuineness has been called in question, and it is unsafe to base any argument upon them.

The gold staters of Cius in Bithynia (**Pl. VIII. 5**) are certainly of later date than those of Lampsacus and Abydos. Their style is considerably later than that of the coins of Chalcidice and of Philip of Macedon; it more nearly resembles that of the money of Pixodarus of Caria (340–334 B.C.). All the known examples come from the two Sidon hoards,[2] which consist of coins dating from the middle to the end of the fourth century. Perhaps the issue of these coins was allowed by Philip or Alexander for some reason which is lost to us, as for services in connexion with the shipment to Asia, since Cius was a landing-place for Phrygia. A parallel may perhaps be found in the issue of gold staters at Philippi in Macedon, apparently by special licence of Philip II. Contemporary with these gold coins of Cius are small silver coins with the same types, weighing 81–83 grains (5·20–5·33 grm.), that is to say, drachms of Persian standard.

Another remarkable gold stater, probably from the Sidon finds, bears on the obverse a head of young Heracles, and on the reverse a Palladium.[3] This is no doubt a coin of Pergamon; a third of a stater with the same reverse, but with the head of Athena on the obverse, is also known.[4] M. Six is probably right[5] in assigning these coins to the period when Heracles, the young son of Alexander, and his mother Barsine established themselves at Pergamon, after

[1] Head, *Coinage of Ephesus*, p. 22. In the *Hist. Num.* they are omitted.
[2] *Revue Numism.*, 1865, 8 (Waddington).
[3] *Revue Numism.*, 1865, Pl. I, 8.
[4] *B. M. Cat. Mysia*, p. 110, No. 4.
[5] *Numism. Chron.*, 1890, p. 200.

the death of Alexander. It is to be noted that the coin in the Sidon finds which has been most worn, and so had probably been longest in circulation, is a stater of Panticapaeum, issued about 390 B.C.

In order to justify us for thus fixing the dates of the coins of Lampsacus, and other Greek cities of the coast, and the circumstances under which they were issued, it will be well to consider some of the contemporaneous gold issues in Greece proper, and the Islands of the Aegean.

The gold coins of Panticapaeum, in the Tauric Chersonese, stand by themselves (**B. M. XXI. 1, 2**). They are of very fine fourth-century work, types Head of Pan and Griffin, and weigh as much as 140 grains (grm. 9·07). The high weight may be the result of an abundance of gold on the spot, to which the modern excavations in the Crimea have borne ample testimony. The contemporary silver coins, bearing as types the head of a satyr, and a bull's head, are didrachms of Persian weight, 182 grains (grm. 11·80), ten of which probably passed as equivalent to the gold stater.

The city of Olynthus in Chalcidice issued gold didrachms of Attic standard in the flourishing time of the Chalcidian League.

Obv. Head of Apollo. *Rev.* ΧΑΛΚΙΔΕΩΝ. Lyre: names of magistrates. (**Pl. VIII. 6.**)

It seems to have been from Olynthus that Philip of Macedon derived his coin standards, both for gold and silver. His issues are treated in Chap. XXI, where the exchange value between gold and silver in the fourth century is also considered.

CHAPTER XVII

COINS OF PHOENICIA AND AFRICA, 480–330 B.C.

§ 1. Phoenicia.

A new and important feature of the period with which we are dealing is the earliest appearance of coins of the cities of Phoenicia. Strange as it may seem, until the middle of the fifth century, the wealthy trading cities of Tyre, Sidon, and Aradus had no coinage of their own. In like manner the great city of Carthage had no coins until nearly the end of the fifth century. Yet Phoenicians and Carthaginians alike must have been perfectly familiar with Greek coins, which circulated in great quantities in the sixth century. And Cyprus, which was half Phoenician, issued money in all the great cities early in the fifth century or before that. Such facts show that we should be mistaken if we supposed either Phoenicians or Greeks to be animated by the keen business spirit, the result of many decades of unbridled competition, which is the ruling factor in modern commercial life.

The occasion of the first issues of money in Phoenicia may have been the collapse of the Athenian Empire. In another chapter I adduce evidence of the determined, and somewhat shameless, way in which Athens insisted on her coins being made the standard of value and the staple of the circulation throughout her empire, and more especially in the islands of the Aegean. The owls of Athens had a wide vogue, and when after the Lamian war they ceased to be produced, imitations took their place inland from Phoenicia. It is reasonable to suppose that at an earlier time, when Athens had been captured by Lysander, and the Persian Satraps began to issue abundant coins in the cities of Cilicia, the maritime towns of Phoenicia began also to feel more keenly the need of a coinage. It is, however, the opinion of the best authorities on the coins of Phoenicia, that the fall of Athens was rather the occasion of a greater plenty in the issue of Phoenician coins than of their first inception. M. Babelon, following M. Rouvier, gives the first issue of coins at Sidon to 475 B.C., Mr. G. F. Hill makes coinage begin at Tyre about 450.[1] The style of some of the coins, which have on their reverse modified incuses, would seem to justify these, or even earlier, attributions. But when one passes away from Greek territory style ceases to be a trustworthy index of date; and certainly the style of coins in Phoenicia is much more archaic than is that of contemporary issues in Greek cities.

It is a suggestive fact that the early coinage of Aradus, in North Syria, is of a different class from the coinages of the cities of Southern Phoenicia.

The city of Aradus, built on an island two or three miles from the coast, began a little before 400 B.C. to issue coin. The ordinary types are—

1. *Obv.* Phoenician letters (*Ex Arado*). Phoenician fish-god, holding dolphin in each hand. *Rev.* Galley with dolphin or sea-horse beneath. Weight, 50–47 grains (grm. 3·25–3·05); 25 grains (grm. 1·63). (**B. T. CXVI.**)
2. *Obv.* Same letters. Torso of fish-god. *Rev.* Prow with dolphin beneath. Weight, 11 grains (grm. 0·68).

One coin is published by Babelon, of the types of No. 1, but weighing 166 grains (grm. 10·77). This is very important, as it makes it clear that the standard is really the Persian, the same as that used in Cyprus and by the Satraps in Cilicia. We have already seen that the Persian stater was often in practice divided into three pieces, which may best be called tetrobols, and which seem to have circulated somewhat above their real value as Chian or Rhodian drachms. We must not press the fact that the coin No. 2 would seem from its type to be the half of some unit, for

[1] *B. M. Cat. Phoenicia*, p. cxxiii.

the torso of the fish-god may be only a substitute for his head, which would well suit the obol.

Early in the fourth century the obverse type is changed; we have a bearded laureate head, possibly of Mel-Karth, in the place of the fish-god (Pl. IX. 6). But the denominations, stater, tetrobol, and obol, still go on at the same weight. The stater sometimes reaches the weight of 165 grains (grm. 10·68), the tetrobol 52 grains (grm. 3·35), and the obol 13 grains (grm. 0·86). There is one exceptional stater[1] which reaches the weight of 258 grains (grm. 16·70), and thus appears to follow the Attic standard. It is possible that this coin may date from the time of Alexander. It is indeed quite archaic in style; but in a Phoenician coin this is not a conclusive indication.

I have placed these two series of coins in the order which seems to me undoubtedly the true one, as it does to Mr. Hill.[2] M. Rouvier and M. Six had transposed them, placing the series with the bearded head first. To assign more exact dates, under these conditions, would be too bold. What is clear is that the coinage of Aradus is under the influence of the Persian Satraps of Cilicia.

The other cities of Phoenicia used the (so-called) Phoenician standard.

Gebal (Byblus) is the next city of Phoenicia, issuing coins before the age of Alexander, to which we come in moving southwards. The earliest coin appears to be the following:

> *Obv.* Galley, containing warriors; beneath, hippocamp. *Rev.* Vulture standing on body of ram (incuse). Weight, 214·5 grains (grm. 13·89), Athens (**B. T. CXVII**); 53·3 grains (grm. 3·45), Brit. Mus.

M. Babelon[3] sees in the reverse type a possible allusion to the overthrow of Evagoras I of Cyprus, on whose coins a ram figures: this, however, is very doubtful. The coin must be given to the first half of the fourth century.

[1] Babelon, *Traité*, ii. 2, p. 521, No. 832.

[2] *B. M. Cat. Phoenicia*, p. xviii.

[3] *Perses Achém.*, p. clxvi.

Next we have the money of a succession of kings, Elpaal, Azbaal, Ainel, of whom only the last can be dated; he was a contemporary of Alexander, if we may regard him as the same as the Enylus of Arrian.[1] He was succeeded, as Mr. Hill has shown,[2] by Adramelek. We may put the full weight of the stater of Byblus at 220 grains (grm. 14·25), and of the quarter stater or Phoenician drachm at 55 grains (grm. 3·58) or less. Smaller coins also occur, notably the trihemiobol of 13 grains (grm. 0·86). There must have been some simple scheme of relations of value between the coins of Byblus and those of Aradus. The drachm of Byblus would naturally be equated with the tetrobol of Aradus, and the trihemiobol of Byblus with the obol of Aradus.

The initial dates of the great coinages of Sidon and Tyre are in dispute. Nor have we any means of determining them, except by a consideration of style, which in cities which were not Greek is apt to mislead. The coins of Sidon which bear the names of kings who may be with some probability identified, belong to the fourth century; but coins having a much earlier appearance are known (**Pl. IX. 7**). M. Babelon makes the series of Sidon begin about 475 B.C., that of Tyre about 470 B.C. Mr. Head places the coins about half a century later. Until more definite data are procured, by the discovery of restrikings, or the composition of hoards, it will not be safe to base arguments upon the supposed dates of the early Sidonian coins.

There is, however, one important line of connexion, if it can be established, between Sidon and Salamis in Cyprus, in the time of Evagoras II, king of the latter city. M. Babelon has tried to show[3] that this king after being defeated in Cyprus was awarded the kingship of Sidon by the Persian king Artaxerxes Ochus for the period 349–346, and there struck coins of the usual Sidonian types.[4] These coins are of a comparatively late style; and they might fairly be used as an argument that the series of Sidon must

[1] *Anab.* ii. 20, 1.
[2] *B. M. Cat. Phoenicia*, p. lxvi.
[3] *Traité*, ii. 2, p. 590.
[4] Compare *B. M. Cat. Phoenicia*, p. 151.

have begun a century earlier. For an attempt to assign other coins to known kings of Sidon I must refer to the above-mentioned work of M. Babelon.

At a period which M. Babelon places at 362 B.C., the end of the reign of Strato (Abdastoret) II, the weight of the coins falls decidedly. The earlier series weigh:

	Grains.	*Grammes.*
Two shekels[1] (4 drachms)	440	28·32
Shekel	220	14·16
Half shekel	110	7·08
Quarter shekel	55	3·54
Sixteenth of shekel	14	0·88

Coins of the later series weigh:

	Grains.	*Grammes.*
Two shekels	400	25·76
Shekel	200	12·88
Half shekel	100	6·44
Quarter shekel	50	3·22
Sixteenth of shekel	12·5	0·80

Mr. Hill makes the suggestion,[2] which is by no means improbable, that this fall of the standard may have been due to a fall in the comparative value of gold, a fall which was in fact in progress in the Aegean region at the time. Taking the weights as above (Mr. Hill places them somewhat higher, but he takes exceptional coins as the standard), we have the following equations: 440 grains of silver at $13\frac{1}{3}$ to 1 are equivalent to 33 grains (grm. 2·14) of gold; 400 grains of silver at 12 to 1 are equivalent also to 33 grains of gold. As the Phoenician silver standard was originally based on the relation of the bar or stater of silver to the bar or stater of gold, and as gold seems to have been the measure of value in Phoenicia, these equations are very probable. If we accept them, four of the double shekels would be equivalent roughly to the daric or the Athenian

[1] Babelon, *Traité*, ii. 2, p. 547. Babelon calls the drachm the shekel; Hill the didrachm.

[2] *B. M. Cat. Phoenicia*, p. cii.

gold stater. They would better fit in with the Athenian gold stater of 135 grains (in fact it seldom exceeds 133 grains) than with the daric of 130–128 grains; but no doubt the daric was the governing coin in Syria at the time. There is, however, some difficulty in seeing how a fall in the relation of gold to silver could take place in Phoenicia, while the Persian Empire went on striking gold and silver at the traditional rates. Mr. Hill also observes that six drachms, in the Athenian silver coinage, would weigh very nearly the same as two shekels of the reduced standard.

The beginning of the coinage of Tyre is assigned by Mr. Hill[1] to 450 B.C.; by M. Babelon to 470. The denominations are:

	Grains.	*Grammes.*
Shekel (didrachm). (Pl. IX. 8) . .	214	13·90
Quarter shekel	54	3·48
Twenty-fourth of shekel	11–10	·70–·60

The owl which figures prominently on the early coins may well be derived from the owl coins of Athens, at the time in the zenith of their fame; but the rest of the types are very markedly Egyptian in character.

With the conquest by Alexander the issue of autonomous coins by the cities of Phoenicia comes to an end; but certain classes of imitative coins, copies of Asiatic or Greek prototypes, for a time go on. (See Chap. XXI.)

While Aradus and Gebal, in the north of Phoenicia, are clearly within the circle of Persian influence, Tyre and Sidon use the old Phoenician standard. As to the exact history and antiquity of this standard we are imperfectly informed. Brandis maintained, with considerable probability, that it corresponded as a silver standard with the ordinary Babylonic gold standard. I have above[2] set forth the equation, 260 grains of gold (grm. 16·84), at the rate of $13\frac{1}{3}$ to 1, are equivalent to 3,458 grains of silver, or 15 shekels of 230 grains (grm. 14·90). This silver unit of 230 grains

[1] *B. M. Cat. Phoenicia*, p. cxxvi.

[2] Chap. I.

stands midway between the Phocaean or Chian unit, which is somewhat heavier, and the Milesian unit, which is somewhat lighter. We have evidence of its use in Phoenicia in quite early times. The numismatic evidence fully confirms its antiquity. It was, for example, in use in the islands of Melos, Carpathos, and Rhodes in the sixth century, and the results of excavation at Cameirus in Rhodes show that this was an early course of Phoenician commerce. Whether the standard of Miletus and Ephesus was derived from it is doubtful. Its adoption at Abdera in the sixth century is a striking fact.[1]

It is almost certain that when so conservative peoples as those of Tyre and Sidon issued coins they would strike them on an ancient standard.

That the same standard was also ancient in Egypt seems to be proved by the issues of King Ptolemy I. He adopted for his silver three standards, one after the other; first the Attic, in imitation of the coinage of Alexander; second the Rhodian, with a view no doubt to convenience in commerce; third, the old Phoenician. And it was the last which prevailed and survived, superseding the others, down to the end of the Ptolemaic régime. An identical standard seems to have been in use in Egypt even under the Old Empire; for we have records of bronze rings weighing about 15 grammes, 232 grains.[2]

Dr. Regling has shown,[3] on the evidence of certain gold coins of Demetrius I of Syria, which bear marks of value, that in the second century B.C. the Ptolemaic or Phoenician drachm was equated with $\frac{5}{8}$ of the Attic drachm. And taking the Phoenician drachm at 56 grains, and the Attic at 67 grains, this exactly corresponds to the proportional weights of the two. We cannot, however, be sure how far this equation was generally accepted, or how far it ruled at an earlier time than the second century.

The above considerations affect the attribution of some

[1] Above, p. 191.

[2] E. Meyer, *Kleine Schriften*, p. 95.

[3] *Klio*, 1905, p. 124.

coins given by M. Babelon to the district of Gaza. Among these are:

1. *Obv.* Phoenician fish-god. *Rev.* Lion at bay. Weight, 162·5 grains (grm. 10·53). (B. T. CXXIII. 7.)
2. *Obv.* Winged goat. *Rev.* Owl facing. Weight, 172–162 grains (grm. 11·11–10·46). (B. T. CXXIII. 8.)

Gaza is known to have issued many imitations of Attic coins, at the time when their issue ceased at Athens.[1] Their weight (like their types) imitates that of Athens. And the name of Gaza appears, according to the reading of M. Six, on drachms of Attic weight, which combine the types of a janiform head and an owl.[2] But the staters above mentioned are of Persian standard, and can scarcely be attributed to any city south of Aradus, such as was Gaza. Possibly, as M. Six held, they may be of Cilicia.

§ 2. Carthage.

Strange to say, the earliest coins which can be attributed to Carthage belong to the last decade of the fifth century. It was on the occasion of the great invasion of Sicily in 410 that the Carthaginians first discovered the necessity of a coinage, no doubt in order to meet the demands of the numerous mercenaries then employed. It is characteristic of the race that they met this demand, not by striking some fresh and distinctive coins, but by making copies more or less faithful of the money already in use in Sicily. Mixed with these, however, some more distinctive types make their appearance, the horse's head, the palm-tree, and a female head in a Persian tiara (Pl. IX. 9). All these silver coins followed the Attic standard, then in universal use in Sicily; and the great mass of them consisted of tetradrachms, though the didrachm, the drachm, and the obol appear as well as the litra with its divisions. They were struck without doubt largely out of the spoil of Selinus, Gela, and

[1] *B. M. Cat. Phoenicia*, p. cxliv; Babelon, *Perses Achém.*, pp. 46, 47; *Traité*, ii. 2, pp. 642–8.

[2] Babelon, *Traité*, pp. 670, &c.; cf. Head, *Num. Chron.*, 1878, p. 278.

other Greek cities. The date of these imitative coins can be fixed with certainty by means of hoards of money found in Sicily. For example, the West Sicilian hoard, examined by Professor Salinas and Sir A. Evans,[1] which was buried at the time of the Carthaginian invasion, about 406 B.C., contained many tetradrachms of this class which were fresh from the die, together with the coins of the Sicilian cities which were destroyed in the course of the invasion.

Combined with these silver coins, however, were issued gold pieces of a less purely imitative kind. The earliest of these are:

1. *Obv.* Head of Persephone. *Rev.* Prancing horse. Weight, 118 grains (grm. 7·64); 24 grains (grm. 1·55). (Pl. IX. 10.)

These coins are given by Evans to the same period as the imitative silver. Somewhat later are the following gold coins:

2. *Obv.* Head of Persephone. *Rev.* Palm-tree. Weight, 36 grains (grm. 2·33).
3. *Obv.* Palm-tree. *Rev.* Horse's head. Weight, 15·3 grains (grm. 0·99).

The gold coins of Syracuse, after the repulse of the Athenians, were of the weight of 90, 45, and 20 grains, equivalent to 20, 10, and 4 or 4½ silver drachms. But the gold coins of Carthage do not seem to have had any satisfactory relation to the silver. They follow an entirely different standard from that of Sicily, or indeed from any Greek gold standard. What that standard is, it is hard to say; but it is used for the later gold and silver coins of the city. Mr. Head calls it the Phoenician standard, with a drachm of 59 grains.[2] But if we turn to the coins of Sidon and Tyre we find that they are minted on a standard not exceeding 55 grains to the drachm. The Carthaginian standard may, however, be a somewhat heavier variety of this, in use in Africa since the foundation of Carthage. In actual

[1] *Syracusan Medallions*, p. 160.

[2] *Historia Numorum*, ed. 2, p. 879.

weight this standard closely corresponds with the Chian or Rhodian.

At a somewhat later time, fixed by Mr. Head to 340 B.C., Carthage strikes at once gold and electrum coins as follows:

Obv. Head of Persephone. *Rev.* Horse standing. Weight, 145 grains (grm. 9·39). Gold.

Obv. Head of Persephone. *Rev.* Horse and palm-tree. Weight, 73 grains (grm. 4·72). Gold.

Obv. Head of Persephone. *Rev.* Horse standing. Weight, 118 grains (grm. 7·64). Electrum.

Obv. Head of Persephone. *Rev.* Horse and palm-tree. Weight, 58 grains (grm. 3·75). Electrum.

Obv. Head of Persephone. *Rev.* Horse looking back. Weight, 27 grains (grm. 1·74). Electrum.

Here the electrum coins are of the same weights as the earlier gold, and belong to the Phoenician rather than the Greek circle of commerce. They may well have been equivalent to ten or twelve times their weight in silver, whether coined or uncoined. The later gold coins are in weight $\frac{5}{4}$ of the electrum, and quite unique in the coinage of the period. At the ratio of 15 to 1, they would be equivalent to 10 silver units of 217 grains; but this ratio seems very unlikely.

It would thus seem that Carthage struck on two different systems at the same time. The silver money struck in or for Sicily followed the Attic standard; that in gold or electrum, struck in all probability mainly for home use, followed a variety of the Phoenician standard. The rates of exchange of the two series against one another remain to be determined. The large silver coins bearing the name and types of Carthage are later, and are the fruit of the silver mines of Spain, where in all likelihood they were struck.

I shall not further examine the coinage of Carthage. It is unfortunate that there is no systematic account of it since Müller's *Numism. de l'anc. Afrique* (1861). It would be a fruitful task to investigate the series in relation to the contemporary coins of Italy and Sicily.

§ 3. Cyrene.

We have seen in a previous chapter (XIII) that the early silver coinage of Cyrene follows a standard practically equivalent to that of Athens, but of independent and of earlier origin. Some of the smaller coins, however, are regulated by the drachm of Phoenicia.

According to Mr. Head, it was at the time of the expulsion of the Battiad kings and the establishment of a republic, about 431 B.C., that a light variety of the Phoenician standard was, in the case of the larger coins, substituted for the Attic; and gold coins were issued on the Attic standard about 400 B.C. But the expulsion of the Battiadae cannot well have been so late as 431, seeing that the last of the kings, Arcesilaus IV, won the chariot-race at Delphi in 466 B.C. The date of 450 is more probable. Whether the change in standard of the silver coins took place then can only be determined by a consideration of the style of the coins themselves. Mr. E. S. G. Robinson, after a careful discussion, is disposed to date the transition to the new standard about 435 B.C.[1] It is not strange that the new standard adopted at Cyrene should be practically that of Samos (stater, 210 grains; grm. 13·60) for two reasons. In the first place, this very standard had long been in use for the divisions of the stater—drachms, and lesser units. And in the second place, there had always been a close connexion between Cyrene and Samos, as is shown by the history of Arcesilaus III, who fled to Samos when he was expelled from Cyrene, and in that island collected an army which restored him to his throne. At Samos the Samian weight for coins, which was for a short period given up at the time of the Athenian Conquest of 439 B.C., was resumed about 430; and it is possible that on that occasion the people of Cyrene adopted it for all their silver.

[1] *Num. Chron.*, 1915, p. 87.

Contemporary with these issues of silver are gold coins on the same standard. The earliest of these is a drachm[1] of somewhat archaic style. (*Obv.* Silphium plant. *Rev.* Head of bearded Ammon: weight, 53 grains (grm. 3·43), Paris.) The half or hemidrachm, and the quarter or trihemiobol were issued certainly before the end of the fifth century. The half drachm has the same types as the drachm; the quarter drachm has various types, especially the heads of Ammon and Cyrene. In the weight of the quarter drachm (13·5 grains, grm. 0·87) Sir A. Evans sees the influence of Sicily, where the silver litra is of this weight. But as 13·5 grains of gold, at the exchange of 15 to 1, are equivalent to three Attic drachms of silver or a Samian tetradrachm in silver, it does not seem necessary to go further to justify the weight.

It would seem then that Cyrene was the first of all cities outside Persia to produce a regular issue of gold coins, as distinguished from a few coins issued by some cities in time of stress. This is very natural, as Egypt was one of the chief sources of gold in the ancient world. We have already seen[2] that Cyrene was also very early in the use of a silver coinage.

Besides these smaller gold coins, we find at Cyrene an abundance of staters of Attic weight. (Pl. IX. 11.)

Opinions as to the date of these gold staters differ widely. Sir A. Evans,[3] in agreement with Dr. L. Müller, assigned them to a period before 415 B.C., and regarded them as having influenced the coinage of Syracuse before the time of Dionysius. M. J. P. Six,[4] on the other hand, with whom Holm agrees, gives them to the time of Magas, 280 B.C., and finds in the enthroned figure of Zeus Ammon, which some of them bear, a copy of the seated Zeus of the coins of Alexander. M. Babelon, also, is strongly of opinion that the gold staters are later than Alexander.[5] The question is not

[1] *Num. Chron.*, 1915, p. 86. Mr. Robinson would date this coin before 485.

[2] Above, p. 218.

[3] *Syracusan Medallions*, p. 63.

[4] *Num. Chron.*, 1897, p. 223; cf. Holm, *Gesch. Sic.*, iii, p. 609.

[5] *Traité*, iii, p. 1085.

one to be easily decided. But my own view coincides with that of Head and Mr. Robinson, that the coins belong to the early part of the fourth century, and are contemporary with the gold staters of Athens, Rhodes, and Lampsacus. The type of the seated Zeus does at first sight remind us of the silver coins of Alexander; but in fact that type more nearly resembles the seated Zeus of the coins of the Persian satraps of Cilicia, which belong to the early fourth century. The chariot also, which is a common type, is nearer to the chariots on the fifth-century coins of Sicily than to that on the coins of Philip of Macedon.

Contemporary with the gold staters are their fractions, the drachm, and hemidrachm of Attic weight. And the older gold coinage of Samian weight seems to have been continued. M. Babelon publishes one gold stater of this weight,[1] 110·5 grains (grm. 7·16), which is quite exceptional. But coins of lesser denomination are common; and as the same magistrates' names occur on them which we find on the staters, the two classes of coins seem to have been contemporary. We have the eighth of a stater of Samian standard weighing 13·5 grains (grm. 0·87).

M. Babelon calls the standard for silver in use in the fifth century Milesian (which is the same as the Samian), and that in use in the fourth century Rhodian. But in fact the coins of the two periods are in weight identical, as M. Babelon himself allows.[2]

We thus have at Cyrene precisely the opposite arrangement to that at Carthage. At Carthage silver was struck on the Attic standard, gold on the Phoenician.[3] At Cyrene gold was struck on the Attic standard, silver on that of Phoenicia. Silver didrachms and drachms of Attic weight were, however, exceptionally issued before the middle of the fourth century; and the magistrates' names on these are in some cases (ΘΕΥΦΕΙΔΕΥΣ, ΠΟΛΙΑΝΘΕΥΣ) identical with those which occur on the gold.

[1] *Ibid.*, p. 1079.

[2] Compare his table on p. 1058 with his table on p. 1080.

[3] *Syracusan Medallions*, p. 63.

CHAPTER XVIII

COINS OF HELLAS, 480–330 B.C.

§ 1. Northern Greece.

In a previous chapter we have considered the origins of coinage in Greece Proper, and carried down its history to the end of the sixth century in the case of a few important cities, Aegina, Chalcis, Eretria, Corinth, Athens, Corcyra. But the Persian War did not make a clear line of division in the coins of Greece Proper, as it did in Asia and Thrace. Nor were the cities of Greece Proper subject, as were those of Asia, to the domination of the Athenian Empire and the Athenian coinage. There is thus usually no marked break in their issues, at all events in the fifth century. And it will be best to treat in the present chapter of the whole of the issues of the cities of Northern Greece and Peloponnesus down to the time of Alexander, except in the case of the great cities above mentioned. The coins of most parts of Greece Proper give few data for metrological inquiries. From Thessaly to Messene they follow, with few exceptions, the Aeginetan standard. But there are many indications of historic value to be gained from the study of some classes of these coins.

Thessaly and Epirus. I begin with Thessaly. The first city of Thessaly to issue coin was Larissa, the city of the Aleuadae, who seem to have obtained a primacy in the region at the time of the Persian wars.[1] It was about 500 B.C. when these issues began. They were followed in the fifth century by those of many other cities, Pharsalus, Pherae, Scotussa, Tricca, and others. The only landmark in the Thessalian series is furnished by the occurrence at

[1] Hdt. vii. 6.

Larissa on some coins of the name Simus, in small letters. It seems reasonable to regard this Simus as the Aleuad who was made Tetrarch of part of Thessaly by Philip of Macedon 352–344 B.C.[1] It is, however, possible that the name may be only that of the artist who made the die; and in fact we hear of a sculptor named Simus at Olynthus at this period.[2] The autonomous silver coins of Thessaly ceased when Thessaly was incorporated with Macedon in 344 B.C.

Alexander of Epirus, who went to Italy in 332 B.C., to aid the Greek cities against the Italians, issued gold staters, which take their place among the coins of Tarentum, and silver didrachms:

> *Obv.* Head of Zeus crowned with oak. *Rev.* ΑΛΕΞΑΝΔΡΟΥ ΤΟΥ ΝΕΟΠΤΟΛΕΜΟΥ. Thunderbolt. Weight, 165 grains (grm. 10·69).[3] (B. M. XXII. 23.)

As the weight of these coins is the same as that of contemporary coins of Corcyra, it is probable that they were issued in Epirus.

Of the same weight as the coins of the Kings of Paeonia (p. 324) are the barbarous imitations of the coins of Zacynthus struck at Damastium, Pelagia, and other Illyrian cities in the middle of the fourth century:[4]

> *Obv.* Head of Apollo. *Rev.* ΔΑΜΑΣΤΙΝΩΝ. Tripod-lebes. Weight, 206–188 grains (grm. 13·34–12·18).

Of these coins, rude as they are, still more barbarous imitations were current. Strabo mentions silver mines at Damastium.

It may be doubted whether these copies are due to the uncivilized Thracian and Illyrian peoples of the district, or to the Gauls, who took advantage of the removal of the Macedonian armies to Asia by Alexander to occupy

[1] *B. M. Cat. Thessaly* (Gardner), p. xxvi. M. Waddington told me that he accepted this attribution.

[2] *Bull. Corr. Hell.*, xiv. 276.

[3] *B. M. Cat. Thessaly*, p. 110.

[4] *B. M. Cat. Thessaly*, Pl. XVI, p. xlii.

most of the country to the north and west of the Macedonian Kingdom.

Very exceptionally, the island of Pharos on the Illyrian coast struck autonomous silver in the fourth century:

Obv. Head of Zeus. *Rev.* Goat standing. Br. Mus. Weight, 41 grains (grm. 2·65).[1]

The weight is that of the coins of Corcyra and Dyrrhachium. The type of the goat seems to be derived from the coins of Paros. A colony of Parians was settled in the island by Dionysius of Syracuse about 385 B.C.; and the silver coin, with others in bronze, was probably minted at that time.

Boeotia. Among the most important series of Greek coins, from the historic point of view, is that of Boeotia. The coinage of Boeotia throughout reflects the history of the cities of the district, their mutual relationships, their rise and fall. The series has received much attention from numismatists, having been carefully worked out, first by Dr. Imhoof-Blumer, then by Mr. Head, and most recently by M. Babelon.[2]

It is unnecessary, in giving a *résumé* of the numismatic history of Boeotia, to specify the weights of the several coins, as all follow the Aeginetan standard, and are of full weight.

The Boeotian coins bear throughout, on the obverse, the shield with inlets at the sides, which seems to be derived from a Mycenaean prototype, and is commonly called Boeotian. This uniformity of type indicates that all through their history the Boeotian cities formed a monetary confederation. The cities, however, began with the issue of drachms of Aeginetan standard, bearing the league type of the shield, the first letter of the name of the issuing city being inserted in the side-openings. Thus we find the aspirate on the money of Haliartus, and T or TA on the money of

[1] *B. M. Cat. Thessaly*, p. 83.

[2] Imhoof-Blumer, *Numism. Zeitschr.*, vols. iii and ix; Head, *Num. Chron.*, 1881; Babelon, *Traité*, ii. 1, pp. 933-76, ii. 3, pp. 211-312.

Tanagra. Thebes seems to have struck coins of this weight and type, but uninscribed. Somewhat later, perhaps about 550 B.C., some cities struck staters or didrachms, with the initial of the city, not on the obverse, but on the reverse, in the midst of the incuse. In this series A represents Acraephium, Ϙ Coroneia, 𐌇 Haliartus, M Mycalessus, Φ Pharae, T Tanagra, ⊕ Thebes (Pl. II. 14). Divisions of the stater were also struck.

It is a somewhat further development, when Thebes places on the reverse of its coins the letters ΘΕΒΑ (archaic), and Tanagra issues staters as follows:

1. *Obv.* TA. Boeotian shield. *Rev.* B in the midst of an incuse. (*B. M. Cat. Central Greece*, Pl. IX. 17.)
2. *Obv.* T or TA. Boeotian shield. *Rev.* B O I in the compartments of a wheel. (Pl. X. 1.)
3. *Obv.* T. Boeotian shield. *Rev.* T A in the compartments of a wheel. (*B. M. Cat.*, Pl. IX. 14.)

Nos. 1 and 2 prove that at an early time Tanagra claimed to represent the League. The occasion has been disputed. Mr. Head thought that it was after the Persian wars, when Thebes was for a time by the confederated Greeks debased from its predominant position. But it is very difficult to bring down No. 1 at all events as late as 480 B.C.; and therefore the view of M. Babelon is preferable. He considers the date of coins 1–3 to be about 507 B.C. He cites tetradrachms of Attic standard, struck at Chalcis in Euboea.

1. *Obv.* Ψ (X) on Boeotian shield. *Rev.* Wheel in incuse-square. (Babelon, *Traité*, ii. 1, p. 973.)
2. *Obv.* Eagle flying holding serpent in beak. *Rev.* ΨΑΛ in the compartments of a wheel. (*Ibid.*, p. 670.)

Chalcis, M. Babelon observes, was destroyed by the Athenians in 507 B.C.; whence both these coins must precede that date. And the occurrence of the shield on No. 1 and the precise correspondence of the reverse of No. 2 with the coin of Tanagra, proves an alliance between the Boeotian and the Euboean city. Herodotus does not say that the Athenians destroyed the city;[1] but they confiscated its territory and so far dominated it, that an alliance with the Boeotians after that date is improbable, whereas there was an alliance before it. It must be observed that the distance between Tanagra and Chalcis is only twelve miles.

There is also an early coinage of Orchomenus; but as the money of this city bears a different type, a grain of wheat, and as it is only of the denomination of an obol, or a half obol, it stands apart. This coinage may go on until the destruction of Orchomenus by Thebes in 368 B.C. It is noteworthy that the incuse on the reverse of the coins of Orchomenus copies the Aeginetan incuse closely, and evidently on purpose.

At the time of the invasion of Xerxes Thebes medized; and when the Persian army was repulsed, the city had to pay for its frailty. For about twenty years we have no coins which bear the name of Thebes. It is a difficult question which city or cities took its place. Tanagra between 479 and its destruction by Myronides in 456 would seem to have held a leading position. And it may well be that some of the coins above cited, bearing the joint names of the Boeotians and Tanagra, may belong to this period. After 456 B.C., the Athenians set up democracies in several of the Boeotian cities, and we should have expected that these would strike coins. We find such coins at Acraephium, Coroneia, Haliartus, Tanagra, and Thebes. The reverses are:[2]

Acraephium. AK. Wine-cup.
Coroneia. KOPO. Head of Medusa.
Haliartus. ARI. Amphora.
Tanagra. TA. Fore-part of horse.
Thebes. ⊕E. Amphora.

About the middle of the century Thebes begins to recover her ascendancy; and after her victory over the Athenians at Coroneia in 446, entirely monopolizes the

[1] Hdt. v. 77, vi. 100.

[2] *Num. Chron.*, 1881, pp. 201–5.

coinage of Boeotia until the Peace of Antalcidas in 387. The staters, which are numerous and in a fine style of art, bear the name of Thebes only, not that of the Boeotians. The types are usually taken from the legend of Heracles: one of them, the infant Heracles strangling the serpents, was copied in the cities of Asia which revolted against Sparta in 394 B.C., a fact which confirms the date of the Theban coin (Pl. X. 3). Some of the Heracles types are, as we should have expected, more archaic in type than this, a few contemporary or later. The head of Dionysus also occurs (Pl. X. 2).

Of exactly the same period, 394 B.C., are certain small coins of pale gold or electrum:

> *Obv.* Head of bearded Dionysus, ivy-crowned. *Rev.* ΘE. Young Heracles strangling serpents. Weight, 46·3 grains (grm. 3); 15·8 grains (grm. 1·02). (B. T. CCI. 1–5.)

This period is that which I have already accepted as the date of the earliest issue of gold staters or didrachms at Athens, the earlier issue having been of drachms and smaller denominations only. Mr. Head has connected this gold issue with the visit to Thebes of the Rhodian envoy Timocrates, who expended the equivalent of fifty talents of silver on behalf of the Persian Satrap Tithraustes, at Thebes and elsewhere, in the promotion of an anti-Spartan alliance.[1] If so, the gold of which these coins were made was Persian. But considering the smallness of the issue we may well consider it as money of necessity.

Thebes followed the Athenian lead, and like Athens struck gold on her accepted silver standard, as did Pisa and Sicyon and other cities which used the Aeginetan weight. As the coins are of electrum, it is probable that the old Asiatic relation of value was preserved, electrum being regarded as ten times as valuable as silver.

The Peace of Antalcidas seems to have had as important effects in Boeotia as anywhere. Many of the cities recommenced their coinage, sometimes with types more distinctive

[1] Xenophon, *Hellenica*, iii. 5. 1.

than of old. Haliartus introduced as type Poseidon striking with the trident (Pl. X. 4); Orchomenus, a galloping horse or an amphora; Tanagra, the fore-part of a horse; Thespiae, a head of Aphrodite. The above cities issued didrachms, but several other cities, including Plataea, were content with striking fractional money.

The League or Confederation was reconstituted by Pelopidas and his friends about 379 B.C., and not long after this begins the series of staters which have not on them the name either of the Boeotians or of any city, but only that of a magistrate; the types, Boeotian shield and amphora, sufficiently identifying the district of mintage. Perhaps these names were those of Boeotarchs, some of them, such as Charopinus, Androcleidas, Epaminondas, and (the younger) Ismenias, being well known to history. Bronze coins are contemporary with these issues in silver, and bear the same names.

After the victory of Philip of Macedon over Thebes in 338 B.C., the city naturally lost its pre-eminence. It was the policy of Philip to restore the cities which Thebes had destroyed, Orchomenus, Thespiae and Plataea. A fresh Boeotian confederation was formed, probably under the leadership of Thespiae. The federal staters and hemidrachms are continued, but in the place of the name of a Boeotarch, they have only the inscription ΒΟΙΩ. The cities of the League also issue bronze coins of uniform pattern, bearing on one side the shield, on the other the first letters of the name of the issuing city, ΑΡΙ for Haliartus, ΘΕΣ for Thespiae, ΛΕΒ for Lebadeia, ΟΡΧ for Orchomenus, ΠΛΑ for Plataea, ΤΑΝ for Tanagra. The absence of the name of Thebes is noteworthy. This coinage may have continued until 315 B.C., when coins began to be issued at Thebes by Cassander with the types of Alexander.

'It is interesting', Mr. Head remarks,[1] 'to observe how, as history repeats itself, the coinage reflects the history. There are three distinct periods in which the influence and

[1] *Num. Chron.*, 1881, p. 250.

importance of Thebes had sunk to the lowest point: first, after the battle of Plataea, 479 B.C.; second, after the Peace of Antalcidas, 387 B.C.; and third, after the battle of Chaeroneia, 338 B.C. On each of these three several occasions a considerable portion of the currency appears to have been issued in the name of the *Boeotians*, while the coinage of Thebes itself either sank for the time being into insignificance or ceased to be issued altogether.'

Locris. The inhabitants of the district of Locris were not homogeneous. The people of Western Locris, the Ozolian Locrians, whose capital was Amphissa, seem to have been not far removed from barbarism.[1] They struck no coins before the second century. Eastern Locris consisted of two districts: the northernmost was called Hypocnemidian, because it lay under Mount Cnemis; its chief places were Scarphea and Thronium; the southernmost was dominated by the city of Opus, which sometimes dominated the whole of Eastern Locris.

In Locris we may trace, if not quite so clearly, the outlines of a similar history to that of Boeotia. The earliest coins of the district which we possess are the obols and trihemiobols bearing only the letter O with an amphora, and the half obols bearing as type half an amphora, and on the reverse the letter Λ. These were struck at Opus: they are given by M. Babelon to the time before 456 B.C., when the people of Opus, with the Corinthians and Thebans, were allies of Aegina. There are also small coins of the fifth century struck at Thronium. After the Peace of Antalcidas, 387 B.C., when federal issues ceased generally, and their place was taken by the coins of separate cities, we find didrachms or staters of Aeginetan standard issued by the city of Opus, and bearing the inscription ΟΠΟΝΤΙΩΝ (Pl. X. 5). Their reverse type is Ajax, the son of Oileus, in attitude of combat.

After the battle of Chaeroneia, 338 B.C., this inscription gives place to ΛΟΚΡΩΝ with a monogram which may be

[1] Thuc. i. 5.

resolved into ΥΠΟ (Hypocnemidian). Here, as in Boeotia, the name of the tribe takes the place of that of a city after Chaeroneia, though our historic evidence is not so clear as in the case of Thebes. The coins which bear the name of Opus, we may observe, have a close resemblance to those of Syracuse, especially to the types of the engraver Evaenetus (compare Pl. X. 5 with XI. 9). The figure of Ajax seems to be a copy of that of Leucaspis on the Syracusan money.

Phocis. The coins of Phocis and Delphi bear traces of the age-long dispute between the two communities for the control of the Delphic sanctuary and festival.

The earliest coins of Phocis which bear the name of the tribe, for there are earlier uninscribed coins (**B. M. V. 19**), seem to begin about 480 B. C.

Obv. ΦΟ or ΦΟΚΙ. Bull's head. *Rev.* Head of Nymph. Triobols, obols, and hemiobols of Aeginetan standard. (B. T. CCV. 1–9.)

Early in the fifth century, on some unknown occasion, the Phocian city of Neon issued obols:

Obv. ΦΟ. Bull's head facing. *Rev.* ΝΕ. Fore-part of boar. (B. T. CCVI. 11.)

When this coin was struck, Neon must have claimed the hegemony in Phocis. Lilaea also struck triobols of the regular Phocian types, but bearing the letters ΛΙ instead of ΦΟ.

It has been suggested that the Phocian coins may have been struck in connexion with the recurring festival of the tribe at Daulis. But the Delphic festival, of which the Phocians exercised control from 448 until the Peace of Nicias in 421 B. C., would seem a more likely occasion. In that case we should have a parallel to the coins issued in connexion with the Olympic festival, and bearing the name of the people of Elis. This view seems to be corroborated by the cessation of the coins (to judge by their style) about 421 B. C., when a full autonomy was secured to the people of Delphi.[1] In the fourth century coinage bearing the

[1] Thuc. v. 18.

name of the people of Phocis is resumed, but the occasion is not certain. In the years 357–346 B.C. the sacred site of Delphi was occupied by the Phocians under their successive generals, Philomelus, Onymarchus, Phayllus, and Phalaecus. Diodorus[1] tells us that Philomelus did not at first seize the treasures laid up on the sacred site; but later, being hard pressed by the Boeotians, he did so. Onymarchus continued the process, and struck abundant coins in gold and silver to pay troops and bribe neighbouring states, as did his successor, Phayllus, by whom the magnificent gifts of Croesus in gold and electrum were melted down. We should have expected gold and silver coins belonging to the Phocian occupation of Delphi to have been abundant, especially as the statements of Diodorus are confirmed by Plutarch, who says that the Phocian gold and silver was dispersed through all Greece. Thus to conjecture what became of the Phocian Delphic money is a difficult problem. No doubt, as being the fruit of sacrilege, the Greeks would melt it down whenever they could. Plutarch tells us[2] that the Opuntians collected some of the silver and made of it a hydria, which they dedicated to Apollo. Notwithstanding such considerations, the total disappearance of the money of Onymarchus and Phayllus is one of the puzzles of numismatics. In fact, the only coins which we can with certainty connect with the Phocian generals are small pieces of bronze, bearing the names of Onymarchus and Phalaecus. Besides, there are known small silver coins:

Obv. Laureate head of Apollo. *Rev.* ΦΩ. Lyre in laurel wreath. Weight, 74 grains (grm. 4·77): with hole in it. (B. T. CCV. 11, 12.)

Obv. Bull's head facing. *Rev.* ΦΩ. Head of Apollo, laureate. Weight, 43–40 grains (grm. 2·80–2·60); 14 grains (grm. 0·90). (B. T. CCV. 13, 14.)

These coins are attributed by M. Babelon[3] to the time of the occupation of Delphi by the Phocians, but it is difficult

[1] Diod. xvi. 24–36.

[2] *De Pythiae oraculis*, xvi.

[3] *Traité*, iii, p. 327.

to believe that these violators would have had the effrontery to use as type the head of the deity whom they had so scandalously robbed. One is rather disposed to attribute them to 339 B.C., when Athens and Thebes reconstituted the Phocian League and rebuilt some of the cities.

Contemporary with these coins are the notable didrachms and drachms which bear the names of the Amphictions:

Obv. Head of Demeter, veiled. *Rev.* ΑΜΦΙΚΤΙΟΝΩΝ. Apollo seated with lyre and laurel-branch. Weight, 184–190 grains (grm. 11·92–12·35); also the drachm. **(Pl. X. 6.)**

Obv. Head of Demeter, veiled. *Rev.* Omphalos entwined by serpent. Weight, 44 grains (grm. 2·82). **(B. T. CCVI. 6.)**

M. Bourguet has shown that there was exactly at this time a renovation of the coinage.[1] The financial Board of the temple in 338 B.C. introduces a distinction between the old coinage, *παλαιόν*, and the new, *καινόν* or *καινὸν Ἀμφικτυονικόν*. The standard of both coinages is the Aeginetan. The Amphictionic coin was struck out of the tribute which the people of Phocis after their defeat were compelled to pay to the Delphic sanctuary. In 338 they had already paid 270 talents in the old money, which was no doubt melted down and reissued.

Delphi is disappointing. We should have expected that, as on the occasion of the Olympic festival abundant coins were struck by the people of Elis, so at Delphi large coins would be abundant. But we have only small pieces, with two exceptions, which will presently be considered. These small pieces work in with those of Phocis in a curious way: the triobol, obol, and hemiobol being Phocian, while the trihemiobol ($1\frac{1}{2}$ obol), the tritartemorion ($\frac{3}{4}$ obol), and the quarter obol are Delphic.[2] All are of Aeginetan weight. Their date is not certain, but they have an archaic air. A few may be later than 421, but most of them would be previous to 448, when Athens placed the presidency of the festival in the hands of the Phocians.

[1] *Administration financière du sanctuaire pythique*, p. 90.

[2] *B. M. Cat. Central Greece*, p. xxxii.

The exceptions are:

1. *Obv.* ΔΑΛΦΙΚΟΝ (archaic). Two rams' heads and two dolphins. *Rev.* Four deep incuses, in each a dolphin.[1] Weight, 276 grains (grm. 17·88). (**B. T. XLII. 16.**)
2. *Obv.* No inscription. Ram's head; beneath, dolphin. *Rev.* Incuse square, quartered; in each quarter, cross. Weight, 186·5 grains (grm. 12·08). (**B. T. XLII. 19.**)

These coins are of the middle of the sixth century, or little later. The second is, naturally, an Aeginetan didrachm. The first is too heavy to be an Attic tetradrachm: can it be an Aeginetan tridrachm, a denomination elsewhere unknown? It is noteworthy that this coin must have been issued at about the time when Peisistratus raised the weight of the Attic tetradrachm.

As a compensation for the jejuneness of the coinage of Delphi, the Delphic inscriptions furnish us with valuable information as to the relations in exchange of the Aeginetan and Attic standards in Phocis. In the temple accounts of the fourth century the sums of money acquired in Attic and in Aeginetan coin are kept apart. Yet they must sometimes have been added together; and the officials made this easy by the adoption of the Attic mina, which consisted, of course, of 100 Attic drachms, and which was regarded as consisting of 70 Aeginetan drachms.[2]

It would seem then that at Delphi an Attic drachm was regarded as normally equivalent to $\frac{7}{10}$ of an Aeginetan drachm.[3] This fairly agrees with the respective weights of the two. We have here definite inscriptional evidence of such adjustments in the normal values of coins of different kinds as I have supposed to exist in many places. There must everywhere have been some generally accepted relation between the staters dominant in the district and other coins

[1] *Rev. numismatique*, 1869, p. 150; cf. Babelon, *Traité*, ii. 1, 993. M. Babelon, by an oversight, gives No. 2 the same inscription as No. 1.

[2] T. Reinach, *L'Histoire par les monnaies*, p. 100. This equation recognized in the time of Aristotle may account for what he says as to the Solonic reform (p. 147).

[3] Bourguet, *Administr. financière du sanctuaire pythique*, p. 18.

which circulated there. In Delphi the local standard was that of Aegina, but Attic money also was largely used.

But this normal equivalence was of course subject everywhere to an *agio* or commission on exchange, according to the temporary demand for one class of coin or the other. Of this *agio* we find examples in the Delphic accounts.[1] In certain transactions recorded a commission, ἐπικαταλλαγή, is mentioned. In some cases the Attic drachm was regarded as equal to $\frac{3}{4}$ of an Aeginetan drachm; sometimes, but apparently only in small transactions, as $\frac{2}{3}$ of it.

The Delphic treasurers on one occasion borrow 190 darics, in order to make gold crowns, and they record a profit on the transaction of 95 staters, that is, one Aeginetan drachm per daric[2]: this is curious, because in this purchase the treasurers were the seekers, not the sought, so that their profit is the more notable. On another occasion, when the treasurers had to pay to the executive 20 Aeginetan talents, they enter in their accounts only a payment of $18\frac{2}{3}$ talents, making a profit (ἐπικαταλλαγή) of $1\frac{1}{3}$ talents.

Euboea. Euboea recovered its liberty in 411 B.C., after which for some years a federal coinage was issued, the types of which indicate Eretria as the mint-city:

Obv. Cow reclining. *Rev.* EYB. Head of nymph Euboea. Weight, 177–184 grains (grm. 11·45–11·94). (B. T. CXCVII. 17, 18.)

These are didrachms of Aeginetan standard, the adoption of which in Euboea is a notable fact, though, as the neighbouring Boeotia used this standard, it is not contrary to all probability.

The confederacy, however, recurred to the Attic standard, probably about 394 B.C., the date of Conon's victory at Cnidus:

Obv. Head of Nymph. *Rev.* Cow standing: inscription EYB or EYBOI. Weight, 249–264 grains (grm. 16·10–17·7). (B. T. CXCVII. 20–22.)

[1] Bourguet, *op. cit.*, p. 20.

[2] *Bull. Corr. Hell.*, xx, p. 464.

Obv. EYB or EYBOI. Head of Nymph. *Rev.* Head of cow. Weight, 61–65 grains (grm. 3·98–4·21). (B. T. CXCVII. 24.)

These are clearly tetradrachms and drachms of full Attic weight, and show the revival of Athenian influence. But after a few years, either at the time of the Peace of Antalcidas (387 B.C.) or at that of the congress at Delphi (369 B.C.), the cities of Chalcis, Carystus, and Histiaea resumed the issue of civic coins, drachms of a somewhat reduced Attic weight, about 56–59 grains (grm. 3·60–3·80). Carystus also struck didrachms on the same standard. That the lowering of the standard was due to the influence of Philip of Macedon who used the Phoenician (Abderite) standard is improbable, as the coins seem earlier than his time.

A Chalcidian drachm of this period bears a very interesting counter-mark, the letters I+N ('Iχν) and a lyre.[1] We cannot hesitate to regard this coin, as does M. Babelon, as marked for circulation at Ichnae in Chalcidice, probably in the dearth of the usual civic coins, when Philip of Macedon was at war with the Chalcidian League.

Athens. There is not much to be said as to the coinage of Athens in the fourth century. I have already given some account of the issue of gold staters and fractions about 394 B.C. The silver coinage of the period after 394 is in style very similar to the gold. It went on to the time of Alexander and the Lamian war. Head assigns a special class of tetradrachms which have on the reverse a subsidiary type beside the owl (a bucranium, prow, rudder, trident, &c.) to the period 339–322; but this is a mere division for convenience, for there is no reason to connect the introduction of a subsidiary type with the battle of Chaeroneia.

What is quite clear is that Athens did not in the time of the Second Confederacy, after 378 B.C., make any attempt to stop the coinage of the allied cities, or to substitute her coins for theirs. The allies had been taught by experience not to submit to any dictation from Athens; and though

[1] *Traité*, iii, p. 186.

the city after 400 B.C. rapidly recovered its power, it did not again acquire a dominating position.

When the Athenian coinage of the older style came to an end, we find in several districts of Asia imitations intended to take its place and continue its vogue. Some of these, struck at an uncertain mint, bear the name of the Persian Satrap Mazaeus, and must have been issued during the campaigns of Alexander. Others seem to be later, and reach us from Egypt, Persia, and even India. As the weight of the Attic tetradrachms and of those of Alexander was the same, the two species of coins could conveniently circulate together.

After the middle of the fourth century the issues of bronze, which has been intermitted after the experiment of the fifth century (above, p. 295), were resumed. Bronze money was also struck at Eleusis.

Aegina. The coinage of Aegina does not give us very clear indications of date. We know the history of the island, and have to fit the coins to that history by their style. But the conservative types, the tortoise and the incuse-square, do not give clear stylistic data. It is, however, probable that numismatists generally are right in supposing that the change of type from a turtle to a land tortoise (**B. M. VI. 29, XIII. 24**) took place about 480 B.C. And M. Babelon is probably right in maintaining that after the Athenian conquest of Aegina in 456 B.C. the people of the island issued no more staters, but only drachms and triobols, the staple of the currency being supplied by the *owls* of Athens.

In 431 B.C. the Aeginetans, having revolted against Athenian domination, were expelled from their island by Pericles, and struck no more coin until they were restored to it by Lysander, after which they resumed the issue of staters and fractions of the stater on their old standard. The bronze coins of Aegina (type, two dolphins) belong to this latter period only. The whole coinage seems to have come to an end about the middle of the fourth century, perhaps in consequence of fresh pressure from Athens.

Megara. The next place which presents us with problems

is Megara. Strangely enough, unless, as M. Svoronos suggests, some of the early didrachms of Attic weight assigned to Euboea are really of Megara, that city strikes no coins until early in the fourth century (**B. T. CXCIV. 6–10**).

1. *Obv.* Head of Apollo. *Rev.* Lyre. Weight, 122 grains (grm. 7·90).
2. *Obv.* Head of Apollo. *Rev.* Five crescents. Weight, 50 grains (grm. 3·24); another, 46 grains (grm. 2·96).
3. *Obv.* Head of Apollo. *Rev.* Three crescents with H. Weight, 23 grains (grm. 1·49).
4. *Obv.* Head of Apollo. *Rev.* Lyre. Weights, 18·2 grains (grm. 1·18); 10·2 grains (grm. 0·66); 4·2 grains (grm. 0·27).

Mr. Head gives up the question to what standard these coins belong. According to all analogy, the five crescents should indicate five units, and the three crescents three units. If the coins are somewhat under normal weight (and they are indeed somewhat worn down), No. 1 might be an Attic didrachm, and No. 2 a pentobol (normal, 56 grains); could No. 3 be a triobol of the same standard and the coins under No. 4 be the diobol, obol and hemiobol?

This seems to me the most reasonable view. The staters of Athens would be used in all large payments. But for small transactions, local coins might be from time to time struck; and there is no reason why they should be of full weight, being intended only for local use.

Coin No. 2 seems to have double marks of value, the five crescents indicating that it is a pentobol, and the H that it is a half drachm of another standard. An Attic pentobol should weigh 55 grains, and an Aeginetan hemidrachm 48 grains. The coin is actually between these limits; but that the intention was that it should pass for one or the other of these does not appear probable. Coin No. 3 should be a triobol; and it is actually almost of the weight of a Corinthian triobol (22·5 grains). It is, however, to be noted that there is no definite evidence that either the Aeginetan or the Corinthian standard was ever in use at

Megara: hence the best view on the whole is that the coins of the city follow the Attic standard.

§ 2. Corinth and Colonies.

The history of Corinth during the period 480–330 B.C. consists of a constant struggle, not always successful, with Athens on one side and Corcyra on the other. Before 480 the predominance of Aegina had driven Corinth into friendliness towards Athens. But after the Persian wars, and especially after the fall of Aegina, the Corinthians came more and more to see that the commercial supremacy in Greece lay between them and Athens. Of Corinthian commerce towards the east we hear very little; probably it scarcely existed in the time of the Athenian Empire. And Corinthian influence towards the west seems to have been in a diminishing course until the time of the fatal Athenian expedition against Syracuse, after which it again increases.

The restrikings of early coins of Corinth in the cities of South Italy, of which I have above spoken (Chap. XI), sufficiently show that the money of Corinth was familiar there down to 480 B.C. or later. But the case seems to have been different in Sicily. For Riccio, in describing finds of fine fifth-century coins of Sicily made near Rhegium,[1] speaks of coins of Athens of the old style as found with them, but not of coins of Corinth. Sir A. Evans gives an account of a hoard found in West Sicily and buried about 400 B.C.,[2] in which he records that two tetradrachms of Athens (of fine archaic style) were found with the hoard, and no coins of Corinth, but several *pegasi* of Leucas of early class, that is, probably, belonging to the time 500–450 B.C. In the Santa Maria hoard, buried about 380 B.C., there were two Athenian tetradrachms, but no Corinthian coins.[3]

[1] *Ann. dell' Inst.*, 1854, p. xl.
[2] *Syracusan Medallions and their Engravers*, p. 167.
[3] *Ibid.*, p. 18.

Thus is established a fact of some importance, the predominance of the Athenian coinage in Sicily and of the Corinthian coinage in South Italy in the period 550–420 B.C. The exceptions may be held to prove the rule. The only coins of Sicily which seem to show Corinthian influence, the didrachms of that standard struck at Zancle, Himera, and Naxos in the latter part of the sixth century, are, as has been shown, really offshoots from the South Italian coinage, and the result of the influence of Cumae. And the only Italian coins which belong to the Attic sphere of influence are those of Thurii, which city was one of the Periclean colonies, and those of Rhegium, which city was almost Sicilian. The line of conflict between the two influences passes through the straits of Messina; to the north of that line we have a predominance of Corinthian, and to the south of it of Athenian influence.

At a later period, in the fourth century, Corinthian coins and imitations of Corinthian coins had considerable vogue in Sicily.

Now that we are aware of the Athenian policy in the fifth century, to force upon the allies the use of Athenian money, and to prevent them from issuing any of their own, we naturally inquire whether such a policy was adopted by other powerful cities. I think it can be traced in the monetary issues of Corinth and her colonies.

Since no detailed record exists of the finds of 'Pegasi' in Italy and Sicily, and since the coins of Corinth and the colonies of Corinth are very hard to date in consequence of the uniformity and conventionality of their types, it is difficult to be sure of the facts in regard to the monetary issues of Corinth.[1] But these facts seem to be as follows:

From 550 B.C. or thereabouts down to 243 B.C., when Corinth joined the Achaean League, there was struck a series of coins of almost uniform types and weight. Accurately to arrange it by date is impossible: there are no fixed points, and the style changes by imperceptible

[1] There is a paper by Professor Oman in *Corolla Numismatica* which deals with the issues of 460–390 B.C.

gradations. Professor Oman has, however, shown that a somewhat abrupt transition from the archaic to the early fine style takes place in the middle of the fifth century.[1]

We must next consider the coins of the so-called 'Colonies of Corinth'. The view of Dr. Imhoof-Blumer, long ago expressed,[2] that this coinage was purely commercial in character, and had little political significance, has been generally accepted, and doubtless it represents at least a side of the truth: it may, however, require some modification in view of recent discovery.

Of the many colonies of Corinth which dotted the coasts of Acarnania and Epirus, one only, Leucas, issues coins from 550 B.C. onwards, of the same weight as the mother-city's and showing the same succession of styles. The coins of Leucas only differ from those of Corinth by having on the reverse, under the Pegasus, the letter Λ instead of ϙ. Down to the middle of the fifth century, these are staters only, not smaller coins. Two other colonies, Ambracia and Anactorium, strike a few (rare) staters of archaic style with Corinthian types: they may be dated about 520–480 B.C. A stater has been published as belonging to Dyrrhachium or Epidamnus, and to the early period, having Corinthian types and the archaic letter Ϝ under the Pegasus.[3] As the coin has not been seen for the last half-century, and as the style of the head of Athena is quite inconsistent with the form of the Ϝ, not being of archaic style, there can be little doubt but that this is a false attribution. The coin is probably of Anactorium, with a F not an E under the Pegasus. The certain coins of Dyrrhachium bear the inscription ΔΥΡ; though an E on the reverse might stand for the old name of the city, Epidamnus.

A very noteworthy fact is that after the early staters

[1] *Ibid.*, p. 210.

[2] *Die Münzen Akarnaniens*, 1878.

[3] *B. M. Cat. Corinth*, p. liii; cf. Lagoy, *Mélanges de Numismatique*, Pl. II, 3. (1845).

of Ambracia and Anactorium there is a great break in the coinage of those cities, which do not resume the issue of pegasi until the end of the fifth century. At some period, the time of which we shall presently consider, not only these two cities, but also other cities of Acarnania, of Illyria, of Italy and Sicily begin abundant issues of staters imitating those of Corinth. It is difficult to account for the intermission of all imitative Corinthian coin, save only at two or three cities, for nearly a century, except by supposing that during that time, covering most of the fifth century, the Corinthians reserved to themselves all striking of coin, and forbade it to their colonies, following the notable example of Athens.

To determine the date of the later outbreak of imitative Corinthian coins is not easy. We must successively consider four groups of cities, those in Sicily, those in Italy, those in Illyria, and those in Epirus and Acarnania.

Syracuse should furnish us with a clue, since the coins of Syracuse have been examined with greater closeness and acumen than those of most cities.[1] The coins of Syracuse are examined in the chapter (XX) on Sicily, where I come to the conclusion that the Pegasus staters bearing the name of the Syracusans were issued at intervals between 380 and 330. The earliest issues appear to be due to the tyrant Dionysius. Other issues were made by Timoleon, 346 B.C., and later.

Of the coins of Corinthian types struck at Locri in Italian Bruttii some are of decidedly early style, and bear the legends ΛΟ or ΛΟΚ.[2] I should be disposed to give these to the time of Dionysius, whose close relation to Locri is well known. Most of the Locrian coins with Corinthian types, however, are of the time of Timoleon and later. Mr. Head[3] suggests for the issues at Terina, Rhegium, Locri (and Medma) the date of 325 B.C., when Alexander of Epirus for a short time released the cities

[1] See especially the monographs of Head and Evans.

[2] *B. M. Cat. Corinth*, Pl. XXIV, 1, 2.

[3] *Hist. Num.*, ed. 2, p. 114.

of the extreme south of Italy from the yoke of the Bruttian Italians. This view is very reasonable.

If the coins of Corinthian types struck in Illyria and Acarnania could be accurately dated, it would be a very interesting task to consider under what political circumstances they were issued; and in what relation they stood to the civic issues of Corcyra, Apollonia, Dyrrhachium, and the Acarnanians. As it is, we can ascertain but little. Many years ago, Dr. Imhoof-Blumer wrote: 'If one goes through the different series of the Pegasus coins (of Acarnania), one finds among them but few the date of which can be placed back before the Peloponnesian War: besides the metropolis Corinth herself, only the cities of Anactorium, Leucas, and Ambracia struck coins with archaic fabric. Next we may place a few coins of Epidamnus, the Amphilochian Argos and Alyzia which may have been struck before the end of the fifth century B.C. All the rest of the staters known at present must be assigned to the two following centuries.'[1]

As regards the archaic issues of Leucas, Ambracia and Anactorium I have already expressed a similar view. But as regards the dates here assigned to the issues of other cities I am doubtful. It seems that a number of cities, Corcyra with its colonies Dyrrhachium (Epidamnus) and Apollonia, and the Acarnanian towns of Alyzia, Argos, Astacus, Coronta, and Thyrrheium, all began to issue Pegasus coins at about the same time.

What was the period or the occasion of that issue we can only conjecture. As Dr. Imhoof-Blumer has observed, the adoption of the types of Corinth by the cities of the Acarnanian League must have been caused by the fact that the Pegasus coins passed freely in the commerce of Sicily, Italy, and the West.[2] It is not possible to bring the beginning of the issue later than 400 B.C., and the first city to attempt it was Ambracia, the coins of which city show the remains of an incuse square, while on many

[1] *Die Münzen Akarnaniens*, p. 11. [2] *Ibid.*, p. 11.

of them there appears the backward curled wing of Pegasus,[1] which seems to belong almost entirely to the fifth century B.C. One is tempted to date the revival of what may fairly be called autonomous coinage, as compared with the adopted coinage of Corinth, at Ambracia, from its defection from Corinth, and its joining the Acarnanian League about 425 B.C., after the terrible defeat the city had suffered from the Athenian Demosthenes. As early as 400 B.C. the example was copied by Anactorium and Dyrrhachium,[2] and (according to Imhoof) by Alyzia and Argos. Before long, even Corcyra so far forgot her secular enmity against Corinth as to issue money of Corinthian types, though perhaps this may not have taken place until the occupation of Corinth by a Macedonian garrison in 346 B.C.

The abundant issues of pegasi early in the fourth century, alike by the mother-city of Corinth and the Corinthian colonies on the Adriatic, accounts for the fact that in Italy and Sicily large hoards of these coins are found. In Sicily, after the almost complete cessation of the issue of tetradrachms about 400 B.C., they must have formed a great part of the money in circulation. And it is very probable, as I try to show (Chap. XX), that the earliest imitations at Syracuse and Leontini were issued in the time of Dionysius himself. After the great Athenian defeat at Syracuse, the commerce and the coins of Athens must have steadily receded before those of Corinth.

It would appear, then, that from 480 B.C. to a time after the middle of the fifth century Corinth succeeded in making her issues the main currency of Acarnania, and, in a less degree, of Epirus and the east coast of Italy. The first city of Acarnania to resume a local Pegasus coinage was Ambracia. Early in the fourth century this example was widely copied on the west coast of Greece, as well as by Syracuse, Locri, and other Italian and Sicilian cities. After

[1] *B. M. Cat. Corinth*, Pl. XXVII; cf. Oman, *l. c.*

[2] A coin of Dyrrhachium in the British Museum has remains of an incuse square. *Cat. Corinth*, Pl. XXVI, 2.

the occupation of the citadel of Corinth by a Macedonian garrison (346 B.C.), we should naturally expect a diminution of Corinthian influence and commerce; and as a result a further outbreak of imitative issues in Acarnania and the West; an expectation confirmed by the facts.

M. Babelon mentions obols in gold as struck at Corinth about 338 B.C.:[1]

Obv. ϙ Pegasus flying. *Rev.* Trident. Weight, 7 grains (grm. 0·44).

He maintains their genuineness; but in the case of small gold coins that is always difficult to establish. The date also, if they are genuine, must be regarded as doubtful: Corinth is far more likely to have struck gold coins, in imitation of Athens, early in the fourth century, than in the time of Philip. There was in the fourth century at Corinth an abundant coinage in bronze.

Corcyra. The coins of Corcyra, like those of Corinth and Athens, give little indication, in type or inscription, of any events of internal or external politics. They are essentially a commercial coinage. The two colonies of Corcyra, Apollonia and Dyrrhachium, after a while begin the issue of staters identical in weight and type with those of the mother-city, but differing in inscription, AΓO or ΔYP standing in the place of KOP. In the *British Museum Catalogue*, these coins, with those of the same style issued by Corcyra itself, are given to the fourth century. 'It is probable that their issue began at some period when the political troubles into which the mother-city fell gave her colonies greater freedom of action, and threw them on their own resources. This may have been when Corcyra was successively overrun by the Athenian Timotheus (375 B.C.) and the Laconian Mnasippus (373 B.C.).'[2] It is probable that Corcyra like Corinth may have taken a leaf from the book of Athenian legislation, and forcibly prevented the striking of autonomous coins by the two colonies, so long as she was able to do so.

[1] Babelon, *Traité*, ii. 3, p. 439.
[2] *Cat. Thessaly to Aetolia* (Gardner), p. xxxix.

A century later Dyrrhachium also issued copies of the staters of Corinth. It is probable that the imitations of coins of Corcyra were made for the trade with the north of the Adriatic, where Corinthian ships did not venture, and the imitations of Corinth for the trade with South Italy and Sicily. If a conjecture already stated, that at Corcyra the local stater was regarded as a tetradrachm of the Corinthian standard, be correct, there would be no difficulty in adjusting the exchange of the two kinds of money in the commerce of the Greek cities of the Adriatic, or in the neutral markets.

There is in fact definite evidence, clear if not conclusive,[1] that the coins of Corcyra issued about 300 B.C. were intended to conform to the two standards. The types are:

1. *Obv.* ΚΟΡΚΥΡΑΙ. Fore-part of cow. *Rev.* Two squares containing floral pattern. Weight, 80 grains (grm. 5·18).
2. *Obv.* Cow with calf. *Rev.* ΚΟΡ. Square containing floral pattern. Weight, 40 grains (grm. 2·59).

No. 1 is indicated by the obverse type to be the half of something, probably the stater of Corcyra, and by the reverse type to be the double of something, probably the Corinthian drachm. No. 2 is shown by both types to be a standard unit, probably a Corinthian drachm. Of course, arguments like these can only establish a probability, not a certainty, but they are quite worthy of consideration.

The weight of the coins of Corcyra tends to fall in the fourth century from 180 grains (grm. 11·66) to 160 grains (grm. 10·36). It is an indication how the earlier metrologists neglected geographical and commercial indications, that Brandis regards these later coins as following the Persian rather than the Aeginetan standard.[2] The extreme improbability of the Persian standard working so far to the West did not convince him. But a much more satisfactory explanation of the fall of standard will be found in the fact that the Corinthian coin also became lighter at this time, though in a spasmodic and irregular fashion,

[1] *Cat. Thessaly, &c.*, p. xv.

[2] *Münzwesen*, p. 129.

while the Italian drachm derived from it sank still faster in weight.[1] If there was a conventional proportion of value between the staters of Corinth and Corcyra, it would be to the interest of both cities to reduce the weight of the stater as far as could be done safely, and without fear of its losing its reputation.

Acarnania. The coins of Acarnania raise interesting problems. For we find that in the fifth century some of them bear the name of the Acarnanians as a confederacy, while others bear the names of cities which probably belonged to that confederacy. The fact that Aristotle wrote a treatise on the Constitution of the Acarnanians proves that there was an organized union of cities. But of the history of that organized union we know very little. And sometimes the coins bearing the name of the tribe and those bearing the names of cities are almost identical in type and style. Without more knowledge of the history of Acarnania it is impossible to discover the relations as regards rights of coinage between the tribe and the cities.

We have the following from the middle of the fifth century (*B. M. Cat. Thessaly*, p. li):

1. *Obv.* Bearded head of Achelous as a river-god. *Rev.* AK. Female head. Weight, 30–29 grains (grm. 1·97–1·87).
2. *Obv.* Head of Achelous. *Rev.* ΣΤΡΑ. Female head. Weight, 36–35 grains (grm. 2·34–2·30).
3. *Obv.* Head of Achelous. *Rev.* F in incuse. Weight, 38–33 grains (grm. 2·48–2·15).
4. *Obv.* Head of Achelous. *Rev.* T in incuse. Weight, 18–16 grains (grm. 1·15–1·01).

No. 1 is a coin of the Acarnanian Confederacy struck at Stratus; No. 2 is a similar coin struck by the city of Stratus on its own account; No. 3 is a coin of Oeniadae. All are of the same standard, the specimens under (1) having lost weight in circulation; the normal weight is about 36 grains (grm. 2·33). No. 4 is of doubtful attribution. The same obverse occurs on a variety of coins which

[1] See Chap. XIX.

have on the reverse the letter T accompanied by other letters, KO, TO, KAΛ, IR. These coins seem to be halves of those previously mentioned. Dr. Imhoof-Blumer[1] leaves the standard and denomination undetermined. But since the district was entirely under the influence of Corinthian commerce, we must seek in that direction for an explanation. The smaller coins (4) seem obviously Corinthian hemidrachms, being of the same weight as the hemidrachms issued in the fifth century at Corinth;[2] and we may fairly regard the letter T as standing for τριώβολον. Coins 1 to 3, being of double the weight, will then probably be Corinthian drachms. They are only a little lighter than the Corinthian drachms struck at Corinth. The contemporary tridrachms at Corinth weigh about 132–128 grains (grm. 8·55–8·30), though they are not very uniform. No doubt these staters were used in the larger commerce in Acarnania; and the local drachms and hemidrachms, being used only for small trade, might well be somewhat under weight.

§ 3. Peloponnesus.

The cities of Peloponnesus were late in starting coinage. Numismatists are disposed, no doubt rightly, to attribute this backwardness to the general use of the coins of Aegina, which the Aeginetan pedlars took with them, and which formed a general or standard currency for most of Greece Proper. Before the Persian wars, it would seem that coins were struck only at Phlius, Sicyon, Aegae, Argos, Heraea, Mantineia, Psophis, Cleitor, and Elis: to which cities are added, in the early part of the fifth century, Cleonae and Troezen, and in the later part, Pheneus, Stymphalus, Tegea, Alea, and Pallantium.

In the history of the coinage of Peloponnesus between the Persian wars and the time of Alexander there are two decided landmarks. One is the alliance between Elis,

[1] *Münzen Akarnaniens*, reprinted from *Numism. Zeitschr.* for 1878, p. 166.
[2] *B. M. Cat. Corinth*, p. 19.

Mantineia, and Argos of 421 B.C. The other is the invasion of Peloponnesus by Epaminondas in 371 B.C., and the foundation by him of Messene and Megalopolis. The first of these events is mirrored in the coinages of Elis and Argos: with the second event begins the issue of the notable staters of the new-founded cities. These events do not introduce any change in the standards used; but they serve as excellent fixed points for the arrangement of the coins.

In 421 B.C. the people of Argos, whose type had hitherto been the wolf, give it up and adopt instead the head of their great goddess Hera, crowned with a round polos, with two dolphins for a reverse type (**Pl. X. 10**).[1] Some of these staters, it is true, have a somewhat early appearance, and the early form R appears on them; we cannot be sure that they may not anticipate the year 421. But the date is safe for the coins of Elis. The people of Elis give up then their old agonistic types of Nike and the eagle, and take instead a head of Hera closely resembling that on the Argive coins, but executed in a far more beautiful style. We may give to the same period the drachm of Mantineia, which city also belonged to the League:

> *Obv.* Bearded male head in Corinthian helmet. *Rev.* MANTI. Head of nymph Callisto ?[2] Weight, 87 grains (grm. 5·63). (**B. T. CCXXVI. 34**),

as Mantineia also until that time had used the simple type of the bear, and now substitutes human heads.

The staters of the period of Epaminondas have long been known and admired:

Messene.

> *Obv.* Head of Demeter, corn-crowned. *Rev.* ΜΕΣΣΑΝΙΩΝ. Zeus Ithomatas striding. (**B. M. XXIII. 35.**)

Megalopolis.

> *Obv.* Head of Zeus. *Rev.* APK in monogram, Pan seated on rock. (**Pl. X. 11.**)

[1] *B. M. Cat. Peloponnesus* (Gardner), p. xxxvii.

[2] *B. M. Cat. Peloponnesus*, p. 185, Pl. XXXIV, 29.

Pheneus.

Obv. Head of Demeter. *Rev.* ΦΕΝΕΩΝ. Hermes carrying the boy Arcas. (**B. T. CCXXV. 6.**)

Stymphalus.

Obv. Head of Artemis. *Rev.* ΣΤΥΜΦΑΛΙΩΝ. Heracles striking with club. (**Pl. X. 12.**)

M. Babelon observes that with the foundation of Megalopolis, Pheneus and Stymphalus cease for a time to issue coins.[1]

Contemporary with these are:

Tegea.

Obv. Head of Athena. *Rev.* ΤΕΓΕΑΤΑΝ. Warrior charging (Hemidrachm). (**B. T. CCXXVII. 28.**)

The reverse type seems to be copied from the charging Ajax of the coins of the Locrians, which belong to the same period.

Hermione.

Obv. Head of Demeter. *Rev.* ΕΡ in monogram, within wreath (Hemidrachm). (**B. T. CCXVIII. 13.**)

Pellene.

Obv. Head of Apollo, laureate. *Rev.* ΠΕΛ in wreath (Hemidrachm). (**B. T. CCXXII. 22.**)

Epidaurus.

Obv. Head of Asclepius. *Rev.* ΕΠ in monogram, within laurel wreath (Hemidrachm). (**B. T. CCXVII. 10.**)

It may, however, be that the occasion of some of these issues was rather earlier than 370, the Peace of Antalcidas, when the several cities of Greece and Asia were recognized as autonomous, and when many of them began to issue coins.

The chief place is taken in Western Peloponnesus by the coinage of Elis, in Eastern Peloponnesus by the money of Argos, and in Northern Peloponnesus by that of Sicyon. In South Peloponnesus, as Sparta did not issue silver coin until the time of Areus, nor Messene until the time of Epaminondas, any silver coin current would have to be borrowed from one of the wealthier neighbours.

[1] Babelon, *Traité*, iii, p. 567.

Arcadia. We begin with Arcadia. It is a rugged and mountainous district; the cities, in their little valleys, stood apart, and the level of civilization was very low. It is natural that Arcadia should never have formed a federal unit like Boeotia or Phocis. Various towns, at different periods of history, claimed not supremacy but hegemony; but none of them held it for long. Generally the Arcadians followed the fortunes of Sparta, and furnished troops to her.

Most remarkable among the early coins of Arcadia are the hemidrachms of Aeginetan standard issued by the Heraeans and bearing their name. They were probably struck in connexion with the festival of Zeus Lycaeus at Lycosura, and passed among the Arcadians as a sort of religious coinage. The earliest issues are inscribed ΕΡΑ; they have as type the head of Demeter or Despoena. They are succeeded about the time of the Persian wars by the hemidrachms which bear, on the obverse, a seated figure of Zeus Lycaeus, on the reverse the head of Despoena, with the inscription ΑΡΚΑΔΙΚΟΝ. These coins seem to show that Heraea was regarded at the time as the leading city of Arcadia. This issue is conjecturally supposed to have come to an end about 418 B.C., when the Spartan hegemony in Peloponnesus was strengthened. Then the name of the Heraeans reappears on an unimportant series of small coins.

The type of the coins bearing the name of the Arcadians bears a striking likeness to that of some of the early coins of Elis; the representation is of Zeus Aphesius, sending out the eagle. In the British Museum is an archaic inscription recording an alliance between the people of Elis and those of Heraea. As the early coins of Elis are nearly all didrachms, and those of Heraea hemidrachms, it may fairly be conjectured that they together constituted the main coinage of Western Peloponnese, which was decidedly of religious character.

Psophis in Arcadia issues in the sixth century the following coins, among others:

Obv. Stag springing to r. *Rev.* Fish placed transversely in incuse. Weight, 61 grains (grm. 3·95); 21 grains (grm. 1·40). (**B. T. XXXVIII. 29.**)

Obv. Fore-part of stag. *Rev.* OΨ. Fish transversely placed. Weight, 13·9–13·5 grains (grm. 0 90–0·86). (**B.T. CCXXVI. 3, 4.**)

Obv. Stag springing to r. *Rev.* E within incuse. Weight, 6·3 grains (grm. 0·40). (**B. T. CCXXVI. 6.**)

The last of these coins is certainly a hemiobol, as is shown by the mark of value E :[1] the coins of twice the weight are probably obols, though the O may not be a mark of value, but the second letter of the city's name. If so, the standard used at Psophis is certainly the Aeginetan; and the coin of 61 grains which looks like an Attic drachm must be an Aeginetan tetrobol. At the same time it must be observed that in the island of Zacynthus, not very far distant from Psophis, we have traces of the Attic standard in the early fifth century, though the larger coins range in weight with those of Corcyra.

It would seem that at some periods Mantineia, and at other periods Tegea, claimed some sort of hegemony among the Arcadians. But their money bears only the name of the city. A definitely organized League of the Arcadians was only formed in the time of Epaminondas's invasion of Peloponnese. Then a new city was built to serve as a federal capital, and received the ambitious name of Megalopolis. To it were transported the inhabitants of several of the townships; and the Arcadians sent deputies to meet in the Thersilion, which has now been excavated.[2] Some towns, such as Alea, Thelpusa, and Pallantium, disappear from the numismatic record; others, like Stymphalus and Pheneus, suspend their coinage. Only Mantineia and Tegea continue uninterruptedly.

The staters struck at Megalopolis are very beautiful:

Obv. APK in monogram; head of Zeus. *Rev.* Pan seated on rock. (**B. M. XXIII. 35.**)

[1] The omission of the aspirate, at a time when the Ionic alphabet was coming in, need not surprise us.

[2] E. A. Gardner and others, *Excavations at Megalopolis*, 1892.

But Megalopolis soon fell into decay, and issued only hemidrachms of careless workmanship.

Elis. From about 500 B.C. onwards we have the very interesting and beautiful series of staters of Aeginetan weight which bear the name of the people of Elis, and were probably issued by them on the successive occasions of the Olympian Festival. The types, Zeus, the eagle, the thunderbolt, Victory, and the heads of Zeus and Hera, all obviously allude to the sacred rites and games of the precinct of Zeus. There is no variety of monetary standard in the coins of Elis; but in the types we may detect a few landmarks, which are of the greater value because of the rarity of such landmarks in the series of Peloponnesus.

The earliest is furnished by the staters which bear the type of Zeus striding and hurling the thunderbolt with the inscription ΟΛΥΜΠΙΚΟΝ (**B. T. XXXIX. 1–2**). They belong to the beginning of the fifth century; E. Curtius conjectured that the occasion of them was the imposition by the people of Elis on the Lepreates of Triphylia of an annual tribute to the Olympic Zeus, the inscription *'Ολυμπικὸν* (*νόμισμα*) marking the coin as belonging to Zeus himself. This conjecture is confirmed by the discovery, based on the inscriptions at Delphi, that it was out of the tribute paid to the sanctuary by the Phocians who had violated it, that the coins were issued marked with the inscription *'Αμφικτιόνων*.[1] This seems an exact parallel.

The earliest introduction of the head of Hera (and that of Zeus) on the coins of Elis must be referred to the occasion of the political alliance between Elis and Argos in 421 B.C., when Argos gave up the wolf type, and Elis the eagle-and-serpent type, in honour of the goddess common to the two states.

A brief interruption of the issues of Elean coins took place in 364–362 B.C., when the Arcadians, after driving the troops of Elis out of the sacred enclosure, melted down some of the treasures to pay their mercenaries, and trans-

[1] Bourguet, *Administr. financière du sanctuaire pythique*, p. 18.

ferred the presidency of the games to the people of Pisa, who had a very ancient claim to it. It must have been on this occasion that certain small gold coins were struck:

Obv. Laureate head of Zeus. *Rev.* ΠΙΣΑ. Three half-thunderbolts. Weight, 24 grains (grm. 1·55).

Obv. As last. *Rev.* ΠΙΣΑ. Thunderbolt, not winged. Weight, 16 grains (grm. 1·04). (B. T. CCXXXV. 13, 14.)

These are evidently a trihemiobol and an obol of Aeginetan weight, struck as money of necessity. The Eleans in a very short time recovered the control of the games.

The head of Zeus on the Pisatan coins is of somewhat noteworthy style, and helps us to assign to the period immediately before or after 364 B.C. coins of Elis which bear a Zeus head of similar character.[1]

Zacynthus. The coinage of Zacynthus, and of the neighbouring cities of Same and Pale in Cephallenia, presents peculiar features. The stater of Zacynthus, in the fifth and fourth centuries, is of the weight of 180 grains normal (grm. 11·66), and so is of Aeginetan standard. But the system of division is not into Aeginetan drachms and obols as elsewhere. The stater is divided into three, the next denomination weighing 60 grains (grm. 3·88). Of this lesser unit, we have the half weighing some 30 grains (grm. 1·94), and the sixth weighing up to 10 or 11 grains (grm. 0·71–0·64). These denominations are clearly the Attic drachm, half-drachm, and obol. This interpretation of the weights is not a conjecture but a certainty, as we have a coin of 8·3 grains (grm. 0·54) marked with O as an obol, and a coin of 4 grains (grm. 0·26) marked with an H as a hemiobol. Zacynthus was in the Athenian alliance at the time of the Peloponnesian War, having been conquered by the admiral Tolmides[2] in 455 B.C. The island was in the circle of Corinthian commerce, and in the third century copies the Corinthian types, but politically it was anti-Spartan, and furnished

[1] For the coins of Elis see my paper in the *Num. Chron.* for 1879; Seltman, *Nomisma*, part ix; and Babelon, *Traité*, vol. iii.

[2] Diodorus, xi. 84. Diodorus says that Tolmides conquered Zacynthus, but brought in the cities of Cephallenia without force.

a refuge to Spartan exiles;[1] we are therefore not surprised to find traces of Attic influence in the coinage. Zacynthus was also in close relations with Sicily, where the Attic standard was in general use.

The coinage of Zacynthus offers us two clear landmarks. The type adopted by the cities of Samos, Ephesus, Rhodes, and other places in 394 B.C., young Heracles strangling the snakes (**Pl. X. 9**), makes its appearance quite unexpectedly on the money of Zacynthus, which may therefore at once be divided into coins earlier than 394 B.C., and coins later than that year. In 357, Dion, then organizing his expedition against the younger Dionysius of Syracuse, made Zacynthus his head-quarters, and struck there, no doubt to pay his troops, a notable coin:

Obv. Laureate head of Apollo. *Rev.* ΙΑ. ΔΙΩΝΟΣ. Tripod. Weight, 174–169 grains (grm. 11·25–10·95). (**B. T. CCXXXVI. 18.**)

The drachm and hemidrachm were struck of Attic weight in Same and Pale in Cephallenia at the time of the Peloponnesian War. The city of Cranium, on the other hand, adhered in all denominations to the standard of Aegina, or perhaps rather that of Corcyra, which was somewhat lower.

Argos. There are few places of which the monetary issues are smaller in proportion to the age, the wealth, and the artistic reputation of the city than Argos. Until the alliance with Elis in 421 B.C., the city issued only small coins—drachms, hemidrachms, obols, and hemiobols—bearing on one side the fore-part or the head of a wolf, on the other side the letter A in an incuse. This coinage probably began about the middle of the sixth century; but it is obviously incomplete; for all larger payments the staters of Aegina must have been used. This may explain the confused notion, common among ancient historians, that the Aeginetan coinage began under the rule of Pheidon of Argos.

[1] Hdt. vi. 70, iv. 37.

In 421 B.C. the head of Hera comes in on the coins:

Obv. ΑΡΓΕΙΟΝ or ΩΝ. Head of Hera, wearing round crown. *Rev.* Two dolphins: between them various devices, the wolf, the tripod, &c. Stater. (Pl. X. 10.)

Obv. As last. *Rev.* ΑΡΓΕΙΩΝ. Diomedes carrying the Palladium. Drachm. (*Ibid.* 18–20.) Also smaller divisions.

As this time is exactly that at which the great statue of Hera was set up by Polycleitus, it is reasonable to see in the coins a reminiscence of the head of that statue; but the style is poor, greatly inferior to that of the contemporary coins of Elis. The issue of the staters and drachms soon ceased, and the city again reverted to the issue of small coins only. M. Babelon speaks of these as Rhodian drachms or Attic tetrobols;[1] there can, I think, be no doubt but that they are hemidrachms of a somewhat reduced Aeginetan standard. The usual weight is about 36–42 grains (grm. 2·33–2·72).

At Argos and at Tegea were issued early in the fourth century a few coins of iron.[2] It is not clear whether they were coins of necessity or deliberately fraudulent issues. The bad state of preservation in which they are found makes assertions in regard to them risky; but it may safely be said that they can have had nothing to do with a regular iron currency, which would be far more bulky.

Phlius. Argos dominated the valley of the Inachus, but the cities of the north coast, which are conventionally placed in Argolis, were in no way subordinate to Argos. They struck coins quite independently, but only the issues of Sicyon are of much importance. The lesser cities must have generally used the coins of Aegina, of Argos, and of Sicyon.

The coins given by Six and Babelon[3] to Phlius which bear on the obverse the letter Φ and a three-legged symbol, and on the reverse an incuse of eight triangles like that

[1] *Traité*, ii. 3, p. 463.

[2] *Ibid.*, pp. 465, 655.

[3] *Ibid.*, ii. 1, p. 813; Six, *Num. Chron.*, 1888, p. 97. One of these coins is said to have been found in Arcadia.

of Aegina, can scarcely be Peloponnesian, considering the fabric and the weight, 110–112 grains (grm. 7·16–7·21). There are, however, coins of Phlius, issued towards the middle of the fifth century, bearing as types a bull walking and a wheel: drachms and hemidrachms of Aeginetan standard. They are continued into the fourth century. Cleonae, on the road between Corinth and Argos, struck a few obols in the fifth century, Epidaurus hemidrachms and obols in the fourth century.

Sicyon. The extensive series of silver coins issued by Sicyon unfortunately offers us no landmarks, but runs on without a break. We may, however, conjecturally regard the letters ΕΥ on the coins as standing for Euphron, tyrant 360 B.C., and ΚΛΕ as standing for Cleander, who also exercised a tyranny in the city.[1]

Troezen. Alone among the cities of Peloponnesus, in the latter part of the fifth century, Troezen struck money on the Attic standard, drachms of 67–56[2] grains (grm. 4·34–3·62) and hemidrachms of 31–30 grains (grm. 2·0–1·94). This remarkable exception may be accounted for partly by the position of Troezen, over against Attica, and partly by the traditional friendship between the two cities. The head of Athena and the trident of Poseidon are the types of the coins. At the time of the Persian wars it was at Troezen that the people of Athens took refuge, leaving their city to the mercy of the Persians. Theseus was said to have been born at Troezen. In the Peloponnesian War, as we learn, Troezen was on the side of Sparta; but probably the sympathies of the people were divided, those who controlled the coinage being Attic in sympathy.

Achaea. Between Patrae on the west and Sicyon on the east lay the cities of Achaea, each possessing a small territory between the Corinthian Gulf and the mountains of Arcadia. None of these cities was of great importance, and none in

[1] *B. M. Cat. Peloponnesus*, p. xxxiv.

[2] *Ibid.*, p. 165. Two coins from the same die weigh, one 67·4 grains, the other 56·7 grains. This fact illustrates the absurdity of basing theories on any minute weighings of single Greek silver coins.

the fifth century made large issues of coins. The Achaean cities had a religious league, of which the centre was the sanctuary of Poseidon at Helice. But this religious unity did not, as in the case of the Arcadians, lead to the institution of a coinage. On the destruction of Helice in 373 B.C. the religious centre of the district was shifted to Aegium, the sacred seat of Zeus Homagyrius and Demeter Panachaea. Then began the earliest federal issues of the Achaeans, who seem to have set up a federal system at the same time as the Arcadians, the Achaeans meeting at Aegium, and the Arcadians at Megalopolis.

The types of the Achaean coins are:

Obv. Head of Artemis. *Rev.* Zeus seated on throne. Stater. (B. T. CCXXII. 19.)

Obv. Same head. *Rev.* Athena charging. Drachm and Hemidrachm.[1] (B. T. CCXXII. 20, 21.)

In the third century the Achaean League extended to all the cities of Peloponnesus. The above coins seem to show that the origins of the League go back to the period of Epaminondas:—an important fact in history; they closely resemble the coins of Pheneus and Messene, struck at that time.

Messene. When the Messenians, under the protection of Epaminondas, rebuilt and reoccupied their city, they struck, for the first time, silver coins:

Obv. Head of Demeter, corn-crowned. *Rev.* Zeus striding, eagle on outstretched arm. Stater. (B. T. CCXXVII. 29.)

We may almost regard these coins, with those of Megalopolis, Pheneus, Stymphalus, and Achaea, as belonging to an anti-Spartan League. Their period of issue was short.

A remarkable stater at Paris, struck at Messene, bears witness to the influence of Philip of Macedon (weight 227·5 grains; grm. 14·73). This coin follows the Abderite weight. That weight had been adopted by the Chalcidian

[1] *Hist. Num.*, ed. 2, p. 416. The smaller coin had been attributed by various authorities to the Thessalian Achaea, but this attribution is now given up.

League; then by Philip of Macedon. M. Babelon[1] sees in it the direct influence of Philip, whose alliance was accepted by the Messenians and who rewarded them after the victory of Chaeroneia by assigning them territory in dispute between Sparta and Messene.[2] If Babelon is right, this will be an almost unique instance of the acceptance of a monetary standard on purely political grounds, and with no regard to commercial convenience. In the time of Alexander, the Messenians adopted for their staters the Attic weight.

There is not in Peloponnesus any phenomenon corresponding to the attempt of Athens to monopolize the coinage of the Delian Confederacy. The reason is obvious. The Peloponnesian League was dominated by Sparta, and the Spartans not only had no notions in the matter of commerce, but had not even any coinage, save of iron bars, until the time of Alexander. Spartan generals, it is true, highly appreciated the gold of Persia, but it does not seem to have been in any way officially recognized. Thus the cities and confederations of Peloponnesus followed their own courses.

§ 4. The Islands.

In Chapter V I have dealt with the sixth-century coinages of the Greek islands, which were nearly all more or less close imitations of that of Aegina. Only of the earliest issues of **Delos** I may here say a few words.

The island of Delos, the religious centre of the Ionian League, and for a time the political centre of the Athenian Confederacy, appears to have struck in the sixth century:[3]

Obv. Δ. Lyre. *Rev.* Incuse square. Weight, 122–126 grains (grm. 7·90–8·16). (**B. T. LXI. 16.**)

Obv. Lyre. *Rev.* ΔΗΛΙ. Wheel. Weight, 5–7 grains (grm. 0·33–0·45). (**B. T. LXI. 20.**)

These coins are of Euboic weight, forming an exception

[1] Babelon, *Traité*, iii, p. 693. [2] Polybius, ix. 28; Strabo, viii. 4. 6.
[3] *Hist. Num.*, ed. 2, p. 485.

among all the coins of the Aegean. Probably they were minted on the occasion of some Ionian festival, and not only for purposes of trade.

The Cyclades, as we have seen above (Chap. XIV), intermitted their coinage at the time of the Athenian Empire, with the notable exception of Melos. Towards the middle of the fourth century some of them resume coinage:

Andros.

1. *Obv.* Head of Apollo. *Rev.* AN. Young Dionysus standing. Weight, 217 grains (grm. 14·08). (**B. T. CCXXXIX. 13.**)
2. *Obv.* Head of young Dionysus. *Rev.* ΑΝΔΡΙΩΝ. Panther. Weight, 55–52 grains (grm. 3·60–3·37). (*Ibid.* **15.**)

Tenos.

3. *Obv.* Head of Zeus Ammon. *Rev.* TH. Poseidon seated. Weight, 260–253 grains (grm. 16·80–16·43). (*Ibid.* **21.**)
4. *Obv.* Similar. *Rev.* TH. Bunch of grapes. Weight, 63–54 grains (grm. 4·12–3·46). (*Ibid.* **22.**)

Delos.

5. *Obv.* Head of Apollo. *Rev.* ΔH. Lyre. Weight, 51 grains (grm. 3·30). (**B. T. CCXL. 14.**)

Naxos.

6. *Obv.* Bearded head of Dionysus. *Rev.* ΝΑΞΙΩΝ. Wine-cup. Weight, 58–56 grains (grm. 3·72–3·65). (*Ibid.* **23.**)

Paros.

7. *Obv.* Goat standing. *Rev.* ΓΑ. Ear of corn. Weight, 32–30 grains (grm. 2·05–1·90). (**B. T. CCXL. 29.**)
8. *Obv.* ΓΑΡ. Goat. *Rev.* Wreath of corn. Weight, 29 grains (grm. 1·85). (*Ibid.* **32.**)

Siphnos.

9. *Obv.* Head of Apollo. *Rev.* ΣΙΦ. Eagle bearing serpent. Weight, 58 grains (grm. 3·72). (**B. T. CCXLI. 5.**)

Melos.

10. *Obv.* Pomegranate. *Rev.* ΜΑΛΙ. Drinking-cup. Weight, 123–115 grains (grm. 7·97–7·44). (**B. T. CCXLIII. 7.**)
11. *Obv.* Similar. *Rev.* Lance head (or Eagle). Weight, 60–54 grains (grm. 3·85–3·48). (*Ibid.* 8, **9.**)

Thera.

12. *Obv.* Head of Apollo, facing. *Rev.* ΘΗΡΑΙ. Bull butting: dolphin. Weight, 95 grains (grm. 6·15: worn). (*Ibid.* **24.**)

It is not easy exactly to fix the dates of these issues. They were probably made either after the Peace of Antalcidas (387 B.C.), or else a few years later (378 B.C.)[1] when a league of the islands was formed, under the patronage of Athens, in opposition to Spartan supremacy. At this time Athens had renounced all attempt at imposing her coins on her allies. All the islands except Tenos seem to have adopted the Chian or Rhodian standard, at that time dominant on the coast of Ionia, rather than the Attic standard, or the Aeginetan standard, which they had used in the sixth century, and which was in use in the Peloponnese and at Thebes. The tetradrachm of Tenos, of Attic standard, is by Babelon assigned to the time of the Lamian War;[2] and in fact the coin is obviously a copy of the money of Alexander. The coin of Thera is of base metal: as it has lost weight, it may be of Rhodian standard.

Crete. In Crete, coins make their first appearance at Cnossus (in the sixth century), Gortyna, and Phaestus. Other cities strike abundantly in the fifth and fourth centuries. They all use the Aeginetan standard; and we have scarcely any means of assigning dates to Cretan coins since we know almost nothing of the history of the island; and a certain barbarism which is common in their execution prevents us even from dating them by style. Thus little is to be made of them from the historic point of view, though many of them are interesting from the mythologic and epigraphic points of view, as well as from that of art.[3]

One point, however, requires a brief mention. In early Cretan laws fines are stated not in cattle as in the laws of Draco, but in λέβητες (bowls) and τρίποδες. It is difficult to suppose that before the use of money so inconvenient a

[1] Cavaignac, *Hist. de l'antiquité*, ii, p. 356. [2] *Traité*, iii, p. 826.

[3] See Babelon, *Traité*, ii. 3, pp. 876–1046; Wroth, *Num. Chron.*, 1884, p. 1, and *B. M. Cat. Crete*; P. Gardner, *Types of Greek Coins*, p. 160.

measure of value as the tripod can have actually been in use. One is tempted to think that in Crete pieces of bronze roughly in the shape of the tripod or the lebes were in circulation, just as in China were pieces of bronze cast roughly in the shape of a shirt or a hoe.[1] Such objects, however, do not seem to have been as yet discovered. Mr. Svoronos[2] thinks that traces of this primitive currency may be found on Cretan coins of the fifth and fourth centuries. There are silver staters (didrachms) of Cnossus, Gortyna, and several other cities, which are stamped with a countermark appearing to represent a circular lebes. A stater of Cnossus also is stamped with a tripod, and the inscription ΝΟΜ, of which the meaning is doubtful. Svoronos's view is that these coins are thus marked to carry on an old tradition, and that they take in circulation the place which had been occupied in earlier times by the actual tripod and lebes. It seems clear, in fact, that some at least of the inscriptions mentioning the tripod and the lebes are as late as the latter part of the fifth century, and that the tripod and the lebes must have had some definite value in the documents of that period. Numismatists are divided as to the admissibility of Svoronos's view.[3] Dr. Macdonald suggests (*Coin-types*, p. 34) that it was rather the bowl *full* of meal or grain which was the unit of value, not the bowl itself. He cites Scottish analogies, and this view seems very reasonable.

[1] Ridgeway, *Origin of Currency*, p. 22.

[2] *Bull. Corr. Hell.*, 1888, p. 405.

[3] Babelon, *Traité*, ii. 3, p. 875.

CHAPTER XIX

COINS OF SOUTH ITALY, 480–330 B.C.

§ 1. Greek Cities.

It is impossible here to discuss the coinage of South Italy in 480–330 B.C. in full detail. It has not yet been carefully worked out by numismatists. Sir Arthur Evans's monograph on the coins of Tarentum is a masterpiece; but we require similar detailed investigations of the numismatics of other cities of South Italy before we can survey the region as a whole. Holm, in his *History of Greece*,[1] has devoted a few pages to the subject, from which I may cite a few general observations: 'Two currents are visible in Western Greece (Magna Graecia) during the first half of the fourth century, one of which, of an autocratic character, has its centre in Syracuse, and the other, allied to freedom, in the league of cities which extends from Thurii to Tarentum. We may further maintain that Heracles, who appears on the coins in the twofold character of a serpent-strangling and lion-slaying hero is the tutelary deity of the league, and that the league, while it certainly has a political connexion with Thebes, from an artistic point of view seems to have cultivated closer relations with Athens.'

Undoubtedly the political history of the Greek cities of Italy is dominated by the relations which those cities held with one another, with the barbarous tribes of Italy, such as the Samnites and Messapians, and with the powerful rulers of Syracuse. In this light their coinages should be investigated. But it would not answer to close these investigations with the date of Alexander the Great, at

[1] *Eng. Trans.*, iii, pp. 143–51.

which their history becomes more interesting, being interlaced with the story of the growth of Roman power. I may cite another interesting generalization of Holm. 'The cities of Bruttium were checked in their development by Dionysius, as were the cities of Sicily, and hence their coinage ceases in 388, Rhegium, Croton, Terina, Temesa, Caulonia; Locri and Hipponium had not yet begun. On the other hand, the cities of Lucania were no doubt hard pressed by the Lucanians, but they retained their independent existence. Thurii was not conquered by the Brettii till 356, and even then was not permanently subdued.' These dates, however, are not accepted in the *Historia Numorum*; and it is clear that further investigation is required. Owing to the unfortunate fact that the *British Museum Catalogue of Italy* was published too early, the chronological relations of the Italian coins are in a more obscure condition than those of other districts. In fact the coinage of Italy must be treated as a whole, and as a continued development; but this cannot be done in the present work.

Most of the cities of South Italy in 480–330 merely continue the coinage in use at the beginning of the fifth century, until they fall into the hands of the Samnites or the Romans, showing progress or decay in art, but no great change in other matters. There are, however, a few points for remark:

(1) The introduction of gold and its relation in value to silver.

(2) Exceptional coinages of a few cities, such as Metapontum, Thurii, and Locri.

(1) According to the most recent view of Sir A. Evans,[1] the earliest gold coins of Tarentum were struck as early as 375 B.C.: they are the beautiful gold staters of Attic weight. (*Obv.* Head of Demeter veiled. *Rev.* Poseidon on a throne welcoming the child Taras.) In the head of these coins Evans sees the work of the Syracusan engraver Evaenetus. If so, the date can hardly be later than he

[1] *Horsemen of Tarentum*, 1889. More recent views in *Num. Chron.*, 1912.

supposes. We have seen that at this time several of the cities of Asia were striking gold staters on this standard; and it seems rather in reference to them and their Attic prototypes of the period beginning in 394 B.C. than in reference to any western issues that the coinage was regulated. The gold coins of Dionysius at the time weighed 90 and 45 grains (grm. 5·83 and 2·91), and though these would work in very well with the Tarentine gold coins, they are scarcely likely to have suggested them. The gold coins of Carthage, at the beginning of the fourth century, weigh 118 and 36 grains (grm. 7·64 and 2·33), and so belong to a different monetary system. But the gold money of Cyrene consists partly of staters of Attic weight, and in them also I would trace the direct influence of Athens and Rhodes.

Succeeding gold coins of Tarentum (Pl. XI. 1) appear to have been issued almost exclusively on the occasions when soldiers from Greece came to aid the people of Tarentum in their resistance to their Italic neighbours. Archidamus was summoned from Sparta about 340 B.C., Alexander the Molossian from Epirus in 334–330 B.C., the Spartan Cleonymus in 302, Pyrrhus in 281. There is a small piece in gold which can be definitely assigned to the time of Alexander the Molossian, since the types which it bears are identical with those on his coins:

Obv. Head of Helios radiate. *Rev.* ΑΛΕΞ. Thunderbolt. Weight, 6·6 grains (grm. 0·42).[1]

Among Tarentine gold coins there are not only didrachms or staters, drachms, tetrobols, triobols, diobols, and obols of Attic standard, but there are also pieces which follow the weight of the silver litra and half-litra, 13·5 grains (grm. 0·87) and 6·7 grains (grm. 0·43). The weights are preserved with noteworthy exactness.

In a find discovered at Taranto some of these coins, though not the earliest of them, were mingled with gold staters of Philip and Alexander of Macedon.

[1] Evans, *ibid.*, Pl. V. 5.

Excluding the doubtful archaic gold coins of Cumae, of which I have already spoken,[1] only Metapontum and Heracleia in Italy besides Tarentum issued gold in the fourth century.

Metapontum.

1. *Obv.* Head of Leucippus. *Rev.* Two ears of corn. Weight, 44 grains (grm. 2·85). Tetrobol. (**Pl. XI. 2.**)
2. *Obv.* Female head. *Rev.* Ear of corn. Same weight.

Heracleia.

Obv. Head of Athena. *Rev.* Heracles seated. Weight, 33 grains (grm. 2·13). Triobol.

These coins are contemporary with those of Tarentum, and probably arose from the same temporary needs.

It is noteworthy that at this time the silver didrachms of Tarentum still weighed 123–120 grains (grm. 7·97–7·77). How these silver coins exchanged against the gold is a difficult question. It appears that until the middle of the fourth century, both in Sicily and in Etruria, gold was fifteen times as valuable as silver. At this rate the gold stater would be worth nearly, but not exactly, sixteen of the silver didrachms: at the rate of twelve to one the stater would be worth about thirteen of the didrachms. A further complication arises from the fact, which seems to be proved by the contents of the hoard of Benevento,[2] that in circulation the silver didrachms of Tarentum, weighing 123–120 grains (grm. 7·97–7·77), were closely mixed up with the silver coins of Nola (110–106 grains), Neapolis (114–110 grains), Velia (112 grains), and Metapontum (119–118 grains). The irregularity in the weights of the coins of Magna Graecia is in any case a most puzzling phenomenon, and one of which no satisfactory explanation has been found.

(2) In the fourth century **Metapontum** places on the bronze coins an inscription indicating value:

1. *Obv.* Hermes sacrificing. *Rev.* Ear of corn. ΟΒΟΛΟΣ. Weight, 130 grains (grm. 8·42).

[1] Above, p. 208.

[2] *Horsemen of Tarentum*, Appendix A.

2. *Obv.* Head of Demeter. *Rev.* Same. Weight, 127 grains (grm. 8·22).[1]

These coins are merely money of account, not of intrinsic value; but the inscription is important as showing that the people of Metapontum did not, like those of Sicily, reckon by litrae of bronze, but in silver, dividing the drachm into oboli.

Thurii was an Athenian colony founded when Athens was at the height of her power, 443 B.C. It is not unnatural that the colonists should have taken with them the full Attic standard, and, almost alone among cities of Italy, should have issued the tetradrachm of 270 grains (grm. 17·50) (**Pl. XI. 4**). The art also of the money of Thurii, which does no discredit to the Athens of Pericles, influences the issues of other cities. We find at Neapolis, Velia, and elsewhere imitations of the head of Athena of Thurii.

It is a curious fact that **Locri** in Bruttii, though a flourishing city from the time of its foundation, struck no coins until the fourth century B.C. The earliest money of the city is a series of staters of Corinthian type and weight, and differing from the coins of Corinth only through bearing the inscription ΛO or ΛOK. Locri was usually on very good terms with the Syracusans, the cement of friendship being the hostility which both cities felt towards the intervening towns of Rhegium and Messana. In the time of Dionysius this friendship became closer, the Tyrant making over to the Locrians the territory of conquered Caulonia, and taking a wife from among the inhabitants. If we are right in supposing that the earliest issue of Corinthian imitations at Syracuse took place in the time of Dionysius, we shall naturally give to the same period the earliest of the Corinthian issues of Locri. These issues went on into the third century. Mr. Head reasonably suggests that they were the main currency of the city for external trade. Contemporary with them, but not earlier than the middle of the fourth

[1] *B. M. Cat. Italy*, p. 259.

century, are the regular issues of money with Locrian type (*Obv.* Head of Zeus; *Rev.* Eirene seated), perhaps intended for the local trade in Italy.

§ 2. Etruria.

The coinage of Etruria may best be treated in the present chapter. The treatment must be necessarily very summary. To go into the question of the *aes grave* of Etruria and Central Italy would involve an investigation of the metrological views of such writers as Haeberlin and Lehmann-Haupt, and of the whole question of the standards used in Italy and Sicily for bronze. This would pass outside the limits of the present work. I will therefore only treat of the gold and silver coins. Some of the silver coins of Populonia and other cities have a decidedly archaic appearance, bearing a type only on one side, while the other is blank. The art of them also is archaic. But it is doubtful if any of them can be given to an earlier date than 480 B.C.

In the fifth and fourth centuries the coins of Etruria show a close relation to those of Sicily, in fact a much closer relation than they exhibit to those of Magna Graecia. They are based upon a silver unit of 13·5 grains (grm. 0·875). This is clearly the Sicilian silver litra, the equivalent of a pound of bronze. It does not necessarily follow that the pound of bronze in Etruria was of exactly the same weight as the bronze litra of Sicily, since the relations of the metals in the two regions may not have been identical; but the difference cannot have been great.

We know that Etruria and Sicily clashed in the early part of the fifth century. Anaxilaus of Rhegium fortified the straits of Messina against the Tyrrhenian pirates, and the great defeat inflicted by Hiero I of Syracuse in 474 B.C. on the combined fleet of Carthaginians and Etruscans seems to have put an end to the thalassocracy of the latter. The coins of Etruria, as well as the Greek vases so common in Etruscan tombs, tell of a more friendly relation.

The facts of the Etruscan coinage are simple. The gold

and silver coins bear marks which precisely determine their value in exchange. There takes place, early in the fourth century, a reduction of standard, by which coins of the usual weights become worth twice as many litrae as before. Sir A. Evans, with great probability, has connected this depreciation with a parallel one introduced at Syracuse by Dionysius I. Dionysius, in his financial extremity, caused the didrachm of Syracuse to pass as a tetradrachm; that is, he caused the stater of 135 grains (grm. 8·74), which had hitherto passed as worth 10 litrae of bronze, to pass as the equivalent of 20 litrae of bronze. And since no mere edict could alter the relations of silver to bronze, this amounted to decreasing the weight of the bronze litra by 50 per cent. Exactly the same reduction is shown by the marks of value to have taken place in Etruria, and probably at the same time. In Etruria the change would not be the result of any financial difficulty. But if the weight of the Sicilian litra of bronze fell, it would be convenient for the maritime cities of Etruria to follow suit.

Gold before 380 B.C. (about): proportion of gold to silver 15 to 1.

Lion's head: plain reverse:

Weight, 44 grains	(grm. 2·85)	↑	=	50 litrae.
" 22 "	(grm. 1·42)	ΛXX		25 "
" 11 "	(grm. 0·71)	XIIC		$12\frac{1}{2}$ "

Young male head: plain reverse:

Weight, 22 grains	(grm. 1·42)	ΛXX	25 "
" 9 "	(grm. 0·58)	X	10 "

Silver before 380 B.C. (about): with plain reverses:

Gorgon-head.

Weight, 130 grains	(grm. 8·42)	X	=	10 litrae.
" 64 "	(grm. 4·14)	Λ		5 "

Head of Hermes.

Weight, 64 grains	(grm. 4·14)	Λ	5 "

Gorgon-head.

Weight, 32 grains	(grm. 2·07)	IIC	$2\frac{1}{2}$ "

Young male head.

Weight, 14 grains (grm. 0·90) I = 1 litra.

Wheel.

Weight, 13 grains (grm. 0·84) I 1 „

Silver, after 380 B.C. (about): reverse plain:

Gorgon-head.

Weight, 131 grains (grm. 8·48) XX = 20 litrae.

Head of Heracles.

Weight, 130 grains (grm. 8·42) XX 20 „

Male head.

Weight, 66 grains (grm. 4·27) X 10 „

„ 32 „ (grm. 2·07) Λ 5 „

Head of Apollo.

Weight, 66 grains (grm. 4·27) X 10 „

„ 29 „ (grm. 1·87) Λ 5 „

Head of Hermes.

Weight, 31 grains (grm. 2·0) Λ 5 „

Female head.

Weight, 60 grains (grm. 3·88) X 10 „

I have mentioned only coins bearing marks of value. There are many other coins not bearing marks of value, but clearly belonging to the same series. In silver we have, before 380, coins with the respective types of the Chimaera and the Boar which are of the weight of Attic tetradrachms and so must have passed as 20-litrae pieces. We have also drachms with such types as the Hippocamp and the Hare which must have passed as 5-litrae pieces.

So far all is clear, and the coinage of Etruria is parallel to that of Sicily. But a complication is introduced by the existence of another series of coins of different standard, and clearly regulated by another unit of value than the litra. As we have in this series the same reduction of the value of the unit to half what it had previously been, which we find in the series already mentioned, Mr. Head suggests[1] that in this class of coins also a change took place about 380 B.C.

[1] *Hist. Num.*, ed. 2, p. 14.

And as the style of the coins agrees with this hypothesis, we may regard it as more than probable.

Silver before 380 B.C.:

Head of Apollo: Reverse plain.
,, ,, ,, wheel.

Weight, 175 grains (grm. 11·34): mark of value V, five units of 35 grains (grm. 2·26).

Other coins of the same weight, but without the mark of value, are:

Head of Zeus: Reverse plain.
Chimaera: ,,
Running Gorgon: ⊙EIL. Wheel.
⊙EILE. Bull's head: Hippocamp.
[This coin weighs only 145 grains (grm. 9·40).]

Also coins of half the weight, about 86 grains (grm. 5·57).

Gorgon-head: Crescent.
⊙EIL. Male head facing: Sphinx.

Silver after 380 B.C.:

Sepia emerging from amphora: Reverse plain.

Weight, 350 grains (grm. 22·67): mark of value XX, 20 units of 17·5 grains (grm. 1·13). Also weight, 178 grains (grm. 11·53), mark X.

Hippocamp: around dolphins. *Rev.* Cerberus: mark V.
Weight, 83 grains (grm. 5·37).

The unit in these coins is no longer the litra of Sicily, but corresponds in weight, in the earlier class, to two Roman scruples of 17·5 grains (grm. 1·13); in the latter class to one such scruple.

An interesting and complicated problem is thus set us. In the first place, we must needs suppose that, if the two series of coins run contemporaneously, they must have been minted by cities in different districts and in different commercial circles. The first class belong, in part at least, to the maritime city of Populonia, which was the chief mart of Etruscan oversea commerce. It was in close contact with the island of Ilva, noted for its valuable iron mines, and must have had constant intercourse with Sicily, as well as

Corsica, Sardinia, and Africa. The second class belonged probably to the interior. The inscription ΘEILE cannot be interpreted with certainty; it was formerly read as Faesulae, but this reading is given up. The coins probably were struck at cities having intercourse with the east coast of Italy. And as the commerce of that coast was dominated by Corcyra, it is natural to see in the Etruscan staters and drachms of 175 and 87 grains, money meant to match the Corcyrean staters and drachms, which are of exactly the same weight. The coincidence of weight with the Roman and Italic scrupulum would be an adjustment. And indeed it is possible that we may here have a reason for a thing which is hard to explain, the fact that the Corcyrean coin-weight, from the very earliest time, never exceeds 180 grains (grm. 11·66) for the stater, and so is below the level of the Aeginetan stater. I have above (Ch. VII) accepted the view that the Corcyrean stater is in fact the equivalent of three drachms of Corinth. But it is quite possible that some adjustment to the copper units dominant in Italy may have also had its influence.

The Roman coinage does not come within the scope of this work, since it is doubtful if any Roman bronze coins were issued before 335 B.C.: the silver denarii were not struck until 268.

§ 3. Spain and Gaul.

A few words must be said as to the coins issued by the Greek cities in the far West. These, Massalia, Emporiae, Rhoda, were founded by Phocaean colonists, perhaps at quite an early time; though Massalia received fresh colonists when the mother-city was taken by the Persians, in the middle of the sixth century. The earliest currency of Massalia is the Phocaean coins, uninscribed and of a great variety of types, which have been found in hoards at Auriol in France[1] and at Cumae. The earliest issues of Massalia, about 400 B.C., are small obols, bearing the heads of Apollo

[1] I have spoken of this find in Chap. XI: see Babelon, *Traité*, ii. 1, p. 1571.

or Artemis, which seem to continue the line of the small Phocaean coins. But about the middle of the fourth century, Massalia issued drachms of a type which long persisted, and served as a model for the rude coins struck by the Gauls in Southern France:

> *Obv.* Head of Artemis. *Rev.* ΜΑΣΣΑ. Lion. Weight, 58–55 grains (grm. 3·75–3·56).

The standard of these drachms is identical with that used at the Phocaean colony of Cumae, and in other Greek cities of South Italy. It is also the standard used for silver at this period at Carthage, and hardly to be distinguished from that of Chios and Rhodes, which was widely used on the shores of the Aegean, or the standard used in Phoenicia.

At Emporiae in Spain also hoards of the little Phocaean coins have been found, some of them rather later in style. They are succeeded by little pieces bearing the head of Athena or Persephone, and sometimes the letters ΕΜ or ΕΜΠ. In the third century both at Massalia and at Emporiae coinage becomes more abundant.

CHAPTER XX

COINS OF SICILY, 480–330 B.C.

§ 1. 480–406 B.C.

The plan of this work does not include an account of the history of the cities and leagues of Greece, except so far as that history affects their coinage and their commerce. And as regards the coins themselves, by far the most important facts for our purpose are those in regard to metal, weights, and denomination. The types, being usually religious in character, are less to our present purpose. Thus there is not much to be here said in regard to the silver coins of Sicily in the fifth century, interesting and beautiful as they are. They adhere strictly to the Attic standard and mostly continue their old denominations.

One issue claims a special mention. The well-known decadrachms or pieces of fifty litrae[1] issued at Syracuse by Gelon after his great victory over the Carthaginians at Himera, and called after his wife Damareteia, are a landmark in numismatic history, because they can be closely dated to the year 479 B.C. or soon after. In days when medals, properly so called, did not exist, it was not unnatural that at a great time of national triumph the mint of a city should strike coins of unusual size, fashioned with special care. We have seen that Athens issued decadrachms in memory of Marathon. At about the same time some of the cities of Thrace and Macedon struck coins of unusual size, octadrachms and decadrachms, which may best be regarded as made in imitation of the Athenian decadrachms, and used on the occasion of the passing of

[1] As to the litra see above, p. 216.

the army of Xerxes. Certainly they were earlier than the large coins struck by Alexander I of Macedon. That Gelon should have followed the precedent set by Athens in 489 B.C. is not a matter for surprise.

The silver coinage of all the cities of Sicily, excepting Syracuse, continues through most of the fifth century unchanged in weight and character, though showing marked progress in style. But stirring political events marked the end of the century, first, the Athenian invasion of 415–413 B.C.; next, the Carthaginian invasion of 409–405 B.C.; and finally, the destructive tyranny of Dionysius. These great events have left noteworthy marks on the coinage.

It is probably to the siege of Syracuse by the Athenians that we must attribute the first issue of Syracusan gold coins. Holm indeed suggests[1] that these were struck after the victory over Athens; but this is improbable. At the time gold coinage was almost unknown in the West,[2] or indeed anywhere, if we except the darics of Persia. There must have been some strong reason for the innovation. The most likely reason is financial pressure. Silver might well in the stress of the siege be running short: to melt down some of the gold plate of the wealthy or the donaria in the temples of the Gods, and to strike gold coins with the proceeds would be a most natural course. We know that the earliest issue of gold coins at Athens took place a little later, in the extreme stress of the contest with Lysander. These Syracusan gold coins were of small denomination:

1. *Obv.* ΣΥΡ. Head of young Heracles in lion's skin. *Rev.* ΣΥΡΑ. Female head in incuse square. Weight, 18 grains (grm. 1·16). (Pl. XI. 5.)
2. *Obv.* ΣΥΡΑ. Head of Athena. *Rev.* Gorgon's head on aegis. Weight, 11–10 grains (grm. 0·71–0·64).
3. *Obv.* ΣΥΡ. Head of Athena. *Rev.* ΣΥΡΑ. Wheel in incuse. Weight, 9 grains (grm. 0·58).

These coins are of somewhat archaic fabric, remains of

[1] *Geschichte Siciliens*, iii. 618.

[2] The only exceptions are the early gold coins given to Cumae, as to the authenticity of which there is grave doubt; and small coins of Cyrene.

the old incuse square being preserved; but the heads on the obverse are not earlier than the last quarter of the fifth century. If at the time the relation of gold to silver stood at fifteen to one, as we have reason to think, we have the following equations:

18 grains of gold	=	270 grains of silver	=	4 drachms.
11 ,, ,,		165 ,, ,,		$2\frac{1}{2}$,,
9 ,, ,,		135 ,, ,,		2 ,,

The notion of a gold coinage having been once started, we cannot be surprised that other cities of Sicily, at the time of the Carthaginian invasion, followed the lead. We have gold coins of the period struck at Agrigentum, Gela, and Catana, or more probably Camarina.

Agrigentum.

Obv. ΑΚΡ. Eagle on serpent: two globules. *Rev.* ΣΙΛΑΝΟΣ. Crab. Weight, 20·5–19·5 grains (grm. 1·32–1·26). (Pl. XI. 6.)

Gela.

1. *Obv.* ΓΕΛΑΣ. Fore-part of man-headed bull. *Rev.* Armed horseman. Weight, 27 grains (grm. 1·74). (Pl. XI. 7.)
2. *Obv.* Similar. *Rev.* ΣΩΣΙΠΟΛΙΣ. Female head. Weight, 18 grains (grm. 1·16).
3. *Obv.* Fore-part of bridled horse. *Rev.* ΣΩΣΙΠΟΛΙΣ. Head of Cora. Weight, 13·5 grains (grm. 0·87).

Camarina.

Obv. Head of Athena, sea-horse on helmet. *Rev.* ΚΑ. Two olive-leaves and berries. Weight, 18 grains (grm. 1·16). (Pl. XI. 8.)

All these appear to be money of necessity. Taking the value of gold compared to silver at fifteen to one, we have the equations:

27 grains of gold	=	405 grains of silver	=	6 drachms.
18 ,, ,,		270 ,, ,,		4 ,,
13·5 ,, ,,		202·5 ,, ,,		3 ,,

It has been suggested that the two olive berries on the coin of Camarina may mark it as the equivalent of two Corinthian staters of 135 grains, and this seems probable.

The two globules on the coin of Agrigentum are a clearer indication of value; it also was probably equivalent to two staters of Corinth. It is somewhat over weight, but this may be an accident: of Silanus (a Greek name) we know nothing.

At an earlier time than the issue of gold coins, some of the cities of Sicily had begun to issue money of bronze. The dates, succession, and occasions of these bronze coins are very difficult to determine. The litra of bronze was the local standard of value in Sicily; and we might fairly have expected to find in the island, as in Italy, bronze coins struck of full weight at first, and gradually diminishing with successive reductions of the litra. There were issued, as we shall see, at a few places, notably at Himera in the fifth century, bronze coins of substantial weight, though not nearly of the full weight. But generally speaking, the bronze coins of the fifth century, which bear marks of value, are of so trifling a weight that it is clear that they were only money of account. These Sicilian coins seem to have been the earliest bronze issues in Greek cities: Hellas followed their lead. This is quite natural, as bronze was at the basis of the coinages of Sicily and of Italy, though the basis is usually hidden from sight.

The bronze money of Himera has been discussed by F. Imhoof-Blumer:[1] an inscribed example proves that the coins belong to Himera, and not, as earlier authorities[2] supposed, to Camarina. The obverse type of all of them is a Gorgon-head: on the reverse is usually only the mark of value. They fall into two classes: for the earlier, Imhoof gives the following weights:

Two ounces (Hexas), grm. 12·05, grains 186.
Three ounces (Trias), grm. 16·40, grains 253.
Four ounces (Tetras), grm. 21·30, grains 330.
Five ounces (Pentonkion), grm. 26·52, grains 410.
Six ounces (Hemilitron), grm. 34·80, grains 538.

[1] *Zur Münzkunde Grossgriechenlands, Siciliens, &c.*, Vienna, 1887.

[2] Including *B. M. Cat. Sicily*.

He observes that we thus arrive at a litra of 72 grammes (1,110 grains), which is about a third of the full weight of the Sicilian litra of 218 grammes, 3,375 grains. The later series is lighter and less regular:

Two ounces (Hexas), grm. 7·40, grains 115.
Three ounces (Trias), grm. 10·70, grains 165.
Six ounces (Hemilitron), grm. 29, grains 450.

The date assigned to these coins is from the middle of the fifth century to the destruction of Himera in 409 B.C.

There is another series having on the obverse the type of a cock, with the Phoenician letters ZIZ and certainly struck under Carthaginian rule:

One ounce (Uncia), grm. 3·85, grains 59.
Two ounces (Hexas), grm. 2·60, grains 40.
Three ounces (Trias), grm. 11·20–5·10, grains 173–79.
Six ounces (Hemilitron), grm. 14·10–8·70, grains 218–134.

Imhoof regards these coins as in part contemporary with the last-mentioned issue, and therefore not struck at Himera, perhaps rather at Solus. But none of the Carthaginian adaptations of Greek coins can safely be given to a time before the great invasion of 409 B.C.; we should therefore prefer, if they were struck at Solus, to assign them to the last years of the century.

Lipara. In the neighbouring island of Lipara coins of greater weight were issued at some time in the fourth century.

Obv. Head of Hephaestus. *Rev.* Stern of Galley.
Litra, grm. 108, grains 1667.
Hemilitron, grm. 51·6–35·7, grains 798–551.
Trias, grm. 25·6–23·6, grains 397–363.
Hexas, grm. 17·81–14·32, grains 275–221.
Uncia, grm. 11·08–8·35, grains 171–129.

Here the litra is somewhat heavier, about half the normal weight of 3,375 grains.

Thus the highest weight which we find for the litra in Sicily in the fifth and fourth centuries is only half of the normal weight. But coins so heavy are exceptional; and we find in the fifth century at many or most of the cities of Sicily small bronze coins bearing marks of value, but of quite irregular and merely conventional weight. Among the earliest of these appear to be the coins of Rhegium.[1]

Obv. Lion's scalp. *Rev.* RECINON. One globule.
Obv. " *Rev.* RE. " "

These appear to be unciae: the letters of the inscriptions appear to show that they were struck before 415 B.C.

A few years later we have at **Syracuse**—

Obv. ΣΥΡΑ. Female head. *Rev.* Cuttle-fish: marks of value.
Trias. Weight, 62–44 grains (grm. 4·01–2·85).

The date of these coins is about the time of the Athenian expedition; and it is not unnatural to connect them with it. In search of an explanation we turn to the coins of Athens, and we find that at that city, as already shown,[2] there were current at the time of the capture of the city, 406–393 B.C., bronze coins issued to take the place of the silver, each bronze coin corresponding in type to a denomination of the silver, and evidently passing as 'money of necessity'. It would be natural to suppose that the same thing may have happened in Sicily at the time of the Athenian invasion. Syracuse, however, does not stand alone: a number of the cities of Sicily issued bronze coins of light weight, bearing marks of value, towards the end of the fifth century. I add a list of some of these:

Agrigentum. The types are: on the obverse, Eagle holding hare or fish; on the reverse, Crab.

Hemilitron. Weight, 359–205 grains (grm. 23·26–13·28).
Trias (three ounces). Weight, 165–60 grains (grm. 10·69–3·88).
Hexas (two ounces). Weight, 132–103 grains (grm. 8·55–6·67).
Uncia. Weight, 64–53 grains (grm. 4·14–3·43).

Camarina. Types: on the obverse, Gorgon's head; on the reverse, Owl with lizard.

Trias. Weight, 65–49 grains (grm. 4·21–3·17).
Uncia. Weight, 20–14 grains (grm. 1·29–0·90).

[1] *B. M. Cat. Italy*, p. 376; *Hist. Num.*, ed. 2, p. 110.
[2] Above, p. 296.

Gela. Types: on obverse, Head of river-god; on reverse, Bull.
Trias. Weight, 73–48 grains (grm. 4·72–3·11).
Uncia. Weight, 15 grains (grm. 0·97).

Himera. Types: on the obverse, Male figure on goat; on the reverse, Nike holding aplustre.
Hemilitron. Weight, 102–91 grains (grm. 6·60–5·89).
Trias. Weight, 36 grains (grm. 2·33).
Hexas. Weight, 35 grains (grm. 2·26).

Selinus. Types: on the obverse, Head of river-god; on the reverse, Selinon leaf.
Trias. Weight, 138 grains (grm. 8·94).

The natural supposition would be that most of these coins were struck at the time of the Carthaginian invasion, during which the issuing cities perished. The example, however, was followed by cities which did not fall into the hands of the Carthaginians:

Segesta. Types: on the obverse, Head of Segesta; on the reverse, Hound.
Tetras. Weight, 132–97 grains (grm. 8·55–6·28).
Hexas. Weight, 113–43 grains (grm. 7·32–2·78).

And the Carthaginians themselves seem to have imitated the procedure:

Solus. Types: on the obverse, Head of Heracles; on the reverse, Crayfish.
Hemilitron. Weight, 116–114 grains (grm. 7·51–7·38).
Trias. Weight, 69 grains (grm. 4·47).

It is to be observed that some of the Sicilian cities had been in the habit of issuing very small coins in silver, bearing marks of value; for example, we find

Leontini.
Obv. Lion's head. *Rev.* Barleycorn.
Hemilitron. Weight, 5·8 grains (grm. 0·37).
Pentonkion. Weight, 4 grains (grm. 0·26).
Hexas. Weight, 1·4 grains (grm. 0·09).

Messana.
Obv. Hare running. *Rev.* ME in wreath.
Hemilitron. Weight, 4·2 grains (grm. 0·27).

Segesta.

Obv. Fore-part of hound. *Rev.* ΣΕΓΕ.
Hemilitron. Weight, 4·5 grains (grm. 0·29).

Obv. Head of hound. *Rev.* ΕΓΕΣΤΑ.
Hexas. Weight, 2·1 grains (grm. 0·13).

Eryx.[1]

Obv. Fore-part of hound. *Rev.* ΕΡΥ and Η.
Hemilitron. Weight, 6·6 grains (grm. 0·42).

Rhegium.

Obv. Fore-part of hare. *Rev.* Two globules.
Hexas. Weight, 2·8 grains (grm. 0·18).

Syracuse.

Obv. Female head. *Rev.* Cuttle-fish.
Trias. Weight, 2·8 grains (grm. 0·18).

These coins are parallel to the small silver pieces of Athens, where, however, we have distinctive types and not marks of value to indicate the denominations. Athens substituted for these, bronze coins of the same types in the last years of the Peloponnesian War: the cities of Sicily substituted for their silver, bronze coins with similar marks of value, but of very small intrinsic worth, in the stress which came on them in the last years of the fifth century.

§ 2. 406–330 B.C.

The coinage issued for Syracuse by the Tyrant Dionysius is interesting for many reasons. It is of great beauty, and of an unusual character; and since we are able to determine many points in regard to it, it throws light on the whole system of coinage among the Greeks. It has been made the subject of careful study, first by Mr. Head[2] and then by Sir Arthur Evans.[3] Evans's treatment is marked by full knowledge and historic method, and is a model of successful research.

[1] *Num. Chron.*, 1896, p. 10.

[2] *Coinage of Syracuse*, 1874.

[3] Freeman's *History of Sicily*, iv, p. 230; *Syracusan Medallions*, 1892; *Num. Chron.*, 1894, p. 216; cf. Holm, *Geschichte Siciliens*, iii, 604.

As all the great cities of Sicily, except Syracuse, had been either destroyed or much impoverished by the military expeditions of the Carthaginians and Dionysius, before 395 B.C., it would be natural to expect that after that date Dionysius's rule would be marked by a great issue of Syracusan money. Until Evans wrote, numismatists had supposed this to be the case, but this opinion must now be modified. Undoubtedly Dionysius required for his fleet and the mercenaries whom he collected from Greece, Italy, and Spain, a great deal of currency of some sort; but he seems largely to have used existing coin.

The years immediately after the Athenian repulse from Syracuse had been years of extraordinary activity in the mints of Sicily. At all the great cities, Syracuse, Agrigentum, Gela, Selinus, Messana, and the rest, we find a plentiful issue of beautiful tetradrachms, the style of which matures with extraordinary rapidity. At Syracuse we have in addition two new phenomena. The great decadrachms by Kimon and Evaenetus were in a special sense a trophy of the victory over Athens. (Pl. XI. 9.) They were probably given as prizes at the Assinarian games, established in memory of the capture of the Athenian army near the river Assinarus. Syracuse also began to issue gold coins. The earliest of these, almost contemporary with the gold coins of Gela and Agrigentum, have already been mentioned. Not much later, and certainly contemporary with the decadrachms, were the following gold coins:

1. *Obv.* Head of Arethusa. *Rev.* Heracles strangling lion. Probably by Kimon.[1] Weight, 90 grains (grm. 5·83).
2. *Obv.* Young male head (perhaps Assinarus). *Rev.* Free horse. Weight, 45 grains (grm. 2·91).
3. *Obv.* Female head. *Rev.* Trident between dolphins. Weight, 20·5 grains (grm. 1·33).

Mr. Head, considering that at the time gold was fifteen times as valuable as silver, equates coins 1 and 2 respectively with 1,350 and 675 grains of silver (grm. 87·47, 43·73),

[1] Head, *Coinage of Syracuse*, p. 20.

that is with two and one silver decadrachms. This relation may be regarded as proved by the fact that a gold coin of the first kind in the Gréau Collection[1] bears two globules as a mark of value. This also confirms the value above given to the small gold coins of Sicily. Coin No. 3 is probably equivalent to a tetradrachm.

Dionysius, when he came into power, no doubt continued the issue of the gold coins and of the decadrachms. But it is a remarkable fact, first established by Evans, that he struck very few tetradrachms; indeed, Evans maintains that he struck none at all after 400 B.C. 'The prolific tetradrachm coinage of Syracuse suddenly breaks off about the end of the fifth century. It may indeed be confidently stated, extraordinary as the phenomenon may appear, that no tetradrachms or silver pieces of smaller denomination are known of this period as late in style as the *pentekontalitra* of Evaenetos, which seem to have formed the sole silver coinage of Dionysius during a great part of his reign. In the great hoards of the period that from time to time have come to light on Sicilian soil, freshly struck pentekontalitra or "medallions" have been found in association with Syracusan tetradrachms of earlier style, and showing traces of wear, though newly coined *pegasi* of Corinth and her colonies, and brilliant tetradrachms of the Carthaginian camp-coinage, accompanied the same deposits.'[2] I think, with Holm, that this statement is slightly beyond the mark, and that some tetradrachms of as late a date as 385 B.C. are known; but broadly put the assertion seems incontestable.

Dionysius is credited by ancient historians, notably by Aristotle and Diodorus, with extreme cruelty and effrontery in his methods of extorting from the people of Syracuse the great sums of money which he required to maintain his army and his fleet. As a palliation we must observe that if Dionysius had not in one way or another procured the means to pay his mercenaries, the Carthaginians would

[1] *Annuaire de Numismatique*, 1868, Pl. III.

[2] Evans, in Freeman's *Sicily*, iv, p. 235.

certainly have sacked Syracuse, as they sacked Selinus and Agrigentum. Of the various operations of fraud and force with which he is credited, I need refer only to two, which may probably have left traces on the coins. In the first place we have extant evidence that he debased the currency, in the form of a bronze coin of the exact type of a decadrachm, and plated with tin, which has been published by Evans,[1] who brings this official forgery into connexion with the statements of Aristotle[2] and Julius Pollux[3] that Dionysius, being in a strait for money, forced upon his creditors tin coins of the nominal value of four drachmae, but really only worth one. No coins of this time in tin are known, but in the coin cited we have a bronze coin plated with tin. Two difficulties, however, beset the proposed explanation. In the first place, the coin is not a tetradrachm but a decadrachm; and in the second place, it is not worth so much as a drachm. It is therefore better to regard Evans's coin as a base official imitation of a silver decadrachm. The expedient of issuing a certain number of plated coins, mixed in with the ordinary productions of the mint, was not unknown to the Roman moneyers. And we have an earlier example of it in the coinage struck by Themistocles at Magnesia.[4]

Aristotle in his *Oeconomica* (ii. 20) also says that on one occasion Dionysius, having borrowed money from the citizens, countermarked the coins in such a way as to double their value as currency, and repaid the debt with such coins, thus actually paying only half what he borrowed. As the extant coins of Syracuse bear no mark of such restriking or countermarking, we may be almost sure that Aristotle or his authority has somewhat misunderstood the transaction. I think that Evans is right in bringing into connexion with it another passage of Aristotle preserved by Julius Pollux,[5] which states that, whereas the earlier talent of Sicily was equal to 24 nummi, the later talent was equal

[1] *Num. Chron*, 1894, p. 219; Pl. VIII, 1.

[2] *Oecon.* ii. 20.

[3] *Onom.* ix. 79.

[4] Above, Chap. XIV, p. 256.

[5] ix. 87.

only to 12 nummi. This shows that at some time, which time is very likely to be the reign of Dionysius, the value of the talent was diminished by half. Originally, as we know from the inscription of Tauromenium,[1] the talent was of 120 litrae; and Evans has shown that the nummus was of 5 litrae, or of the value of an Attic drachm, and not, as had been supposed on the authority of Pollux, of the value of a litra.

The hoards of coins, buried during the reign of Dionysius, which have been discovered explain in some degree the gaps in his own coinage. From these 'it appears that the silver currency of the Sicilian cities was at this time supplied more and more by imported *pegasi* of Corinth and her Adriatic colonies. In the West Sicilian hoard' (of about 400 B.C.), 'the early didrachms (tridrachms) of Leukas were numerously represented. In the great Naxos hoard' (of about 410 B.C.), 'these *pegasi* already occurred in considerable abundance. Add to these a copious supply of Athenian tetradrachms of early style, and, later, the abundant Siculo-Punic coinage, and it will be seen that, without drawing on native Hellenic sources, there was no dearth of silver currency at this time in Sicily.'[2] In these same finds are also many Syracusan decadrachms, and abundant tetradrachms issued by the other cities of Sicily before their destruction.

If, as is probable, the reduction in the value of the talent to half took place in the time of Dionysius, that talent, having before been of the value of six tetradrachms, would later be only of the value of three tetradrachms or six Corinthian *pegasi*. If Dionysius borrowed talents of the former value, and repaid them with talents of the reduced value, it would account for the statement of Aristotle. And the obscure statement as to the fresh type or countermark may be readily explained if the Corinthian *pegasi* became the main coinage in place of the old tetradrachms. It even appears probable that Dionysius did not content himself with using the *pegasi* of Corinth, but struck imitations of them himself.

[1] *C. I. G.* 5640, 41.

[2] Evans, *Syracusan Medallions*, p. 151.

The earliest coins of Corinthian types struck at Syracuse are the following:

Obv. Pegasus to left. *Rev.* ΣΥΡΑΚΟΣΙΟΝ. Helmeted head of Athena to right. Stater.

Little later in style are another series in which the inscription ends with ΩΝ instead of ΟΝ (Pl. XI. 10).

The Padre Romano long ago suggested that the former class of these coins was issued in the time of Dion, 357 B.C.[1] Mr. Head, Mr. Hill, and Sir A. Evans all assign the former class to the time of Dion, the latter to the time of Timoleon, 346 B.C.[2] M. Six, however, preferred for class I an earlier date, that of Dionysius I, and found their occasion in the foundation by that tyrant of the cities of Issa and Lissus on the Illyrian coast, which might bring Syracuse into the circle of Corinthian commerce.

To this last argument we cannot attach very much value, since the coast of Illyria was more dominated by the commerce and the coins of Corcyra than by those of Corinth. The colonies of Dyrrhachium and Apollonia made their issues of coins at this time uniform with those of the former, not those of the latter, city. But there are serious reasons for thinking that after all Six was right, and that Dionysius may have struck the earliest Pegasus coins.

It is difficult to find a reason for which Dionysius should be supposed to have imported coins from Corinth instead of striking them himself. Nor is it any argument against the attribution to Dionysius that the coins under consideration do not bear his name or signet; for the same thing is to be observed in case of the decadrachms, which were confessedly issued by Dionysius.

Sir A. Evans, as we have seen, does not give these coins to Dionysius but to Dion. The chief reason which he adduces for this attribution is the existence of closely parallel coins also of Corinthian types, bearing the inscrip-

[1] *Alcune monete scoperte in Sicilia*, p. 23.

[2] Head, *Hist. Num.*, ed. 2, p. 179; Hill, *Coins of Sicily*, pp. 117, 150; Evans, *Syracusan Medallions*, p. 156

tion ΛΕΟΝΤΙΝΟΝ, Dion having been closely connected with Leontini. But it may be replied that Dionysius was still more closely connected with that city, which, in fact, he refounded and peopled with his mercenaries. Contemporary with these *pegasi* struck at Syracuse and Leontini are the rare Corinthian staters of Terina,[1] having on the obverse the monogram Ꚍ. Terina was closely connected with Dionysius and dependent on him.[2] Dion had no special connexion with Corinth, and I know of no reason why he should have used the types of that city. The only coins known to have been issued under his authority bear the types of Zacynthus. I am therefore disposed to prefer the attribution to Dionysius.

The somewhat later Pegasus coins with the inscription ΣΥΡΑΚΟΣΙΩΝ are universally attributed to the time of Timoleon. And this is most reasonable: Timoleon was a citizen of Corinth, sent by that city to the help of the people of Syracuse when they were in great straits. In other coins of the time of Timoleon Corinthian influence may be traced. But it is unlikely that the Corinthian influence began in his time. From the time of the disastrous Athenian expedition against Syracuse, the influence of Athens and the Athenian owls came to an end in Sicily. Corinth, as the chief commercial city of the Peloponnesian allies, would naturally take her place. The tetradrachm ceased to be struck. The silver decadrachm, and experimental coins in gold, silver, and bronze, arranged on the basis of the litra of 13·5 grains, took the place of the regular 4, 2, and 1 drachm issues. The very fact that in the time of their distress the Syracusans applied to Corinth for aid is in itself eloquent.

A coin has been published of Corinthian types, having beneath the Pegasus Carthaginian letters which appear to stand for the name of Eryx.[3] As most of these Punic

[1] Evans in *Num. Chron.*, 1912, p. 56; Pl. IV. 26.

[2] *Ibid.*, p. 53.

[3] Imhoof-Blumer, *Die Münzen Akarnaniens*, p. 6. The present locality of the coin is unknown.

imitations of Greek issues belong to the time of Dionysius, a fresh argument is furnished for the Dionysian date of the earliest Sicilian coins of these types.

The abundant and remarkable coinage of pale gold or electrum which in the middle of the fourth century makes its appearance at Syracuse, has been given by Romano, Six, and Holm to the time of Dion. It presents us with an entirely fresh set of types, among which the head and attributes of Apollo are conspicuous:

1. *Obv.* Head of Apollo. *Rev.* Head of Artemis. (Pl. XI. 11.)
2. *Obv.* " " *Rev.* Tripod.
3. *Obv.* " " *Rev.* Lyre.
4. *Obv.* Female head. *Rev.* Cuttle-fish.

The weights are as follows:

1. 112·5 grains (grm. 7·28) = 100 silver litrae of 13·5 grains (grm. 0·86).
2. 56·2 grains (grm. 3·64) = 50 silver litrae of 13·5 grains (grm. 0·86).
3. 28·0 grains (grm. 1·82) = 25 silver litrae of 13·5 grains (grm. 0·86).
4. 11·2 grains (grm. 0·72) = 10 silver litrae of 13·5 grains (grm. 0·86).

This gives a proportionate value of electrum to silver of twelve to one. It appears that in the time of Dion, and down to the great issues of gold coins by Philip of Macedon, gold in Sicily was fifteen times as valuable as silver. These electrum coins, therefore, would seem to have been reckoned as of four-fifths the value of gold.

A comparison with coins struck by Dion at Zacynthus—*Obv.* Head of Apollo. *Rev.* ΙΑ ΔΙΩΝΟΣ Tripod—and with the fact that Dion regarded himself as in a special degree under the protection of Apollo, seems to furnish conclusive reasons for assigning these coins to his influence. Mr. Head, who in the first edition of the *Historia Numorum* assigned them to the time of Timoleon, in the second edition transfers them to Dion.

Besides the imitations of Corinthian money, the attribution of which to Timoleon I have justified, there are coins in gold and bronze which may with confidence be given to his time.

Obv. Head (and name) of Zeus Eleutherius. *Rev.* ΣΥΡΑΚ. Pegasus: three pellets. Weight, 33 grains (grm. 2·15–2·12).

This coin was formerly mixed up with the electrum of Apolline types, but it is really of pure gold. The marks of value show that it was equivalent to three staters of Corinthian type, 405 grains of silver, giving us a relation between gold and silver of 12 to 1 instead of 15 to 1. And such an increase in the value of silver, or such a fall in the value of gold, actually took place in Europe about 350 B.C., in consequence of the acquisition and development of the gold mines of Thrace by Philip of Macedon. In Macedon, and in the Aegean district generally, the fall went beyond 12 to 1, as far as 10 to 1; but the change in value would probably be less rapid in Sicily.

The alliance coinage, issued by the cities of Sicily in the time of Timoleon, mostly in bronze, and bearing such inscriptions as ΣΥΜΜΑΧΙΚΟΝ and ΟΜΟΝΟΙΑ, is of great interest. It was first identified by Head, and is fully discussed by Evans in Freeman's *History of Sicily*, vol. iv, p. 349. Timoleon succeeded in establishing something like a free Commonwealth of Sicily, which, had it but lasted, might have greatly affected the history of Italy and the West.

Mostly of the time of Timoleon, though some of them may have been struck by Dion, are some bronze coins of substantial weight, belonging to Syracuse and to other cities.

Obv. ΣΥΡΑ. Head of Athena. *Rev.* Star-fish between dolphins. Some of these are marked with a pellet, showing them to be litrae. Weight, 630–420 grains (grm. 40–27).

Obv. ΣΥΡΑ. Head of Athena. *Rev.* Hippocamp. These bear no mark of value; but they were probably the trias. Weight, 139–78 grains (grm. 9–5).

Obv. ΣΥΡΑ. Female head. *Rev.* Dolphin and mussel. A pellet on the reverse marks this coin as an uncia. Weight, 62–47 grains (grm. 4–3).

The weight of these coins is somewhat more carefully regulated than is that of those above mentioned: they constitute a real bronze coinage. In the fourth century they are extensively used by the other cities of Sicily as blanks whereon to restrike their own types. Contemporary, and indeed sometimes restruck on coins of Syracuse, are the following of Mytistratus:

Obv. Head of Hephaestus. *Rev.* ΜΥ in wreath.
Hemilitron. Weight, 448–427 grains (grm. 29–27).
Uncia. Weight, 103 grains (grm. 6·67).

It is noteworthy that this hemilitron is restruck on the litra of Syracuse. This shows how little importance was attached, even in the case of these more weighty issues, to the intrinsic value of the coins. On the whole it is quite clear that though bronze may have passed by weight in Sicily, yet when it was in the form of struck coins, the size and weight of these had little relation to their value. The coinage follows the analogies of Greece, and not those of Italy, where bronze coins of full value were issued, though not before the fourth century. Thus the coins of Sicily do not help us to solve the vexed question of the successive reductions of the litra.

Besides the electrum coins, the silver Pegasi, and the large bronze coins struck at Syracuse, a variety of interesting coins struck in several cities bear witness to the influence of Timoleon. Agrigentum and Gela resumed their issues of silver, though they only struck small denominations. We find inscriptions on coins commemorating Zeus Eleutherius at Syracuse and Agyrium, commemorating Apollo Archegetes at Alaesa and Tauromenium, commemorating Demeter at Enna, and testifying to an adoration of Sicilia at Adranum. One city stamps its coinage with the word ΚΑΙΝΟΝ, new. In fact it seemed that Sicily was born anew, and a fresh devotion to the chief deities of the island arose in many places. But in twenty years the enthusiasm had vanished, and before long Sicily fell under the sway of a tyrant as bad as Dionysius, Agathocles. The coinage of Agathocles also is characteristic, and Evans devotes some interesting pages to it. But it falls outside the period treated of in this book.

CHAPTER XXI

COINS OF PHILIP AND ALEXANDER

THE accession to the throne of Macedon of Philip II, in 359 B.C., is one of the most important dates in the history of the world. The Macedonian kingdom had hitherto counted for little in that history; the reigns of its rulers had been short and turbulent, and it was surrounded by powerful enemies. But the population, mainly of Thracian and Illyrian blood, was numerous and hardy; and when Philip had secured the gold mines of Pangaeum, which brought him in a great revenue, and had imported Greek science and culture to bear on his rude people, and had especially developed the art of war, the greatness of Macedon was assured.

The coinages of Philip and Alexander reflect the political expansion of Macedon. They are of enormous extent, and soon assumed a dominant position in relation to money in the whole ancient world.

The chief types of Philip's coins are:

Gold.

Obv. Head of Apollo, laureate. *Rev.* ΦΙΛΙΠΠΟΥ. Two-horse chariot. Stater of about 133 grains (grm. 8·6).

Obv. Head of young Heracles in lion's skin. *Rev.* ΦΙΛΙΠΠΟΥ. Fore-part of lion. Half-stater. Also the quarter, the eighth, and the twelfth of the stater.

Silver.

Obv. Head of Zeus, laureate. *Rev.* ΦΙΛΙΠΠΟΥ. Boy-rider on horse, carrying palm or crowning horse. Tetradrachm of about 224 grains (grm. 14·5).

Obv. Head of young Heracles. *Rev.* ΦΙΛΙΠΠΟΥ. Youth on horse. Didrachm, octobol, drachm.

Also smaller divisions and bronze coins.

The most noteworthy and abundant of these coins are the gold staters with chariot type, and the silver tetradrachms with the victorious horse. Plutarch tells us that Philip was very proud of his victories at Olympia, and placed the chariot on his coins in memory of them.[1]

It is probable that the gold staters (a complete innovation in the Macedonian coinage) were first struck when Philip gained possession of the Thracian gold mines. It does not appear likely that the silver tetradrachms were issued before the victory with the race-horse (κέλης) at Olympia which coincided with the birth of Alexander, 356 B.C. And in fact there are other tetradrachms of Philip which may be earlier, and fill the gap 359–356:

Obv. Head of Zeus, laureate. *Rev.* Bearded Macedonian horseman, hand raised.

This type Philip may have given up in 356 in favour of the jockey type.

The head of Zeus on the silver tetradrachms clearly represents the Olympian form of the God. Philip's close connexion with Olympia is also indicated by his setting up a circular building there containing his portrait and those of his family. Evidently he regarded the great Father of the Greek race as his especial patron.

The head on the obverse of the gold staters is commonly regarded as an Apollo; and in some cases it certainly is Apollo, with long hair falling over the neck. But more usually it is a head with short hair and bull neck, and very different in character from the Apollo of the Olympian coins. As, on the money of the Mamertines of Sicily, an imitation of the head on the Philippi is inscribed ΑΡΕΟΣ, one may suspect that the type of Philip was really Ares, the war-god of Thracian and Macedonian. It was very natural that Alexander should substitute the head of Athena for that of Ares.

Philip seems to have taken the standard alike of his gold and silver coins from Olynthus. The gold coins follow

[1] *Vita Alexandri*, 3, 4.

the Attic standard, which had since 394 B.C. been almost universally dominant for gold. The silver coins are nearest to the old standard of Abdera, which had been powerful in Thrace early in the fifth century, but which Abdera had herself abandoned towards the end of that century. One would naturally have expected Philip to use the Chian or Rhodian standard for silver, which in his time had great vogue, and was followed by the powerful Mausolus of Caria. The reason for the preference of a somewhat lighter weight may have been the desire to make gold and silver better correspond together. It would seem that in the middle of the century, at all events in Macedon, gold had fallen as low as 10 to 1. At this rate a gold stater of 133 grains would be equivalent to 1,330 grains of silver, that is, to six tetradrachms of 224 grains (nearly) or twenty-four drachms of 56 grains (grm. 3·62). This drachm may well have been equated with the Persian tetrobol, or two-thirds of a drachm, as the Rhodian drachm was equated in Asia. The kings who preceded Philip had probably reckoned the daric, which was their standard gold coin, as equivalent to 130 × 12 or 1,560 grains of silver, that is, to ten of their staters of about 160 grains or 20 drachms of Persian weight. That Philip did not reckon 20 of his silver drachms to the gold stater, but 24, seems to be proved conclusively by the fact that he issued fourths, eighths, and twelfths of the gold stater. Reckoning 24 drachms to the stater, these would be equivalent to 6, 3, and 2 silver drachms; reckoning 20 drachms to the gold stater, they would be equivalent to 5, $2\frac{1}{2}$, and $1\frac{2}{3}$ silver drachms, which is far less likely.

It would have been simpler had Philip, like his successor Alexander, struck gold and silver on the same standard, as did Athens, where, the ratio between gold and silver being 12 to 1, and both metals being struck on the same standard, 24 silver drachms went to the gold stater. Had Philip taken this line, any fall or rise in the value of gold would not have been of any practical inconvenience. The gold stater would have been the standard coin, and 24 or 22 or

20 silver drachms would have exchanged for it as the value of gold fell. That would have been the adoption of a monometallic currency. For this apparently Philip was not prepared; he remained a bimetallist, and it was left to Alexander boldly to accept monometallism.

The fall in the value of gold about the middle of the fourth century may be proved by the evidence of the accounts of the Treasurers at Delphi.[1] In 331 B.C. the value of the daric is there stated as 15 Aeginetan silver drachms, which according to the current reckoning were equivalent to 20 Attic drachms, which gives nearly the ratio of 10 to 1. The value of the gold Philippi is given in the same series of records as 7 Aeginetan staters or 14 drachms.[2] No doubt Philippi were regarded as of the same value as the daric, the difference between 15 and 14 drachms being accounted for by the *agio* of the moment. The Philippi are a few grains heavier than the daric.

These records raise a curious point. It seems scarcely possible that in the last years of the Persian Empire the daric should at Delphi have been equivalent to 20 Attic drachms while on the continent of Asia Persian drachms (sigli) of 86 grains (grm. 5·57) should still have been, as in the fifth and early fourth centuries, passing at 20 to the daric. But we must remember the immobility of the Persian Empire, of the 'law of the Medes and Persians which altereth not'. A commercial empire would have lowered the weight of the siglos; but probably, as the value of silver rose, all payments in Persia would be made in gold except in the case of small amounts.

Two cities founded by Philip, or at all events renamed by him, Philippi in Macedon and Philippopolis (Gomphi) in Thessaly, were allowed by the founder to issue coin for a time. The coins of Philippi are gold staters, with the types of the head of Heracles and a tripod, and silver coins with the same types, but of the weight of Philip's silver tetradrachms. The coins of Philippopolis are:

[1] Bourguet, *Administration financière du sanctuaire pythique*, p. 25.

[2] *Bull. Corr. Hell.*, xxiv, p. 136.

Obv. Head of Hera. *Rev.* Zeus Acraeus seated. Weight, 183 grains (grm. 11·85).

This is a didrachm of Aeginetan standard: the drachm was also struck. These coins are remarkable, since the weight does not conform to the Macedonian but to the Thessalian standard. Probably they were issued before Philip incorporated Thessaly, and brought the Thessalian coinage to an end.

Alexander adopted the Attic standard, both for gold and silver. The acquisition of enormous supplies of gold from Ecbatana and other fortified cities of Asia conquered by Alexander must have tended to keep down the proportionate value of gold to silver to 10 to 1.

The chief types of Alexander are:

Gold.

Obv. Head of Athena, helmeted. *Rev.* ΑΛΕΞΑΝΔΡΟΥ or ΑΛΕΞΑΝΔΡΟΥ ΒΑΣΙΛΕΩΣ. Winged Victory, holding naval mast and spar. Distater, stater, and fractions.

Silver.

Obv. Head of young Heracles in lion's skin. *Rev.* Inscr. as the gold. Olympian Zeus seated on throne, holding eagle. Decadrachm, tetradrachm, didrachm, drachm, and fractions.

Bronze.

Obv. Head of young Heracles. *Rev.* ΑΛΕΞΑΝΔΡΟΥ. Club and bow.

Alexander's types carry on the Zeus of his father Philip, and the Heracles of his ancestors. The introduction of the head of Athena is a personal innovation; probably a result of Alexander's Homeric proclivities, Athena having been the guardian goddess of the Greeks at Troy. Victory is also an innovation: the mast must refer to some victory at sea.

We reach next a question which is very difficult. In 337 B.C. Philip convened a congress of the Greek cities at Corinth, when he was proclaimed chief and leader of an anti-Persian confederacy, Philip taking the place of Athens as head of the island-league. In the next year Philip was assassinated; but Alexander, soon after his accession, again called together a congress of deputies from the cities of Greece at Corinth, and received the same appointment as his father. Each Hellenic city was to be free and autonomous, and was guaranteed against hostile attack and the intrigues of would-be tyrants. But certainly Alexander claimed not only the command of the Greek army in Asia, but also a general headship in Europe.

The question is whether these arrangements involved any change in the free striking of coins by the Greek cities. The immense abundance of the gold and silver coins of Philip and Alexander shows that in practice they were everywhere dominant; but what was their legal status? Was the coinage Macedonian or imperial?

To begin with Philip. Though he brought to an end the coinage of the cities of Macedon, and of Thessaly when it was incorporated with Macedon, he does not appear to have interfered with that of Greece south of Thermopylae. We have in Boeotia a fresh and distinctive coinage (see p. 359 above), which begins with the fall of Thebes in 338 B.C.; and in Locris a similar phenomenon occurs. Athens certainly did not cease to strike coins after the battle of Chaeroneia, nor after the congress at Corinth in 337. Philip could no doubt have stopped the issues of money in Boeotia, Locris, and Athens, had he chosen to do so; and the fact that he did not choose is notable. He had lived as a hostage in Thebes, and must have been aware that when Thebes dominated the Boeotian League in 446–387 B.C. all the coinage of Boeotia had been Theban, and there had been no local issues at the other cities. He must also have been aware of the monetary policy of the Athenian Empire of the fifth century. But if Philip did not interfere with the issues of Northern Greece, it is highly improbable that the coinages either of Peloponnesus or of Asia would be at all affected by his financial measures. And the coins themselves furnish no evidence of any marked change. We may therefore confidently say that Philip's coins are Macedonian only.

The problem in regard to Alexander is more intricate. The power of Alexander was both wider and more despotic. He must have been well aware of the monopoly claimed in Asia by the Kings of Persia for the gold daric: a privilege he would be unlikely to give up. And he must have known of the financial policy of the Athenian Empire in its flourishing days. Had Alexander lived a few years longer, he might have established a world-coinage like that of the Roman Emperors, and forbidden all other mintage in Europe, Asia, and Egypt. But his ceaseless campaigns left him little time or opportunity to attend to matters of finance.

The gold and silver coinages of Alexander, like those of his father Philip (which seem to have been continued after Philip's death in certain districts), were immense. Alexander's mint cities extended from Pella to the Far East; and finds of his coins have been constantly made over a great part of Asia and Europe. The subject of his mints from which coins were issued has not yet been systematically attacked since L. Müller wrote, half a century ago. Müller's classification is quite out of date, and would not now be accepted by any one. The editors of the Coin-Catalogues of the British Museum when the volume of the Catalogue including Macedon was issued (by Head, 1879) set aside the coinages of Philip II, Alexander III, and Philip III of Macedon and their successors for future treatment; and the pledge then given of a separate volume on the subject has not yet been redeemed. Mr. Newell is working on the coins of Alexander,[1] and it is to be hoped that he may succeed in ordering them satisfactorily.

Meantime any attempt to make a final classification of the coins which bear Alexander's name would be premature. We can only feel our way towards a few conclusions in regard to them.

Alexander's gold staters succeeded and superseded the

[1] *Num. Chron.*, 1915, p. 294, and *Amer. Journ. of Num.*, 1911, 1912.

daric, though it is possible, as M. Babelon suggests, that for a short time he struck darics himself. Almost certainly some of the double darics which reach us from the Far East (B. M. XXVII. 1) were struck during his lifetime, and by his authority. But no other gold appears to have been permitted, except in the case of the Kings of Cyprus (above, Chap. XVI), who seem to have continued their coinages. The city of Cius may also have been specially privileged.

But while Alexander, according to all probability, preserved the prerogative of the Persian Kings as regards the coinage of gold, he seems not to have interfered with issues of silver, but to have left his tetradrachms to make their way rather by their own merits than by legislation.

We may summarize the situation as follows. In the last third of the fourth century, we find many competing coinages:

(1) The gold and silver of Alexander himself, whether struck under his direction or in civic mints by his permission, or after his death.

(2) The gold and silver of Philip III, Alexander's brother, who succeeded him in parts of his dominions; and (in Egypt) the coins of Alexander IV, his son by Barsine.

(3) The gold and silver of the Greek Kings of Macedon, Syria, and Egypt: several of these rulers assumed the title King about 306 B.C.; after which they issued abundant coins, in their own names, in many of the cities of their dominions.

(4) The continued coinages of the Greek cities which preserved their autonomy: the issue of gold was confined to the Kings of Cyprus, and the city of Cius; but many cities continued to mint silver, and on various standards. Also in some districts of Persia the old coinage seems to have persisted.

(5) Coins issued, apparently as a special privilege in some of the cities founded by the Diadochi and others.

We had best begin by citing a few series of coins of

classes (4) and (5) which can be definitely dated, as such coins give us fixed points for the comparison of other series.

Paeonia. Audoleon, son of Patraus, continued in Paeonia to the north of Macedon the coinage of his predecessors. He is known, from an inscription,[1] to have been reigning about 286 B.C.: the reign may have begun about 315. His earlier coinage is as follows:

Obv. Head of Athena. *Rev.* ΑΥΔΩΛΕΟΝΤΟΣ. Free horse. Weight, 200–188 grains (grm. 12·96–12·18).

Also the half, the quarter, and the sixth of this stater. At a later time (after 306 B.C.) we have staters of Attic weight with the types of Alexander, but the name of Audoleon. The standard of the former set of coins may be that of Philip II, decidedly lowered.

Samothrace. A mint which issued silver coin for the first time in the period 330–280 B.C. is that of the island of Samothrace:

Obv. Head of Athena. *Rev.* ΣΑΜΟ. Kybele seated on throne. Weight, 125 grains (grm. 8·10). Br. Mus. Probably a didrachm of Attic standard which has lost weight.

The head on the obverse is certainly copied from the gold of Alexander, which gives the date. The issue is probably connected with the festival of the Cabeiri, which increased in reputation in Hellenistic times, to which times also belongs the temple at Samothrace excavated by A. Conze and his party.

Uranopolis in Chalcidice was founded about 300 B.C. by Alexarchus, brother of Cassander, who is described by Athenaeus[2] as a notorious euphuist and eccentric. This man issued silver coins on the standard used by Philip II of Macedon:

Obv. Sun, moon, and stars. *Rev.* ΟΥΡΑΝΙΔΩΝ. Aphrodite Urania. Weight, 209 grains (grm. 13·54). Also the half and quarter.

[1] *C. I.* ii. 312; where a convention between Athens and this king is recorded.

[2] iii. 98 E.

His coins, however, are rare, and were probably regarded as curiosities.

Lysimachia, earlier Cardia, in the Thracian Chersonese, struck a few silver coins, no doubt during the lifetime of its founder, Lysimachus.

Obv. Head of young Heracles. *Rev.* Victory holding wreath and palm. Weight, 82 grains (grm. 5·31).

The obverse type is taken from the silver of Alexander, the reverse type from his gold. The weight is that of a Persian drachm or Attic octobol.

Demetrias, in Thessaly, founded by Demetrius Poliorcetes, struck hemidrachms or tetrobols of the same standard.

Obv. Bust of Artemis. *Rev.* ΔΗΜΗΤΡΙΕΩΝ. Prow of ship. Weight, 36 grains (grm. 2·33).

Lamia, in Thessaly, struck coins at the same time.

Obv. Female head wearing fillet. *Rev.* Heracles seated. Weight, 86 grains (grm. 5·57).

The head is conjectured to be that of Lamia, queen or mistress (for at the time the two were scarcely distinguished) of Demetrius Poliorcetes, to whom the Athenians raised a temple. We have a similar commemoration of Arsinoe, wife of Lysimachus, at Ephesus.

Euboea. A district in Central Greece where we find a fresh departure in coinage is Euboea. Histiaea, in the north of the island, seems to have struck coins for a short time, probably when the cities of Euboea had revolted against the Macedonian supremacy after Alexander's death.[1]

Obv. Head of Maenad, vine-crowned. *Rev.* ΙΣΤΙΑΕΩΝ. Nymph Histiaea seated on a Galley, holding mast or trophy-stand. Weights, 89 grains (grm. 5·76), 42 grains (grm. 2·72).

Head calls these coins octobols and tetrobols of Attic standard; and as they had to work in with the money of Athens and of Macedon this seems likely. On the other hand, they might well pass as drachms and hemidrachms of Aeginetan weight;

[1] *B. M. Cat. Central Greece*, p. lxiii.

and this standard was in use in the neighbouring Boeotia until the Lamian War or later.

Carystus at the same period, if we may judge by style, issued the following:

Obv. Cow suckling calf. *Rev.* ΚΑΡΥΣΤΙΩΝ. Cock. Weight, 119 grains (grm. 7·71).

Obv. Head of bearded Heracles. *Rev.* ΚΑΡΥ. Bull lying. Weight, 27 grains (grm. 1·74).

These coins seem to be of Attic standard. The Carystians fought on the side of Athens in the Lamian War.[1]

In Greece proper, the end of the Lamian War is a clearer landmark than the battle of Chaeroneia, or the destruction of Thebes by Alexander. After that war the grip of Macedon on Greece grew tighter; and it is probable that in many cities the silver coins with the name and types of Alexander took the place of the old civic issues. This may have happened in Boeotia and Thebes; there is, as we shall see directly, some evidence that it took place at Sicyon[2] and other cities. But on this question further research is needed.

Several of the cities of Peloponnesus continued their issues at this period, probably not regularly but spasmodically, when they could recover autonomy. At other times they struck tetradrachms with the types of Alexander or his successors. In 1850 there was discovered near Patras[3] a large hoard of Alexanders, of noteworthy fabric, which seem to have been in great part minted at Sicyon, as the accessory types in the field—Apollo holding a long fillet, and the Chimaera—belong to that city. A notable feature of these coins is that two small figures of Nike are placed on the back of the throne of Zeus. Other cities beside Sicyon may have struck some of these coins.

Among the continued issues of Peloponnesian cities about 300 B.C. we may note the following: Elis, Zacynthus, Argos,

[1] Diodorus, xviii. 11.

[2] Head, *Hist. Num.*, ed. 2, p. 411.

[3] Newton in *Num. Chron.*, 1853, p. 29.

Arcadia (Megalopolis) continue their previous issues, without change of type or weight, though the latter tends to fall.

Messene, retaining the type of the thundering Zeus, passes from the Aeginetan to the Attic standard. The date of this transition we are unable to fix exactly; it may be about 280.

Lacedaemon issues silver coins, for the first time in its history. Areus, king 309–265 B.C., struck coins bearing the types of Alexander but his own name. It is probable that the tetradrachms of Attic weight, having on one side a king's head and on the other the archaic Apollo of Amyclae, were also struck by Areus, though the coins bear only the inscription ΛΑ, and the portrait has been variously identified.

Epidaurus, not earlier than 330 B.C., issues remarkable coins.

Obv. Head of Apollo.. *Rev.* E. The seated Asclepius of Thrasymedes. Weight, 61 grains (grm. 3·95).[1]

The type, evidently suggested by the seated Zeus of Alexander's coins, and the weight, both agree with the date above assigned.

The cities of Crete seem to have been little affected by the expedition of Alexander, though Crete no doubt supplied many mercenary soldiers to his army. They continue the old types and standard, though the issue of coins is far less abundant, until the second century, when imitations of the later coinage of Athens, minted on the Attic standard, come in.

Most of the islands of the Aegean continue their coinages into the third century. We have silver coins of early Hellenistic style at Amorgos, Andros, Ceos, Delos, Melos, Naxos, Paros, and Tenos. But in all cases the standard is no longer the Aeginetan, but the light Rhodian. They also

[1] Mr. Head suggests (*Hist. Num.*, ed. 2, p. 441) that this may be an Aeginetan drachm of light weight, but this is improbable.

issue bronze money. In the standard adopted we may see the influence of the Ptolemies of Egypt, whose wealth was great and whose commerce extensive. The islands were frequent subjects of contention between the Kings of Egypt, Syria, and Macedon, and we have scanty materials for following their destinies in detail.

We hear, however, from the writers on metrology of an island drachm, *δραχμὴ νησιωτική*,[1] and this may well be the drachm used in the islands in the Hellenistic age, when there existed a confederation of islands, *Κοινὸν τῶν Νησιωτῶν*,[2] having its centre in Tenos.

We pass northwards to the Propontis. There occurs, in the time of Alexander, an unusual separation between the coinages of the twin cities Byzantium and Calchedon. Byzantium does not appear to have struck silver coins after the memorable siege by Philip of Macedon (340 B.C.) until the death of Lysimachus (280 B.C.). Probably it was attached at that time to the Macedonian Kingdom. We find, however, the initial letter of the city's name, ΓΥ in countermark, on some of the coins of Ptolemy I of Egypt,[3] which were struck at Sidon and Tyre, and adopted at Byzantium. As Byzantium in the fourth century went over to the Rhodian standard, there is nothing to surprise us in this; the coins of Ptolemy would run very well with the civic issues; but it seems to indicate a poverty, which may easily be accounted for by the plundering invasions of the Gauls at that time. Calchedon, on the other hand, seems to have continued, during Alexander's time, the previous coinage. In the days of Lysimachus tetradrachms and drachms with his types were struck in the city.[4]

In Asia Minor the best proof that Alexander's coinage did not bring to an end the local issues will be found in the

[1] Hultsch, *Metrologici scriptores*, i. 301 ; ii. 143.

[2] *C. I.* xii. 5, Nos. 817, 824.

[3] *B. M. Cat. Thrace*, p. 110.

[4] *Hist. Num.*, ed. 2, p. 512.

coins bearing the names of rulers and founders. The following are noteworthy:

Heracleia Pontica. Dionysius 337–305 B. C.

Obv. Head of young Dionysus, holding thyrsus. *Rev.* ΔΙΟΝΥΣΙΟΥ. Young Heracles, setting up trophy. Weight, 148-150 grains (grm. 9·59–9·72). Also the half and quarter.

Amastris in Paphlagonia. The city was named after Amastris, wife of Dionysius of Heracleia.

Obv. Male head in tiara. *Rev.* ΑΜΑΣΤΡΙΕΩΝ. Goddess seated on throne, holding Victory.

Obv. As last. *Rev.* ΑΜΑΣΤΡΙΟΣ ΒΑΣΙΛΙΣΣΗΣ. Goddess seated on throne, holding Victory or Eros. Weight, 144–148 grains (grm. 9·33–9·59).

These coins belong clearly to a light variety of the Persian standard.

We may trace the course of the coinage after the invasion of Alexander in a few other Asiatic cities. Sinope and Amisus, the chief mints (with Heracleia) on the Asiatic coasts of the Black Sea, continue to strike coins after Alexander; but Amisus changes its standard. Up to the end of the fourth century the city adhered to the Persian (or Aeginetan, for the weights fluctuate); in the early third century it goes over to the Rhodian.

Sinope.

Obv. Head of Sinope, turreted. *Rev.* ΣΙΝΩ. Prow. Weight, 36–38 grains (grm. 2·33–2·46).

Amisus.

Obv. Head of city, turreted. *Rev.* Name of magistrate, not of the city. Owl standing on shield. Weight, 22–27 grains (grm. 1·42–1·74).

Perhaps the coins of Sinope may have been regarded as Rhodian tetrobols: the coins of Amisus were probably light hemidrachms of that standard.

Cyzicus, Lampsacus, and Parium in the Propontis do not seem to have struck civic coins, at all events in silver, between 330 and 200.

In speaking of the land-ways from Europe to Asia in the time of Alexander, we must free ourselves from the notion, natural to a modern, that they lay through Byzantium and the opposite Calchedon. The sea-way to the Euxine necessarily lay between these two cities, and gave them their importance; but the ordinary route from Macedon to the East lay through the Thracian Chersonese, and the crossing between Sestos and Abydos. This had been the route of Xerxes, and it was that of Alexander. Thus the districts of Bithynia and Mysia to the east and south of the Propontis were somewhat out of the way of military forces. Some of the cities of these districts, Cius, Elaea, and Aegae, for instance, seem to have kept their autonomous coinage; Cius until it was occupied by the kings of Bithynia; Elaea, and Aegae until the rise of the Kings of Pergamon. At the same time **Lesbos** issued some remarkable coins:

Obv. Head of Athena. *Rev.* ΑΙΟΛΕ. Thunderbolt. Weight, 35 grains (grm. 2·26).

These are supposed by Imhoof-Blumer[1] to have been struck at Methymna for the people of Lesbos.

At **Ephesus** the civic coinage is continuous, until Lysimachus (about 288 B.C.) altered the name of the city to Arsinoeia, and struck octobols bearing that name. But at the same time he seems to have struck in the city gold staters and silver tetradrachms bearing his own name: at least they bear the subsidiary type of the bee, which points to Ephesus.

At **Samos**, after the restoration of the people to their island by Lysimachus, in 322 B.C., there appears an abundant civic coinage on the debased Chian or Rhodian standard, which goes on into the third century. The coins with Alexander's name, marked with a galley, and probably struck at Samos, appear from the fabric to belong to the second century.

It would seem that the only regular coinages in Caria, of

[1] *Zeit. f. Num.*, iii, p. 312.

the beginning of the third century, are those of the islands Cos, Calymna, Rhodus, and Cnidus, the latter city being practically on an island, as the long peninsula on which it stands is almost free of the mainland. These islands, being subjects of contention among the successors of Alexander, enjoyed periods of autonomy. Rhodes, in particular, was a powerful state, and its coins give us the best indication of date, for the head of Helios, which is their regular type, appears radiate after the time of Alexander; and Head[1] is probably right in supposing that the occasion of the change was the setting up by Chares of the colossal figure of Helios beside the harbour of Rhodes. This occurred after the unsuccessful siege of Rhodes by Demetrius Poliorcetes, about 292–280 B.C.

Certain bronze coins, struck by Eupolemus, a general of Cassander—

> *Obv.* Three Macedonian shields. *Rev.* ΕΥΓΌΛΕΜΟΥ. Sword in sheath,

are supposed to have been issued in Caria in 314 B.C.,[2] as they are found in that region, and are conjecturally ascribed to Mylasa.

Several of the cities on the southern coast of Asia Minor continued their autonomous coinages into the third century.

Aspendus continues the issue of the staters of Persian standard, of the types of the wrestlers and the slingers, coins of which many barbarous copies have come down to us, struck probably by the barbarous Pisidian tribes of the interior of Asia Minor. Also at Etenna in Pisidia there appear copies of these coins, with the wrestling group on the obverse, and on the reverse a warrior with a dagger and the legend ΕΤΕΝΝΕΩΝ.[3] Selge, as in earlier times, issues coins of the same types as those of Aspendus, but with the inscription ΣΕΛΓΕΩΝ.

The important cities of Cilicia—Issus, Mallus, Soli, and

[1] *Hist. Num.*, ed. 2, p. 639.
[2] *Num. Chron.*, 1891, p. 135 (Wroth); *B. M. Cat. Caria*, p. lxiii.
[3] Imhoof-Blumer, *Kleinas. Münzen*, Pl. XIII. 1.

Tarsus—whence had been issued great quantities of silver staters of Persian standard by the authority of Persian satraps, seem to have, into the third century, continued their civic issues. These bear, on the obverse, the name of Baal of Tarsus, with his figure seated; on the reverse, Lion killing bull, above city-wall, or, Bust of Athena facing. The initials of the four cities, I M Σ and T, appear on the separate issues. From the destruction of the Persian Empire, places like Mallus and Soli decayed. Alexander fined the people of Soli 200 talents for their attachment to Persia:[1] probably the city was almost ruined.

Phoenicia, unlike Cilicia, seems with Alexander to have come more into the stream of the world's commercial activity. At Sidon, according to M. Rouvier,[2] dated coins both of gold and silver were issued as early as 327 B.C. bearing the name of Alexander. We are told that when Alexander took Sidon, in 333 B.C., he deposed the reigning King Strato II and set up in his place one Abdolonymus. After that, history fails, and we cannot say whether Abdolonymus continued in the kingdom; but we hear of later kings. The dated coins of Sidon seem to take the place of the abundant earlier coinage of the city; and we should suppose that the silver, at all events, was locally controlled. Certainly the bronze coins with the types of Alexander, which were struck in many cities, would be merely local issues. Mr. Newell[3] maintains that the Alexander coins struck in Cyprus were issued by the local rulers, in the place of the previous abundant silver. But the Cypriote kings also, as we have seen (Ch. XVI), went on with their issues, even of gold coins, after the expedition of Alexander.

After this brief survey, we must endeavour sum up the evidence, though any conclusions can be only tentative.

[1] *Anab.* ii. 5. 5.

[2] *Journ. Int. d'archéol. numism.*, 1902: cf. *Nomisma*, iv. 6.

[3] *Num. Chron.*, 1915, p. 299.

The cities of Greece Proper, when they continued to issue coins, used their accustomed standards, with some tendency to fall; and this was the case also generally in Asia. The light Rhodian or Ptolemaic drachm is aggressive among the islands. But we do not find, at all events until the third century, any general disposition among the cities to conform to the new monetary conditions established by Alexander.

Generally speaking, the ceasing of the current coinages in Europe and Asia appears to have been gradual and not sudden. The local coinages went on in most places until they gradually stopped, not as illegal, but as superfluous. When, after the defeat of Antiochus III by the Romans, some of the cities of Asia regained their liberty, they took to issuing tetradrachms with the types, and of the weight, of those of Alexander, from which, however, they are easily distinguished by their peculiar flat fabric.

Thus the coinage of Alexander lasts over two centuries, and has to be studied in connexion with the civic issues of the third and second centuries, as well as with the coinages of the kings of Macedon, Syria, Egypt, and other realms.

The coins of Philip belong to a definite geographical area, and no doubt are the state coinage of the enlarged kingdom of Macedon. Within that kingdom only a few privileged cities, like Philippi and Gomphi, were allowed to strike money. But, outside it, Philip does not seem to have exercised any power over issues. But the coins bearing the name and types of Alexander seem sometimes to be imperial, and sometimes merely civic or local.

To disentangle the whole confusion, and to separate the occasions of the Alexander coins, the coins bearing the names of his successors, and the civic issues, would be a great task, and unfortunately a task for the satisfactory fulfilment of which the materials at present hardly exist.

There was a great outbreak of barbarous or semi-barbarous copies of the gold coins of Philip and Alexander. The coinage of Philip worked westward: it was copied from tribe to tribe as far as Britain. It is probable that the Gauls, when they invaded Greece in 279 B.C., acquired a quantity of *Philippi* as spoil; and that it was from that beginning that the use of imitations spread among the Celts, though there was another line of influence through Massilia. The imitations of Alexander's coins, both in silver and gold, reach us from the Oxus valley and North India.

GENERAL INDEX

INDEX TO PLATES

PLATE I. ELECTRUM AND GOLD OF ASIA, 700–480.

1. Uncertain mint. Fore-part of lion. = Oblong sinking between two squares.
2. Uncertain mint. ΦΑΝΟΣ ΕΜΙ ΣΗΜΑ (retrograde).[1] = As last.
3. Phocaea. Φ. Seal. = Two incuse squares.
4. Cyzicus. Tunny-fish bound with fillet. = Two incuse squares.
5. Croesus of Lydia: *gold*. Fore-parts of lion and bull face to face. = Two incuse squares.
6. As last: *silver*.
7. Persia: *gold*. The King advancing: holds javelin and bow. = Oblong incuse.
8. Chios. Sphinx seated. = Incuse square.
9. Lampsacus. Half of winged horse. = Incuse square, quartered.
10. Uncertain mint. Sow. = As last.
11. Samos. Fore-part of bull looking back. = As last.
12. Uncertain mint. Cock; above it, palmette. = As last.
13. Uncertain mint. Horse prancing. = As last.
14. Clazomenae. Half of winged boar. = As last: *silver*.

PLATE II. SILVER OF GREECE, 700–480.

1. Aegina. Sea-tortoise. = Incuse.
2. Naxos. Wine-cup, ivy-leaf, bunches of grapes. = Incuse square, quartered.
3. Eretria. Gorgon-head. = Incuse square; in one section lion's head.
4. Eretria. Gorgon-head. = Bull's head.
5. Chalcis. Wheel. = Incuse square.

[1] In this and other cases it is not thought necessary to reproduce exactly the archaic lettering, which is better seen in the plate.

6. Athens. Owl. = As last.
7. Corinth. ϙ. Pegasus. = Incuse square.
8. Corinth. ϙ. Pegasus. = Mill-sail incuse.
9. Athens. Head of Athena helmeted. = AΘE. Owl and olive-spray.
10. Athens. As last.
11. Athens. As last, barbarous.
12. Athens. As last, fixed type.
13. Corcyra. Cow suckling calf. = Two oblong incuses: in each a pattern.
14. Thebes. Boeotian shield. = ⊙ in incuse.

Plate III. Silver of Asia, 700–480.

1. Cos. Crab. = Larger and smaller incuse.
2. Cyme. Fore-part of horse. = Two incuses; in each a pattern.
3. Chios. Sphinx seated. = Larger and smaller incuse squares.
4. Teos. Griffin seated. = Incuse square, quartered.
5. Chersonesus in Caria. Head and paw of lion. = XEP. Fore-part of bull in incuse.
6. Cnidus. Head and paw of lion. = Head of Aphrodite in incuse.
7. Camirus in Rhodes. Fig-leaf. = Two oblong incuses.
8. Tenedos. Janiform head. = TENE. Bipennis.
9. Ephesus. Bee. = Incuse square.
10. Samos. Lion's scalp. = ΣA. Bull's head.
11. Poseidion in Carpathos. Two larger and one smaller dolphin. = Two oblong incuses.
12. Ialysus in Rhodes. Half of winged boar. = IEΛYΣION. Eagle's head and palmette.
13. Phaselis in Lycia. Fore-part of galley. = ΦAΣ. Stern of galley.
14. Calymna. Head of bearded warrior. = Lyre in incuse.

Plate IV. Thrace and Macedon, 600–480.

1. Thasos. Satyr carrying nymph. = Incuse square.
2. Lete. Satyr pursuing nymph. = As last.
3. Lete. As last.

4. Zacelii. ΙΑΙΕΛΕΩΝ. Centaur carrying nymph. = Incuse square.
5. Neapolis. Gorgon-head. = Incuse square.
6. Abdera. ΗΡΑΚ. Griffin seated; locust. = Incuse square, quartered.
7. Edoni. Man leading two oxen. = ΓΕΤΑΣ ΗΔΟΝΕΩΝ ΒΑΣΙΛΕΥΣ around a square.
8. Bisaltae. ΒΙΣΑΛΤΙΚΟΝ. Horseman walking beside his horse. = Incuse square, quartered.
9. Macedon, Alexander I. Horseman walking beside his horse. = ΑΛΕΞΑΝΔΡΟ around square.
10. Acanthus. Lion slaying bull. [= Incuse square, quartered.]
11. Potidaea. Poseidon on horseback, star. = Incuse square.
12. Terone. Amphora and bunches of grapes. [= Incuse square.] (Restruck on coin of Acanthus.)

Plate V. Italy and Sicily, 600–480.

1. Caulonia. ΚΑΥΛ. Apollo, striking with bough, winged figure on arm: stag. = Obverse type, incuse and reversed.
2. Tarentum. ΤΑΡΑΣ. Taras on dolphin; shell. = Obverse type, incuse and reversed.
3. Tarentum. ΤΑΡΑΣ. Taras on dolphin, holds cuttle-fish. = Sea-horse; pecten shell.
4. Croton and Sybaris. ϘΡΟ. Tripod. = ΣΥ. Bull looking back, incuse.
5. Metapontum. Ear of corn. = Same, incuse. (Restruck on a coin of Corinth.)
6. Zancle. ΔΑΝΚΛΕ. Dolphin in harbour. = Pecten in incuse pattern.
7. Rhegium. Lion's scalp. = ΡΕΓΙΟΝ. Calf's head.
8. Messana. Lion's scalp. = ΜΕΣΣΕΝΙΟΝ. Calf's head.
9. Syracuse. ΣΥΡΑ. Four-horse chariot. = Female head in incuse.
10. Syracuse. ΣΥΡΑΚΟΣΙΟΝ. Female head in the midst of four dolphins. Four-horse chariot crowned by Victory.
11. Syracuse. Same inscr. Female head, wearing wreath, in the midst of four dolphins. = Four-horse chariot crowned by Victory; lion.

Plate VI. Athenian Empire. I.

1. Electrum of Lampsacus. Fore-part of winged horse in wreath. = Incuse square.
2. Electrum of Cyzicus. Heracles kneeling, holding club and bow; tunny. = Incuse square.
3. Melos. Pomegranate. = ΜΑΛΙ. Incuse device.
4. Melos. Pomegranate. = ΜΑΛΙ. Crescent.
5. Siphnos. Head of Apollo. = ΣΙΦ. Eagle flying; barleycorn.
6. Samos. Lion's scalp. = ΣΑΜ. Fore-part of bull; olive-spray; monogram.
7. Samos. As last. = ΣΑ. Fore-part of bull; olive-spray.
8. Chios. Sphinx seated; amphora. = Incuse square, quartered.
9. Methymna. Boar. = ΜΑΘΥΜΝΑΙΟΣ. Helmeted head of Athena.
10. Cos. ΚΟΣ. Discobolus; tripod. = Crab in incuse square.
11. Themistocles, Magnesia. ΘΕΜΙΣΤΟΚΛΕΟΣ. Apollo standing. = ΜΑ. Eagle flying.
12. Colophon. ΚΟΛΟΦΩΝΙΩΝ. Head of Apollo. = Lyre in incuse.

Plate VII. Athenian Empire. II.

1. Termera, Tymnes. ΤΥΜΝΟ. Heracles kneeling. = ΤΕΡΜΕΡΙΚΟΝ. Lion's head in incuse.
2. Sinope. Head of nymph. = ΣΙΝΩ. Sea-eagle on dolphin.
3. Amisus. Turreted female head. = ΠΕΙΡΑ, ΔΙΟΓ. Owl facing, on shield.
4. Dardanus. Male figure on horse. = ΔΑΡ. Cock; monogram.
5. Calchedon. Bearded head. = ΚΑΛΧ. Wheel.
6. Thasos. Satyr carrying nymph. = Incuse square.
7. Thasos. Head of bearded Dionysus, ivy-crowned. = ΘΑΣΙΟΝ. Heracles shooting; shield.
8. Abdera. ΑΒΔΗΡΙ. Griffin. = ΜΗΤΡΟΦΩΝ. Vines, in incuse.
9. Aenus. Head of Hermes. = ΑΙΝΙ. Goat; crescent, ivy-leaf.
10. Macedon, Archelaus I. Male head. = ΑΡΧΕΛΑΟ. Horse with loose rein.

11. Amphipolis. Head of Apollo facing. = ΑΜΦΙΠΟΛΙΤΕΩΝ, Α. Torch in square.
12. Acanthus. Lion devouring bull. = ΑΚΑΝΘΙΟΝ. Square pattern, quartered.

Plate VIII. Asia Minor, 400–330.

1. Aenus, *gold.* Head of Hermes. = ΑΙΝΙΟΝ. Archaic figure on throne; caduceus.
2. Lampsacus, *gold.* Young Heracles strangling serpents. = Fore-part of winged horse.
3. Lampsacus, *gold.* Head of Athena. = As last.
4. Clazomenae, *gold.* Head of Apollo, facing. = ΚΛΑΞ ΑΘΗΝΑΓΟΡΑΣ. Swan; fore-part of winged boar.
5. Cius, *gold.* Head of Apollo. = ΑΓΝΩΝΙΔΗΣ. Prow of ship; eagle.
6. Chalcidice, *gold.* Head of Apollo. = ΧΑΛΚΙΔΕΩΝ ΕΠΙ ΕΥΔΩΡΙΔΑ. Lyre.
7. Samos. ΣΑ. Lion's scalp. = ΣΥΝ. Young Heracles strangling serpents.
8. Hecatomnus of Caria. Carian Zeus. = ΕΚΑΤΟΜ. Lion.
9. Mausolus. Head of Apollo facing. = ΜΑΥΣΩΛΛΟ. Carian Zeus.
10. Ephesus. ΕΦ. Bee. = ΑΡΙΣΤΟΔΗΜΟΣ. Fore-part of stag; palm tree.
11. Cnidus. Head of Aphrodite; prow. = ΕΟΒΩΛΟ. Head and paw of lion.
12. Byzantium. ΒΥ. Ox on tunny. = Incuse.
13. Byzantium. As last; monogram. = Incuse.
14. Cyzicus. ΣΩΤΕΙΡΑ. Head of Persephone. = ΚΥΞΙ. Lion's head, tunny.

Plate IX. Asia, Africa, 480–330.

1. Tiribazus. ΑΜΙ. Ormuzd. = Aramaic inscr. (Tiribazou). Zeus standing.
2. Pharnabazus. Female head facing. = Aramaic inscr. (Pharnabazou). Bearded helmeted head.
3. Datames, Tarsus. Aramaic inscr. (Baaltars). Baal of Tarsus. = Aramaic inscr. (of Datames). Persian satrap seated, solar symbol.

4. Persian Satrap. BA. Bearded Persian head. = ΒΑΣΙΛΕΩΣ. King as on the darics; galley.
5. Persian Satrap. Bearded Persian head. = ΒΑΣΙΛ. Lyre.
6. Aradus. Head of Melkart. = Aramaic inscr. (from Aradus). Galley on waves.
7. Sidon. Galley before fortress; below, lions. = King in chariot; goat incuse.
8. Tyre. Deity on winged hippocamp; dolphin. = Owl; sceptre and flail.
9. Carthage. Female head in tiara. = Inscr. (Shâm machanat). Lion and palm tree.
10. Carthage, *gold*. Head of Persephone. = Horse.
11. Cyrene, *gold*. Nike in quadriga. ΠΟΛΙΑΝΘΕΥΣ. = ΚΥ-ΡΑΝΑΙΟΝ. Zeus Ammon, incuse altar.
12. Cyrene, *silver*. Head of Zeus Ammon. = ΚΥΡΑΝΑ. Silphium plant.

Plate X. Hellas, 408–330.

1. Boeotia, Tanagra. Shield. = ΒΟΙ in wheel.
2. Thebes. Shield. = ΘΕ. Head of bearded Dionysus, ivy crowned.
3. Thebes. Shield. = ΘΕ. Young Heracles strangling serpents.
4. Haliartus. Shield: on it trident. = ΑΡΙΑΡΤΙΟΝ. Poseidon striking with trident.
5. Opus. Head of Persephone. = ΟΠΟΝΤΙΩΝ ΑΙΑΣ. Ajax charging.
6. Amphictiones. Head of Demeter. = ΑΜΦΙΚΤΙΟΝΩΝ. Apollo seated with his lyre; tripod.
7. Athens, *gold*. Head of Athena. ΑΘΕ. Owl, olive-spray, calathus.
8. Athens. Head of Athena. = ΑΘΕ. Owl, olive-spray.
9. Zacynthus. Head of Apollo. = ΙΑΚΥΝΘΙΩΝ. Young Heracles strangling serpents.
10. Argos. Head of Hera with crown. = ΑΡΓΕΙΩΝ. Two dolphins; wolf.
11. Arcadia. Head of Zeus. = Monogram, ΟΛΥ. Pan seated on rocks.
12. Stymphalus. Head of Artemis. = ΣΤΥΜΦΑΛΙΩΝ ΣΟ. Heracles striking with club.

PLATE XI. ITALY, SICILY, 480–330.

1. Tarentum, *gold.* Head of Hera, veiled. = ΤΑ . ΚΥΛΙΚ. Young rider crowning horse, rudder, buccinum.
2. Metapontum, *gold.* ΛΕΥΚΙΠΠΟΣ. Head of Leucippus. = ΜΕ ΣΙ. Two ears of barley.
3. Sybaris. Head of Athena. = ΣΥΒΑΡΙ. Bull looking back.
4. Thurii. Head of Athena, Scylla on helmet. = ΘΟΥΡΙΩΝ. Bull butting; fish.
5. Syracuse, *gold.* Head of young Heracles. = ΣΥΡΑ. Female head in incuse.
6. Agrigentum, *gold.* ΑΚΡ. Eagle devouring serpent; two pellets. = ΣΙΛΑΝΟΣ. Crab.
7. Gela, *gold.* ΓΕΛΑΣ. Bull, barleycorn. = Horseman.
8. Camarina, *gold.* Head of Athena, hippocamp on helmet. = ΚΑ. Olive leaves and berries.
9. Syracuse. ΣΥΡΑΚΟΣΙΩΝ Δ. Head of Persephone amid dolphins. = Quadriga crowned by Victory: beneath, arms, ΑΘΛΑ.
10. Syracuse. Same inscr. Head of Athena. = Pegasus.
11. Syracuse, *electrum.* Same inscr. Head of Apollo, bow. = ΣΩΤΕΙΡΑ. Head of Artemis, bow.

1
2
3
4
5
6
7
8
9
10
11
12
13
14
700–480

)-480

PLATE III

1

2

3

4

5

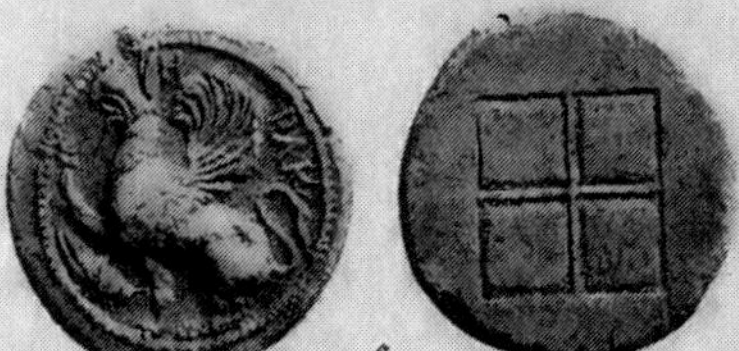

6

7

8

9

10

11

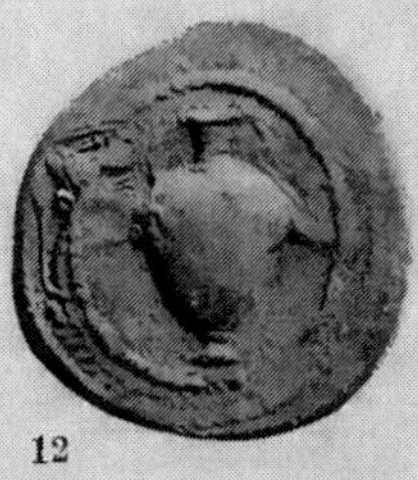

12

PLATE V

PLATE VI

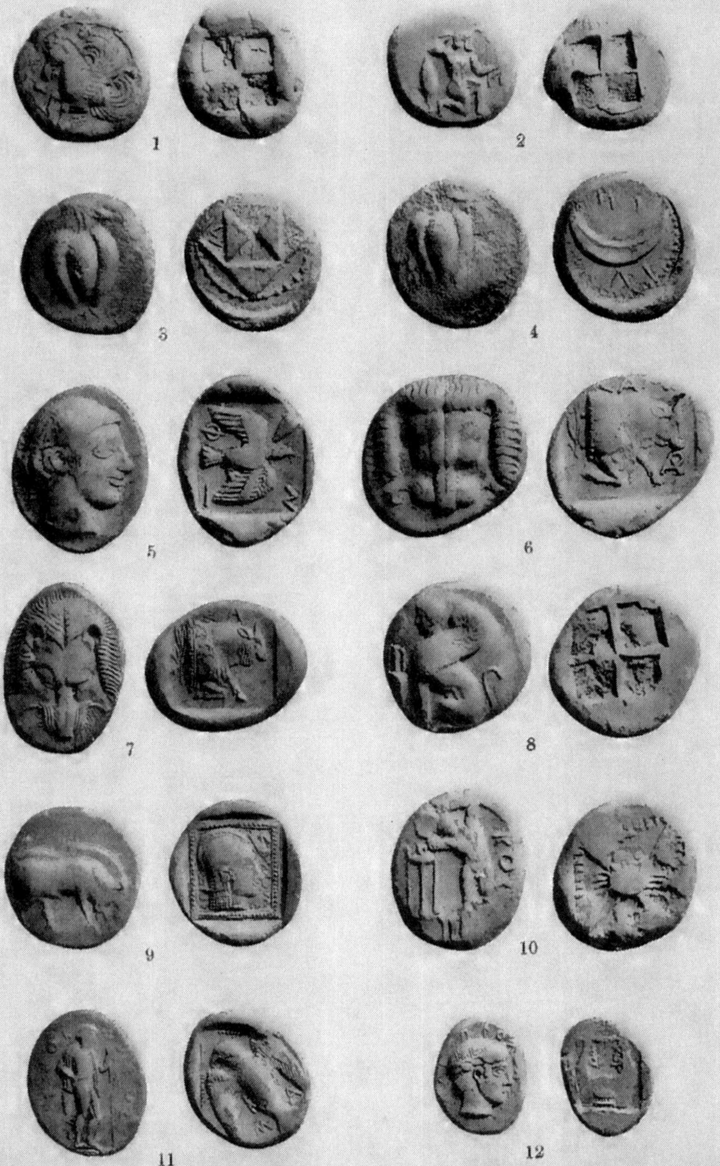

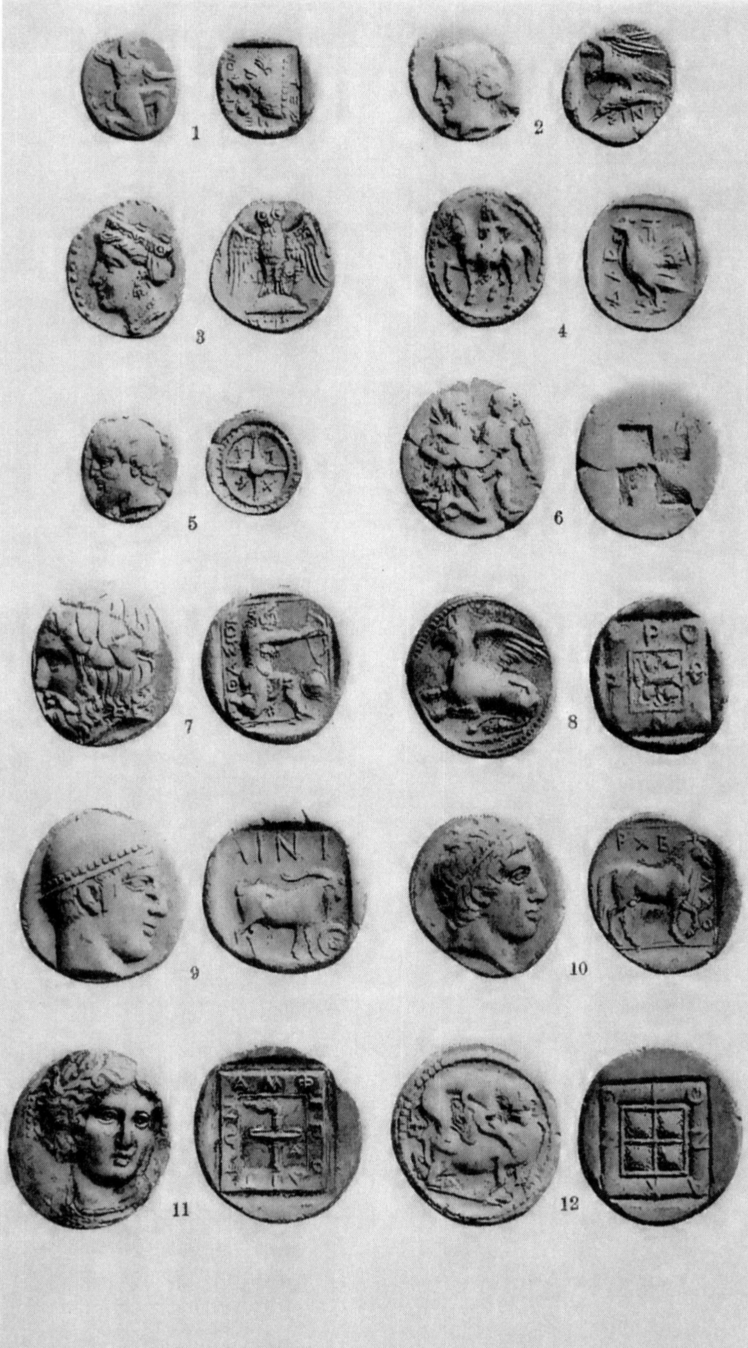

II

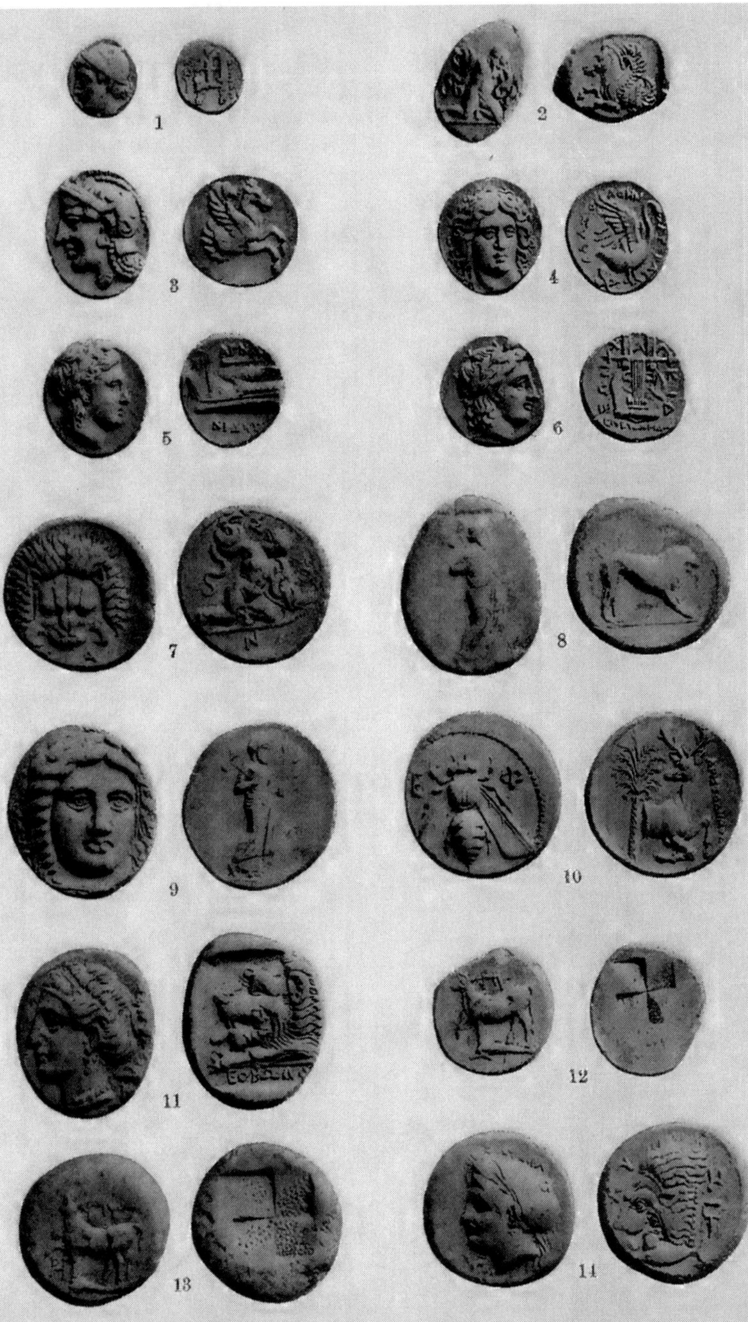
1
2
3
4
5
6
7
8
9
10
11
12
13
14

PLATE IX

PLATE X

PLATE XI

1

2

3

4

5

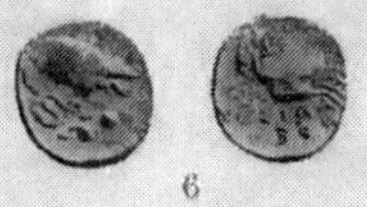

6

7

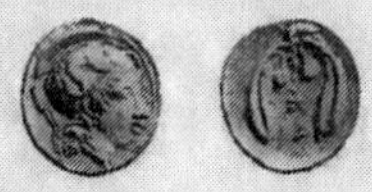

8

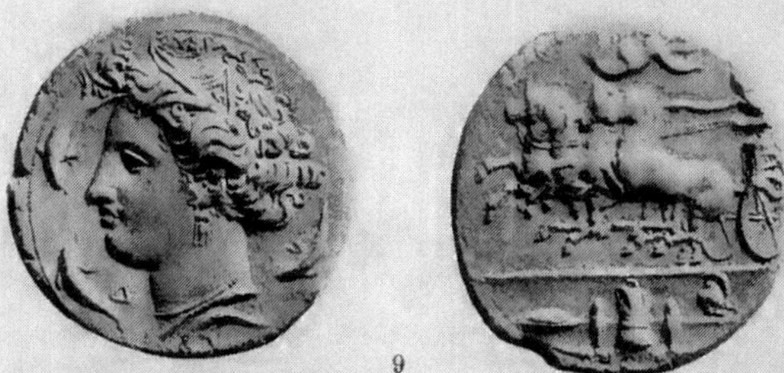

9

10

11